PENGUIN REFERENCE BOOKS

THE PENGUIN DICTIONARY OF COMPUTERS

Anthony Chandor was educated at Epsom College and New College, Oxford. A Fellow of the British Computer Society, he has been a member of Council and, since its inception, a member of the Examinations Board for professional examinations. In over twenty years of computer experience, he has twice been appointed by the United Nations as data processing adviser. He was a director of the National Computing Centre, a founder and managing director of Aragon International Ltd, and is chairman of Mandarin Communications Ltd, the electronic publishing specialists. He is the author of a number of books including *Choosing and Keeping Computer Staff* and, with John Graham and Robin Williamson, *Practical Systems Analysis*.

●

John Graham entered the computer industry in 1959 and in addition to his wide experience in systems, programming and data processing consultancy, he also has considerable experience of management in the data processing industry. He is a director of Aregon International Ltd. A Member of the British Computer Society, he is the author of *Systems Analysis in Business*, *Making Computers Pay*, *The Penguin Dictionary of Telecommunications* and *Personal Computers*.

●

Robin Williamson was educated at Tonbridge School and Magdalen College, Oxford. He entered the computer industry in 1963 and has been a systems and programming manager responsible for major computer projects. He has regularly lectured on systems analysis and development and spent some time in New York as manager of ICL Dataskil's USA operations. He is a director of Mandarin Communications Ltd and a Fellow of the British Computer Society.

THE PENGUIN DICTIONARY OF
COMPUTERS

ANTHONY CHANDOR

WITH

JOHN GRAHAM
ROBIN WILLIAMSON

Third Edition

PENGUIN BOOKS

Penguin Books Ltd, Harmondsworth, Middlesex, England
Viking Penguin Inc., 40 West 23rd Street, New York, New York 10010, U.S.A.
Penguin Books Australia Ltd, Ringwood, Victoria, Australia
Penguin Books Canada Ltd, 2801 John Street, Markham, Ontario, Canada L3R 1B4
Penguin Books (N.Z.) Ltd, 182–190 Wairau Road, Auckland 10, New Zealand

First published 1970
Reprinted 1970, 1972, 1973, 1974, 1975
Second edition 1977
Reprinted 1977, 1978, 1979, 1980, 1981 (twice), 1982, 1983, 1984
Third edition 1985
Copyright © Anthony Chandor, John Graham, Robin Williamson, 1970, 1977, 1985
All rights reserved

Made and printed in Great Britain by
Hazell Watson & Viney Limited,
Aylesbury, Bucks
Typset in 9/11pt VIP Times

PREFACE TO THE FIRST EDITION

EVERY day more and more of us find that computers have become part of our daily background: magazines we read have been typeset by computers, architects have designed our houses with the help of computers, our payslips are printed by computers, we pay bills prepared by computers, using cheques marked with computer symbols, and the payments result in bank statements prepared by computers. Even more directly associated with the machines are those who use them in their day-to-day work – scientists and storekeepers, clerks and directors, soldiers and sailors, accountants and engineers – besides the growing numbers of computer personnel who are responsible for making the machines do the work. Each of us, whether layman, computer user or computer technician, will have problems with computer terminology from time to time, and it is the purpose of this book to provide a ready means of solving these problems.

Requirements of the Book

Since the early 1950s, when computers first began to be used commercially, many hundreds of everyday words have been given new meanings, and words which had a peaceful existence on their own in ordinary English dictionaries have been joined together in the computer world to make phrases which are quite unintelligible to anyone unaware of their specialist meaning. For example, neither *crippled leap-frog test* nor *graceful degradation* includes an unfamiliar word but both phrases have a specific technical meaning. In addition to the 'plain English' words, there are, of course, numbers of purely technical words which need defining in simple terms. This book provides a glossary giving as much information as possible, and the overriding aim has been helpfulness rather than deftness or lexicographical terseness. It is designed to satisfy both the layman whose association with computers is still only indirect and the technical reader already familiar with many of the terms but searching for a definition of a word used in a branch of computer technology he has not yet mastered.

5

To cater for these main categories of reader the following primary guide-lines are necessary:

For the layman:

Basic words must be explained in simple English and not in terms of each other.

Basic concepts must be explained at some length if necessary.

Advanced words must be extensively cross-referenced to make it possible to follow a word through a series of entries.

For the technical user:

Specialist words and jargon in common use must be included as well as the more generally recognized terms.

Some subjects (such as *Law and Computers* and *Audit of Computer Systems*) must be given a more discursive treatment than the conventional entries.

Structure of the Book

To meet these requirements the book has been organized in the following way. First there is a general article called *Introduction to Computers* for all readers to whom the subject of computers is entirely new. This explains very simply what computers are and how they are used, and sets the background for the rest of the book. It is followed by conventional dictionary entries for technical words and phrases, and widely used jargon expressions. The power and pervasiveness of the acronym are also recognized and those in common use (such as *PERT* and *ALGOL*) are included. Interspersed with the definitions, in the same alphabetical sequence, are seventy general articles dealing concisely with a specific topic which requires more generous treatment than can be given in a conventional definition. Each topic has been selected to satisfy the requirements of the different categories of reader and is written at an appropriate technical level. For example, the article on *Programming* is written in simple language for the layman, as it is unlikely that an experienced programmer would need to refer to so general a heading. The article on *Information Retrieval Techniques*, however, is written for the informed reader, as it is improbable that a complete beginner will be looking up this subject.

Not all the articles are on strictly technical subjects. In the same way that, for example, an accountant may use this book to refer to the article on *Systems Analysis*, a computer professional may wish to inform himself generally on some aspect of accounting for which a computer is to be used – perhaps *Discounted Cash Flow* or *Budgetary Control*. Several such activities in which computers are commonly used are described in the book, and they are there to provide a background reference for the young computer technician. Similarly certain subjects related to the use of computers are described, such as *Allocation, Forecasting* and *Model Building*.

At the end of this preface, on page 11, there is a list of the general articles indicating the category of reader for whom the article is intended. Those shown as suitable for the man-in-the-street provide a background of information as simply as possible, and assume no prior knowledge other than that obtained from the *Introduction to Computers* on page 14. The articles shown as 'technical' will provide useful information for those starting a career in computers, for scientists and engineers using computers directly in their daily work, and, it is hoped, may provide agreeable browsing for computer personnel who are already established.

There is detailed cross-referencing throughout the book, and in any definition all those words themselves defined elsewhere in the book are printed in italics the first time they are used. In general the natural lead word of a phrase is taken to be the master word even if it is an adjective qualifying a noun – for example, *bufferred computer* appears under the letter B and *overflow bucket* under O. With some terms it is not easy to see which the 'natural' lead word is, and for these a cross-reference is given under the appropriate words: for example, *machine-spoilt work time* appears under the letter M but there is also a reference from *work time, machine-spoilt*. Each definition is given in an attempt to explain the actual usage rather than to suggest any standard; various admirable attempts have been made to bring order to the anarchistic plethora of overlapping and conflicting usages of technical terms, but the terms are still used with a variety of meanings in different contexts and this book therefore explains each term with no attempt to give 'preferred' definitions only. The entry under *background processing* is not untypical: three different meanings and two of them directly contradictory, but all three in general use. Where appropriate the definitions include synonyms, antonyms, directly related words and, where this would help to expand the definition, a reference to one of the general articles.

Haslemere, 1970   ANTHONY CHANDOR

PREFACE TO THE SECOND EDITION

THE vigour and dynamism of the computer industry continues to be reflected in its words and phrases and the pace of growth of the industry is still matched by the speed at which new phrases become established. Men and women associated with computers are as quick to adopt new phrases to describe new techniques and advances in technology as they are ingenious in inventing the processes which require such labels. It has been pleasantly noticeable during the years since the compilation of the first edition of this dictionary that, in general, it is the imaginative phrase which establishes itself rather than its pedestrian equivalent: such words as 'de-updating' still emerge, but phrases like 'deadly embrace', 'menu selection' and 'slave store' find swift acceptance; computer people would clearly rather use a compelling phrase than mangle an already tortured word. One notable failure has been an improvement on the somewhat sinister phrase 'computer people' (the even less agreeable 'liveware' having been mercifully rejected). Perhaps a user of this dictionary has already observed the use of a suitable phrase? Over the past few years I have been most grateful for suggestions for inclusion of new words from readers all over the world, and look forward to receiving many more. If one such suggestion allows a replacement for 'computer people' without leading inexorably to 'informatician' a great advance will have been made!

Haslemere, 1977   ANTHONY CHANDOR

PREFACE TO THE THIRD EDITION

In the eight years which have passed since the second edition two great changes have taken place: the practice of distributed computing, with terminals used not only for data collection but also for local processing; and the introduction of personal computers, which have done so much to remove myths that the use of a computer is an arcane skill reserved for the initiated and twice-blessed. Each of these changes has generated its own new words, while at the same time rendering many others obsolete. The new ones have been collected and now appear in this new edition – *card cage* and *daughterboard, game chip* and *telesoftware*. The obsolete ones have not been removed: it is the task of this dictionary to explain words which might be found in books and articles, not to act as an arbiter of correct usage. Often, therefore, the tense has been changed in the definition, and general articles on such objects as *paper tapes* have been shortened and new general articles on, for example, *network architecture* and *microcomputers* have appeared.

There still seems to be no satisfactory single word for 'computer people'. Perhaps as more and more people treat computing as part of their daily lives, there is less and less need for a special word. How very fortunate!

Haslemere, 1985   ANTHONY CHANDOR

ACKNOWLEDGEMENTS

THE help received from many individuals and organizations is most gratefully acknowledged. It is not possible to make particular acknowledgement except to those whose contribution was substantial; many thanks, therefore, to:

Maryanne Bankes	G. J. Mansell
T. Hugh Beech	David Rogers
R. R. Campbell	J. Wale
H. J. P. Garland	Erik Westgard
Rudu Malir	W. J. Woodward

LIST OF GENERAL ARTICLES

As explained in the preface, the following topics are dealt with at greater length than conventional definitions. They are grouped below according to whether they are more suitable for the layman or the technical reader and, except for *Introduction to Computers*, appear in the main text within the alphabetical sequence.

Articles for the layman

Introduction to Computers

Analog computers
Central processors
Computer personnel
Data processing department
  organization
Digital computers

Hybrid computers
Input devices
Output devices
Programming
Punched cards
Storage devices
Systems analysis

Articles for the technical reader

ALGOL
Allocation
Auditing computer systems

BASIC
Boolean algebra
Budgetary control

Character recognition
Check digits
COBOL
Communications devices
Control totals

Cost analysis systems
Critical Path Method

Data base management systems
Data preparation
Data processing standards
Debugging
Decision tables
Discounted cash flow
Documentation – systems
Documentation – programming
Dump and restart

A NOTE ON SPELLING

THROUGHOUT this book, a programme of events is distinguished from a computer program by the convenient – and generally recognized – difference in spelling, and a similar distinction between analogue and analog computer and disc and magnetic disk has been adopted.

See references are denoted by an arrow: ⟡

See also references are denoted by a double arrow: ⟡⟩

INTRODUCTION TO COMPUTERS

The purpose of a computer

A computer is a tool. A tool operates by taking raw material and converting it into a product by means of a device which performs a process. The process is determined by people. To take an analogy from everyday life: a blunt pencil (raw material) is converted into a sharp pencil (product) by means of a penknife performing the process of sharpening, as determined by a schoolboy. The device – the penknife – can of course be turned to several other uses, such as extracting stones from horses' hooves, or carving initials on a desk. But its scope is basically limited to one type of process and one type of material.

In all essentials, computers are tools, and in describing them we can consider each of the functions of any tool: the raw material, the product, the device, the process and the people.

The raw material

First, the raw material: facts (or *data*). A fact is a thing or event known to exist or have happened: something which can be described in precise, measurable terms. A fact may be an amount of £13 as written on a cheque; a line on an architect's plan; a measurement in a scientific experiment; a membership number; an address; an item on an invoice; a forecast in a plan. An individual fact, on its own, does nothing more than provide the single piece of information it represents.

The product

The product that a computer generates from this raw material is *information*. By the relation of facts of the same type or different types, something useful is obtained. In isolation, a cheque for £13 is of little interest to the bank manager: related to an overdraft of £88 and an agreed maximum of £100 for Mr Smith, the isolated fact becomes informative, with unfortunate consequences for Mr Smith. The single line on the architect's drawing is meaningless: related to all the other lines on the drawing it plays a part as representing an outside wall, or a room divider or a drain. The single experimental measurement may be insignificant: related to hundreds of other measurements, the fact may become crucial in the proof of a scientific theory. The process carried out by the computer is the converting of isolated facts into information by relating them to each other. This is a process with which we are all familiar in daily life – figuring out how much has been spent on a shopping spree by jotting down facts, isolated purchases, and adding them up to form a grand total. Looking up an address in a street atlas is, again, the conversion of an isolated fact, an address, into information: the relationship of the address to a locality, and thus to a way of getting there. We are also familiar with tools used to process facts: the cash register, the adding machine, the library catalogue, the slide rule, even a dictionary, all are used to process facts into information.

The device: distinguishing features

How does the computer compare with other information-processing tools? The three main distinguishing features of a computer are speed, capacity and versatility. An example of speed: an average person might take about a minute to add up ten 7-digit numbers. In the same time, some computers could have added up 1000 million or more numbers. Further, the average man would feel some unease about the accuracy of his addition of 1000 million numbers: the computer sum would be correct. An example of storage capacity: the contents of a hundred volumes of the London telephone directory could be accommodated in one typical storage unit: in one second, 15,000 entries could be looked up. Examples of versatility: the same computer could be used to print bank statements; draw perspective drawings from outline sketches; calculate betting odds; calculate satellite orbits; match aspiring lovers; calculate population statistics. There are few fields of human activity in which the computer cannot be applied.

Instructions

The computer achieves such prodigious feats not because of any superhuman powers of intelligence, but because it is able to carry out a few extremely simple operations accurately and very quickly. We are all familiar with the principle of doing something complex by performing a set of simple instructions: a knitting pattern tells one how to make a garment by following a set of simple stitches; a do-it-yourself construction kit works in the same way. Just as the knitting pattern insructions consist of a few basic steps written in a special code (K1, P1 means knit one stitch, purl one stitch) so the computer has a repertoire of basic operations which it can carry out on data. These operations can be loosely grouped into control operations, which enable the computer to operate various devices which feed data into it for processing, and which accept results after processing; arithmetic operations, enabling the computer to add and subtract, and thus multiply and divide as well; and logical operations, which enable the computer to select different sets of instructions as a result of tests made on items of data.

Hardware

Hardware is the term given to all the electronic and mechanical gadgetry which together forms a computer system, as distinct from the sets of instructions which are used to operate them. A computer system consists of three basic types of machine. First, there is that part of the system which can perform operations as a result of instructions. This part is known as the *central processor*. Second, the unit used to store the raw material on which the processor is to set to work: this is known simply as a *storage device*, although the term *memory* is also used, as an analogy in human terms. Finally, there are devices (a) to place data into storage and (b) to extract the finished product from the system. These are known collectively as *input devices* and *output devices*. A computer is thus a collective noun used for a group of devices: a central processor, storage, input and output devices. In fact, the picture is not quite as clear-cut as this. Central processors contain a special type of storage device known as high-speed or *immediate access store*. The power and speed of a computer depends on the amount of this storage available, since all instructions are held in this storage device, as well as that part of the data which is being immediately affected by the instructions. As high-speed store is expensive (even after the astonishingly sharp declines in price ever since the introduction of integrated circuits on silicon), large quantities of data are held on *backing stores* which are cheaper, but from which it takes longer to extract individual items of data. Basic data still has to be placed into the backing store, so a common sequence of events is for this raw material to be put onto a backing store in one operation, and then be processed from the backing store before becoming the final product. Indeed, several stages of processing may take place, the intermediate results of each being transcribed to backing store, before the final product is available.

The central processor is usually placed in one box or cabinet, and input, output and storage devices each in their own boxes; for this reason the latter are all collectively known as *peripheral units*. Nowadays a computer system is much like a child's construction kit in that the user can buy the 'Mark 1' version and then improve his kit by buying new peripheral units and plugging them into his system. Or he can keep his peripheral units and change the central processor for a bigger and faster one. 'Bigger' will mean a larger immediate access store with the ability to hold larger and more complex sets of instructions; 'Faster' will mean that the instructions themselves will be carried out more quickly.

Types of computer

What we have described so far has been mostly concerned with computers used for commercial applications, and also by scientists and engineers engaged in the processing of large numbers of mathematical calculations. This sort of computer is known as a *digital computer*. It works on data held as a large number of distinct items, and operates in a series of steps or instructions. But 'raw material' or unprocessed data is not always in the form of individual and separate items – cheques, bills, bookings. In some cases this raw material is something which lasts over a length of time and changes its value over that time. For example, the speed of a car over a journey is in a sense an item of data, which lasts as long as the journey takes, and varies continuously over that journey. We may need to process this data item to obtain information, for example to detect a speed in excess of 70 m.p.h. and slow down. We are all familiar with a machine which does just this: the car speedometer displays the speed at any time, and by watching this we can control our vehicle. *Analog computers* are a type of computer which can accept data as a quantity varying over a length of time, rather than as a series of distinct items each with a unique value. Analog computers are used for scientific purposes, to measure the results of experiments, or to simulate processes which can be described in terms of quantities varying according to known rules over lengths of time. They are also used for process control of industrial operations, constantly measuring some varying quantity, for example voltage or gas pressure, and causing operations such as switching off circuits or opening valves when the quantity being measured reaches pre-determined values. *Hybrid com-*

puters are yet another type of machine, combining some of the properties of both digital and analog computers. A varying input accepted by the analog computer can be converted into a series of distinct values which can then be processed by the digital part of the machine. Digital processing is usually faster and more sophisticated than the processing which can be done by analog machines, so *hybrid* processing gives the advantages of both types of device.

Processing – programs

We have said that the computer is a tool, and the job it does is processing facts to obtain information. But the same could be said of adding machines, cash registers and a number of other accounting and calculating machines. The great difference between a computer and other information-producing equipment is versatility: unlike the other machines, which in general perform one fixed type of operation, the computer's operations can be varied without limit. How does this happen? We have already explained how the computer performs a complex task by a series of relatively simple steps, and how the heart of the machine is a *central processor* in which the instructions are stored and obeyed. The storage unit of the processor can be likened to a large filing cabinet, with quantities of empty files or pockets each with a reference number. To start things off, one instruction is placed in each 'pocket'. In the computer system this is done by means of an input device 'reading' the set of instructions or program. The computer is then directed to start working. The first instruction is extracted from the first pocket and whatever this instruction says is obeyed. Then the next instruction is extracted from the next pocket, and so on until the sequence of instructions is completed. Data which is to be processed is placed in pockets in the same way; one instruction might be to fill up a number of pockets with data; another might be to empty pockets containing results. In the computer's processor, pockets or *storage locations* hold *characters, words* or *bytes*; they are the smallest unit of information with which the machine can operate. If we were to go to any storage location and extract its contents, we could not tell whether the 'number' was an instruction, a data item or the *address* of another storage location, for these are all held in exactly the same way in store. Since instructions are thus the same sort of thing to the computer as numbers, they can be *modified*. This means that once a program of instructions is placed in store, it can be changed by its own action: a program of instructions can thus be made to react to each problem it has to face, and this enables extremely sophisticated and complex operations to be performed. However, there is one difficulty – and it is a very significant one. The computer can only do what it is told: it slavishly obeys each instruction it extracts from successive storage locations, without any discrimination: it cannot say to itself 'that doesn't seem sensible', or 'I wonder what that means': it just obeys. So instructions must be carefully worked out to make sure that in no circumstances will the computer be asked to do anything illogical. Therefore, when a computer issues a final demand for payment of a bill for £0, it is not the machine that has done something stupid: it is correctly obeying a stupid instruction. The illogicality has been caused by the human operator who has failed to foresee the situation and give the computer appropriate instructions. The art of *programming* is thus an exacting one, for every combination of circumstance must be considered by the programmer and taken care of by an appropriate set of instructions.

Software

We have described the term 'hardware' already: it refers to all the machinery, electronic or mechanical, which together makes up a computer. Programs can be produced by individual computer users to perform specific jobs in which the user alone is interested. But many types of problem are more general, and programs written to solve one instance of a general problem may be used to perform the same job for others faced with similar problems; these programs are known as '*software*'. In particular, manufacturers of computers spend large sums of money on developing this sort of software. A computer is obviously much more useful to a user if it comes with a number of ready-made programs which can be put to use at once: also the user is saved the time and expense involved in working out the programs for himself. This sort of software covers a great range of programs, from quite short and simple routines (for example programs to work out taxation for payroll users) to large and sophisticated programs (such as those for *critical path method* analysis used in scheduling complex production programs).

Languages

Some of the most important pieces of software provided by manufacturers are computer *languages*. Instructions in the form operated on by the internal circuitry of a processor consist of a numeric code. Instructions operate on items of data stored with the program in the processor, and each item has its own 'pocket' or storage location, again identified by a number. Programs stored in the processor are thus a combination of numbers making up instructions and storage locations. To work out the numerical equivalents for all the instructions in a program is a tedious and difficult task, requiring great attention to detail and the obeying of exacting rules. But computers themselves are very good at tedious and repetitive tasks, obeying exacting rules. So programming can be simplified by inventing a way for instructions to be written out in a form more easily comprehensible to the user, and making the computer itself translate this into the numbers and codes which are required to use the program on the computer. For example, the programmer can write 'SUBTRACT TAX FROM PAY'; this is then translated for him into the computer code, say 100 326 475, which is then used by the machine to perform the specified calculation. The nearer the language used by the programmer to the code used by the machine, the lower the 'level' of the language. High level languages are what is known as *problem orientated*, that is, they are designed to simplify the writing of instructions for certain types of problem, either commercial or scientific.

People

We have attempted to explain the concept of a computer as a device (*hardware*) using a process (*software*) to turn a raw material into information. But none of this can be achieved without human control over this powerful tool. Perhaps the most exacting task is that which falls on the *systems analyst*. He has to consult his client, the potential user of the machine, to establish the problem to be solved. He must then examine in detail existing procedures: when he has understood exactly what is required, he must design a complete solution to the problem, covering not only computer procedures, but all associated operations, clerical and other. He has to decide what product he is trying to produce: what sort of *information* his system is designed to extract. He decides the raw material required to obtain this, and devises the procedures by which this 'raw data' is collected, fed to the computer, processed and finally dispersed to those who are to use it. He must be skilled not only in analysing a problem and devising a solution, but in communicating his solution to the client or management specifying the requirements, to the users of the information, to those involved in collecting raw data and distributing information and to the other computer professionals involved in the development of the computer side of the system.

There are two associated groups of people: programmers and operators. *Programmers* obtain from the analyst detailed descriptions of specifications of individual jobs which the computer has to perform to make up the overall system. Each such job will require a program to be stored in the computer to perform the tasks. The programmer is responsible for preparing the detailed instructions, and making sure that his program is correct and will in fact perform the required job accurately. Computer *operators* are responsible for the day-to-day operation of programs once these have been specified by the analyst and written by the programmer. They load programs into the processor, check the operation of the various peripheral units and make sure that the correct raw data is read into the computer when required and that the finished product, the information output, is returned to its correct destination.

The future

As the information explosion multiplies day by day, so the enormous problem of keeping this explosion under control becomes more and more acute. Computers, with their ability to process great quantities of facts at vast speeds, are the only means we have of creating some sort of order out of apparent chaos. Computers can give management the information they need to make correct decisions; politicians the facts on which to base policy decisions; research workers the details of results obtained by others in specific fields; architects up-to-date information about available materials and designs; doctors case histories of patients with specified symptoms; lawyers precedents; airline pilots flight plans. The list is endless, and it is endless just because we are continually devising new tasks for the computer and developing computers to perform them.

A

aberration A defect in the electronic lens system of a *cathode ray tube*.

abnormal termination *Termination* which takes place when an error condition is detected by hardware, indicating that a particular series of actions previously initiated cannot be completed correctly.

abort To abandon deliberately a previously initiated activity, generally causing an abnormal termination. Usually implies a controlled termination once a process is recognized as being unable to reach a successful completion.

absolute address The actual *address*[2] of a *location* in *store* expressed in terms of the *machine code* numbering system.

Also known as actual address, direct address, machine address, real address, specific address.

absolute addressing To *address*[3] *locations* in *store* by their *absolute addresses*.

absolute code A programming code using *absolute addresses* and *operators*.

Also known as actual code, direct code, one level code and specific code.

absolute coding Program *instructions* which have been written in *absolute code*, and do not require further processing before being intelligible to the computer.

Also known as basic coding, specific coding.

absolute error The magnitude of deviation of a computed result irrespective of sign.

absolute value computer A computer in which data is processed in its absolute form, all variables maintaining their full values; contrasted with *incremental computer* in which changes in the variables are processed as well as the values of the variables themselves.

acceleration time The time which elapses between the interpretation of an *instruction* to a *peripheral unit* to *read* or *write*, and the moment when transfer of information from the unit to *store* or vice versa could

23

begin; e.g., the time taken to accelerate the *tape transport* on a *magnetic tape* unit.

access Used as a verb describing 1. the process of obtaining data from a *peripheral unit* or retrieving it from a *storage device*; 2. the process involved in obtaining an *instruction* from *memory* in order to obey it. ◊ *fetch*.

access arm A device used to position the reading and writing mechanisms of a *storage device*.

access control register A *register* used to record the *access level* allocated to an active procedure. Part of the protection system built into a computer to ensure that interference does not occur between different software modules.

access level Within many computer systems there are a number of levels at which control mechanisms (*hardware* and *software*) may exist to prevent interference between modules of software. These access levels are numbered to represent different degrees of *security* – for example, the highest levels of security would be applied to check attempts to initiate routines in the *kernel* of an *operating system* which would be responsible for coordination of activities in the total hardware/software system.

access method The way in which data in a file is selected for processing; e.g., a *direct access storage* system can contact files which are accessed in a number of different ways – *serial access, random access*, and *selective sequential access*. ◊ general article on *Updating and file maintenance*.

access permission A response given to an attempt to initiate a software routine, when access control mechanisms have determined that the attempt has correct status and satisfies predetermined security checks. ◊ *access right*.

access right The level of *access* granted to users of a system; e.g., *read* a *file* only, or *write* to a file.

access, simultaneous Synonymous with *parallel access*.

access time The time taken to retrieve data from a *storage device* or to obtain data from a *peripheral unit*; measured from the instant of executing an *instruction* to call for the data to the moment when the data is stored in the specified *location*.

accountable file A *file* whose use needs to be taken into account when a system is evaluated, as opposed to *pass-through* files which have an ephemeral use only.

accountable time The time in which a computer system is available to users, and excludes time when the computer is switched off; undergoing scheduled or unscheduled maintenance; or closed down because of external factors.

accounting journal   A journal maintained as a file by an *operating system* to record events relating to various jobs which are active in the computer and to provide a basis for subsequent analysis in order to assess charges to users.

accounting machine   Used to describe *keyboard* machines which prepare accounting records, but more specifically to describe a *punched card tabulator* capable of reading cards and producing lists and totals.

accumulator   Originally used to describe an electronic device performing arithmetic on *operands*; usually a part of the *arithmetic unit* consisting of a special register and associated circuitry. Now used frequently to refer to any *store* location in which arithmetic results are created. The implication is that an accumulator stores one value and on receipt of a second value it creates and stores the sum of these values.

accumulator register   Synonymous with *accumulator*.

accuracy   The size of error or range of error, the degree of conformity to a rule. High accuracy implies small error, but accuracy is contrasted with precision, e.g., three places of decimals properly computed are less precise but more accurate than four places of decimals containing an error.

AC dump   The removal of all alternating current from a system or part of a system; this may be intentional or accidental.

ACK   ◊ *acknowledgement*.

acknowledgement   1. A message given in reply to a message or signal within a computer system when an immediate response to initiate another action is not required. 2. A message which indicates the status of a message passed in the opposite direction on a *network*. The message ACK is a positive acknowledgement confirming that the message has been correctly received, while the message *NAK* is a *negative acknowledgement* indicating that the message was not correctly received and should be retransmitted.

ACM   Abbreviation for association for computing machinery.

acoustic coupler   A device which allows a telephone handset to be connected to a telephone network for *data transmission*, and allows serial digital data to be converted into a frequency in the audio range. Used for connecting portable *terminals* to remote computers.

acoustic delay line   A *delay line* containing a medium which reacts to the propagation of sound waves.

Also known as sonic delay line.

acoustic memory   Synonymous with *acoustic store*.

25

acoustic store A *regenerative store* using an *acoustic delay line*. Also known as acoustic memory. ⊘ *delay line store*.

acronym A group of letters formed from the initial letters of the words in a pronounceable phrase, e.g., FORTRAN from FORmula TRANslator. Sometimes any appropriate letters are chosen, e.g., the word *bit* comes from *b*inary dig*it*, and all too often the acronym is thought of first and a tortuous phrase is invented to fit it.

action message A message generated by a *program* or an *operating system* indicating that a condition has occurred requiring operator action.

action period The time during which data stored in a *Williams tube store* may be read or new data may be written to the store.

active element 1. That part of a computer system capable of performing operations. 2. A circuit receiving energy from a source other than a main input signal.

active star A *network* in which the external *nodes* are all connected to a single central node, which processes all messages from external to central and from external, via central, to external. ⊘ *network architecture*.

activity 1. In PERT and *critical path method* an activity is the representation on the network of an actual task consuming time and resources necessary for progress from one *event* to another. Where interdependencies consume neither time nor resources they may be shown as activities, which may also represent waiting periods and transfers of information as well as actual jobs to be performed. 2. A *read* or *write* operation carried out on a *file*. The *activity ratio* is analysed to allow available resources to be optimized.

activity ratio The ratio of the number of *records* which have moved in a *file* being updated to the total number of records in that file.

actual address Synonymous with *absolute address*.

actual code Synonymous with *absolute code*.

actual decimal point A decimal point which appears on a screen or as a printed character on a *print-out* and for which an actual *location* has been allowed in *store*. Contrasted with *assumed decimal point*.

actual instruction Synonymous with *effective instruction*.

actuator 1. Any device which, under the control of a signal, can carry out mechanical action. 2. The mechanism of a *magnetic disk drive* which causes the *read/write head* to be moved to the *track*.

Ada A *programming language* developed for US Department of Defense specifically for *real-time* systems and in particular for systems in which computers are used for control. Ada therefore includes facilities for concurrent programming and allows development of very large systems with program development tools specified in an Ada Programming Support Environment (APSE). The language is named after Lord Byron's daughter Augusta Ada Lovelace, who worked with Charles Babbage and is not unjustly described as the first programmer.

adaptive channel allocation A method of controlling a communication channel by an *adaptive control system* so that the channels are allocated in accordance with changing requirements rather than in a fixed pattern. ⇨ *multiplex*².

adaptive control system A control system which continuously monitors its own behaviour and, by adjusting its *parameters*, is able to suit itself to a changing environment.

adaptive routing A method of *routing* messages on a *network* in which the route is adapted to avoid line failures or to cope with a new traffic pattern. A feature of *packet switching* services.

addend One of the *operands* used in performing the function of addition. A distinction is usually drawn between the addend and its counterpart the *augend*. The addend is added to the augend to form a *sum*, in such a manner that the augend is replaced by the sum and the addend remains in its original form.

adder A device performing the function of addition using digital signals. It receives three inputs representing *addend, augend* and a *carry* digit; and will provide two outputs representing the *sum* and a carry digit.

It is also known as digital adder, and is sometimes referred to as a full adder to distinguish it from *half adder*.

adder, binary half ⇨ *binary half adder*.

adder-subtracter A device which acts as either an *adder* or a *subtracter*.

addition An arithmetic operation in which two *operands* – the *addend* and *augend* – are added to form a *sum*.

additional characters Synonymous with *special characters*.

addition record When a *file* is being updated a *record* added to the file, as opposed to one which amends an existing record, is known as an addition record.

addition table In computers which use *table look-up* techniques for addition, the area of *memory* holding the table of numbers to be used is known as the addition table.

addition without carry Synonymous with *exclusive-or operation*.

address 1. That part of an *instruction* which specifies the location of an *operand*. 2. The location of an identified position in the topology of a network, recognizing that systems with layered *protocols* such as X.25 may have different address forms for different levels. 3. Used as a verb, to indicate a specific location. ⟫ *real address, physical address, virtual address*.

address bus   A *bus* used only for the transmission of *address data*.

address computation   An operation on the *address* part of a *program instruction*. Related to *arithmetic address*.

address, direct   Synonymous with *absolute address*.

address format   The way in which the *address* part of an *instruction* is arranged.

address generation   A technique used to retrieve *records* from a randomly stored *direct access file*.

address, indirect   ⟫ *indirect addressing*.

addressing   An *address* is that part of an *instruction* which specifies the location of an *operand*. Each *word* or *byte* of *store* is allocated a number which is part of the coding system used by the *program controller* to perform operations on data; by specifying the number of a particular word as part of a program instruction, access is obtained to the operand stored within the word. To simplify the *assembly* of large programs a system of *relative addressing* is often used, in which the programmer does not use the *absolute addresses* which form the *machine code*. Instead addresses are specified relative to a *base address*[2] which is added to the *relative address* during assembly of the program or when the program is *loaded*. Thus *segments* of a program can be written independently by different programmers each using relative addresses. When programs are written in a programming language names are allocated to operands and these names, sometimes referred to as *symbolic addresses*, are used to specify the operands to be processed by particular instructions.

address, instruction   The *address* of a *location* containing an *instruction*.

addressless instruction format   Synonymous with *zero address instruction format*.

address, machine   Synonymous with *absolute address*.

address mapping   Conversion of data used to represent the physical location of *fields* or *records* and the process by which records or *blocks* of information are assigned to *storage* locations. For example, the translation of a *virtual address* to an *absolute address* or *real address*.

address modification   The process of changing the *address* part of an *instruction* by means of a *modifier*, so that the instruction will operate upon a different *operand* each time the *routine* containing the instruction is performed. ↷ *instruction modification, program modification.*

address, multi- ↷ *multiple address.*

address, one ↷ *one address instruction.*

address, one-plus-one ↷ *one-plus-one address.*

address part The part of an *instruction* in which is given the *location* of an *operand*.

address, real ↷ *real address.*

address register A *register* in which an *address* is stored.

address, specific Synonymous with *absolute address*.

address, three ↷ *three address instruction.*

address track A *track* on a *storage device* (e.g., on a *magnetic drum*) which contains *addresses* to facilitate *access* to data stored on other tracks.

address translation slave store A *hardware* entity used to assist in the translation of *addresses*, e.g., a *virtual address* to a *real address*.

address, variable Synonymous with *indexed address*.

address, virtual ↷ *virtual address.*

address, zero level Synonymous with *immediate address*.

add-subtract time The time required by a computer to add or subtract, exclusive of the *read time* or *write time*.

add time The time required by a computer to perform one addition, exclusive of the *read time* or *write time*.

ADP Abbreviation of *automatic data processing*.

advance feed tape *Paper tape* in which the leading edge of the *feed holes* is in line with the leading edge of the (larger) character holes, thus making it possible to distinguish between the front end and the tail end of a piece of perforated tape. Contrasted with *centre feed tape*.

after-look journalizing In a system in which extensive recovery facilities are needed to safeguard against system failure, a journal is made of amendments to files. This term signifies that an entry is made to the journal after each change made to the file concerned. ↷ *before-look journalizing*.

agenda A set of operations which form a procedure for solving a problem. In *linear programming*, a group of programs used to manipulate a problem matrix.

agendum call card In *linear programming*, a *punched card* containing one item of an *agenda* used to manipulate a problem matrix.

AI Abbreviation for *artificial intelligence*.

ALGOL ALGOL is an acronym for ALGOrithmic Language. It is a *problem oriented high level* programming *language* for mathematical and scientific use, in which the *source program* provides a means of defining *algorithms* as a series of statements and declarations having a general resemblance to algebraic formulae and English sentences.

An ALGOL program consists of *data items, statements* and *declarations*, organized in a program structure in which statements are combined to form compound statements and blocks.

Every data item processed in an ALGOL program is termed a variable, and is assigned a general name or identifier by the programmer. Groups of similar items of data can be processed as *arrays*, individual items within the *array* being identified by means of the identifier of the array followed by a *subscript*.

Every operation a program is to perform is represented as a statement. Statements may be assignment statements or conditional statements. An assignment statement has the form 'Variable := Arithmetic Expression' where the symbol ':=' means 'becomes', and the arithmetic expression includes variables, numbers and a series of standard functions, combined by the *operators* $+$, $-$, $\times$, $/$, $\uparrow$ (*exponentiation*). An example of an assignment statement is

$$x := (-b + sqrt(b \uparrow 2 - 4 \times a \times c))/(2 \times a)$$

Any statement may be labelled by an identifier, which may be used subsequently as a reference for a branch statement. Conditional statements are used to express branches if specified conditions are satisfied. 'For statements' are used in the construction of *loops*. ALGOL also includes facilities for logical or *Boolean operations*. Certain variables can be declared as capable of taking only the values 'true' or 'false', and such variables can appear in statements containing the logical operators 'and', 'or', 'not', 'implies' or 'equivalent'.

Declarations are used in ALGOL to provide the compiler with information about quantities appearing in the remainder of the program. The 'type declaration' is used to specify whether a variable is an *integer* (a whole number falling within a range determined by the capacity of the computer being used), a 'real number' (a number expressed in *floating point representation*) or a 'Boolean variable' (capable of taking the values 'true' or 'false'). An 'array declaration' specifies not only the type of the elements but the range of *subscripts*, e.g., integer array Table [1:12, 1:15], which specifies storage for 12×15 integer elements, referred to as Table [1, 1] to Table [12, 15]. The 'procedure declaration' permits the programmer to give a series of statements an identifier, and to use this series of statements as a *subroutine* merely by quoting this identifier.

The structure of an ALGOL program consists of a series of consecutive statements separated by semicolons. A series of statements may be combined to form a compound statement by enclosing the statement between the statement parentheses 'begin' and 'end'. A block has the form of a compound statement but contains at least one declaration. A complete program will normally consist of a number of blocks. This block structure of ALGOL is of great value because it permits parts of a program to be written by different programmers with no risk of duplication of identifiers; and it permits the compiler to produce an efficient and economical program by sharing storage between separate blocks. This is equivalent to the use of *segments* and *overlays* in other languages.

ALGOL was originally known as IAL or International Algebraic Language, and was developed in Europe at the same time as FORTRAN was being developed in the United States.

algorithm A series of instructions or procedural steps for the solution of a specific problem.

algorithmic Pertaining to a method of problem-solving by a fixed procedure; ⟡ *algorithm*. Contrasted with *heuristic approach*.

algorithm translation A translation from one language to another by means of an *algorithm*.

allocate As a result of an action performed by an operator, a *program instruction*, or automatically by an *executive program*, to place a *peripheral unit* or *memory* area under the control of a program. The *hardware* allocated may be *released* and made available to some other program, in contrast to the situation where hardware is *assigned* to a program for a whole *run*. ⟡ *storage allocation*.

allocation Any planning needs, above everything else, to allocate the available resources to provide the best possible result, but before the resources can be allocated the meaning of 'best possible result' must be established, and it will be necessary to devise some criterion to judge the economic effect of each complete set of such allocations. In most business applications this criterion will be either total profit or total cost and the objective is to find the allocation which will maximize or minimize these respectively. Of course adjustments will have to be made for appreciation of investment and depreciation of inventory, but even so the problem would basically be a simple one if each resource could be examined independently. Unfortunately this is invariably not the case: the allocation of a resource limits the allocation of some or all of the other resources. If we decide to develop a new product, then this will require some of our manpower to be scheduled into this activity,

31

which will in turn affect our recruitment campaigns, etc. The problems now become very complex since out of the many possible allocations the 'best' allocation of resources is not immediately obvious.

Methods of mathematical programming have been designed to solve such allocation problems. Mathematical programming can be considered in two separate categories: the treatment of linear forms, and the treatment of non-linear forms. In the linear category the objective (e.g., total profit) must be a linear function of the variables (cost per item, etc.); i.e., for each unit being considered the other variables must have fixed profit, cost, etc. If one costs £1, two must cost £2 and three £3. In the non-linear category this restriction is much weaker, the relationship between cost per unit and number of units, etc., need only be expressable as a function.

allocation, dynamic storage ⟡ *dynamic allocation (of memory)*.

all-purpose computer Synonymous with *general purpose computer*.

alphabetic Pertaining to a *character set* or a field of data in which the coded characters relate to letters of the alphabet only. As this is sometimes loosely used to include symbols, such as /@ $ £, it is as well to qualify the term when using it.

alphabetic code A system of coding data by the use of combinations of letters to represent items of information, either as abbreviations or *mnemonics*. ⟡ *alphabetic*.

alphabetic string A *string*[2] in which the characters belong to a set of words including an *alphabetic* set.

alphageometric In *videotex*, *picture description instructions* transmitted to a *terminal* resulting in the graphic display of line drawings, colour-filling of polygons, approximately curved lines, etc., as well as text and character display. An accepted standard for alphageometric display is the North American Presentation Level Protocol Syntax. ⟡ *alphamosaic, alphaphotographic*.

alphameric code Synonymous with *alphanumeric code*.

alphamosaic In *videotex* and *teletext*, a method of coding which allows signals transmitted to a *terminal* to be displayed in a mosaic of 2×3 rectangles. This method uses a simple and inexpensive decoder, but is restricted to text and pictures which do not rely for their effect on curved or diagonal lines (both of which take on a staircase-like effect). ⟡ *alphageometric, alphaphotographic*.

alphanumeric code Pertaining to a *character set* or *field* of data in which the coded characters may represent numerals or letters of the alphabet. In its strictest sense does not contain coded characters relating to symbols such as /@ $ £.

alphaphotographic In *videotex*, a method of coding which allows signals transmitted to a *terminal* to be displayed with photographic quality. The time needed for transmission and complexity of decoding restricts use of such coding. ⟡ *alphageometric, alphamosaic*.

alteration Synonymous with *inclusive-or operation*.

alteration switch A *switch*³ in which the path selected can be determined either manually or by *program*. Related to *indicator*.²

alternative denial Synonymous with *not-and operation*.

ALU Acronym for *Arithmetic and Logic Unit*.

Alvey programme A collaborative programme of work on fifth-generation computing undertaken in the UK, with research results shared between participants. John Alvey chaired the working party which recommended the programme.

ambiguity error An error occurring in the reading of a number when its digital representation is changing: imprecise synchronization may, for example, cause the number 399 to be read as 499 when it was in fact passing to 400. ⟡ *guard signal*.

amendment file Synonymous with *change file*.

amendment record Synonymous with *change record*.

amendment tape Synonymous with *change tape*.

amplifier A device which is capable of accepting an *input* signal in wave form and of delivering a magnified signal of the current or voltage applied to it.

amplifier, DC ⟡ *directly coupled amplifier*.

amplifier, inverting Synonymous with *sign-reversing amplifier*.

amplifier, sign-changing Synonymous with *sign-reversing amplifier*.

amplitude The magnitude of a variable, usually its maximum value whether or not it varies with time.

analog The representation and measurement of the performance or behaviour of a *system* by continuously variable physical entities such as currents, voltages, etc. ⟡ general article on *Analog Computers*. Contrasted with *digital*.

analog adder A device which provides one output variable which is a weighted sum of two input variables.

analog channel A channel, such as a *voice channel*, on which the data transmitted can be of any value between fixed limits defined by the channel.

analog computers Analog computers are machines designed to perform arithmetical functions upon numbers, where the numbers are represented by some physical quantity. For example, in mechanical analog computers the numbers are often represented by the physical dimensions of the members forming the various functional units, for instance by the angular rotation of shafts or gear wheels. In electrical analog machines voltages are used to represent the input variables.

Essentially an analog computer must be able to accept inputs which vary with respect to time, and directly apply these inputs to various devices within the computer which perform the computing operations of addition, subtraction, multiplication, division, integration and function generation. The output from the system may be in the form of a graph produced by a plotting pen, or a trace on a cathode-ray tube, and again the output signals might be used directly to control the operation of some other machine or process.

The computing units of analog computers are able to respond immediately to the changes which they detect in the input variables, and the connexion of these various units in a particular fashion can cause an analog computer to perform very complex arithmetical functions at high speed while the actual process under study is in operation. This ability to operate in *real time* mode means that analog computers have many applications in the scientific and industrial fields in simulating various physical systems or automatically controlling industrial processes. They are widely used for research into design problems, particularly where the solution is required speedily without difficult setting-up problems.

Analog computers do not have the ability of digital computers to store data in large quantities, nor do they have the comprehensive logical facilities afforded by programming digital machines. And although the arithmetic functions performed by the computing units are more complex in analog machines than in the digital systems, the cost of the hardware required to provide a high degree of accuracy in an analog machine is often prohibitive.

Some analog machines are designed for specific applications, but most electrical and electronic analog computers provide a number of different computing devices which can be connected together via a plugboard to provide different methods of operation for specified problems.

⟡ *digital computers* and *hybrid computers*.

analog/digital converter A unit which converts output signals from an *analog computer* into *digital* representation for use in a digital computing system.

analog network A circuit representing physical variables in such a way that mathematical relationships can be shown directly by examining measurable quantities continuously.

analog representation   A representation of a variable by a physical quantity (such as voltage) whose magnitude is directly proportional to the variable.

analogue   ◇ *analog*.

analyser   A *program* which analyses other programs submitted to it, summarizing references to *locations* in *store* and following the sequences of *branch instructions*. Such a program is an aid to *debugging*.

analyser, digital differential   ◇ *digital differential analyser*.

analyser, electronic differential   ◇ *electronic differential analyser*.

analyser, mechanical differential   ◇ *mechanical differential analyser*.

analysis   The study of a concept or *system* by breaking it down to the separate elements that form the whole structure in order to determine the functional relationship between these elements. Contrasted with *synthesis*.

analysis, systems   ◇ *systems analysis*.

analyst, systems   ◇ general article on *Computer Personnel*.

analytical function generator   A *function generator* in which the *function*² is a physical law.

  Also known as natural law function generator, natural function generator.

and circuit   Synonymous with *and element*.

and element   A *logic element* operating with *binary digits* which provides one output signal from two input signals according to the following rules:

Input		Output
1	0	0
1	1	1
0	1	0
0	0	0

Thus a 1 digit is obtained as output only if two 1 digits are present as coincident input signals. See also *Boolean algebra*.

  Also known as and gate, coincidence gate.

and gate   Synonymous with *and element*.

and operation   A logical operation applied to two *operands* which will produce a result depending on the *bit patterns* of the operands and according to the following rules for each bit position:

Operands		Result
p	q	r
1	0	0
1	1	1
0	1	0
0	0	0

For example, operating upon the following 6-bit operands,

$$p = 110110$$
$$q = 011010$$

$$r = 010010$$

Also known as conjunction, logical product, intersection, meet operation. ⟡ *Boolean algebra.*

annotation Synonymous with *comment.*

anomalistic period The interval of time between one passage of a satellite through its *apogee* and the next consecutive passage.

ANSI Acronym for American National Standards Institute.

anticoincidence circuit Synonymous with *anticoincidence element.*

anticoincidence element A *logic element* operating with *binary digits* which provides one output signal from two input signals according to the following rules:

Input		Output
1	0	1
1	1	0
0	1	1
0	0	0

Thus a 1 digit is obtained as output only if two differing input signals are received. Synonymous with *exclusive-or element.* ⟡ *Boolean algebra.*

anticoincidence operation Synonymous with *exclusive-or operation.*

aperture plate A small part of a piece of ferromagnetic material constituting a *magnetic cell.*

APL Abbreviation of a programming language, a language which provides a set of powerful operators for the handling of multidimensional arrays and also allows the user to define his own operators.

apogee The point in its orbit at which a satellite is at its maximum distance from Earth.

application The particular kind of problem to which *data processing* techniques are applied; applications are usually referred to as being either 'computational', i.e., requiring considerable computing capacity, or 'data processing', i.e., where data handling capacity is of greatest importance.

application level One of the seven layers of the *ISO Seven Layer Reference Model*. The application level is the seventh layer. It provides direct support of application processes and *programs* of the end user and the management of the interconnexion of these programs to the communication entities.

application package A *program* or *suite of programs* designed to perform a specific type of work (e.g., payroll, sales ledger, or storm sewer analysis). The package may contain a number of functions pertaining to the field of application, but individual users can select functions required and vary their *input* and *output* requirements by using *parameters*.

application program A *program* forming part of a user's job and written by the user, as distinct from programs forming part of the general purpose *software* used to manage the operation of the total computer system.

application system A system designed to perform a particular task; a term used to distinguish a user's system from the various compiling systems and systems management software with which an *application* will co-exist within the computer.

application virtual machine Relates to a user's system operating in a computer system which is able to provide a *virtual machine environment*. Each application is allocated certain *hardware* and *software* resources, so that to the user his particular *application* appears to be operating within a computer system dedicated to his task. Each user job is, therefore, said to occupy a virtual machine.

APSE Acronym for Ada Programming Support Environment. ◊ *Ada*.

arbitrarily sectioned file A *file* which has been organized in a simple manner to allow for the addition and removal of *sections* automatically.

arbitrary function generator Synonymous with *general purpose function generator*.

architectural protection Relates to the *hardware* and *software* facilities built into a computer system by the manufacturer to provide for the security of processes and data handled within the system. For example, facilities intended to prevent one user *application program* from interfering with others with which it may co-exist.

architecture The design of a computer and the way in which *hardware* and *software* interact to provide basic facilities and levels of performance. Computer manufacturers design computers to meet the needs of particular segments of the market and any particular model is designed to meet some or all of a number of design objectives. The architecture of the machine relates to the way in which hardware and software are constructed to achieve the objectives of the design. (Examples of design objectives: speed of throughput, resilience to system failure, cost, protection and security of user applications, ease of maintenance, ability to control several applications at once, orientation to specific types of work.)

archived file A *file* which has been *stored* on some backing medium (e.g., *magnetic disk*) and not held permanently *on-line* to the *main store*. The file will not appear in the *operating system*'s catalogue of current files, but can be reconstituted should the need arise. Archiving provides a cheaper method of storing data not required frequently, and the removal of files of this type from the *filestore* can greatly improve the efficiency of a computer system.

archiving The process of creating and maintaining *archived files* within a computer system – one of the functions which will be performed by an *operating system* under the control of the operations staff.

area Any part of *memory* assigned to hold data of a specified type. Such assignation may be at the programmer's discretion or determined by *hardware*.

area, common storage ◊ *common area*.

area search The scanning of a large group of *records* to select those of a major category or class for further processing.

area, working ◊ *work area*.

argument 1. A variable used to reference a table – the *key* which specifies the *location* of a particular item. 2. Synonymous with the *fixed point part* of a number in *floating point representation*. 3. A variable factor the value of which determines the value of a function.

arithmetic address An *address* obtained by performing an arithmetic operation on another address. Related to *address computation*.

arithmetical instruction An *instruction* which specifies an arithmetic operation upon data, e.g., addition or multiplication. Arithmetical instructions form a subset of the machine *instruction set* to be considered separately from *logical instructions*.

arithmetical operation An operation performed using the arithmetic instructions, e.g., addition, subtraction, multiplication and division. Performed upon numerical *operands* and yielding a numerical result according to the rules for arithmetic. ⇨ *logical operations*.

arithmetical shift To multiply or divide a numerical *operand* according to the number base inherent in the structure of the word holding the number. For example, if a number is stored in *decimal notation* as in a *character oriented* word, a *left shift* of n places has the effect of multiplying by 10^n. Similarly, a *right shift* has the effect of dividing by the appropriate power of ten. With numbers stored in *binary notation* a left shift has the effect of multiplying by 2^n and conversely, a right shift of dividing by 2^n. Contrasted with *logical shift*.

arithmetic and logic unit The *hardware unit* of a *central processor* which deals with arithmetical and logical operations.

arithmetic check The verification of an arithmetical process by means of a further arithmetical process, e.g., multiplying 33 by 18 to produce an arithmetic check of the result of 18 multiplied by 3 multiplied by 11.

arithmetic, floating-decimal ⇨ *floating point arithmetic*.

arithmetic instruction ⇨ *arithmetical instruction*.

arithmetic, multi-length ⇨ *multiple-length arithmetic*.

arithmetic operation ⇨ *arithmetical operation*.

arithmetic organ Synonymous with *arithmetic unit*.

arithmetic overflow ⇨ *overflow*.

arithmetic register A *register*, usually part of the *arithmetic unit*, constructed for containing the *operands* and results of arithmetic functions on data.

arithmetic shift ⇨ *arithmetical shift*.

arithmetic unit A unit within a computer performing *arithmetical operations* on *operands*; may also perform *arithmetic shifts, logical shifts* and other *logical operations* on data.

Also known as arithmetic organ. ⇨ *arithmetic and logic unit, arithmetic register*.

ARPANET Acronym for Advanced Research Projects Agency Network, an early *packet switching service*.

array An arrangement of items of data each identified by a *key* or *subscript*. Constructed in such a way that a *program* can examine the array in order to extract data relevant to a particular key or subscript. The dimension of an array is the number of subscripts necessary to identify an item; e.g., if an array consists of the days of the year, the array is one-dimensional if any day is identified by its number, e.g., 32 for 1 February, and two-dimensional if identified by day and month, e.g., (1, 2) for 1 February.

array processor A computer whose *architecture* allows it to process *arrays* of numbers by including a set of processors which work simultaneously, each one working on one element of the array in parallel.

artificial intelligence A term used to describe the use of computers in such a way that they perform operations analagous to the human abilities of learning and decision taking. Often used to embrace *expert systems*, *knowledge-based systems* and *decision support systems*, although strictly speaking neither of these requires a learning ability.

ASCII Acronym for American Standard Code for Information Interchange.

ASR Abbreviation of *automatic send-receive set*.

assemble To put a *program* through the process of *assembly* by means of an *assembly program*.

assembler Synonymous with *assembly program*.

assembly The operation on a *symbolic language program* which produces a complete program in *machine language*. Basically, assembly consists of (*a*) the translation of symbolic operation codes and *addresses* to machine language form, and (*b*) the grouping of the resultant machine language program from its constituent parts, e.g., the inclusion of *library software*, consolidation of program *segments*, adjustments to *links*, etc. ⟡ *compiler*, from which it is distinguished by the fact that assembly produces machine *instructions* on a one-for-one basis from relative instructions, while compiling usually produces many machine instructions from one *pseudo instruction*. ⟡ general article on *Languages*.

assembly language Any *symbolic language* used for programming which must go through an *assembly* in order to be converted into the *machine code* required for operation on a computer.

assembly list A list which may be produced during *assembly* to show the details of the *symbolic language* and the corresponding details of the *machine language* form created by assembly. The comparison of the two languages is particularly useful for any *debugging* which may be necessary.

assembly program The *program* which operates on a *symbolic language* program to produce a *machine language* program in the process of *assembly*.

Also known as assembler, assembly routine.

assembly routine   Synonymous with *assembly program*.

assembly unit   Part of a *program* capable of being incorporated into a larger program by the process of *assembly*, e.g., a *subroutine* forming part of the *library facilities* of the system.

assign   To reserve a part of a computing system (usually a *peripheral unit*) for a specific purpose. This reservation is normally permanent for the duration of a *program*. Contrasted with *allocate*.

associative memory   Synonymous with *associative store*.

associative store   A *store* whose *locations* are identified by their content rather than by their specific *address*.

Also known as associative memory, content-addressed storage, parallel search storage.

assumed decimal point   The position where a decimal point would appear when decimal fractions are printed or stored continuously with their *integral* part. Contrasted with *actual decimal point*.

asynchronous computer   A computer which operates on a method of *asynchronous working*.

asynchronous data transmission   A method of slow speed *data transmission* in which the transmission of successive characters is initiated on the completion of the reception of the preceding character. Contrasted with *synchronous data transmission*.

asynchronous working   Mode of operation for a machine in which the completion of one operation initiates another. Contrasted with a machine in which operations are synchronized to a schedule provided by a clocking device (*synchronous working*).

asyndetic   Omitting *connectives*.

attended time   Time during which the computer is attended for serviceable operation (*up time*) or out of service for maintenance or engineering work.

attentuate   To cause the reduction in amplitude of a signal.

attenuation   The difference in amplitude between a signal at transmission and at reception.

Also known as loss.

atto-   Prefix denoting one million-million-millionth or 10^{-18}.

audio   Used to describe frequencies capable of being heard by the human ear, i.e., between 15 cycles and 20,000 cycles per second.

audio response unit   Pre-recorded responses held in a digitally coded form on a computer *storage device* can be linked by an audio response unit to a telephone network to provide audible responses to inquiries.

audit of computer systems   Ever since the earliest commercial *punched card* systems the *audit trail* has been in danger and auditors, both internal and external, have come to feel that much of their job lies in defending the trail from the possible ravages of *systems analysts* and *programmers*. The difficulty arises in ensuring that good intentions about liaison do not deteriorate into the sudden realization that a *source document* can no longer be traced through to its final home in the company's financial statements.

The first step is usually to ensure that no *systems definition* may be passed for *programming* or implementation until it has been formally approved by both internal and external auditors. (Systems definitions usually have to be signed off by other authorities such as the user departments, operating authority, etc., and the formal addition of the auditors to this cycle presents no problems.) Approval must also, of course, be given to any amendments to the system that are made later, and although it can be a tedious business getting approval for every small amendment to a new system, anarchy will prevail if this is not made a firm rule.

Even the regular approval of new systems is not the whole answer to ensuring that oversight or over-sophistication do not destroy the audit trail: anyone who has been given a three-inch thick systems definition and asked to approve it will appreciate that a prior knowledge of the design and workings of the system is invaluable in checking a definition for flaws. Auditors can acquire this by being present regularly at the design stage of a new system, and many companies now make it a rule that representatives of the auditors discuss new systems with analysts on a once-a-week basis. This ensures at least that the completed definition is not entirely new ground, and also allows the auditor to suggest amendments to the system before such amendments involve a laborious rewriting and re-drawing of a large part of the definition.

Having made sure that a new system has adequate controls and that the audit trail is satisfactory, the auditor now needs to consider methods of ensuring that the systems he has approved are the systems which are in fact operating. The main check here will be on the *programs*, and it is usual for auditors to maintain a secure copy of each program (perhaps in a fire-proof locked cabinet) and to compare these programs on a regular basis with those which are actually being used. The auditor must also constantly satisfy himself that adequate disciplines are being maintained in all the data processing areas – programming, *data preparation, work assembly*, operating and control – and his best chance of making sure that the disciplines he watches are indeed adequate is to ask for written standards of procedure against which he can check actual procedure.

So far we have outlined only an extra burden for the auditor, but computer systems can also be of great benefit to him and the more familiar an auditor is with computers the more readily he will call for special audit programs. Such programs might select particular transactions for a manual audit, either on a random basis or on an exception rating, i.e., all transactions which exceed a certain norm; or information obtained by audit staff at remote centres can be processed and compared with *master records*, saving audit time and increasing its breadth of operation. Again, details of transactions can be reframed and analysed in ways designed by the auditor, perhaps as part of the regular system so that special audit runs are made at the end of each job.

The computer can be a great help to an auditor, but it is clear that this is possible only when the auditor is to some extent familiar with the abilities – and requirements – of a computer. Regular discussion with the data processing personnel should give him this familiarity, and a once-a-week check on the design of new systems is perhaps the most satisfactory way of achieving this.

audit trail A record of processes and events relating to a specific record, transaction, or *file*. In a computer system the trail will be stored as a file and is created during the routine processing of data as a separate activity, thus allowing the system to be audited or subsequent reconstitution of files. ⬙ general article on *Audit of Computer Systems*.

augend One of the *operands* employed in addition, used specifically to denote the operand that is replaced by the *sum* on completion of the operation. ⬙ *addend*.

augment To increase a quantity in order to bring it to a required value.

augmenter A quantity added to another in order to bring it to a required value; an augmenter may be either positive or negative.

auto-abstract ⬙ *automatic abstract*.

autocode Once synonymous with *basic language* or *high-level language*.

autodial To initiate a process which activates an *autodialer*.

autodialer A device which, when activated by a short code or mnemonic key or, in *videotex*, by the selection of a number from a *menu*, causes the dialling of a prerecorded telephone number and subsequent connexion to a computer.

automatic abstract Key words selected from a document and arranged in an order meaningful to human beings; the selection and arranging is carried out automatically in accordance with certain criteria *programmed* previously.

automatically cleared failure A failure which is corrected by the system itself, e.g., a *parity* failure which has been overcome by retransmission of the data *blocks* concerned.

automatically corrected error An error which is detected and corrected by a system without the aid of an operator. Relates to the data handled by a system and is not necessarily caused by a failure of *hardware* or *software*.

automatic carriage A control device on, for example, typewriters and automatic *key punches*, which can control automatically the spacing, skipping, feeding and ejecting of paper, cards, preprinted forms, etc.

automatic check Any facility, *software* or *hardware*, for automatically performing a check for the absence of specific errors. Sometimes contrasted with *programmed check* and used only in the sense of *hardware check*.

automatic coding Any technique using a computer to assist in the clerical work of programming.

Also known as automatic programming. ⊄› *relative coding, symbolic coding*.

automatic data processing Any form of processing performed by automatic equipment. The term was at one time used to distinguish work performed by electro-mechanical equipment (e.g., *punched card machines*) from electronic data processing work carried out on electronic computers.

The distinction is now obsolete and both terms are used with equal validity.

automatic dictionary In *information retrieval* systems, an automatic dictionary substitutes codes for words and phrases. In a language translating system it provides a word-for-word substitution from one language to another. ⊄› *dictionary*.

automatic error correction A technique which makes use of *error detecting codes* and *error correcting codes* and (usually) automatic retransmission. Errors in transmission are automatically corrected.

automatic exchange A transmission exchange in which communication between terminals is effected without intervention from operators.

automatic feed punch Synonymous with *automatic punch*.

automatic hardware dump A *dump* arising from a system error and used to provide information for diagnostic purposes, e.g., concerning the internal state of the *instruction code* processes. The information will be dumped to a medium which is conveniently analysed by the maintenance staff.

Also known as hard dump, hardware dump.

automatic interrupt   An interruption to a *program* caused by a *hardware* device or *executive program*, acting on some event occurring independently of the interrupted program.

Also known as automatic program interrupt.

automatic message switching centre   ⟡ *switching centre*.

automatic paper tape punch   Synonymous with *automatic tape punch*.

automatic program interrupt   Synonymous with *automatic interrupt*.

automatic programming   1. Synonymous with *automatic coding*. 2. The process of generating a *program* automatically without first having to describe the required result in a *procedural language*; the objective might be, for example, the automatic generation of programs to process documents whose descriptions and relationships have been provided.

automatic punch   A *key punch* in which *punched cards* were passed through the machine automatically. Contrasted with *hand punch*.

Also known as automatic feed punch.

automatic restart   A *restart* effected automatically by an *operating system* without reference to the computer operators.

automatics   The theory of *automation*.

automatic send–receive set   A *teletypewriter* which both receives and transmits.

automatic stop   A computer may be programmed to stop when an *automatic check* detects an error; the halt is then known as an automatic stop.

automatic switching centre   ⟡ *switching centre*.

automatic tape punch   A *tape punch* activated automatically by signals transmitted from a *central processor* or over some *data transmission* circuit.

automatic verifier   A *punched card* machine used for *card verifying*.

automation   The automatic implementation of a process; the control of a process by the use of automatic devices.

automonitor   A *program* which causes a computer to keep a record of its own processing operations. ⟡ article on *Debugging*.

autopolling   Referring to a party-line transmission circuit; each station is allowed to transmit according to a predetermined arrangement. ⟡ *poll*.

auxiliary equipment   *Data processing* equipment not under the direct control of a central processor. ⟡ *backing store, off-line equipment*.

auxiliary store   Synonymous with *backing store*.

availability ratio   Synonymous with *operating ratio*.

available machine time   Synonymous with *available time*.[1]

available point   A position on a *terminal screen* capable of being *addressed* and for which such characteristics as colour and intensity may be specified.

available time 1. The time during which a computer is not under maintenance and has the power switched on and is otherwise ready for use. 2. The amount of time a computer is available to a particular user.

AVL tree A *binary* search tree arranged so that for each *node* the heights (levels) of the sub-trees do not differ by more than one, and thus produce a tree in which the heights are balanced. Named after its original identifiers, Adelson, Velskin and Landis.

axiomatic semantics A technique of describing, for a particular *program statement*, what should be true after the statement has been *executed*; the description is made in terms of what was true before execution, and the technique of describing in 'axioms' is thus important in attempts to prove that a program is fault-free.

B

back-end processor A *processor* which is dedicated to carrying out a specific function (such as *data base management*) as part of a complete process. Contrasted with *front-end processor*.

backgrounding ⟡ *background processing*.

background job A *job* in an *operating system* which has a lower priority than jobs being run simultaneously which involve any *on-line* activity. ⟡ *background processing*[1].

background processing 1. In a *multi-access* system, processing which does not make use of *on-line* or interactive facilities. 2. High priority processing which takes precedence (as a result of *program interrupts*) over *foreground processing*. 3. Low priority processing over which foreground processing takes precedence. Note: as definitions 2 and 3 are directly contradictory and definition 1 has a related but different meaning, this phrase should be used with caution. Definition 3 is the most commonly used.

Also known as backgrounding.

background program A *program* which requires *background processing*.

background reflectance In *optical character recognition*, the degree of reflection caused by those areas around an inked character.

backing store A store of larger *capacity* but slower *access time* than the *main memory* or *immediate access store* of a computer.

Also known as bulk store, auxiliary store, secondary store.

backplane The *board* by means of which a *central processor* communicates with its *peripheral units*. A backplane usually consists of a board with a number of sockets connected to the internal wiring of the computer in such a way that peripheral units can be connected through interface cards inserted into the sockets.

Also known as *motherboard*.

backspace In *sequential processing, punching* or typing: to move backward one unit at a time.

backup A facility intended to provide a service in the event of loss of

47

service from some other resource; any resource necessary for effective *recovery*.

backup storage   A section of *storage* not normally available to users but used within the computer system under the control of system management *software* to provide security copies of certain classes of file.

Backus Naur form   An early, widely used formal notation to describe the *syntax* of a *programming language*. It was invented by John Backus and introduced to describe the syntax of *ALGOL 60* by Peter Naur, the editor of the ALGOL 60 Report.

backward recovery   A mode of system *recovery* in which transactions previously applied to a *file* are processed to reinstate the file to an earlier condition.

badge reader   A *data collection* device (used, for example, in *in-plant* data communications systems) capable of reading data recorded as holes in prepunched cards, or plastic badges or more complex magnetic coding. Sometimes these devices are also fitted with keys so that data can be entered manually.

balanced error   When all values in an *error range* have an equal probability and the maximum and minimum values in the range are equal in value and opposite in sign, then the range has a balanced error.

balance error   In *analog* computing, an error voltage which occurs at output of analog adders and is a multiple of the *drift error*.

band   1. A group of magnetic *tracks* on a *magnetic drum* or *magnetic disk store*. 2. A range of frequencies between two defined limits.

bandwidth   The range of frequencies passed by a transmission channel. For convenience, in voice and data transmission terminology, frequencies are often classified as *narrow band* (up to 300 Hz), *voice band* (300–3000 Hz), and *broad band* or wide band (over 3000 Hz).

bar code   A pattern of vertical lines distinguished from each other by width. These can be read by a *bar-code scanner* to provide data to a computer. For example, coding on food packages is read at check-out terminals. In Europe the European Article Numbering Code is a standard, while the Universal Product Code is the North American standard.

bar-code scanner   An *optical character reader* which can automatically read data from documents bearing characters formed with a special bar code. The characters are translated into *digital* signals which may be entered directly into a *central processor* or recorded on some data medium such as *magnetic disk*.

barrel printer   A *printer* in which all the characters for printing are placed round the surface of a cylinder (the barrel), the entire *character set* being placed round the cylinder at each *print position*. *Print hammers* opposite each print position can be activated by the computer, striking the paper and bringing it in contact with a continuous ink ribbon between the paper and the surface of the barrel. The barrel rotates at high speed, the appropriate character being selected as it reaches a position immediately opposite the print hammers.

Also known as *drum printer*. ⟡ *on-the-fly printer*.

base 1. Synonymous with *radix*. 2. ⟡ *data base*.

base address 1. In *address modification*, an address to which a *modifier* is added in order to obtain a variable *operand* address. 2. During the *assembly* or *loading* of a *program*, an address added to the address component of each *instruction* in order to obtain *absolute addresses*. ⟡ *addressing*.

baseband signalling The transmission of a digital signal without *modulation*. Only one signal at a time can be present on a baseband channel. Baseband networks may use twisted pair or coaxial cables. Contrasted with *broadband signalling*.

base notation Synonymous with *radix notation*.

base number A quantity which specifies a system of representation for numbers. ⟡ *radix*.

BASIC is a *high level programming language* originally designed for developing programs in *conversational mode*, in an *on-line programming* environment. The name is an acronym for Beginner's All-purpose Symbolic Instruction Code. Because of its simplicity and comparative power, the language is much used on *personal computers*.

In a conversational system each element of the program is input in sequence directly to the computer, which carries out elementary checking and validation of each step before the next one is input. BASIC is designed to simplify conversational programming by avoiding any complications of structure or format, and providing extensive diagnostic facilities as an aid to *debugging* and error correction. The BASIC language contains two main parts, the *source language* statements themselves, which are the instructions forming the actual program, and system commands, which allow the user to control the use of the BASIC *compiling* system.

The *source language* facilities are comparable with *FORTRAN* (see general article on that language) with additional facilities for handling data transfers to and from files and powerful *matrix* handling facilities.

The particular feature of BASIC is the ability it allows the user to interact with the program while it is being *executed*. The basic element of a program is the 'line', which consists of a *statement* of the source language identified by a unique line number. Line numbers define the logical sequence of statements within the program and act as *labels*[2]. Since the sequence in which statements are executed depends on their line number, the order in which they are input by the user is immaterial. This means that insertions and corrections can be input without the need to copy out the whole program, provided the correct line number sequence is maintained.

Examples of source language statements used in BASIC may be found in the article on *FORTRAN*.

System commands allow the user to use the control and editing facilities of the language.

Editing facilities allow the user to delete parts of a program, or add parts of a different program without typing in all the statements line by line. Facilities also allow the user to output all or part of any program onto a terminal.

File maintenance facilities allow the user to set up and maintain files of program statements which can be retrieved and executed or combined into other programs.

Instant calculation facilities allow the user to perform any arithmetic function available within the source language without creating and compiling a program in order to do so.

Examples of system commands in BASIC are:

RUN	execute a program held in a BASIC work file
DELETE	remove a program from a work file
LIST	print a listing of a program on an output device
TYPE	execute the arithmetic function following this command (e.g., TYPE SQRT for executing the square root function)
HELP	print an analysis of an error condition to assist in *debugging*.

Although most personal computer manufacturers adopted BASIC, they developed their own dialects so that programs written for one type are seldom directly *portable* to another.

basic coding Synonymous with *absolute coding*.

basic instruction In *instruction modification* the basic instruction is the *instruction* form which is modified to obtain the instruction actually obeyed.

Also known as presumptive instruction or unmodified instruction.

basic language Synonymous with *low level language*. But ⊄ *BASIC*.

basic linkage A *linkage* which is standard for a given *routine* or *program* and is used repeatedly following the same rules each time.

basic mode A communications line control procedure based on the International Standards Organization 7-bit code. Interactive processing between a *terminal* and its *main frame* processor.

batch A collection of *transactions*, in the form, for example, of *source documents, punched cards* or a group of *records* on some *magnetic storage device*. Any group of records processed as a single unit, e.g., a *block*.

batching Synonymous with *blocking*.

batch job A *job* run in *batch processing mode*.

batch mode ◊ *batch processing mode*.

batch processing A method of processing data in which *transactions* are collected and prepared for input to the computer for processing as a single unit. There may be some delay between the occurrence of original events and the eventual processing of the transactions. Contrasted with *real time* processing in which transactions are dealt with as they arise and are automatically applied to files held in a *direct access storage device*.

batch processing mode In *real time* systems there is usually some aspect of the *data processing* work that does not require to be handled on a real time basis. *Transactions* falling in this category may be batched on a daily/weekly/monthly basis and be accepted into the system for processing against *sequential* files. Thus, at certain periods of relatively low activity, a real time system may operate in batch processing mode; alternatively *batch processing* jobs may form *background processing*[3] work to real time operations in a *multiprogramming* environment.

batch total A total developed by adding certain *fields* of a series of *records, source documents*, or *punched cards*, in order to provide a check that all records are present at successive stages of processing. The total may be a meaningful accumulation of a quantity or value field, or it may be a *hash total*.

baud A unit used to measure the number of times per second that a *data transmission* channel changes state. Named after Baudot, a pioneer of telegraphic communication, one baud is equivalent to one half-dot cycle per second in Morse code, or, in a binary channel, one baud is equal to one *bit* per second. Since, even in a binary channel, the baud rate includes all elements transmitted including coordination elements, the baud rate is not necessarily equivalent to the data rate, and baud is not necessarily synonymous with bit per second.

BCD Abbreviation of *binary coded decimal*.

BCPL A *systems programming language* from which the language *C* was derived.

BCS British Computer Society.

bead In a program a small *module* which performs a specific function. Beads are usually written and tested individually and then strung together and tested in groups sometimes known as *threads*. In this way programs can be written and tested in a modular way and this provides a sound method for controlling the development of complex programs. ⟐ general article on *Modular Programming*.

beam store Any magnetic *storage device* in which electron beams are used to activate storage cells; e.g., a *cathode ray tube* store.

beat A unit of time related to the execution of an instruction in the *program controller* of a *central processor*. For example, in a two-beat machine one beat may be required to interpret the instruction and set up the necessary circuits to perform the specified operation, while a further beat is required to perform the function.

before-look journalizing Relates to a system in which entries in a *log* or journal are made before each attempt to update a *record* on a *file*. Thus the status of the file can be reconstructed should *recovery* be needed. (Contrasted with *after-look journalizing*.)

beginning of file label A *record* at the beginning of a *file* which provides identification of the file, and information about the boundaries, and perhaps method of organization, of the file.

beginning of file section label A *record* identifying a specific section of a file and providing information about its physical limits.

beginning of volume label A label at the beginning of a unit of magnetic storage (e.g., *magnetic tape* or *disk*) which provides identification of that specific unit and its contents.

beginning of information marker An area of reflective material on a *magnetic tape* which indicates the beginning of the recording area. ⟐ *load point*.

benchmark A task to be performed in a computer system, designed to measure the performance of the system under certain conditions or to evaluate its effectiveness in performing certain classes of work. Benchmarking is a method used by some purchasers to evaluate the proposals for the supply of *hardware* and/or *software*.

benchmark problem A particular calculation used to measure the performance of different machines or *programs*. ⟐ *benchmark*.

bias 1. An error range having an average value not equal to zero; contrasted with *balanced error*. 2. A voltage applied to an electrical component to control the operating characteristics of a circuit.

bias testing A test used to check the operation of equipment, in which the operating characteristics are changed to reduce the safety margin of the various circuits against faults. ⟅> *marginal testing*.

bi-conditional operation Synonymous with *equivalence operation*.

Bildschirmtext The public *videotex* system in the Federal Republic of Germany.

billi- A prefix denoting one thousand million or 10^9, synonymous with *giga*.

bimag core A magnetic storage *core* having two states of magnetization.

binary Pertaining to a pair. As in the *binary notation* system in which only the digits 0 and 1 are used.

binary arithmetic operation Any *arithmetical operation* in which the *operands* are *binary numbers*.

binary Boolean operation Synonymous with *dyadic Boolean operation*.

binary cell A storage element able to represent one *binary digit*.

binary chop Synonymous with *dichotomizing search*.

binary code A *code* in which *characters* are represented by groups of *binary digits*. For example, a common coding system employs 6-bit groups to represent different characters and allows for up to 64 separate characters to be represented, each by a unique *bit pattern*.

binary-coded character A *character* represented by a *binary code*.

binary coded decimal notation A method of using groups of *binary digits* to represent decimal numbers, with each digit position of a decimal number being allocated four *bits*.

binary coded decimal representation ⟅> *binary coded decimal notation*.

binary coded digit Any numeral represented by a coded group of *binary digits*. For example, the use of four *bits* to represent a *decimal digit*, or the use of three bits to represent a digit in the *octal* scale of notation.

binary coded octal Representation of an *octal digit* by its three *bit binary* equivalent.

binary counter A *counter* able to accumulate numbers recorded in the *binary* scale of notation.

binary digit A digit in *binary notation*; i.e., either 1 or 0. Generally abbreviated as *bit*.

binary dump A *dump* of the contents of *memory* in *binary* form onto some external medium such as *magnetic disk*.

binary half adder A *half adder* operating with digits representing *binary* signals, capable of receiving two inputs and of delivering two outputs.

binary image An exact representation in *store* of each hole in a *punched card* or *paper tapes* as distinct from the character represented by a combination of holes.

binary incremental representation A form of *incremental representation* in which the value of an increment is represented by one *binary digit*, after being rounded to either plus one or minus one.

Input		Output	
Augend	Addend	Sum	Carry
1	0	1	0
1	1	0	1
0	1	1	0
0	0	0	0

binary notation A *positional notation* system for representing numbers in which the *radix* for each *digit position* is two. In this system numbers are represented by the two digits 0 and 1. In the same way that in the normal decimal system a displacement of one digit position to the left means the digit is multiplied by a factor of 10, so in the binary system displacement means multiplication by 2. Thus the binary number ˙10ʼ represents two, while ˙100ʼ represents four.

binary number Any number represented in *binary notation*.

binary numeral One of the two digits 0 and 1 used for representing numbers in *binary notation*.

binary operation A term used to refer to any *operation* using two *operands*, i.e., a dyadic operation. This term is, however, also used to mean any operation involving the use of operands in binary form – a *binary arithmetic operation*.

binary pair Synonymous with *bistable circuit*.

binary point The binary point performs the same function in the *binary notation* system as the decimal point in the decimal system, i.e., it separates the integral from the fractional part of a number.

binary representation ⬦ *binary notation*.

binary search Synonymous with *dichotomizing search*.

binary synchronous communications An IBM *data communications protocol* for the synchronous transmission of data between *main frame* computers and *remote terminals*. The protocol is *character-oriented*. Often known as bisync.

binary-to-decimal conversion Conversion of a number represented in the *binary notation* to its equivalent decimal notation. A *routine* to perform this conversion automatically.

binary variable   A *variable* which can have one of two values (0 or 1). Also known as two-valued variable.

bionics   The study of the functions and characteristics of living systems in relation to the development of *hardware* designed to operate in a similar manner.

bipolar   An input signal is defined as bipolar if different logical states are represented by signals of different electrical voltage polarity. Contrasted with *unipolar*.

biquinary code   The representation of a number (n) by a pair of numbers (x, y) where n=x+y and x=0 or 5, y=0, 1, 2, 3 or 4. The pair may be represented in a *binary* code using the following table:

Decimal	Biquinary	Binary Representation
0	0+0	0000
1	0+1	0001
2	0+2	0010
3	0+3	0011
4	0+4	0100
5	5+0	1000
6	5+1	1001
7	5+2	1010
8	5+3	1011
9	5+4	1100

bistable   Capable of assuming either one or two stable states. ⟡ *flip-flop*.

bistable circuit   A circuit which can be triggered to adopt one of two stable states.

Also known as binary pair, bistable trigger circuit, trigger pair.

bistable magnetic core   A *magnetic core* which can adopt one of two states of magnetization.

bistable trigger circuit   Synonymous with *bistable circuit*.

bisync   ⟡ *binary synchronous communications*.

bit   An acronym for *B*inary dig*IT*, one of the two digits (0 and 1) used in *binary notation*. The term is extended to the actual representation of a binary digit in different forms, e.g., an element of *memory*, a magnetized spot on a recording surface, a pulse in an electronic circuit.

bit, check   A binary *check digit*.

bit density   The number of *bits* stored per unit of length or area.

bit handling   The technique adopted in some *programming languages* to manipulate individual *bits* of a *byte* or *word*.

bit location   An element of *main memory* capable of storing one *bit*.

bit mapping   A technique used in *graphics* display in which the information displayed on a *screen* corresponds, *pixel* by pixel, with *bits* held in *main memory*.

bit pattern   A sequence of *bits*. Bit patterns may be used to represent *characters* in a *binary code*.

bit position   The *digit position* of a *bit* in a *word*, referenced as the first, second, third, etc., position from the least significant bit.

bit rate   Relating to the speed of a device, e.g., the speed with which *binary digits* can be transferred over a communications channel. May be measured in *bits per second* or *bauds*.

bit, sign   A *binary sign digit*.

bit slice   ♦ *bit slice microprocessor*.

bit slice microprocessor   A *microprocessor* using a computer *architecture* which uses a number of high performance processing units chained together. Each of these units (slices) represents a width (e.g., 2, 4 or 8 *bits*) of an *arithmetic and logic unit*. These are *microprogrammed* to form a processor of any desired *word* length out of standard units.

bit string   A continuous sequence of *binary digits* to represent data in coded form, in which each *bit* has significance according to its position in the *string*[2] and its relation to other members of that string.

bit track   A term sometimes used to refer to a physical track on a *disk* or a *drum*, along which a *read/write head* reads or records data serially as successive *binary digits*. Compare with *byte track* or *logical track*.

blank   A blank character in the repertoire of an *automatic data processing* code; e.g., in a computer's internal *machine code* or in a *paper tape code*. Not necessarily indicated by an empty position on the medium; e.g., in internal *memory* a blank character usually has a specific *bit pattern* in the same way as any other numeric or alphabetic character.

Also known as space character.

blank form   Synonymous with *blank medium*.

blank medium   The representation of a *blank* by means of an empty position on the medium concerned; e.g., the absence of punching in a *card column* or in a *row* position on *paper tape*.

Also known as blank form.

blank tape The representation of *blanks* on *paper tape* indicated by the presence of *sprocket holes* only in the *row* positions concerned.

blast 1. Synonymous with *blow*. 2. A term sometimes used in relation to *dynamic storage allocation*; to *release* external or internal *memory* areas so that they become available for re-allocation to other *programs*.

bleed Related to the printing of characters for *optical character recognition*; the flow of ink beyond the specified limits of printed characters.

block A group of *records* or *words* treated as a logical unit of data; e.g., data is transferred between *memory* and *peripheral units* as individual blocks. Blocks may be fixed in length or may be of variable size.

block copy To copy a file from one medium to another without changing its contents. ⋗ *block transfer*.

block diagram The diagrammatic representation of any system (e.g., a computer *program*, an electrical circuit) in which logical units of the system are represented by labelled rectangles or *boxes* and the relationship between units is shown by means of connecting lines. ⋗ general article on *Flowcharts*.

block header *Words* or *bytes* at the beginning of a *block*, used to describe the organization of the *file* and the relationship between blocks.

block ignore character A character associated with a particular *block* to indicate that the block contains errors; e.g., errors stemming from *data preparation*.

blocking The grouping of individual *records* into *blocks*, usually to achieve a greater efficiency for *input/output* operations, by reducing the number of *read* or *write* operations required.

Also known as batching.

blocking factor The maximum number of *records* of a given size which can be accommodated in a single *block*.

block, input ⋗ *input area*.

block length The size of a *block*, measured in the number of *characters*, *words* or *records* it contains. In certain cases, blocks may be restricted to a minimum and/or maximum length, by either *hardware* or *software* requirements.

block list A printed representation of a *file*, or print of a file, in which *records* and *fields* are listed in the sequence in which they appear with just enough reformatting to make the information understandable. Used, for example, as a diagnostic aid.

block mark A special character used to indicate the end of a block. Employed particularly for systems in which *variable blocks* are used.

block, output ⊳ *output area.*

block sort Particularly related to sorting with *punched card sorters*; the file to be processed was sorted first in the highest digit position of the *key*, thus reducing the operation to a number of smaller sorting operations which could be done independently, and the separate sections were then joined.

block transfer The movement of data as *blocks* rather than as individual *records*; e.g., in internal *memory* transfers or in transfers between a *central processor* and its *peripheral units*.

blow To write *data* into a *PROM* or variant. Also known as *blast, burn.*

BNF Abbreviation of *Backus Naur form.*

board The rigid rectangular sheet of insulating material on which an *integrated circuit* is mounted. Boards themselves are mounted on a *chassis.* ⊳ *printed circuit board.*

bobbin core A type of *magnetic core* formed by winding a length of ferro-magnetic tape around a bobbin.

Boolean algebra Boolean algebra (named after the mathematician George Boole, 1815–64) uses algebraic notation to express logical relationships in the same way that conventional algebra is used to express mathematical relationships. In conventional algebra, an expression such as p+q=r is a general expression consisting of variables p, q and r, which can take numbers as values, and symbols standing for mathematical operations such as addition. In Boolean algebra the same sorts of expression are used, but the variables do not stand for numbers but for statements, e.g., 'the cat is on the mat', and the logical operations which relate such statements, e.g., 'or', 'and'.

The relevance of Boolean algebra to the logic of computers lies in a simplification of the system in which the values of the variables are restricted to the two possible 'truth values' of a statement, i.e., 'true' and 'false'. These values may be represented by the digits 0 and 1, thus enabling the logic of Boolean algebra to be applied to the *binary* logic of computers. The truth value of a complex logical statement made up of variables and the relations between them depends on the *truth table* of each variable and the logical relationships between them. Basic logical relationships or operations are defined by means of truth tables which give the 'truth value' of the expression for all combinations of values for the constituent variables. An example of a Boolean operation holding between two *operands* is the *and operation* (also known as the logical product, conjunction, intersection or meet). This can be represented symbolically as p & q, p.q, pq, Kpq. The truth table for the result r of the *and* operation on the operands p,q is as follows:

Operands		Result
p	q	r
1	0	0
0	0	0
0	1	0
1	1	1

This can be interpreted as meaning that the operation *and* results in the truth value 1 only if both operands have this value, but is 0 if any one of the variables has this value. Boolean operations on two operands are known as *dyadic Boolean operations*. Truth tables for the following dyadic operations can be found under their appropriate article: *inclusive-or operation, exclusive-or operation, equivalence operation, not-and operation, nor operation, conditional implication operation, not-if-then operation*. Two Boolean operations are known as *complementary operations* if the result of one is the opposite or negation of the result of the other; e.g., the or operation is complementary to the nor operation. Two Boolean operations are known as *dual operations* if the truth table of one can be transformed into the truth table of the other by negating each value in the table; e.g., the or operation is the dual of the and operation.

In general, a Boolean operation is an operation in which the result of giving each of a set of variables one of two values is itself one of two values. Since the internal states of a digital computer can only have one of two values, circuits can be designed to simulate the Boolean operations. These devices are known as *logic elements*, or *gates*. For example, the *and element* corresponds to the Boolean and operation, and is a logic element which produces an output signal of 1 only if all its input signals are also 1. The use of logic elements is fundamental to the operations by the digital computer: all the operations available to the programmer are ultimately executed by means of some combination of signals passing through logic elements.

Boolean calculus Synonymous with *Boolean algebra*.
Boolean complementation Synonymous with *negation*.

Boolean connective A *connective* used to connect the *operands* in a statement of a *Boolean operation*, indicating the type of operation concerned.

Boolean logic Synonymous with *Boolean algebra*.

Boolean operation An *operation* which operates in accordance with the rules of *Boolean algebra*.

Boolean operation, dyadic ⟡ *dyadic Boolean operation*.

Boolean operation table A table which indicates, for a particular *Boolean operation*, the values that will result for particular combinations of *bits* in the *operands*. When the values are interpreted as true or false, known as a *truth table*. ⟡ *Boolean algebra*.

bootstrap The technique of *loading* a *program* into a computer by means of certain preliminary *instructions* which in turn call in instructions to read programs and data. Since the preliminary instructions are usually set manually or pre-set and called into action by the use of a special *console* switch or message from a console typewriter, the machine does not quite 'pick itself up by its own bootstraps'.

bootstrap input program ⟡ *bootstrap*.

bootstrap routine, tape ⟡ *tape bootstrap routine*.

border-punched card Synonymous with *margin-punched card*.

borrow A carry signal which arises in *subtraction* when the difference between digits is less than zero.

box A *flowchart symbol* used to represent a logical unit of a system or *program*. ⟡ general article on *Flowcharting*.

box, connexion ⟡ *connexion box*.

boxed mode In *teletext*, a method of displaying characters of one colour on a rectangular background of another colour and superimposing the whole on a broadcast picture displayed on a television set.

branch A departure from (or to depart from) the normal sequence of *program* steps. This is caused by a *branch instruction* which can be *conditional* (i.e., dependent on some previous state or condition in the program) or *unconditional* (i.e., always occurring regardless of previous conditions). A branch of a program consists of a sequence of instructions between branch instructions.

Also known as jump, Go To instruction. ⟡ general article on *Programming*.

branching ⟡ *branch*.

branch instruction A *program* is normally performed by obeying a series of *instructions* stored in successive *locations* of *memory*. This sequence of operation can be altered by special *branch* instructions which can direct the *program controller* to execute a specific series of instructions. Thus, the program can be considered as consisting of several branches which are entered according to branch instructions written into the program itself. A branch instruction specifies the address of the next instruction to be performed; sometimes a branch will be mandatory but often it may or may not be performed according to conditions occurring during execution of the program.

Also known as control transfer instruction, discrimination instruction, jump instruction. ⟡ *unconditional branch instruction, conditional branch, switch*.[3]

branchpoint The point in a *program* where a *branch* takes place. Related to *switch*[3] and contrasted with *break point*.

breadboard A mock-up or experimental model of any device.

breakdown A failure of *hardware* or *software* requiring the attention of an engineer or technical support specialist.

breakpoint A point in a *program* where the normal sequence of operations is interrupted by external intervention (e.g., by an operator signal) or by a *monitor routine* used in *debugging*. The normal sequence is resumed after the interruption has served its purpose, e.g., after visual checking, printing out. Contrasted with *branchpoint*, which is an internal interruption in the sequence of events due to a *branch instruction* within the program.

breakpoint instruction A *program instruction* located at a *breakpoint* which will cause the program to take action on recognizing an external intervention (e.g., an operator's signal) or transfer control to a *monitor routine* in *debugging* operations.

breakpoint symbol A symbol used in *programming* to indicate a *breakpoint* at a specific *instruction*.

bric A *cartridge* used as *main memory*.

bridge limiter A device used in *analog* machines to prevent a variable from exceeding specified limits.

bridgeware *Hardware* or *software* aids used to transcribe *programs* and *data files* written for a particular type of computer into the format necessary for operation on another type of computer. ⟡ general article on *Transition*.

bridging The process of converting systems written for a particular type of computer into an appropriate format and structure to be run on another type. ⟡ general article on *Transition*.

broadband A *band*[2] covering a wide range of frequencies, usually greater than those required for voice communications. ⟡ *bandwidth*.

brush An electrical conductor used in some systems as a means of sensing the presence of a hole in a *punched card*.

brush compare check On some *punched card* reading and card punching machines a check was performed by means of *brushes* at different *brush stations*; the information read by one set of brushes was compared in a brush compare check with the information read by the other set.

brush station The location of *brushes* in a *punched card* reading or card punching machine using the brush sensing method of establishing the presence of a hole in a punched card.

brute-force approach An attempt to apply computer techniques to the solution of problems which cannot be solved by a precise mathematical or logical approach.

BSC Abbreviation of *binary synchronous communications*.

bubble memory A method of representing *data* in *memory* as magnetic bubbles which can be magnetized in the opposite direction from that of the rest of the medium. Manufacturing costs have tended to constrain the initial high promise of this technology.

bucket In *direct access storage* a bucket is a unit of storage as distinct from the data contained in the unit. The data is *accessed* by reference to the bucket in which it is located.

budgetary control Budgetary control is a system used by management in which targets (budgets) are set and actual performance compared with them. The purpose is to establish where, how and why actual results are diverging from the budget and what action is needed to achieve the budget. Computers are often used for recording and reporting the information required in a budgetary control system (for example, on *spreadsheets* on personal computers), and a brief summary is therefore given here.

The main steps in operating a budgetary control system are: (i) The objectives of the organization and their relative importance are determined. For example, the importance of volume of orders as against profit from orders might be decided. In a normal trading business the key budgets are orders, revenue, production, manpower, capital expenditure, cash flow, profit and return on capital employed. (ii) A total budget is drawn up which would result in the achievement of the objectives. Certain of the resources available may be insufficient to attain the budget. Perhaps skilled labour is limited; or money. It is then clear that some definite action is needed to make the budget achievable. Perhaps a training programme needs to be set up; or financing arrangements made. This stage stimulates forward planning. (iii) The detailed budgets are set and each manager should be involved so that he fully accepts his own budget. Budgets should only include those items for which a manager has been given authority. (iv) Many of the individual budgets are interdependent and therefore have to be compatible so that the total budget is a realistic whole. For example, the sales manager's budget for revenue is dependent upon the production manager producing enough goods and at the right times. (v) There should now be a reliable total budget built up from the individual budgets to which each manager is committed. (vi) The actual results are recorded in the same form as the budget, compared with it and variances from the budget established. (vii) The causes of variances are analysed and reported to the appropriate levels of management. Each manager has to explain his variance and either to justify it or take action to remedy it.

The frequency of reporting will differ according to need and to the ability to take immediate action; e.g., cash may be reported daily whereas manpower may be monthly.

Attention is concentrated on the exceptions from the required results.

Budgets may be set for any length of time but if taken too far ahead become less reliable. They are often set annually, and should not be revised too frequently because there is then a danger of their becoming forecasts of expectations rather than targets for achievement.

Budgets may be fixed amount or flexible according to level of activity; e.g., a salesman's budget for entertainment may be a fixed sum or a percentage on orders taken, i.e., flexible. Flexible budgets are more complex but often give more useful information than fixed budgets.

The advantages of the system are that it provides: (i) definition of objectives; (ii) anticipation and planning; (iii) personal involvement of all levels of management; (iv) delegation of controllable items; (v) coordination of activities; (vi) concentration on exceptions; (vii) a basis for corrective action.

Budgetary control encourages management to anticipate as well as concentrating attention on those results which are deviating from the budget. Both of these effects are vital pillars in the structure of management control.

budgeting In computing, the process of allocating resources to a particular development activity in order to constrain the resources utilized for the project. For example, restrictions may be placed upon *programmers* to limit the amount of *main store, backing store*, and *peripherals* utilized by their *programs* as a policy to promote operational efficiency in the installation.

buffer Synonymous with *buffer store*.

buffer amplifier An amplifier used to isolate a signal source (e.g., an

63

buffer, double

oscillator) from another circuit being driven by that source. This prevents the driving circuit from being affected by the characteristics of the driven circuit.

buffer, double ⟡ *double buffering.*

buffered computer A computer in which *buffer stores* are provided to match the speed of the *peripheral units* to the higher speed of a *central processor.*

buffered input/output Relating to the use of *input/output buffers* to increase efficiency when data is transmitted to and from a *central processor.*

buffer store Generally used as a means of temporarily storing data when information is being transmitted from one unit to another; e.g., between a *central processor* and its input/output *peripheral units.* The purpose of a buffer is to compensate for the different speeds at which the units can handle data. Sometimes a *buffer* may be a permanent feature of a peripheral unit (e.g., as in a buffered *printer*) and in other systems *internal memory* areas may be assigned temporarily to act as buffers for particular units.

bug Any mistake or malfunction of a computer *program* or system. ⟡ general article on *debugging.*

built-in check Synonymous with *hardware check.*

bulk storage Synonymous with *backing store.*

bulk store Synonymous with *backing store.*

burn Synonymous with *blow.*

burst 1. To separate sheets of continuous *stationery* by means of a *burster.* 2. The transmission of a group of *records* in a *store*, leaving an interval to allow *access* to the store for other requirements (cf. a burst of machine-gun fire).

burster A device used *off-line* in a computer system to separate individual forms in a set of continuous *stationery* produced as output from a *printer.*

burst mode A mode of data transfer between a *central processor* and a *peripheral unit* in which a signal from the peripheral unit causes the central processor to receive data until the peripheral unit signals that a transfer has been completed. ⟡ *burst.*[2]

bus Synonymous with *highway.*

bus driver, output ⟡ *output bus driver.*

byte A set of *bits* considered as a unit; normally consists of 8 bits and corresponds to a single *character* of information.

byte mode A mode of data transfer between a *central processor* and a *peripheral unit* in which the unit of transfer is a single *byte* at a time.

64

byte track   A number of *tracks* on the surface of a *disk* or *drum*, along which *read/write heads* move in parallel to read or record data representing a unit of information (e.g., *byte*). Compare with *bit track*; synonymous with *logical track*.

C

C A *high level programming language* designed for *system programming*, usually (but by no means exclusively) for software development in the *Unix* environment.

cache memory A high speed *buffer memory* that sits between *processor* and main memory and thus is appropriate for high performance systems.

CAD Abbreviation of *computer aided design*.

CAI 1. Abbreviation of *computer aided instruction*. 2. Abbreviation for *computer assisted instruction*. (The two terms are synonymous and CAI can therefore safely be used for both.)

calculating punch A *calculator* equipped with a *card reader* and a *card punch*. Data to be processed was input on *punched cards* and, after a sequence of arithmetical calculations, results were punched into specified *fields* of the same cards or on other cards.

calculator A *data processing* machine designed to perform arithmetic (e.g., addition, subtraction and multiplication) and a limited range of *logical operations* on data. For example, a *punched card* machine capable of processing data input on punched cards and of generating results on punched cards. Some early calculators were able to follow a simple step-by-step *program* but were not usually able to *modify* their own programs.

calendar time The total time available in a given working period, e.g., $6 \times 24 = 144$ hours in a working week of 6 days.

call A *branch* to a *closed subroutine*.

call direction code A special code, used in telegraph networks, transmitted to an outlying terminal to switch on automatically the teleprinter equipment at the terminal.

calling sequence The set of *program instructions* whose purpose is to set up initial conditions necessary before a *call* is made to a *subroutine*. Also the instructions within a subroutine used to provide the *link* with the main program.

call instruction An *instruction* which causes the *program control unit* to *branch* to a *subroutine*. The call instruction may also specify *parameters* required on entry to the *subroutine*.

CAM Abbreviation of *computer aided manufacture*.

Cambridge ring A *local area network* developed as a *ring* network. Designed at Cambridge University under the leadership of Professor Roger Needham, it pioneered many aspects of network design.

capacitor store A type of storage unit commonly used in early *punched card calculators*, in which each *bit* of information was represented by a capacitor.

capacity 1. The number of *words* or *characters* that can be contained in a particular *storage device*. 2. The upper and lower limits of numbers which can be processed in a *register*.

capstan On a magnetic *tape transport*, a shaft on which a reel of *magnetic tape* is mounted and which drives the tape past the *read/write head*.

card 1. Synonymous with *printed circuit board*. 2. Synonymous with *punched card*.

card back The unprinted side of a *punched card*; the obverse of the *card face*.

card bed Synonymous with *card track*.

card cage A structure in which *printed circuit boards* can be mounted and which contains a *backplane*.

card code The combination of holes in a *punched card* used to represent letters of the alphabet, numerals or special symbols.

card column The lines of a *punched card* parallel to the short edge of the card. Each column was treated as a unit for the purpose of punching and holes in one column represented a specific character. Contrasted with *card row*. (Some systems used to divide the columns in two, upper and lower, or allow punching in between the rows in a column thus making each column do the work of two.)

card, edge-punched ⬦ *margin-punched card*.

card, eighty-column ⬦ *eighty-column card* and *punched card*.

card face The printed side of a *punched card*; the side uppermost when the first *card column* punched was on the left-hand side. The obverse of the *card back*. Cards were usually made with one corner cut, so that, when cards were grouped in a *pack*, it was possible to ensure that all were facing the same way.

Also known as face.[2]

card feed A mechanism which moved *punched cards* one at a time into the sensing, reading or punching mechanism of a machine.

card field A group of consecutive *card columns* in a *punched card* containing a unit of information. For example, columns 6 to 9 might contain a four-figure staff number: these columns made up the staff number field.

card fluff When *punch knives* cut holes in *punched cards*, the edges of the holes were not always clean and the slightly burred effect – card fluff – could cause mis-feeding or mis-reading later.

card format A description of the contents of a *punched card*, usually provided as part of a *systems definition* or *program specification*.

card hopper A device for holding *punched cards* and making them available as required to a *card feed* mechanism, e.g., on a *card reader* or *card punch*.

Also known as input magazine. Contrasted with *card stacker*.

card image An exact representation in *store* of each character in a *punched card*, as distinct from the *binary image* representation.

card jam Synonymous with *card wreck*.

card leading edge The edge of a *punched card* which led when the card was transported along a *card track*. Contrasted with *trailing edge*.

card loader A routine used to *load* a *program* from *punched cards* into *store*.

card, margin-notched ⋄ *edge-notched card*.

card, ninety-column ⋄ *ninety-column card* and *punched card*.

card punch A machine which caused holes to be punched in *punched cards*, thus allowing data to be stored and later conveyed to other machines which could read or sense the holes. A card punch could be *on-line* (when holes were punched as a result of signals from a *central processor*) or *off-line* (when holes were punched as a result of operator action). ⋄ *automatic punch, hand punch*.

card punch buffer Before a *punched card* was punched by an *on-line card punch*, the data was transmitted to the card punch *buffer store*. If for any reason the card punch was unable to punch the data in the buffer, e.g., because the input *hopper* was empty and there were no blank cards, the card punch would become inoperative and the data remained in the buffer.

card punch, duplicating Synonymous with *reproducer*.

card punching The punching of holes into *punched cards*. The holes had particular significance according to the code being used, and the punching allowed the data to be stored and later conveyed to other machines which could read or sense the holes. This was one of the basic methods of preparing data for input to a computer system. Contrasted with *paper tape punching* and *character recognition*. ⋄ general article on *Data Preparation*.

card reader A machine for reading information represented by holes in a *punched card* and converting it into another form for processing by a computer. ⋄ general article on *Input Devices*.

card reproducer   A machine which read a *punched card* and punched a copy of the card. The machine could be set to reproduce a specified number of copies from one card, and to copy only selected parts of the original card.

card row   A line of *punching positions* on a *punched card* parallel to the long edge of the card. There were, for example, twelve rows on a normal 80-column card. Contrasted with *card column*.

card stacker   An *output device* for holding *punched cards* (stacking them in a *pack*) after they had passed through, for example, a *card reader* or *card punch*. Contrasted with *card hopper*.

card systems   Computer systems which had no input *peripheral unit* other than a *card reader*, and no output peripheral unit other than a *card punch* and a *printer*. Such systems did not have a *backing store*.

card-to-card   In *data transmission*, the operation of transmitting data on *punched cards* to a remote terminal where the data was reproduced onto other punched cards.

card-to-magnetic-tape converter   A device which read batches of data from *punched cards* and wrote them as logical *records* on to *magnetic tape* ready for subsequent processing. This type of equipment was designed to permit data *input* and *validation* to be undertaken without monopolizing the *central processor* of the main configuration. Such devices became largely obsolete when comprehensive *time sharing* and *multiprogramming* facilities became available.

card-to-tape   1. The operation of converting data on *punched cards* to *paper tape*, performed on *card-to-tape converters*. 2. A routine for transferring data on punched cards to *magnetic tape* on a computer by means of a special *program*; the program could also *edit* and verify the data at the time of transcription.

card-to-tape converter   A device used for converting from one unit of storage (*punched cards*) to another (*paper tape*). The data contained in the punched cards was read, converted into the new character code and punched into paper tape. ⬧ *card-to-magnetic-tape converter*.

card track   That part of a *punched card* machine which transported cards through the various *reading stations* and/or *punching stations*, from the input *hopper* to the *stacker*.

Also known as card bed.

card trailing edge   The edge of a *punched card* which trailed when a card was transported along a *card track*. Contrasted with *leading edge*.

card, verge-perforated   Synonymous with *margin-punched card*.

card verifier   A *punched card* machine used for *card verifying* after data had been punched into cards.

card verifying   Checking the accuracy of punching in *punched cards*. *Direct data entry* has largely replaced the process of card verifying, which was usually carried out by placing the *punched cards* in a device similar to the *card punch* (a *card verifier*) which had keys similar to those of the card punch. The operator (not the one who did the original punching) read the *source documents* and depressed the verifier keys; if these corresponded with the original punching the card was accepted as valid, but if there was a discrepancy the keyboard locked and the card was rejected. In some systems the original holes were altered (e.g., round holes ovalized) and the *pack* of cards was then passed through an automatic verifier which rejected all holes without an altered shape. Most systems, however, depended on the fact that one operator keyed original punching and another keyed what should have been the same information into the same cards. ⋄ general article on *Data Preparation*.

card wreck   A fault condition that occurs when one or more *punched cards* become jammed along the *card track* of a punched card machine.
    Also known as card jam.

carriage return   The operation causing an *automatic carriage* to be returned so that the next character is printed or punched at a pre-set left-hand margin. On *personal computers* and *word processors* the phrase is still often used although the carriage does not return anywhere.

carriage tape   Synonymous with *control tape*.

carrier system   A system which allows several independent communications signals to share the same circuit.

carry   The digit added to the next high digit position when the sum of the digits in the lower position exceeds the radix or number base.

carry, addition without   Synonymous with *exclusive-or operation*.

carry-complete signal   A signal developed by an *adder* to indicate that all arithmetic carries relevant to a particular operation have been generated. ⋄ *carry*.

carry, ripple-through   Synonymous with *high-speed carry*.

carry, standing-or-nines   Synonymous with *high-speed carry*.

carry time   A system required to add a *carry* into the next higher digit position.

cartridge   A container for a magnetic medium designed in such a way that the medium resides permanently in the cartridge, which can then be loaded so that the operator does not touch the medium itself. Usually serves as *backing store*, but can be in-built *main memory brics*.
    Also known as *cassette*. ⋄ cassette.

cartridge drive   A *drive* or transport for handling *disk cartridges* or *cartridge tapes*.

cartridge tape   *Magnetic tape* housed in a *cartridge*.

cascade control   A system of automatic control in which control units are organized in sequence so that each unit controls its successor and is in turn controlled by its predecessor.

cascaded carry   A *carry* into a digit position resulting in a carry out of the same digit position; uses the normal adding circuit, unlike a *high-speed carry*.

cassette   Synonymous with *cartridge*, but sometimes reserved for a container similar to a standard domestic audio tape cassette.

casting-out-nines   A particular form of *modulo n check* in which *n* is equal to nine.

catalogue   A file of named objects used or handled within a system. For example, in an *operating system*, the catalogue may contain details of devices, users, and files currently maintained and allocated.

category   This term is sometimes used to describe a group of *direct access disks* or *volumes* containing a given set of information. For example, *files* used for *program* development work may be placed in a particular category.

category storage   A section of the *filestore* used by an *operating system* containing a number of *categories*.

catena   A series of items recorded in a *chained list*.

catenate   To arrange a series of items in a *catena* or *chained list*.

cathode follower   A form of *buffer amplifier* in which a thermionic valve is used, and in which the potential of the cathode follows that of the grid.

cathode ray tube   An electronic tube in which a beam of electrons can be controlled and directed by an electronic lens so as to produce a visible *display* of information on the surface of the tube or to *store* data in the form of an energized portion of the tube's surface. Abbreviated as CRT. Often known as screen.

cathode ray tube visual display unit   A *visual display unit* in which a *cathode ray tube* is used as the medium for the output of data.

CD Rom   A *compact disk read only memory*: a storage device using *optical laser storage* techniques.

Ceefax   The *teletext* system provided by the BBC.

cell   1. The smallest unit of a *store* capable of storing a single *bit*. 2. An area of storage used to *extend* or *reduce* the size of a *dynamic buffer*.

cellar   Synonymous with *push down store*.

center   ◊ *centre* for all entries.

central control unit   Synonymous with *program controller*, but sometimes used specifically to denote a unit which has control over one, or more, subordinate *control units* operating in the same system.

centralized data processing The grouping of all data processing requirements of an organization at a single *data processing centre*.

central processing unit Synonymous with *central processor*.

central processors The central processor is the nerve centre of any *digital* computer system, since it coordinates and controls the activities of all the other units and performs all the arithmetic and logical processes to be applied to data. All program *instructions* to be executed must be held within the central processor, and all data to be processed must first be *loaded* into this unit. It is convenient to consider the central processor as three separate *hardware* sections: *internal memory, arithmetic unit* and a control section.

This article concentrates mainly on the latter, the role of the other two sections being defined in more detail elsewhere in this book. The functions of the control section are more difficult to classify since they embrace a wide range of activities analogous to the central nervous system of a human being. It is, however, possible to distinguish the *program control unit* as a primary member. This unit, also known as the *program controller*, examines one by one the individual instructions in the user's program, interprets each instruction and causes the various circuits to be activated to perform the functions specified. Essentially these functions involve the selection of required *operands* from internal memory, and the activation of the arithmetic unit to perform the specified operation on these operands.

Internal memory consists of a series of magnetic storage devices organized to hold data or program instructions in a series of *locations* as either *words* or *characters*. In many computing systems the internal memory is stored within the cabinet housing the other sections of the central processor, but in large systems separate cabinets may be used to contain sections of internal memory. Nevertheless the memory can always be considered as part of the central processing unit.

The arithmetic unit consists of a series of special *registers* and circuits which are able to perform arithmetic and logical operations upon one or more operands selected from memory. For example, the arithmetic operations of addition, subtraction, multiplication and division may be performed, as well as various *shift* operations and comparisons including the *logical operations*, 'or', 'and', 'not', etc.

The control section has many complex functions to perform but to simplify the situation we will first consider the basic instruction cycle within the central processor. First the program control unit will select an instruction from memory and will store it within one of a number of special *control registers*. Here the instruction is decoded to ascertain the particular arithmetic or logical operation to be performed, and to ascertain the memory locations involved. Then the instruction is executed, causing the required operands to be selected from the specified memory locations and to be routed via the arithmetic unit and back again to the same or some other specified memory locations. The time required to perform an instruction is usually considered in two phases – the time to select the instruction and the time required to execute it. During the execute phase the arithmetic unit operates under the aegis of the program control unit to perform the required arithmetic or logical process on the selected operands.

The cycle is repeated for each instruction in the program: call an instruction, decode and execute the instruction, call an instruction, and so on. Each complete cycle is performed at high speed and takes place as a series of discrete pulses; e.g., during the execute phase the various digits of the operands are often handled one after the other as individual digit pulses. The control section has the function of generating the basic timing pulses to control the activities of the many circuits operating within the system to ensure that each instruction occupies a predetermined period, referred to as the *instruction time*. Furthermore the individual stages during the instruction time must be completed to a basic schedule governed by the timing pulses.

Thus it can be seen that the control section of the central processor coordinates the activities of the other sections, but it must also control the operation of *peripheral units*. In most computing systems the number of locations available within internal memory are comparatively few and data must be stored in some other peripheral unit (e.g., on a *magnetic disk*) until required for processing. Sometimes it is also necessary to write a program as a number of separate *segments*, each of which are called into memory as and when required.

Peripheral units are generally activated by instructions written in the user's program, often organized to call for data to be processed in *blocks*, so that the program control unit must decode *read* and *write* instructions in the user's program in order to initiate transfers to and from the central processor.

Once the program control unit has initiated a read or write operation the control section must continue to monitor the operation to ensure that it is satisfactorily completed. For example, *parity* errors or peripheral failures may be encountered and it is then necessary to provide a signal to the user's program and perhaps to the operating *console* to ensure that the situation can be corrected. Communications between the computer operator and the central processor are also handled via the control section. This aspect of the control function is often referred to as *input/output control*.

The function of the control section does not cease at this point, for in most *minicomputers* and *main frame* computers *time sharing* is incorporated and it is necessary for the control section to coordinate several concurrent peripheral operations while data is processed internally within the central processor. The extension of this technique into the field of *real time* data processing implies also that the central processor must be able to receive *interruptions* from distant terminals at any moment in time; here the control section has very complex functions to perform in coordinating the receipt and transmission of data over perhaps several communications channels. In this sort of situation specialized communications control units often have to be connected to the central processor and in any highly developed time sharing system some kind of *executive program* is usually necessary. Such programs are stored permanently in internal memory and can effectively be considered as part of the hardware of the central processor, since as well as providing an economic and flexible control over concurrent operations they perform many of the routine functions otherwise done by hardware in more conventional systems – e.g., the complete coordination of all input/output control functions and the handling of all communications between the operator and the computer.

central terminal   A *hardware* unit which coordinates communications between a computer and a number of outlying terminals. It may receive messages at random from the terminals, store them until they can be handled by the *central processor* and then return them to the terminal concerned.

centre, automatic switching   ◊ *switching centre*.

centre-feed tape   *Paper tape* with *feed holes* aligned exactly with the centres of the character holes. Contrasted with *advance feed tape*.

centre, semi-automatic switching   ◊ *switching centre*.

centre, torn-tape switching   ◊ *switching centre*.

chad   The piece of paper removed when a code hole is punched in *paper tape* or a *punched card*.

chadded tape   *Paper tape* punched in such a way that the *chads* are only partially removed and remain attached to the tape.

chadless tape   *Paper tape* with the *chads* completely removed.

chain   1. A *routine* consisting of *segments*, each of which uses in turn the output from the previous segment as input. 2. A set of items organized as a *chained list*.

chain code A sequential arrangement of *words* in which adjacent words are linked by the rule that each word is derived from its neighbour by displacing the *bits* one position left or right, dropping the leading bit and inserting a bit at the end, so that a given word does not recur until the cycle is complete.

chained list A set of data ordered in such a way that each item contains an *address* to locate the next item in the set. The items may be stored in any sequence, and may be retrieved by a *chaining search*.

chained record A *file* of *records* in which the records are arranged in a random manner in *memory* or *backing store* but are linked by means of a control *field* in each record which gives the *address* of the next record in the series. The first such record is known as the *home record*.

chaining search A method of searching a set of data organized as a *chained list*. An initial *key* is transformed to obtain the *address* of a *location* which may contain a direct reference to the item required or may indicate another item in the chain. The search continues through the chain until the required item is located or until the chain is completed.

chain printer A high-speed *printer* in which the type is carried past the paper by the links of a continuous chain.

change dump A *print-out* or other output of all *locations* which have changed since a previous event (usually another change dump). Used in *debugging*.

change file A collection of *change records* used in *batch processing* to update a *master file*.
　Also known as amendment file, transaction file.

change, intermediate control ◊ *intermediate control change*.

change, major control ◊ *major control change*.

change, minor control ◊ *minor control change*.

change of control A logical break in the sequence of *records* being processed which initiated some predetermined action (e.g., the printing of *control totals*) before the next group of records is processed. ◊ *comparing control change*. 'Change of control' was sometimes also used for *transfer of control*.

change record A *record* whose function is to change information in a corresponding *master record*.
　Also known as amendment record, transaction record.

change, step ◊ *step change*.

change tape Synonymous with *transaction tape*.

channel 1. A path along which information flows. When all elements of a digit are sent in parallel, a channel is made up of parallel paths. 2. A *paper tape* channel is a longitudinal row in which code holes may be punched in paper tape. 3. The part of a *store* accessible to a reading station.

channel, paper tape   ↘ *channel²*.

channel, peripheral interface   ↘ *interface*.

channel status table   A table maintained by an *executive program* to indicate the status of the various *peripheral unit interface channels*, so that control can be exercised over input/output operations.

channel-to-channel connexion   The transfer of data between computers by means of connecting appropriate *channels* from each system.

chapter   A self-contained section of a *program*, synonymous with *segment*.

character   One of a set of symbols in a *data processing* system used to denote, for example, the numerals 0–9, the letters of the alphabet, punctuation marks, etc. Each character is represented by a unique code of *bits*, holes in *punched cards*, holes in *paper tape*, etc.

character-at-a-time printer   A *printer* which creates each line of print by consecutively printing each *character* from left to right along the line; e.g., a teleprinter or electric typewriter used as an output device.
   Also known as character printer. Contrasted with *line printer*.

character code   The specific combination of elements (*bits*, holes in *punched cards*, etc.) used to represent *characters* in any system.

character code, forbidden   ↘ *forbidden character code*.

character crowding   ↘ *pack²*.

character density   The number of characters that can be stored per unit of length, e.g., on *magnetic tape*. (↘ *packing density*.)

character emitter   An *emitter* which outputs a *character* at timed intervals.

character, erase   ↘ *ignore character*.

character fill   To fill a number of specified storage *locations* by repeatedly inserting a nominated *character*; e.g., to indicate an error condition.

character, functional   ↘ *control character*.

characteristic   An alternative for *exponent*, when reference is made to *floating point representation*. The characteristic is the signed integer which serves to indicate the position of the *radix point* for the *fixed point part* of the number.

characteristic overflow   A condition arising when *floating point arithmetic* is used if an attempt is made to develop a *characteristic* greater than an upper limit specified for the particular *hardware* or *software* system employed.

characteristic underflow A condition that arises when *floating point arithmetic* is used if an attempt is made to develop a *characteristic* less than some specified lower limit for the particular *hardware* or *software* system employed.

character modifier A constant used in *address modification* to reference the *location* of a specific character.

character oriented Pertaining to a computer in which individual character *locations* can be *addressed* rather than *words*. Each *operand* in *memory* is addressed by specifying the first and last character location, thus permitting *variable length* operands to be used.

character printer Synonymous with *character-at-a-time printer*.

character reader A device which can convert characters input in a form legible to human beings into machine language. ⟡ *magnetic ink character reader, optical character reader* and general article on *Input Devices*.

character reader, magnetic ink ⟡ *magnetic ink character reader*.

character reader, optical ⟡ *optical character reader*.

character recognition Human beings are taught to recognize patterns from an early age. In the first year of life a baby can be induced to make more or less consistent vocal responses to pictures, for example saying 'dog' whenever it is shown a picture of one. Later, children are taught to identify letters and numbers and subsequently to read and perform arithmetic. When children grow up some of them may spend their lives manipulating letters and numbers, recognizing patterns quite automatically.

The ideal *data processing* system is one in which data is captured at source and processed as soon as possible, and it would therefore be very desirable for machines to recognize symbols and numbers directly in the same formats as those used by human beings in their everyday social and commercial activities.

At present the patterns that most computers can recognize are not conveniently read by human beings. Similarly, data originating from people is not usually input directly into the computer. Data handling, therefore, is typified by a conversion process from 'human' format to computer format.

The objective here is to enable the computer to read source documents directly. The problem of converting a pattern on an input document into electronic signals suitable for processing by a computer is one of pattern recognition.

It is necessary to strike a balance between a pattern convenient for people to read and one that is convenient for the computer. There are two main systems for automatically recognizing printed characters: *optical character recognition* (OCR) and *magnetic ink character recognition* (MICR). In the former, characters are printed in conventional type formats or as *bar codes*, usually in black ink on a white surface, and the characters are scanned by measuring their optical reflectivity when subject to illumination. In MICR systems however, characters are printed in a highly stylized format using an ink impregnated with magnetizable particles. When MICR documents are read the ink is magnetized before the characters are presented to a *read head*. The output signals generated are governed by the magnetized particles passing the head and for any character are proportional to the vertical projection of the character. *Mark reading* is also a form of character recognition and it is common to find mark reading and optical character recognition used within the same system. Despite the fundamental differences in these systems, the equipment utilized in each case contains similar types of unit. There is always a scanner, which reads characters and converts them into electronic signals, and this unit is associated with a normalizing unit, which examines each signal to improve its quality without changing its basic characteristics.

The signal thus generated is then examined to determine the basic properties of the character and a decision mechanism is used to analyse these properties and identify the character concerned. If the decision mechanism is unable to identify the character unambiguously then the character is rejected.

The ability of machines to recognize characters printed in a format easily recognizable to human beings has great advantages in reducing the task of *data collection* and thereby speeding up the flow of data in a system. Costs for *data preparation* can be considerably reduced and improvements in accuracy can often be achieved as compared with more conventional methods.

The development of character recognition systems has taken place in many different organizations and has led to a wide number of special type founts being developed. As improvements have been made in techniques of character recognition some degree of standardization has been evident but there are still many differing founts in use. In the field of MICR there has tended to be less variation and two founts, known as E13B and CMC7, are more or less accepted as standard on an international basis. In OCR systems there are more variations although the International Standards Organization has proposed two standard founts known as OCR'A' and OCR'B'.

In some respects there appears to be less flexibility in MICR founts than in OCR. The MICR system requires that characters should be printed in a highly stylized format and with a high degree of accuracy, but this system of recognition relies on the magnetized particles forming each character and is not therefore so vulnerable as OCR systems are when handling damaged and folded documents, or with documents that have been soiled or have overwritten characters. OCR systems require less stylized formats and the characters can often be printed by the use of conventional machines such as typewriters; this aspect allows for cheapness and flexibility in establishing data collection points. In both systems characters to be read must be printed in certain specified areas of the documents with a fairly high standard of print registration.

MICR has been used for cheques in banking throughout the world. MICR sorter/readers are used to sort automatically the cheques in clearing houses for distribution to various branches, the cheques being preprinted with a branch code. The cheque number and customer's account number are also preprinted, and at a later stage the amount of the transaction can be added using an MICR *encoder*. Details from such cheques can be read automatically into a computer *memory* to update subscribers' accounts.

OCR documents have been used as *turn-around documents* in hire-purchase accounting and similar applications, each customer being issued with a book of vouchers preprinted with the amount due for each payment in the hire contract. In some credit card *applications* customers are given a plastic ticket which is embossed with their own account number; this card has to be presented at point of sale to act as a plate in printing a record of the transaction. The record is then used to provide automatic input to OCR equipment.

OCR equipment is often used in gas and electricity accounting; a common system is to combine mark reading and character recognition techniques to enable meter reading staff to input details of consumption from turn-around documents, the actual consumption figures being entered as marks on preprinted areas of the forms. Bar codes are, of course, familiar on most packages of consumable items.

Character recognition techniques are used with great advantage where large numbers of transactions in a fairly regular format are involved. They are best suited to applications where only a limited number of variable characters have to be entered, and in this context provide a speedy and accurate method for recording data.

character, redundant ⏵ *check character*.

character repertoire The range of *characters* available in a particular code, or, for example, on each *print member* of a *line printer*.
  Related to *character set*.

character set The set of *characters* forming a particular group or code accepted as valid by a particular computer and not *illegal characters*. For example, a 64-character machine code might consist of the ten numerals (0 to 9), twenty-six alphabetic characters (A to Z) and 28 *special characters* including *blank*.

character space In *videotex*, the space on a screen display occupied by a character or graphic symbol.

character string A one-dimensional *array* of *characters* in *memory* or some other storage medium.

character subset A selection of characters from a *character set*; e.g., the subset that embraces alphabetic characters only.

charge coupled device A *semiconductor* device which can be used for storing data, suitable for applications where *memory* is *accessed serially*.

chart Any diagram used as an aid in analysing or solving a problem when developing a system or *program*, or when documenting any system or procedure. ⏵ *flowcharting*.

chart, systems ⏵ *systems flowchart*.

chassis The metal base, e.g., in a *microcomputer*, on which are mounted the sockets and wiring. Often also equipped with a structure designed to accept a *backplane* and *printed circuit board*.

check Any operation performed to test the validity or accuracy of an *operand* or result; e.g., to test for the presence or absence of certain specified conditions. *Data processing* requires both machine checks and clerical checks in order to verify the accuracy of data handling and the correctness of machine operations. Machine checks may be especially *programmed* or may be performed automatically by *hardware*.

check bit A *binary check digit*.

check character A *character* forming one of a group of characters, the value of which is dependent on the other members of the group. Its sole function is to act as a check on the other characters when data is stored or transferred, and it is redundant in so far as its information content is concerned. ⏵ general article on *Check Digits*.

check digits In most *data processing* applications it is necessary to ascribe numbers, or codes, to people or objects in order to process data about them. People are given staff numbers; spare parts are given numbers; almost everything, for data processing purposes, is given a number.

At some stage in the data processing these numbers are handled by people to whom they are meaningless. Although part number 24573986 may mean a washer to an engineer, and customer number 25679467 may mean Peter Smith & Co. of Brighton to a salesman, they are meaningless to a data input clerk and the possibility of transcription errors looms large.

In many applications such errors are not important; the probability of them occurring is small and the effort to recover from them when they do is not great. If we are selling nuts and bolts in threes and fours it is not too terrible if, through such an error, we reduce the stock of the wrong nut by three when we stock thousands of them. On the other hand it would be embarrassing if, because a keying error went undetected, we charged the wrong customer for an oil tanker!

In applications where the risk of errors must be reduced to a minimum, check digits, generated by the machine performing the data processing, are often used. In a computer installation the extra processing time needed to take care of check digits is negligible.

A check digit is simply one or more digits added to a number; one method of calculating the digit is by finding the remainder when the original number is divided by a fixed number. Thus if we are using the number 7 to generate check digits, instead of 127 we would write 1271, the 1 being the remainder when 127 is divided by 7; instead of 324 we would write 3242, 2 being the remainder when 324 is divided by 7. These remainders are calculated by the machine when the system is initiated, and thereafter remain as part of the number, the machine checking that the remainder given is correct each time the number is processed.

The use of check digits reduces considerably the probability of an undetected error. If the probability of an error escaping the verification stage is one in a thousand, then the addition of a two-digit check digit will reduce the probability of an undetected error to, at most, one in a million.

The choice of method used to generate the check digits is not material. Several well-known techniques are available and choice will depend on the particular application requirements.

Before the decision is taken whether or not to use check digits in a data processing system, a study should be launched to find the incident rate of undetected errors and their effect; if it is found that the incidence rate is too high for tolerance the use of check digits will considerably reduce it.

check indicator A method of showing that a check has failed. The indicator may be a *hardware* indicator, causing a *console* display or an internal *switch* to be set which may be tested by *program*; or it may be a programmed indicator causing an error message to be printed.

checking program A *program* which diagnoses errors in other programs by identifying, in the format of the various *instructions*, mistakes resulting from incorrect coding or mispunching. Used in *debugging*.

checking routine Synonymous with *checking program*.

check, marginal ⟡ *marginal testing*.

check number Synonymous with *check digit*.

checkout routine Synonymous with *debugging aid routine*.

checkpoint A point in a *program* at which details concerning the state of the program are recorded to assist in *recovery* should it be subsequently necessary. ⟡ *dump and restart*.

checkpoint dump The process of recording details in the progress of a job to allow for the possible need for *recovery* after a failure. ⟡ *dump and restart, checkpoint*.

checkpointing The practice of writing a *program* in such a way that it automatically *dumps* information at frequent intervals throughout a job, to enable the job to be restarted in the event of a *failure*. ⟡ *dump and restart, checkpoint*.

check problem A problem with a known solution used to check that a *program* or machine is working correctly.

check, redundant ⟡ *redundancy check*.

check register A *register* used to store input data temporarily before it is compared with the same data input at a different time or by a different path. A form of *transfer check*.

check row A *row* (or rows) on *paper tape*, forming part of an item *field* on the tape and attached to the field to act as a *check symbol*, permitting a *summation check* to be made for that item when the tape is used as input to a computer.

check sum A *sum* generated using individual digits of a number and employed as part of a *summation check*. Sometimes used as a synonym for *hash total*.

check symbol A digit or digits generated for a particular item of data by performing an *arithmetic check* on the item. These digits are then attached to the item and accompany it through various stages of processing so that the *check* can be repeated to validate the item at each stage.

check total Synonymous with *control total*.

check word   A *word* appended to a *block* of *records*, and containing data generated for that block, to act as a *check symbol* when the block is transferred from one *location* to another.

chip   A small section of a silicon *semiconductor* which forms a substrate impregnated with a pattern of impurities to form one or a number of semiconductor devices in an *integrated circuit*. ⟡ *silicon chip*.

chip-slice   ⟡ *macrologic*.

chip tray   A small receptacle positioned beneath the *punching station* of a *card punch* or *tape punch* to collect pieces punched from the *punched cards* or *paper tape*.

chopper   A device for interrupting a current or a beam of light to produce a pulsating signal. Sometimes done to achieve timing pulses, as for example in a photo-electric cam. In the case of a continuous current signal a chopper *amplifier* is often used in order to amplify the signal in the presence of *noise*.

chopper-stabilized amplifier   A device which includes a *modulator*, an a.c. coupled *amplifier* and a *demodulator*, to stabilize fluctuations in a circuit. The modulator acts as a *chopper*.

circuit   A set of physical transmission resources (e.g., *lines* and *exchanges*) which provide for two-way transfer of messages from source to destination in a *telecommunications* system.

circuit, and   ⟡ *and element*.

circuit board   ⟡ *board*.

circuit diagram   The physical representation of components and interconnections which define a specific *hardware functional design*. ⟡ *printed circuit*.

circuit, duplex   ⟡ *duplex channel*.

circuit, half-duplex   ⟡ *half-duplex channel*.

circuit noise level   A measure of the disturbance in a *data transmission* circuit, usually expressed as a ratio of the *noise* measured in a circuit in relation to some chosen reference level.

circuit, simplex   ⟡ *simplex channel*.

circular shift   Synonymous with *logical shift*.

circulating register   A *register* in which digits can be shifted around in circular fashion, in such a way that digits removed from *locations* at one end of the register are automatically inserted at the other end.

CIS-COBOL   Acronym for Compact Interactive Standard *COBOL*. A version of COBOL designed to run on, and be portable between, a number of *personal computers*.

clear   To replace data in a *storage device* with some standard *character*, e.g., zero or *blank*. Contrasted with *hold*.

clear band In relation to *optical character recognition*, any area on a document which must be kept free of printing.

clock Any electronic device which provides pulses at fixed intervals to monitor, measure or synchronize other circuits or units operating within the same system. For example, a device to measure the frequency of a circuit or to measure the time used for particular activities.

Also known as clock signal generator.

clock pulses Electronic pulses which are used to control the timing of all circuits within a machine. The pulses are emitted repetitively from a *master clock* to synchronize the operations carried out by the machine.

A clock pulse is also known as a clock signal.

clock rate The frequency at which pulses are emitted from a *clock*.

clock signal Synonymous with *clock pulses*.

clock signal generator Synonymous with *clock*.

clock track A track on a magnetic recording medium which provides *clock pulses* to control *read* and *write* operations.

closed loop 1. A continuous *loop* in a *program* from which there is no exit except by operator intervention or by action on the part of some *executive program* monitoring the operation of the *program* concerned. A closed loop is usually an error, and may be signalled by a *hoot stop*. 2. Referring to a system in which there is no human intervention and in which the output from the system is fed back to adjust the input. For example, in certain *process control* applications in which the computer is able to set switches, valves, etc., to control directly the process concerned.

closed shop Describing a method for running a computer installation, particularly with regard to the testing and running of *programs* under development. The programming staff are not allowed to be in attendance when their programs are run on the computer but are supplied with their results and with reports generated by *diagnostic programs*, including *memory prints, file prints*, etc. The objective of the closed shop system is to minimize the computer time spent in *debugging* programs and to ensure that only specialized operating staff are allowed to run the machine. Contrasted with *open shop method*. ⊳ general article on *Remote Testing*.

closed subroutine A *subroutine* which generates a re-entry point for returning to the *main program* according to conditions established on entry to the subroutine. Contrasted with *open subroutine*.

closed user group A number of subscribers to a public information service such as a *videotex* network who can access information updated by members of the group. Non-members cannot access the information even though they subscribe to the other services on the network.

cluster A group of devices such as *magnetic tape units* or *terminals* interfaced to a *communications network* or *host processor* through a cluster controller. This is done in such a way that the *software* is not necessarily aware that one controller is allowing a number of devices to share an *interface*.

cluster, tape Synonymous with *magnetic tape group*.

clutch point On *card punches* and *card readers* the movement of cards along the *card track* was initiated by engaging a clutch to transmit the drive to the card transport mechanism. The clutch could often only be engaged at one, or more, fixed points in the feed cycle – these were known as clutch points.

CMOS Abbreviation of complementary metal oxide semiconductor.

COBOL COBOL is an acronym for COmmon Business Oriented Language. It is an internationally accepted programming *language* developed for general commercial use, originally under the sponsorship of the American Department of Defense. COBOL is a *problem oriented high level language* in which the *source program* is written using statements in English of a standard but readable form.

A COBOL program is written in four divisions; these are: Identification Division; Environment Division; Data Division; Procedure Division.

The Identification Division contains descriptive information that identifies the program being compiled.

The Environment Division deals with the specification of the computer to be used for operating the object program (the *object computer*), including such information as the size of *memory*, the number of *tape decks*, *printers* and other peripheral devices that will be used; a description of the computer to be used for compiling the source program (the *source computer*) is also given.

The Data Division is used to allocate identifying names or *labels* to all units of data on which operations are to be performed. All input and output *files* are defined and associated with the *peripheral units* to be used for input and output. *Records* and *fields* within the files are described, as are all *constants* used by the program and any *working store* required.

The Procedure Division gives the step-by-step *instructions* necessary to solve the problem. These steps are specified by means of instructions expressed in stylized but meaningful English statements which can be

85

recognized by the *compiler* and translated into a sequence of *machine code* instructions capable of being used by the computer to solve the problem. These statements are compounded of (i) *reserved words* which have a special significance, enabling the compiler to generate the appropriate machine instructions for the particular operation required, and (ii) identifying labels used by the programmer to reference units of data described in the Data Division, or used to identify other sections of the Procedure Division. The following statements are given as examples:

ADD OVERTIME TO NORMAL-HOURS

In this example, ADD . . . TO . . . are reserved words instructing the compiler to generate the machine coding necessary to perform addition, and OVERTIME and NORMAL-HOURS will be labels defined in the Data Division to refer to units of data.

READ INPUT-A AT END GO TO FINAL

Here READ causes the compiler to produce the coding necessary to activate an input device; AT END GO TO produces a *branch instruction* when the last item on the input device is recognized; INPUT-A will be the name given by the programmer to a particular input file, described in the Data Division and there associated with its peripheral device; and F I N A L will refer to the name given by the programmer to another section of the Procedure Division in which is specified the action to be taken when all items have been accepted from the input device.

Other examples of COBOL statements are:

WRITE LINE-3 AFTER ADVANCING 2 LINES
IF STOCK LESS THAN MINIMUM GO TO REORDER
MOVE SPACES TO LINE-4

Development of COBOL is coordinated by a body known as CODA-SYL, an acronym for COnference on DAta SYstems Languages. COBOL *compilers* supplied by manufacturers do not always provide all the facilities of full COBOL, so it is possible that programs written with a particular compiler in mind will not be acceptable to another compiler with a slightly different subset of facilities. In general terms, the advantages of using COBOL are that it is relatively simple to learn, and programs can be quickly written and tested; programmers can easily understand programs not written by themselves, and thus associated documentation can be simplified; and programs can be used on other machines, within the limitations noted above. Disadvantages are (i) the relative inefficiency of the resulting object program as compared with a program written in *machine code* or a machine oriented language and (ii) the lack of flexibility imposed by the restrictions on the type of instructions and methods for performing operations inherent in a highly standardized language. ⟡ general article on *Languages*.

code 1. The representation of data or *instructions* in symbolic form; sometimes used as a synonym for *instruction*. 2. To convert data or instructions into this form.

code, alphameric Synonymous with *alphanumeric code*.

code area An area of *main storage* containing, at a particular moment, executable *code* representing processing *instructions*, as distinct from areas containing only data.

code, binary ⟡ *binary code* and *binary notation*.

code, column-binary ⟡ *column-binary*.

code, computer Synonymous with *machine code*.

code, cyclic Synonymous with *Gray code*.

coded decimal A notation in which each decimal digit is separately represented in coded form, e.g., by the *binary notation* of the digit. ⟡ *binary coded decimal notation*.

code, direct Synonymous with *absolute code*.

code-directing characters Characters attached to a message to indicate the routing and destination of that message.

coded stop Synonymous with *programmed halt*.

code elements The basic elements from which a code is constructed; e.g., the individual *bits* that make up a 6-bit *character code*.

code, error checking ⟡ *error checking code*.

code, error correcting ⟡ *error correcting code*.

code, error detecting ⟡ *error detecting code*.

code holes Holes punched in *paper tape* or *punched cards* to record data.

code line A *program instruction* in written form.

code, macro ⟡ *macroinstruction*.

code, micro ⟡ *microinstruction*.

code, minimum latency Synonymous with *minimum access code*.

code, mnemonic operation ⟡ *mnemonic operation codes*.

code, numeric The representation of data as coded groups of *bits* to denote numerals; e.g., in *binary-coded decimal* format. Contrasted with *alphabetic code*.

code, one-level ↄ *absolute code.*

code, optimum ↄ *minimum access code.*

code position Any part of a data medium into which a code may be inserted.

coder A person who writes computer *instructions* from *flowcharts* prepared by others, as distinct from a *programmer*, who prepares the flowcharts as well as *coding* from them.

code segment An area of *storage*, representing a subdivision of the storage allocated to a *process*, and containing executable *instructions*. Other segments forming part of the process include *data segments* and *dump segments*.

code, self-checking ↄ *error detecting code.*

code, single-address ↄ *single-address instruction.*

code, specific Synonymous with *absolute code.*

code, symbolic Synonymous with *symbolic instruction.*

coding The writing of *instructions* for a computer. Coding is part of the activity of *programming*.

coding check A check performed to ascertain whether a *routine* contains errors. Usually performed initially by following the logic of the routine on paper using test data. ↄ *dry running.*

coding sheet A form on which computer *instructions* are written before being transferred to an input medium, e.g., *punched cards.*

coding, specific Synonymous with *absolute coding.*

coefficient Synonymous with *fixed point part.*

coincidence element Synonymous with *equivalence element.*

coincidence gate Synonymous with *and element.*

collate To produce a single ordered *file* from two or more files which are in the same ordered sequence. Synonymous with *merge*, although collate was more usually used when the files were *punched card* files.

collator A machine for merging two *punched card files* (sorted into the same sequence) into a single file, which would be in the same sequence. Cards which matched could also be separated from those which did not match; thus a collator could also be used for card selection.

Also known as *interpolator.*

collector A *software module* used in *compiling*; collates various compiled *program* modules into a form suitable for *loading* onto the computer system for subsequent *execution*.

column ↄ *card column.*

column binary A method for representing *binary numbers* on *punched cards*; consecutive *punching positions* on each *card column* were considered as consecutive digits in a binary number. Contrasted with *row binary*.

column binary code   ⬦ *column binary*.

column 1 leading   The way in which *punched cards* were placed in the feed *hopper* of some punched card machines; i.e., with a short edge leading and with column 1 read first.

column split   The facility on a *punched card* machine for reading two parts of a *column* as two separate codes or characters.

COM   Acronym for Computer Output on Microfilm.

combined head   Synonymous with *read/write head*.

combined read/write head   Synonymous with *read/write head*.

command   Synonymous with *instruction*.

command chain   Part of a *process* which can be *executed* independently as a sequence of *input/output instructions*.

comment   Written notes which can be included in the coding of computer *instructions* in order to clarify the procedures, but which have no effect on the computer itself, i.e., are not translated into *machine language*.

Also known as *annotation, narrative*.

commercial data processing   *Data processing* concerned with or controlling a commercial application; e.g., *inventory control*, payroll. Contrasted with *industrial data processing, scientific data processing*.

commercial language   A *language* designed for the writing of *programs* for commercial applications such as payroll, invoicing. ⬦ *COBOL*.

commission   To instal a computer to the point where it is capable of successful operation. Commissioning may precede a *customer acceptance test*.

common area   An *area* of *memory* which can be used by more than one *program*, or more than one *segment* or *routine* of the same program. ⬦ *multiprogramming* and *overlay*.

common business oriented language   ⬦ *COBOL*.

common carrier   A business which offers general communication services to the public.

common language   The representation of data in a form intelligible to the many different units of a *data processing system*, so that information can be transferred between parts of the system.

common storage area   ⬦ *common area*.

common target machine   A *target machine* is a machine represented by some, or all, of the resources in a computer installation, and is a particular set of resources intended for an *application*: for example, a hypothetical machine in a *virtual machine environment*. The common target machine represents the full potential machine available from a particular *hardware/software* system. ⟡ *compiler target machine*.

communication channel A channel for transmitting data between distant points; e.g., to connect a remote data station to a central computer system.

communication devices The collection of data from remote locations for centralized processing has long been necessary in both business and scientific organizations. This need has increased as more powerful and expensive computer systems have been installed and as applications based on centralized *on-line* files have been developed. This process has led to the development of many types of communications device to suit the varying needs of users in terms of the volume and speed of transmission required.

In the earlier stages of the development of data transmission there was a tendency to use existing forms of equipment to transmit data, for example, the teleprinter and associated *paper tape* machines were used to transmit data over conventional telegraph circuits. Such a system usually required that data was prepared and input as paper tape at one terminal, and was transmitted to a central location where a duplicate tape was punched automatically to be taken by hand to a *paper tape reader* for loading into the computer. This type of system had many disadvantages: the speed of transmission was only about 50 *bits* per second, the handling of paper tape at the sending and receiving terminals limited the system to *batch processing* applications and introduced time delays which were unacceptable for many systems, and the lack of inbuilt error detection and correction facilities was a severe restraint – a single bit transposed could generate very significant errors in subsequent processing.

To deal with these problems equipment was developed to meet the following needs: (i) to allow for the capture of original data by automatic *data collection* techniques to distant stations; (ii) to transmit the data automatically at high speed to a central computer; (iii) to check all transmissions to detect and automatically reject or correct transmission errors; (iv) to accept data at the central location and to present it directly to the computer for processing, e.g., against *files* maintained there, if necessary using a *multiplexor* to enable the central computer to control perhaps a hundred or more *communication channels*; (v) to enable the central computer to prepare data for transmission back to the terminal; and (vi) to enable data to be displayed or recorded at the distant terminal.

Of course not every system requires all these needs to be satisfied: some systems may control only a few communication channels, some or all of which may be required to operate in batch processing mode only; and again volumes may be such that a fairly low speed of transmission may be suitable in some off-peak period.

In straightforward data collection systems terminals such as *badge readers, keyboard* machines, *direct data entry* terminals and videotex terminals may be available at distant locations. These units can be connected to a communication channel by special transmission units designed to *interface* the appropriate data collection device to the particular channel used.

In remote inquiry systems the remote stations will also include output devices such as *page printers, visual display units, intelligent terminals*, videotex terminals, etc. Thus an inquiry transmitted to the central computer can be processed and a reply is automatically transferred back to the terminal. (Airline reservation systems provide an example of this.) In inquiry systems the distant terminals are connected to their communication channels by transmit/receive data terminal units.

In large organizations a data processing capability may be required at several decentralized locations, even though a large degree of centralized data processing is maintained. Depending upon the volume of traffic and the type of application, such a situation could give rise to high speed links directly from one computer to another, or more conventional transmission techniques, e.g., from *magnetic tape* at one terminal to magnetic tape at another.

At the centralized location the computer can simply accept input in the form of some input medium such as magnetic tape or paper tape, but this type of input would not be suitable for *real time* inquiry applications, and instead some form of high speed link might be required. Here a special transmission control unit, perhaps incorporating a *multiplexing* facility, is used to connect the computer to the various communication circuits. Such systems often require very complex *software/hardware* facilities to accept and transmit data to and from a large number of channels on a *time-sharing* basis.

In order to achieve the advances listed above there has been a considerable development in data transmission techniques, improving both the speed of transmission and the facilities for error detection and correction.

The limitations of distortion and attenuation in circuits, particularly over long distances, make for slow transmission speeds by conventional

91

telegraph methods. However by transmitting a modulated carrier wave much higher speeds can be obtained depending upon the quality (e.g., band width) of the transmission circuit used.

Error detection and correction techniques rely for the most part upon the use of a *redundancy code*. For example, *parity* checks may be applied to each *character* at the receiving terminal. Another method, known sometimes as a *loop check*, requires data to be transmitted in blocks, which when received are sent back to the transmitting terminal via a special return circuit for comparison with the data originally transmitted. If a transfer is incorrect the block is then retransmitted until a 'correct' transfer is signalled. Using re-transmission techniques an error rate better than a single error in 10^7 characters can be achieved.

communication link Synonymous with *communication channel*, but sometimes used to include *data terminal* equipment.

communications line control procedure A particular procedure used in a communications network to control signals from a particular class of device or method of transmission.

communications link controller A *hardware* device containing *software* or *microprograms*, and designed to interfere between a *main frame* system and a communications network. May contain various buffers for a wide range of line speeds and for different *communications line control procedures*.

commutator pulse One of a group of pulses used to set the limits of a *digit period*.

Also known as P-pulse (abbreviation of position pulse).

compact disk A storage device using *optical laser storage* techniques and thus providing robustness, ease of handling and greatly enhanced storage capacity.

comparator A device for comparing two items and producing a signal dependent on the result of the comparison. This may be used to compare two different items or two versions of the same item in order to check data transference.

compare To determine the relationship between two data items and to signal the result. This may be any one of the possibilities 'equal to', 'greater than', 'less than'. The result may be signalled by setting an *indicator* or by a *conditional branch*. Also used in *file processing* to refer to comparing the contents of two or more *files* in order to check for similarities or discrepancies in data.

comparing control change A change in the value of *control fields* in a *record* which caused defined actions to take place, e.g., the production of totals on a *punched card tabulator*. Also known as *control break*, control change.

compatibility   Compatibility is said to exist between two computers if *programs* can be run on both without alteration. A computer is said to be 'upwards compatible' with another if a program written on the first can be run on the second, but not vice versa.

compatibility, equipment   ◊ *compatibility.*

compilation   The process of using a *compiler* to create an *object program* from a *source language.*

compilation time   The time at which a *program* is *compiled*; contrasted with *run time.*

compile   To create an *object program* by means of a *compiler.*

compiled module format   An intermediate format used in the process of *program compilation*, usually created prior to the consolidation or collection of program *modules* into the final form ready for *loading.*

compiler   A complex *program* which converts computer *instructions* written in a *source language* into *machine code*. The resulting *object program* can then be read and acted upon by the computer. In order to produce the object program the compiler (a) translates each language *statement* into its *machine code* equivalent, (b) incorporates into the object program any *library subroutines* requested by the user, (c) supplies the interconnecting links between the parts of the programs. A compiler is distinguished from an *assembly program* by the fact that a compiler usually generates more than one machine code instruction for each source statement, whereas an *assembly* language is one-for-one with machine code. ◊ *languages.*

compiler-compiler   A *program* capable of accepting the syntactical and semantic description of a *language* in order to generate a *compiler* for that language.

compiler diagnostics   Relating to the facilities incorporated in a *compiler* to detect, and indicate to the user, errors in *source programs*. Such routines provide the programmer with listings both in the *source language* and *machine code* form, these listings being accompanied by error messages and references to potential sources of error in the program.

compiler manager   *Software* which controls the *compilation* process – usually part of the *operating system.*

compiler target machine   The machine potentially available from a specific *hardware/software* system, for which a *compiler* is capable of generating *programs*. Most applications will run in a subset of the total resources available and each application therefore has its own *target machine.* ⟡ *common target machine.*

compiling system A collection of *software modules* forming part of an *operating system*, used to convert *source language* into *object code*. The compiling process may consist of several stages including *compilation, collection* and *loading.* ⟡ *compiler.*

complement A number which is derived from another by one of two rules: (i) subtract each digit from one less than the *radix* or number base (e.g., 9 for the decimal system), then add one to the result; (ii) the same as (i), but do not add one to the result. Method (i) is known as the *radix or noughts* or *true complement*. 770 is the true complement of 230 in the decimal system. Method (ii) is known as the *diminished radix complement, radix-minus-one complement* or, in the decimal system, *nines complement*, and in the binary system, *ones complement*. 769 is the nines complement of 230, 010 is the ones complement of the binary number 101. The complement of a number is frequently used in computers to represent the negative of a number, and the act of making a number negative is known as *complementing*.

complementary operation A *Boolean operation* which has a result which is the *negation* of the result of another operation is said to be a complementary operation to the other, e.g., the *or operation* is complementary to the *nor operation*. Contrasted with *dual operation*.

complementing The method of producing the negative of a number by obtaining its *complement*. Contrasted with *negation*.

complete carry The result when a *carry* arising from the addition of carries is allowed to generate a carry. Contrasted with *partial carry*.

complete operation The complete implementation of a computer *instruction*, involving the *accessing* of the instruction and associated *operands*, obeying the instruction and placing the results in *store*.

complete routine A *routine*, usually supplied by the computer manufacturer, which does not need any user modification before use.

compute mode The operating mode for an *analog computer* in which the input signals are connected directly to the computing units to develop a solution. Contrasted with *hold mode* and *reset mode*.

computer Any machine which can accept *data* in a prescribed form, process the data and supply the results of the processing in a specified format as information or as signals to control automatically some further machine or process. The term is used generally for any kind of computing device, the three main categories being *digital computers, analog computers* and *hybrid computers*; there is a general article on each of these. There is also a general article under the heading

Introduction to Computers at the beginning of this book. Digital computers are *main frame* computers, *minicomputers* and *personal computers* or *microcomputers*.

computer aided design   The process of applying computer technology to design, so that a designer uses a computer *terminal* as a window to necessary data, a draughting board, and a tolerance analysis tool.

computer aided instruction   A tutorial method, using a computer as a base for managing the student's progress.

computer aided learning   A computer-based tutorial method which uses the computer to pose questions, provide remedial information and chart a student through a course.

computer aided manufacturing   A computer-based system of integrating a number of aspects of manufacturing systems, so that inventory control, manpower scheduling, order processing, etc. are integrated with design and process control.

computer, all-purpose   Synonymous with *general-purpose computer*.

computer applications   A general term for the uses to which a computer may be put. ⟡ *application package*.

computer code   Synonymous with *machine code*.

computer, digital   ⟡ *digital computer*, also *computer*.

computer efficiency   A measure of the reliability of a computer. Various definitions of efficiency will be found under *serviceability ratio*, *operating ratio* and *utilization ratio*.

computer graphics   Display of computer output information in pictorial form (as opposed to textual form) either on a *visual display unit* or on a *printer* or *plotter*.

computer instruction   ⟡ *instruction*, and general article on *Instruction Formats*.

computer operation   ⟡ *operation*[2].

computer, parallel   ⟡ *simultaneous computer parallel processing*.

computer personnel   The general article on *Data Processing Department Organization* shows the kinds of task which have to be undertaken in a data processing department and the staff levels at which they are usually carried out. As indicated in the article, these levels are by no means mandatory and usually the allocation of jobs depends very much on the people available. This article will look at some of the qualities ideally found in each of the prototype jobs in an ideal installation and will give some indication of the sort of things those concerned with the installation will be called upon to do. The jobs described are Data Processing Department Manager, Systems Analyst, Programmer, Senior Systems Analyst, Chief Programmer, Computer Operator,

Tape Librarian, Keyboard Operator, Control Clerk, Operations Manager.

First, the manager of the department: although it is certainly true that he requires technical ability and practical data processing experience it should not be forgotten that he is primarily a manager and that without the qualities associated with management – clear, energetic thinking, tenacity, tact, imagination and ability to control – he will never be able to run a data processing department. Added to these qualities must be certain specialist ones such as the technical competence to control staff with specialized skills; the ability to absorb technical writings so that he can advise his superiors of new developments in data processing relevant to their problems; and a general receptiveness to new ideas. As with managers of most other departments, his best asset will be the ability to remain unruffled in all circumstances.

The systems analyst's job must begin and end in communication, although, as will be seen in the general article on *Systems Analysis*, the design stage of his job requires maturity and imagination. The ability to communicate is all-important, however, and this must include conversational ability (i.e., being able to mix with people) and the ability to express himself on paper. He must be able to work methodically and precisely (errors of fact or of omission can be extremely expensive) and must ally a creative imagination with a willingness to undertake considerable drudgery at times. Since he is nearly always working with other people rather than alone, it is a great help if he is generally likeable, but it is even more important that he should be determined to get things right and then be able to put them on paper.

The programmer must be able to reason logically and clearly and must have the patience and tenacity to see his way through to the end of a problem. He must be able to cope with routine work and, when the chance of doing something clever but perhaps impractical appears, must be able to curb himself if, in the end, the best answer is the simple and straightforward one. It is by no means necessary to be a mathematician (unless, of course, the programming work involves some of the techniques of *operational research* or the computation of statistics) but the usual qualities of mathematicians are found in programmers; these are the ability to reason logically, a precise awareness of detail and the self-discipline to work within prescribed standards. As will be seen from the general articles on *Programming* and *Documentation – Programs* the programmer must also be able to work well in a team and must be able to work in an orderly way, documenting his work carefully.

Leading the systems analysts and programmers are the senior systems analyst and chief programmer who are 'technical management' rather than 'line management', i.e., they are experienced technicians themselves, able to undertake the work, at any level, of those they lead, and able to control in detail the work of their teams. Since both systems analysts and programmers are often called upon to reduce large work loads in a short time, the senior systems analyst and chief programmer must also both be able to maintain a good team spirit amongst those they lead.

General responsibility for the day-to-day efficiency of the computer and ancillary machines will rest with the operations manager who will manage the computer operators, the data control staff, the librarians and the data preparation staff. This may easily add up to forty or more people and the operations manager must be a skilled manager as well as technician. He is closer to the output of the installation than anyone else, and since this will inevitably result in crises at times, it will often be his task to make the best possible use of limited means. Perhaps the best qualities for an operations manager are resourcefulness and good humour.

One of the most important things he has to do is to ensure a high standard of computer operating, and the computer operators he trains must have a considerable interest in the job and be willing to accept responsibility. *Operating systems* help to solve the problem of finding computer operators able to handle routine work and yet with enough mental alertness to cope with *multiprogramming* machines, but any operator needs to be sufficiently self-reliant to take on responsibility for very expensive equipment, which, when badly operated, can become even more expensive as lost minutes cost money.

Librarians and work assemblers are needed to control the storage, issue and control of all magnetic media, and, as these jobs usually call for a monitoring of the work flow into and out of the computer room, they require a considerable organizing ability and some technical knowledge of programming and operating.

Keyboard operators and all other operators who are responsible for preparing input and output need to be accurate, able to work under pressure and have a sense of responsibility. This last will depend largely on the machine room supervisor, who will have to be ready at all times to cope with unexpectedly large loads or other sudden re-arrangements of work.

In general the data processing department needs to work very closely as a team: the systems analyst is as dependent on good operating as the operator is on good operating instructions, and the work of both can be set back by poor data input. Perhaps the most important quality for all new members of the department is that they should be well liked by the others.

computer program ⬦ *program.*

computer, stored program ⬦ *stored program computer*, also *computer.*

computer system A *central processor* and associated *peripheral units*, which are or can be *on-line* to the processor, form a computer system.

Also known as *configuration.*

computer word ⬦ *word.*

computing amplifier An amplifier in which the output voltage is related by *negative feedback* to the input voltage.

Also known as operational amplifier.

conceptual modelling A method of problem-solving whereby a *mathematical model* is constructed to suit the results obtained from an experiment; the model is used to conduct further experiments to ascertain whether the model is correct. ⬦ general article on *Model Building.*

concurrent conversion The simultaneous running of *conversion programs* with normal programs ⬦ *multiprogramming.*

concurrent processing Synonymous with *multiprogramming.*

condensing routine A *routine* for transferring an *object program* from *memory* or a *storage device* onto *punched cards* in such a way that the maximum number of *instructions* possible was contained on each card.

conditional branch instruction A *branch instruction* which will transfer control to another *program* instruction if, and only if, some specified condition is satisfied; e.g., if a nominated item of data is zero or less than zero. If the specified condition is not satisfied the program proceeds directly to the next instruction.

Also known as conditional transfer or conditional jump. Contrasted with *unconditional branch instruction.*

conditional breakpoint A *breakpoint* at which the particular sequence of *instructions* to be followed after the external instruction has occurred may be varied by setting specified conditions.

conditional breakpoint instruction A *breakpoint instruction* which acts, after the external intervention has occurred, as a *conditional branch* by which alternative courses of action may be entered.

conditional implication operation A Boolean *operation* in which the *result* for the values of the *operands* p and q is given by the table:

Operands		Result
p	q	r
0	0	1
1	0	0
0	1	1
1	1	1

Also known as if-then operation, implication, inclusion, material implication.

conditional jump Synonymous with *conditional branch*.

conditional stop instruction An *instruction* which can cause a *program* to be stopped if some given condition is detected. For example, the program may be required to stop if it finds that a *console switch* has been set by the operator.

conditional transfer Synonymous with *conditional branch instruction*.

conditional transfer of control To *transfer control* to another part of a *program* by means of a *conditional branch*, i.e., depending upon certain specified criteria.

configuration The general term given to a *computer system*, usually used to indicate the physical units of the system.

configuration block A collection of *hardware* devices which respond to a particular type of *command* given by the operator when configuring the computer for operation. ⋄ *configuration state*.

configuration state Relates to the status of a device in a computer *configuration* and indicates its availability for allocation to an *application*, e.g., configured-in – available for use, configured-out – available for certain privileged users, configured-off – not available.

configuration table A table maintained in a computer by the *operating system* to signify the status of individual units of the system. ⋄ *configuration state*.

configured-in ⋄ *configuration state*.

configured-off ⋄ *configuration state*.

configured-out ⋄ *configuration state*.

conjunction Synonymous with *and operation*.

connection box ⋄ *connexion box*.

connective A symbol representing an *operation* between two *operands* which is written between the operands, e.g., the symbol used to represent the *logical connective* 'and', written P & V in order to relate the variables P, V.

connector 1. A symbol used in *flowcharting* to indicate the connexion between different points on a flowchart. 2. A mechanical means of allowing the connexion or separation of one or more electrical circuits.

connexion box A mechanical device used in some *punched card* machines for controlling operations by means of variable linkages. The mechanical equivalent of a *plugboard*.

connexion (of a node) A link between an *application program* and a resource (e.g., a *peripheral* device) established under control of an *operating system* and represented by entry in the *catalogue*.

consistency check 1. A check performed by *program* to ensure that a *record*, or *transaction*, does not contain contradictory data. 2. A check performed to ensure that a result is *accurate*, achieved by using alternative techniques to derive answers which are then compared.

console The unit of a computer used for all manual communication with the computer. The console provides a display of information from the computer, either through a *printer* or by means of screen messages, and provides a means for the operator to put messages into the computer, again either through a typewriter or by the depression of switches.

console, data station ◊ *data station console*.

console display register A special *register* into which data can be loaded by program, or under operator control, to allow data to be displayed by a visual indicator on the *console*.

console switch A *switch* which can be set from an *operator's console*, enabling a *program* to alter its actions according to the setting it detects.

console typewriter A unit of the *console* whereby the computer can display messages to the operator and the operator can input instructions to the computer. Console typewriter messages may be of two types: messages informing the operator of actions required, e.g., *disk drives* needing attention, paper running low on the *printer*, and messages output from a running *program* giving information on the progress of the *run*, e.g., the printing of *control totals*.

constant area The part of store *allocated* by a *program* used to hold *constants*.

constants In a *program* constants are items of data which remain unchanged for each *run*, e.g., page headings or numerical constants required for calculations, such as the constant 12 required for dividing dozens to obtain units.

construct A statement in a *source program* which will produce a predetermined effect when executed.

container file Synonymous with *controlling file*.

content The content of a *location* in *store* is the data held in the location.

content-addressed storage Synonymous with *associative store*.

contention The condition which arises when using *multiplexor channel time sharing*, and more than one unit attempts to transmit at the same time.

continuous stationery A continuous supply of paper consisting of perhaps several hundred individual sheets separated by perforations and folded to form a pack. The stationery is designed for automatic feeding through the print unit of a *line printer* and sprocket holes are punched for this purpose in the margins of each sheet.

contrast In *optical character recognition* (OCR), the difference in colour or intensity between the character and its background.

control The function of interpreting and acting upon *instructions*, or performing required operations when certain specific conditions occur.

control break A *key change* which occurs in a *control data*[1] field. This term is more commonly used in connexion with computer *report programs* whereas comparing *control change* was used in *punched card* terminology.

control card 1. A *punched card* containing data required for control purposes, e.g., *control totals*. 2. A synonym for *parameter card*.

control change ⟡ *comparing control change*.

control change, intermediate ⟡ *intermediate control change*.

control change, major ⟡ *major control change*.

control change, minor ⟡ *minor control change*.

control character A character whose function is to initiate controlling operations over *peripheral units*, e.g., a paper-feed control character will specify the amount of paper to be passed through a *printer* before the next line is printed.

Also known as functional character.

control circuits The circuits in a computer's *control unit* used to carry out the operations initiated by the computer *instructions*.

control computer A computer used in *process control* where the process under control feeds signals to the control computer, which in turn sends signals back which directly control the operation of the process.

control counter A synonym for *control register*.

control data 1. Pertaining to *records* in *punched card* practice which bear *keys* or information of certain significance in *batching* and sequencing the records. For example, a group of records might need to be sorted into order according to data in three separate *fields* of each record; the first field might specify COUNTY, the second TOWN and the third STREET. The first field would be the *major control data*, the second *intermediate control data* and the third *minor control data*. 2. Information used to influence the operation of a *routine*, either by selecting it or by modifying it. In this sense, associated with *parameter*. ⟡ *control statement*.

control field A *field* within a *record* where *control data* is held. The presence or absence or change in value of the contents of the control field will cause specified *operations* or *routines* to occur.

control, flow ⟡ *job flow control*.

control holes Punchings in a *punched card* which indicated how further data in the card was to be treated in the machine.

Also known as function holes, designation holes or control punchings.

control, input/output traffic ⟡ *input/output traffic control*.

control language In an *operating system*, the set of *commands* available to the user for the organization and control of the *programs* and *resources* available in the computer system.

Also known as job control language (JCL), system control language (SCL).

control language interpreter A *software* routine which is used to *read*, *interpret* and *execute* statements written in a *control language*.

Usually part of an *operating system*.

controlling file A section of *storage* which occupies a number of complete *cylinders* on a *magnetic disk*, and which can be expanded or contracted in size to contain a number of *files*. Synonymous with *container file*.

control loop Synonymous with *control tape*.

control mark Synonymous with *tape mark*.

control-message display A device which displays control information (e.g., information on the operation of a given *program* as it is being run), in plain language. A *console typewriter* is an example of a control-message display.

control, numerical ⟡ *numeric control*.

control panel 1. A panel on a computer *console* containing manual switches used for direct communication with the *central processor*. 2. Also used for the unit containing engineers' controls. 3. In *punched card* machines, control panel was synonymous with *plug-board*.

control punchings Synonymous with *control holes*.

control register A *register* whose function is to contain the *address* of the next *instruction* in the sequence of operations. The term is also used for the register which holds the address of the current instruction, normally known as the instruction register.

Also known as control counter, program counter.

control sequence The normal order in which *instructions* are acted on in a computer. A *transfer of control* is said to occur when a *branch instruction* alters the normal sequence.

control stack A *hardware* mechanism consisting of a number of *storage locations*, and used to provide procedural control over processes within the computer, to assist in the *dynamic allocation* of work space, and to perform arithmetic. It is an *architectural* feature of some computer models and provides an efficient means of calling procedures and ease of implementation of *re-entrant code*.

control statement In a *high level programming language* in which the expression *statement* is used to refer to an *instruction*, a control statement is a *directive* to the program used to cause actions to take place according to specified conditions. The expression is also used for directives present in a *source program* which control the operation of the *compiler* without affecting the resulting *object program*, e.g., directions for a page change on the *printout* of the *source language* during compilation.

control tape A closed *loop* of punched *paper tape* or plastic tape used to control the operation of printing devices.

Also known as paper tape loop, carriage tape, control loop.

control total A total established for a *file* or group of *records* during a specific operation (e.g., a computer *run*) to check that the processing operation has been applied to all records. The total may be significant in itself, as for example a total of a value *field*, but ⬦ *hash total*.

Also known as check total. ⬦ general article on *Control Totals*.

control totals Control totals are used during the processing of data as a check upon accuracy. Their purpose is to ensure that the processing has been done correctly without having to check each individual item.

Where many documents are being handled during a series of clerical processing operations there is always a risk of loss or error. If a total of the results is taken after processing and this agrees with the control total of the data before it was processed, considerable detailed checking can be avoided.

In addition, where documents are being sent from one person to another they can be supported by the control total. By totalling the documents and comparing them with the control total supplied, the recipient can be sure that he has received all the documents sent to him.

As an illustration, a system for recording suppliers' invoices can be considered. The clerk receiving the invoices would check them for price, etc., put them into batches and produce batch control totals of the amount payable and number of invoices. The control totals might be produced on a manual add-listing machine.

Each batch of invoices together with a slip giving the batch control total would be sent to the data control section. An entry would be keyed for each invoice and the entries then printed so that batch totals for each list could be checked with the batch control slips. It would then be certain that the invoice values had been punched correctly and that no invoices or entries had been mislaid. This certainty will have been achieved without any detailed checking.

Where any errors occur then a comparison of the batch totals indicates immediately the incorrect batch. If the number of documents in each batch is kept to a manageable quantity then the number which have to be checked, in the case of an error, is minimal. Errors can be found quickly.

Control totals are an extremely useful device as a total check on the processing of data and one which avoids checking each item in detail.

control transfer   The departure from the normal sequence of *program instructions* which occurs when a *branch instruction* is obeyed.

control transfer instruction   Synonymous with *branch instruction*.

control unit   That part of computer *hardware* which *accesses instructions* in sequence, interprets them and initiates the appropriate operation required. ⟡ *central control unit, program controller.*

control unit, peripheral   ⟡ *peripheral control unit.*

control word   A *word* in *store* which contains information used for control purposes. These purposes depend on the type of control involved. In a *subroutine* the control word acts as a *parameter* directing the specific action required; the control word associated with data *blocks* may contain information about the size of the block or the type of data held in the block.

conventional   In describing *punched card* equipment, used to distinguish *tabulators, sorters, collators*, etc., from *computers*. Coined at a time when computers were unconventional.

conversational compiler   A *compiler* which uses the *conversational mode* of computer operation in which the user enters each *source language statement* in turn to the computer, which immediately checks its validity and informs the user if he can proceed or must correct a mistake.

conversational mode A method of operation in which the user is in direct communication with the computer and is able to obtain immediate response to his input messages.

Also known as interactive mode.

conversion 1. The process of transcribing a *file* from one format to another on to the same or a different *storage* medium – *file conversion*. 2. The process of converting a *source program* from one *dialect* of a language to another (e.g., when converting programs written for a specific range of computers to another range) – *program conversion*.

conversion equipment Equipment used for performing data conversion without involving a *processor*, e.g., a *card-to-tape converter*. Such devices are known as *converters*.

conversion program 1. A computer *program* designed to perform data *conversion*. 2. A computer program designed to convert programs written for one computer system into programs capable of being run on a different system. ⟡ *simulator routine*.

converter ⟡ *conversion equipment*.

coordinate store Synonymous with *matrix store*.

copy To reproduce data from one *storage device* to another, or another part of the same store, without altering the original data.

CORAL A *high-level language* for *real-time applications*.

cordless plug A *plug* with connectors incorporating no flexible part.

core, core store A term once used to refer to the *main store* or *main memory* of a computer, derived from the fact that such storage devices were made up of small ferrite cores capable of holding a magnetic charge (⟡ *core storage*). In modern computers the main store is no longer composed of cores and the term is not therefore entirely apposite.

core dump Transferring the contents of *core storage* to an *output device*, e.g., a *line printer* or *paper tape punch*. Synonymous with *memory dump*, although strictly should only be used for memory composed of cores.

core memory A computer *memory* or *store* composed of *magnetic cores*.

core memory resident A *routine* which is retained permanently in *core storage*.

co-resident When two or more *routines* are held in *main memory* at the same time they are said to be co-resident.

core storage A type of *memory* composed of magnetic *cores*, in which data is held in *binary* form by means of the property of cores of retaining a positive or negative charge. The pattern of charges serves to represent the coded data.

corner cut   A corner removed from a *punched card* to ensure that all cards in a *pack* were stacked the same way round before being fed to a machine. '

correction, automatic error   ◊ *automatic error correction.*

corrective maintenance   Work required to correct a machine fault; maintenance in addition to *routine maintenance.*

corruption   The mutilation of *data* or *code* caused by a failure of *hardware* or *software* or an error in an *application program.*

cost analysis   The purpose of cost analysis is to ascertain the cost of production of any job, process or service in an industrial or commercial organization. If standard costs or budgets have been previously set up, deviations from the norm can be brought to the attention of management. The routine tasks of sorting and manipulating data involved in cost analysis, and the subsequent tabulation of data and production of summary reports have been undertaken by computers for many years, and an outline of the main factors of such systems is given below.

Systems of cost analysis are designed by cost accountants; basically their purpose is to break down the total expenditure involved in production, administration and marketing into a number of subdivisions. For example factory costs may be broken down into direct labour costs, direct material costs and overheads. Direct costs are those which are completely incurred in the production of a certain unit. Overheads include indirect items which cannot readily be assigned to any particular process, such as rent, rates and insurance.

Once costs have been broken down the cost analysis data processing cycle consists of the generation of records each of which represents a unit of expenditure under some cost subdivision. As well as cost each record will specify an account chargeable, usually a job or department.

For example, a simple form of cost analysis system might involve the generation of the following types of record: labour; stores; purchases and expense.

Each of these types would contain at a minimum the following *fields*: date, record type number, job or account number and quantity. (Other fields might be included if the cost analysis system were part of a large data processing system.) Thus a labour record would have information detailing the date, a man number, a job or account number and the hours worked by that man during the period concerned. The stores and purchases records show quantities of direct materials issued to jobs, a stores item being generated if the material comes from stock, and a purchases item if material is bought from outside. The last record, expenses, details incidental costs such as packing or delivery.

Data recorded might be written to *magnetic disk* under a computer system, and processed in various ways. First of all the data would be *sorted* into some useful sequence, for example job number, within cost type. Then the quantity fields in the records would need to be converted into monetary costs. For example, labour cost would be found by multiplying hours worked by a rate for the job. Then the data might be re-sorted to cost type within job number, and passed against a work-in-progress file *updating* it to give the latest cost position. *Printouts* might be required at stages during the computer run, to agree *control totals* and to summarize information for management.

It is likely that a cost analysis system implemented on a computer would be more sophisticated than that described above, which is intended to illustrate only the basic principles. For example, the power of a computer makes it possible to set up an integrated *production control* system of which costing would be a small part. Again it is likely that a *standard costing* technique would be embodied in the data processing cycle to enable management to compare actual with expected results.

count A cumulative total of the number of times a specified event occurs, e.g., a count of lines printed or *records* read. A count is also used in *programming* to mean a total of the number of times a particular *instruction* or *routine* is performed, and is used for control purposes, determining the operation of the process concerned.

counter Any device used to accumulate totals. For example, an electro-mechanical device on a *punched card* machine, or in a *digital computer* a *memory* location or *register* used as an *accumulator* or to record a number of repeated *loops* in a *program*.

counter, control ◊ *control register*.

counter, program address ◊ *program address counter*.

CPM 1. Abbreviation of *critical path method*. 2. Abbreviation of *cards per minute*.

CP/M An *operating system* designed for *personal computers*.

CPS Abbreviation of character-per-second or cycles-per-second.

CPU Central processing unit. ◊ general article on *Central Processors*.

crash A system failure, usually one which requires *operator* attention before the *run* can be resumed.

creation A term in *file processing* referring to initial *data collection*, and the organization of this *raw data* into a *file*.

crippled leap-frog test A variation of *leap-frog testing* in which the

107

test arithmetic is performed on only one part of *store*, not on different *locations*.

crippled mode   A machine operates in crippled mode when certain parts are not working, but the system is still able to operate at reduced capacity. Related to *graceful degradation*.

criterion   A *constant* used in decision-taking as the standard against which variable data is compared to determine action to be taken.

critical path method (CPM)   This is a technique used in planning, scheduling and controlling major industrial, technical or commercial projects. An alternative term for CPM is PERT (*Project Evaluation and Review Technique*). Originally slightly different in concept, the two terms are now interchangeable, and both are referred to as *network planning*. CPM is useful in conjunction with projects which require the combination of varying amounts of different resources at different times and which involve a large number of interrelated events and activities.

The first stage in planning a project using CPM techniques is the drawing up of a network, a special type of chart made up of circles and arrows. Each circle represents an *event*, i.e., something that happens at a particular point in time. The circles are joined up by arrows which represent *activities*, i.e., jobs of work that are spread over a period of time. An event cannot occur until all the activities leading up to it have taken place.

A network will always start with an event, for example 'Authorization of Project', and will always end with one, for example 'Product Launched'. In between the first and last events there will be a number of intermediate events, each preceded and followed by one or more activities. Thus any intermediate event will be dependent on the completion of certain activities and will itself control the start date of later activities.

Each activity on a network is given a time estimate which represents the time that activity is expected to take. A common convention for networks is that time flows from left to right. Each event is given a number, later events having a higher number than earlier events. It is not necessary to number events in sequence however, and gaps in sequence are often left to facilitate later insertions on a network.

Sometimes it is not possible to give an accurate estimate of the likely duration of activities. In these circumstances it is usual to specify three time estimates; optimistic, pessimistic and most likely. Another peculiarity of activities is that no actual work need be done in the time allotted to them. Awaiting delivery of a component is an example of this sort of activity. It is also possible for an activity to take up no time at all. Although this appears to be a negation of common sense, activities of zero duration are a convention used to simplify the drawing of networks. Activities which require no resources and/or no time are known as dummy activities.

The drawing up of a network is a useful discipline because it causes the designer to consider the interrelationship between the various activities. The real value of a network, however, lies in the use that can be made of it in scheduling and controlling projects. First of all it is possible to process a network in order to establish how long the project is likely to take from start to finish. This is known as isolating the critical path.

The critical path of a network is determined by considering each event in turn and calculating the earliest possible time at which the event can occur. If an event depends on several activities the earliest time is determined by the activity which takes longest to finish. Thus the critical path is the sequence of interconnected events and activities which will require the longest time to accomplish. The sum of all the time estimates of the activities on the critical path will be the shortest time in which a project can be completed.

The characteristic of events and activities on a critical path is that if any of the time estimates are not met, the completion date of the project will be affected. Conversely time estimates not on the critical path can change (within limits) without affecting the overall completion date. The degree to which a time estimate is free to change is known as the degree of *float*. The total float of any activity is the maximum time that can possibly be made available for its completion minus the duration of the activity. Any expansion or movement in an activity in excess of its total float will change the critical path and increase the overall project time. Deliberate use can be made of knowledge of float times in order to divert resources from non-critical activities and concentrate them on activities on the critical path. It should be stressed that the critical path in a network can never possess float.

Critical path techniques enable a project to be controlled as well as scheduled. Control will obviously need to be tightest for events which lie on the critical path. The technique used is to insert actual performance times on the network, which is then re-analysed to see the effects of the work done. This will enable management to take action on anything which is likely to jeopardize the future progress of the project. It is evident that any slipping on a critical activity will delay completion of the project. To correct this, it may be possible to transfer resources from non-critical activities.

Critical path analysis is usually thought to be a technique associated with electronic computers. This need not necessarily be the case, but when a project involves more than a few hundred activities, or any additional operation apart from simple scheduling is required, it is probably essential to use a computer in order to cope with the volume of calculation. Most computer manufacturers offer CPM or PERT packages as part of their standard *software*, and these programs can be run either on the user's own computer or by computer bureaux which sell computer time. As well as the analysis of the critical path, the computer can also handle problems associated with re-allocation of resources, and the effect of resource *allocation* can be immediately tested by *simulation*.

The main features of a computer CPM or PERT system may be summarized as follows:

(a) The handling of events and activities and their changing values.

(b) The ability to interrelate networks of different levels.

(c) The ability to accept progress data and to produce progress reports.

(d) The ability to determine the critical path through a network.

cross-check   The checking of the result of a routine or calculation by obtaining the result by different methods and comparing.

cross compiler   A *compiler* used on one computer system to provide *object code* in accordance with the format needed to run on a different type of computer.

cross talk   The appearance of signals from one telephone circuit on another circuit, causing interference.

CRT   Abbreviation of *cathode ray tube*.

cryogenics   The study of the operating characteristics of electronic devices at temperatures approaching absolute zero.

CUG   Abbreviation of *closed user group*.

current instruction register   A special *register* in which *instructions* are stored so that they can be executed under the aegis of the *program controller*.

cursor   A *special character*, usually a flashing square block or underline, which indicates the position on a screen at which the next information character will be displayed.

customer acceptance test   A test designed by, or on behalf of, an organization purchasing a computer system to test the performance, facilities, and reliability of the system. May include tests of *hardware* and *software*, and perhaps *application* systems developed for the customer. Usually such a test takes place on the customer site after the computer has been *commissioned*.

customizing The modification of a standard *hardware* or *software* product to meet the needs of a specific *user*.

cybernetics The study of the theory of control systems with particular regard to the comparisons between machines and the nervous system of animals and men.

cycle 1. A sequence of operations performed repetitively in the same order. 2. The time required to complete a given set of operations.

cycle count A count of the number of times a given cycle has been performed, or a count of the number of repetitions still required.

cycle index counter A *counter* used to count the number of times that a given cycle of *program instructions* has been performed. The cycle index counter can be examined at any selected time to ascertain the number of repetitions still required in a *loop*.

cycle reset Setting the *cycle count* to its initial value or some other selected value.

cycle time The time taken to complete a *cycle* of operations. Store cycle time is the minimum time required to retrieve an item of data from *store*.

cyclic code Synonymous with *Gray code*.

cyclic redundancy check A check carried out on a *storage device* or in a *communication* circuit to detect errors. ⟡ *summation check*.

cyclic shift A *shift* in which a *string* of *characters* or *bits* is treated as if it were a *closed loop*, so that data from one end of the string is re-entered at the other end. For example, if the string 123456 is given a cyclic shift of two places to the right the result will be 561234.

cyclic store A *storage device* in which the storage medium is arranged in such a way that access to individual *locations* can be obtained at only fixed points in a basic cycle; e.g., a *magnetic drum*.

cylinder Synonymous with *seek area*.

D

dagger operation Synonymous with *nor operation*.

daisychain A number of devices connected to a controller by a method which allows a cable to connect one device to the controller and then allows a separate cable to connect the first device to a second; a third cable connects a third device to the second, and so on.

daisywheel printer An *impact printer* in which the type font is held on a removable disc which has spokes radiating from a central hub. The type is at the end of the spokes and, when it is opposite the printing position, is struck by a single hammer against the inked ribbon and paper. Imaginative technologists liken the disc and spokes to a daisy.

DASD Acronym for *Direct Access Storage Device*.

data A general expression used to describe any group of *operands* or *factors* consisting of numbers, alphabetic characters or symbols which denote any conditions, value or state, e.g., all values and descriptive data operated on by a computer *program* but not the program itself. The word data is used as a collective noun and is usually accompanied by a singular verb: 'data are' may be pedantically correct but is awkward to say and therefore awkward to understand. Data is sometimes contrasted with *information*, which is said to result from the processing of data, so that information derives from the assembly, analysis or summarizing of data into a meaningful form.

data acquisition control system Relating to a *computer system* in which high speed data channels are used to connect a central computer to distant locations. Essentially a system designed to operate in *real-time* applications, receiving data from a number of remote stations, and transmitting data to them under *program control*. The *data collection devices* within such a system may cater for both *analog* and *digital* forms of data *input* and *output*.

data adapter unit A unit designed to allow a *central processor* to be connected to a number of data *communications channels*; for example, for connexion to distant terminals over telegraph channels or to a number of local *in-plant data collection* points.

data administrator A person responsible for control of data within an organization implementing a *data management* system. He is responsible for the design of data structures, and for ensuring standards of accuracy and mutual integrity within the computer system and in the organizational environment. ⟳ general article on *Data Base Management Systems*.

data analysis display unit　Relating to the facilities offered by *cathode ray tube visual display units* for an *on-line* analysis of data.

data area　An area of *store* containing *data* rather than *executable code* forming part of the system *software* or *application program*.

data bank　A comprehensive *file* of *data*, usually stored in a *direct access storage device*. Data stored in a data bank is usually available to a large number of users by means of remote terminals, and is often updated by means of a *real-time* system.

data base　A file of data so structured that appropriate applications draw from the file and update it but do not themselves constrain the file design or its content. A file which is not designed to satisfy a specific, limited application.

data base management systems　Computer users have increasingly accepted the concept that the various sub-systems of an organization should be integrated to form a total system. Thus all users of data within the organization share common records of information and the information available to staff and management at every level is drawn from the same source, providing mutually consistent levels of accuracy to all users. This concept constitutes an ideal condition which has seldom been achieved in practice, there being two major requirements which militate against complete success: (i) Large complex organizations find it difficult to organize the control of basic operational data since this demands standards of accuracy and quality spanning departmental boundaries and requires extensive coordination outside the needs and objectives of individual departments. (ii) The *software* systems required to manage the data within the computer system are complex and demand large investments from both computer manufacturers and user organizations. Such systems have the general title of Data Base Management Systems.

Some organizations have achieved a degree of success by integrating the various sub-systems which constitute a major part of their business activity. The boundaries of such systems usually have to be restricted to groups of systems with a major operational significance. This article seeks to describe the general nature of such systems and the characteristics of the software needed.

The first concept which characterizes the nature of data base systems is that data should be recorded once only, and be shared by the various sub-systems and users of the system. Thus to eliminate the duplication of data it must be structured and organized to include the requirements of all users. Information should not be recorded in local files designed for specific applications.

The data base concept is also strengthened when data is captured and recorded in the data base at the time when events in the organization give rise to the transactions concerned. Thus there is a trend towards *real time* processing. Although this ideal takes time to evolve within an organization, the objective is to ensure that files are updated as events occur and the computer is able to communicate relevant information to people in many different places at the same time, thus overcoming problems of communication in large organizations. The data base system needs to ensure that data is accurate and available to users who need it, but also needs to protect the *security* and confidentiality of information.

Thus the Data Base Management Systems (DBMS) which manage the information must be able to ensure that files are accessed concurrently and yet be protected from corruption. A high degree of *resilience* is necessary to handle breakdowns which might destroy the mutual consistency and accuracy of data.

The gradual development of a data base system requires the originators of data to be responsible for its accuracy, and it is usually accepted that a *data base administrator* should be appointed to monitor the quality of data and to be responsible for the development and organization of the files. ◊ *data administrator*.

An essential feature of a DBMS system is to enable application programs to operate against a background of changing file structures; this is achieved by providing independence of methods of file access from the application program logic. The appropriate record access mechanism is allocated to programs at *run time* (e.g., the program need not know whether a file is *sequentially* or *randomly* organized). The method of file access is not the only feature to be handled in this way. The structure of records will change in the evolution of a data base, and routines are necessary in the DBMS to mask out unwanted *fields* automatically. Thus the data base can be developed without the need to *recompile* individual programs which were previously written to address records according to an earlier form of file organization.

This concept is described by a number of different terms. For example the term *data independence* is used; and also the term *transparency*, which relates to the notion that the DBMS provides each application program with a specific view of the data base structure relevant to the application concerned. This facility is usually made available in DBMS by a Data Description Language (DDL). At any time there is only one complete description for the total data base but there may be many sub-descriptions which delineate data structures for specific application programs. The complete description of the data base is referred to as a *schema* whereas the sub-descriptions are known as *sub-schema*. The DDL facilities enable the data base administrator to describe the physical extent of the data base as it is *mapped* onto the hardware – it defines also all data elements, records and all logical relationships between records, and the sub-schema enables the data administrator to name the fields, records, and logical sets which he wishes to make available to individual applications.

A DBMS system usually provides *data dictionary* facilities, giving a variety of reports to the data base administrator to assist in the control of the data base.

In some cases, the records stored in a data base are not organized into files in the form conventionally associated with free-standing applications. The reason for avoiding conventional structures is that they do not provide methods of access suitable for all possible uses of the data base. It is preferable to store data as a number of networks which permit many complex logical relationships between data elements to be expressed. This ability to support such logical relationships is one of the factors to be considered in evaluating the effectiveness of a particular DBMS The logical relationships are usually described as *sets*, and there are often options for describing the order of member records within a set. For example a record may be a member of a number of sets, and at the same time be the owner of one or more sets of records. A record will, however, appear only once in the data base as a prime location to be updated by transactions which relate to it.

The members of a set are automatically linked in forward or reverse directions by pointers enabling a chain of records to be processed in a desired direction.

As previously described, an application programmer can gain access to records in the data base only by means of a sub-schema. The sub-schema is provided to the application in its working storage area in response to statements written in the data manipulation language (DML). The DML is the language used to describe processes to be performed upon data by application programs. In many DBMS the DML is provided as an extension of the *COBOL* language. The DML provides facilities to store, delete and modify records; to insert and

115

remove records from sets; to find and get records by key and/or according to set relationships.

A DBMS system must provide privacy facilities to prevent users from gaining access to data elements or records which they are not authorized to examine. The same facilities may be used to prevent users from updating or deleting data elements, which they may otherwise examine.

Although in some DBMS, records may be stored in the form of conventional files, the individual application program may still regard the records as being organized into particular files. For example, allowing a file to be accessed by a variety of keys enabling each user to view the data as a file with a desired field as the key. This is sometimes referred to as the *alternate key* facility.

Where records in a data base have to be accessed in more than one hierarchical grouping then the more complex facilities described earlier are needed. The logical sets available in such systems are sometimes referred to as owner coupled sets. Almost all the DBMS have been developed by computer manufacturers, or *software* houses – the skills and investment required to develop such large general purpose systems is usually beyond the scope of individual computer-using organizations.

data capture ⟡ *data collection*[2].

data carrier A general term referring to a medium for recording data, e.g., *magnetic disk*.

data carrier store Describing any form of *data storage* in which the storage medium is external to the computer. For example, both *magnetic disk* and *laser cards* can be used to store data, and they must be loaded on to a *peripheral unit* before the data can be *accessed* for automatic processing. Contrasted with *inherent store*.

data cell drive Sometimes used in reference to a *direct access storage* device, particularly where a number of such devices are connected to a single *central processor*. Thus, each device or data cell drive represents a module of storage within the total storage capacity of the system, perhaps running into billions of characters of information.

data channel multiplexor A device, usually associated with a central computer, servicing a number of *communications channels*, any of which may be transmitting or receiving data from the computer. The communications channels may operate at varying speeds according to the needs of the system, but the *multiplexor* will operate at a much higher speed to service these channels successively one *character* at a time.

data collection 1. The process of capturing *raw data* for use within a *computer system*. Also known as *data gathering*. Related to *file creation*. 2. In modern business systems the term is often used to imply the *capture* of information at the instant of a transaction occurring. For example, requiring the use of *data transmission equipment* to connect distant locations with a central computer where the transactions are recorded and processed.

data collection and analysis Related to a system in which a number of *data collection* points are connected directly to a *central processor*, so that data can be collected and automatically analysed as events arise. Such techniques may be used in both *real time* commercial systems and in industrial *process control* applications.

data communications Synonymous with *data transmission*. Concerning the use of communications equipment to transfer coded data by telephone, telegraph or radio communications circuits. ◊ general article on *Communications Devices*.

data communications exchange A special *hardware unit* that connects a control unit of a *central processor* to a communications network. Used in *real time* applications where data is to be transmitted and received simultaneously over several *communications channels* perhaps operating in many different modes.

data communication terminal A distant or *in-plant* terminal at which *input* and *output devices* may be stationed and connected via a *channel* to some central computer system. For example, *paper tape readers* and *punches* are often used for communication with a *central processor* from distant locations. When the terminal equipment is not being used for *data transmission* it can often be used for *data preparation* and editing in an *off-line mode*.

data control Related to the control of data entering or leaving a data processing system. For example, in *batch processing* applications input documents may be collected and vetted to ensure that they have been correctly coded and batched.

data conversion ◊ *conversion*.

data conversion language A language used to describe the data structures of *files* to be transcribed under the operation of a file *conversion* routine.

data delimiter Synonymous with *separator*.

data description The specification of an element of data in a *source program* written in accordance with the rules for a particular programming *language*. For example, an entry describing a *data-name* as written

117

in the *data division* of a *COBOL* program. The description specifies the *data name*, the length in characters, whether the item is numeric, alphabetic or alphanumeric, and the *data level* of the element in relation to others.

data description language A language used in a *data base management system* to describe the structure of *records*, *data elements*, *files* and their relationships.

data description library A *record* composed of accumulated data definitions in a *data management system*, and representing a definition of the entire *data base*. Used by the *data administrator* to control and manage the system.

data display unit A term sometimes used when referring to a *visual display unit* in which data stored in *memory* can be selected and displayed as characters or graphs upon a screen. Sometimes a *data display unit* may incorporate a *light pen* to enable graphs to be modified by a user under *program control*.

data division ♢ *COBOL*

data element Any item of data which for a given situation may be considered as a unit, e.g., *field*, *record*.

dataflow computer A computer in which *data* values flow from operations which produce them to the operations which use them as *operands*. An example of *non von Neumann architecture*.

data format A description of the way data is held in a *file* or *record*, e.g., whether it is in *character form*, is a *binary* number, etc.

data gathering Synonymous with *data collection*.

datagram A self-contained *packet* that contains enough routing information to allow it to reach its destination on a *packet switching network*.

data handling equipment In the broadest sense any equipment used to process data, but more specifically equipment used in *automatic data processing systems*.

data independence Providing a distinction between *logical records* as recognized by user *programs* and physical records as stored by the system. Processing can then be described without specific reference to the way the *data* is held.

data item A unit of data within an *application* system, one of the logical elements contained in a *record* and describing a particular attribute (e.g., name, address, age). May require a number of *characters*, *words*, *bytes*, or perhaps just a single *bit* to represent the entity concerned.

data level Relating to the rank of a particular *data element* in relation to other elements specified as part of the same *record* in a *source*

118

language. For example, in the *data division* of a *COBOL* program each data element is described, and that description includes a reference number which specifies for the COBOL *compiler* the relationship between that element and other elements in the same hierarchy.

data link level In the ISO *seven layer reference model* for communications *protocols*, the second level which controls the accuracy of data transfer. ⬦ *high-level data link control*.

data logging The recording of data and data movements occurring at a specified point in a system.

data management The process of handling data in a controlled environment; including the control of data having complex relationships by various system management routines without loss of integrity and without interference to other processes within the total system. ⬦ general article on *Data Base Management Systems*.

data management utility system A *data management* system based on a number of parameter-driven routines.

data manipulation instructions ⬦ general article on *Instruction Classification*.

data manipulation language In a *data base management system* a procedural language used to define the processes required by users.

data matrix An array of values stored as a series of rows and columns representing variables and the values they may take.

data-names In writing a *program* in a programming *language*, items of data are allocated data-names which are specified as part of the *source program*. These names are used as *operands* in the source program *instructions* and replace the *addresses* of the items of data that they represent. When the source program is compiled the *compiler* will usually allocate *relative addresses* to these items of data and will substitute the appropriate relative addresses as operands in instructions which quote the data-names. When the *object program* is finally loaded, the *loading routine* will allocate an *absolute address* to each relative address and thereby each data-name originally specified in the source program will relate to a specific address in the *memory* at *run* time. ⬦ *addressing*.

data net A *data communications exchange* for controlling the transfer of messages to and from remote terminals and a central computer.

data phone A device which permits data to be transferred over a telephone channel.

data plotter A device designed to give a visual display, usually in the form of a graph on paper, by plotting the course of coordinates.
   Also known as X–Y plotter.

data preparation Computers can process information with virtually unerring accuracy, but if a computer is presented with inaccurate information to process, the result produced will be useless. Great care must be given to the systems and procedures concerned with the preparation of data, and the way in which this data is loaded into a computer.

The data to be processed may be generated in a number of different forms – it could, in an order processing system for example, arise from a telephone conversation in which a customer identifies himself giving name, address, items ordered, quantities, credit card number and delivery address. It is easy to imagine the difficulty and confusion which could arise if errors were made in the transcription of this data: for example, goods could be delivered to the wrong address; the wrong goods could be sent to the right address; or the charge could be made to the wrong customer's account. Instead of increasing efficiency, the computer could simply be creating confusion at a very fast rate. Data preparation systems are therefore designed to: avoid errors in transcription of data from one medium to another; verify that data items are consistent with information stored in existing computer files; and then check the consistency of information within *data elements* and the relationship between data elements in the input data itself.

In the early days of computing, data was prepared for input to the computer on *punched cards* or *paper tape*. This often meant that transactions recorded on forms or documents had to be read, *field* by field, by a *key punch* operator who punched relevant items on a keypad which caused a mechanical punching unit to be activated to punch holes into a card or a paper tape. This process had several potential sources of error: the original document might be illegible; the punch unit itself might fail or create errors; or the operator might depress incorrect keys on occasions. To overcome these problems the whole process was usually carried out twice – once by the original key punch operator, and secondly by another operator using a *verifier*. A verifier was a machine purposely designed to compare the position and significance of holes in a card or tape with key depressions made by the verifying operator. When there was a discrepancy, the verifying machine was halted and the verifying operator was obliged to re-examine the original document and decide on the correct character. Very high degrees of accuracy could be obtained by such methods, but it required an extensive degree of manual labour to create such input, and significant delays, sometimes days or weeks, could arise before data could be organized and entered into a central computer.

To speed up this process, data entry and verification machines were designed to record data directly on to a medium such as *magnetic tape* or *magnetic disks*. These machines were known as *key-to-disk* or *key-to-tape* systems. The basic operation was still the same: an initial input operation, and a second verification stage. Magnetic media could be handled more quickly and efficiently than cards or paper tape, but systems were still essentially delayed by the need to batch data and go through the basic stages: collection and batching of source documents; initial keying of input; second stage verification and correction of input; and loading into the computer. Great benefits were to be obtained by cutting down this cycle and, if possible, by capturing transactions at the point and time of their occurence.

Today many computers operate *on-line*, with the users inputting directly into the computer using a *terminal*. This greatly speeds up the efficiency and avoids the delays inherent in the batch preparation process described above. However, it will be appreciated that errors can be created in this on-line process. To avoid getting rubbish into the system, a combination of manual as well as automatic computer procedures can be applied. When data is entered, checks are imposed upon all fields which are keys and which control the entry of data on to files, e.g., customer numbers, item numbers, personnel numbers.

A name and address file is never maintained simply by name. Names can easily be confused even if qualifying initials are used. Each customer is given an account number in which some part of the number consists of a self-checking code. When the entire number is entered, the computer automatically performs a calculation to determine whether the number is a valid one. If the number is invalid, the user is prevented from entering further details of the transaction.

The system known as Modulo 11 provides an example of a self-checking system; a unique code is obtained by performing a calculation upon a number to derive a remainder, which is then appended to the number for use in data processing operations. For example, the number 14710 has a remainder of 3 attached to become 147103. To check the validity of this number, the computer detaches the remainder and multiplies each digit by a statistically selected weighting factor as follows:

121

Digit	Weight	Result
1 ×	1	= 1
4 ×	2	= 8
7 ×	5	= 35
1 ×	3	= 3
0 ×	6	= 0
		47

The total is divided by 11 to give a remainder of 3. Such check-sums will expose transcription errors in keys, but other checks are needed: for example, numeric fields must not contain non-numeric codes; numeric fields may have to fill in a defined range of values; and comparisons of descriptive data already stored in computer files can be made against details given by the user. A series of such checks will, when combined, greatly reduce the probability of errors in data preparation.

Other methods are in use to reduce data preparation costs and input errors. Some of these methods are intended to capture data automatically by greatly reducing or even eliminating the use of keystrokes to capture data. For example, in retail operations, transactions can be captured by having magnetic recording devices attached to cash registers so that data can be transmitted on-line to a central computer at frequent intervals. Point-of-sale machines also exist which can read bar codes imprinted on goods so that movements to or from stock are captured automatically. These techniques capture data as a by-product of an everyday operation using methods which entail little special consideration by the person performing the operation.

The development of techniques for the automatic recognition of preprinted characters by machines has led to some improved concepts in data collection. These techniques are described in more detail under the heading *character recognition*, but some details are given here. The essential principle involved is that the original transaction document is used as input to the computer system. Machines are available which can read documents bearing either magnetized-ink characters or special characters for *optical recognition*; these machines can be connected directly to a *central processor* to facilitate the automatic transcription of the data from the documents on to a storage medium such as a *magnetic disk*. These techniques are suitable for many applications involving large volumes of data to a fairly standard format; for example the use of magnetized-ink characters on bank cheques. They are particularly suitable where *turn-around documents* can be used and where the details to be entered for each transaction involve relatively few items of data. Gas, electricity and hire purchase accounting are examples.

The development of *real time* data processing applications requires data collection devices to be held permanently *on-line* to the central processor via some form of data transmission or *in-plant* communications network. Here *interrogating typewriters, cathode ray tube visual display units, key-to-disk* units and other keyboard input devices come to prominence. The data preparation limitations can be virtually eliminated as far as the recording of transactions is concerned, and the system can be designed to respond immediately to each transaction as it arises.

In all forms of data preparation it is usually preferable to allow the computer to perform a range of validity checks on every item of data as it is transcribed from the input medium. In this way it is possible to ensure that each record entering the system conforms to a prescribed pattern in the number and type of characters in specified fields, and in the logical relationship between fields for certain transaction types. These types of check are even more important in real time applications.

In *batch-processing* applications it is also necessary to maintain *control totals* throughout the stages of preparation and transcription to ensure that individual transactions or complete batches are not lost.

Generally, all data preparation is concerned with accuracy of transcription or transmission, and the eventual integrity of data depends very largely on this initial accuracy.

data processing The operations performed on *data*, usually by automatic electronic equipment, in order to derive information or to achieve order among *files*. A data processing system may incorporate clerical functions and ancillary machine operations as well as all arithmetic and logical operations performed by a computer.

data processing, automatic ◊ *automatic data processing*.

data processing centre The general term used when referring to the offices or buildings in which automatic data processing equipment is installed, including the equipment itself and all the programming, operating and systems staff necessary to run the centre. It is common to find such a unit organized as a single management group providing a service to the company or organization within which it operates.

Senior Management	Line Management	Junior Line Management
Policy	Communications	*Systems Analysis*
Company organization	Application selection	Budget control
Budget setting	Budget control	Resource allocation
Objective setting	Resource planning	Personnel
Senior personnel selection	Personnel training	Training
	Physical planning	System selection
		User contact
		Programming
		Budget control
		Resource allocation
		Personnel
		Training
		Program strategy
		Operations
		Budget control
		Resource allocation
		Personnel
		Control
		Statistics and reporting
		Training
		General
		Documentation and standards
		Data administration

124

	Systems Analysis	Programming	Operations	General
Technical Management	Supervision Feasibility studies Systems specification Maintenance Standards writing Clerical	Supervision Program organization Maintenance Standards writing Clerical	Scheduling – operations – data control – data preparation Supervision Clerical	
Staff	Informal training Analysis and design Implementation	Informal training Programming and testing	Work assembly Computer operating Data control Data preparation Informal training Library	Stock control Typing and copying
Trainees	Undergoing training			

Functions of a Data Processing Department

data processing department organization A great deal has been written about organizational structure in data processing departments, but what is not always recognized is something far more important than the titles of the members of the department: the question of whether all the functions which should be carried out are being carried out. The charts on pages 124 and 125 show the main functions and it is possible to draw up an organizational structure to suit any organization – and indeed any personalities in an organization – by ensuring that the different functions are covered. The functions are shown on different levels of responsibility as a guide only: it is quite possible for one man to fulfil functions on several different levels. The charts on pages 128 and 129 show two standard organizational structures. These structures are variable, but act as a useful guide-line for the brief outlines of jobs given below. Remarks on the qualities needed for each job are given in the general article on *Computer Personnel*.

The data processing manager is the centre of the organization, and on his imagination, determination and flexibility will depend much of the success of the department. He is responsible for deciding policy within the department and ensuring that the systems analysts, programmers and computer operations staff are all working towards the same end (and this is by no means automatic!). He should have a clearly defined position in the company, preferably one with an immediate contact at policy-making level. This is not only because he will need to influence policy, but also because one of his most important functions is communication: he must constantly ensure that the service his department offers is well known throughout the company, and he must encourage initiative in utilizing these services.

The systems analysts design systems and procedures (including documenting them) and implement them throughout the company. Sometimes such systems will be restricted to those which utilize, either directly or indirectly, computer time or *terminal* time and in this case *organization and methods* staff or *operational research* staff are employed in another department. More usually, O and M and OR activities are considered to be part of the data processing activities of the company. In the design stage, systems analysts will be as much concerned with people as with machines, and before any system can be approved for implementation it must be fully documented ($\lozenge$ general article on *Documentation – Systems*).

The functions of the *programmers* are to prepare, test and document computer programs from written specifications prepared by the systems analysts, and include amending existing programs to meet changing

126

requirements. Further information on programming strategy, tactics and design are given in the general article on *Programming*, and this is supplemented by the general article on *Documentation – Programming*. After the program has been *coded*, *desk-checked*, tested and documented it will be ready for productive *runs*, and may be passed to the computer operations staff for running as required.

The computer operations staff are responsible for the day-to-day running of the data processing equipment, which may include *data control* and *editing*, data preparation and computer operating. Data control and editing functions include the following: ensuring work progresses satisfactorily by supervising the passage of a job through the department according to work schedules; receiving and preparing clean '*raw data*' from other departments for the data preparation section; ensuring the enforcement of *control total* and error procedures and checking them; collecting and preparing all input data, and issuing programs and operating instructions for the jobs to be run by the computer operating section; controlling the issue of all programs and current files which are held in a *magnetic disk* or *magnetic tape* or *punched card library*: ensuring that output is dispatched to the correct addresses; and filing input data after use.

Data preparation includes the following functions: preparing actual computer input by recording raw data received from the data control section in a computer input medium controlling the whole process whereby data may be input directly from terminals intelligent or otherwise. The data may be input on-line, directly updating data files and the data preparation unit is responsible for ensuring that data security procedures are properly applied and checked. The unit is also responsible for arranging the computer input in a prescribed manner; updating master files, etc., as instructed by the data control section.

Computer operating includes the following functions: operating equipment in the computer area, processing data as instructed and supplied by the data control section; and maintaining log-books giving details of machine utilization.

Many data processing department managers have found that a service section can relieve a great deal of the load of non-productive work from other sections. Among tasks which can be handled by such a section are maintenance of standards manuals and organization manuals, control of documents including technical literature and records of *file layouts*, print layouts, etc; the organization of training; internal communications; and administration such as ordering new desks, recording absence and holidays and controlling stationery usage.

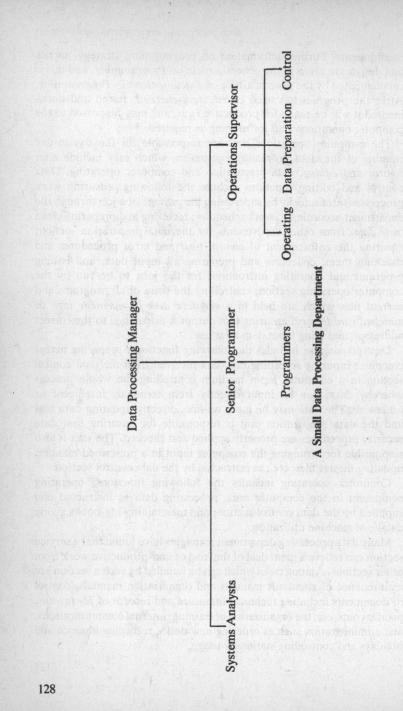

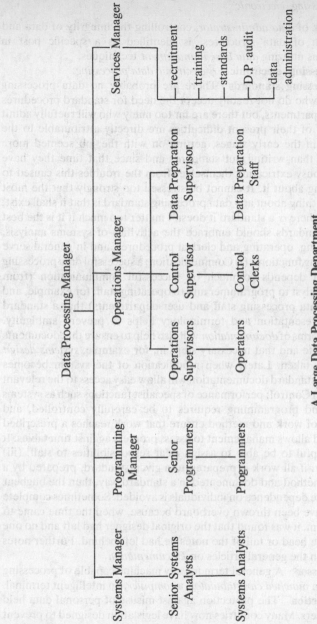

A Large Data Processing Department

Data Processing Manager

- Systems Manager
  - Senior Systems Analysts
  - Systems Analysts

- Programming Manager
  - Senior Programmers
  - Programmers

- Operations Manager
  - Operations Supervisors
    - Operators
  - Control Supervisor
    - Control Clerks
  - Data Preparation Supervisor
    - Data Preparation Staff

- Services Manager
  - recruitment
  - training
  - standards
  - D.P. audit
  - data administration

The task of *data administrator*, controlling the integrity of data and the design of data structures, is identified as a specific post in installations utilizing *data base management* techniques.

data processing, electronic ⟩ *electronic data processing*.

data processing standards There are probably no data processing managers who do not readily accept the need for standard procedures in their departments, but there are far too many who will ruefully admit that many of their present difficulties are directly attributable to the fact that, in the early stages, getting on with the job seemed more important than writing out standards and since that time they have been too busy extricating themselves from the troubles this caused to do anything about it. It cannot be stressed too strongly that the most important thing about any data processing standard is that it shall exist; so long as there *is* a standard it doesn't matter too much if it is the best or not. Standards should embrace the activities of systems analysis, programming, operating and clerical procedures, and in general serve the following functions. (i) Communication: a successful data processing installation depends so much on successful communication (from systems analyst to programmer and to operating staff, for example, and between data processing staff and user departments) that a standard form of presentation and terminology helps to prevent ambiguity. Standard forms of *documentation* will also help to ensure that documents are complete and that necessary steps in, for example, *systems design* have been taken. Later, when modification of the system becomes necessary, standard documentation will allow easy access to the relevant section. (ii) Control: performance of specialist functions such as systems analysis and programming requires to be carefully controlled, and standards of work and method ensure that work reaches a prescribed quality and allows management to assess progress against timetables. It is also helpful to be able to assign clear responsibilities to staff. (iii) Continuity: if all work is prepared to a given standard, prepared by a standard method and documented in a standard way, then the bugbear of complete dependence on individuals is avoided. Sometimes complete systems have been thrown overboard because, when the time came to amend them, it was found that the original designer had left and no one could make head or tail of the notes he had left behind. Further notes are given in the general articles on *Documentation*.

data processor A general term for any machine capable of processing data, e.g., a *punched card tabulator*, a *computer*, an intelligent terminal.

data protection The protection against misuse of personal data held on computers. Many countries now have legislation designed to prevent

exploitation of such data without the agreement of the individual concerned. 2. The process of safeguarding against the loss of data.
 Also known as data security.

data purification The process of validating and correcting data to reduce the number of errors entering a data processing system.

data record A *record* containing a unit of data for processing by a computer *program*.

data reduction The selection and *editing* of *operands* to derive facts from large volumes of *raw data*. To summarize information for subsequent processing or for presentation to management.

data reduction, on-line To accept data from a source directly *on-line* to a computer and to *edit* and arrange that data into an ordered format.

data representation The use of characters (i.e., numerals, letters and special symbols) to represent values and descriptive data. In a digital computer all *program instructions* and data are recorded as electrical impulses arranged in a coded form (⍺ *binary notation* and *binary-coded decimal notation*).

data retrieval ⍧ *retrieval, Information Retrieval Techniques.*

data security The protection of *data* against unauthorized access, loss or destruction.

data segment A sub-unit of the *storage* allocated to a particular *process*, used to contain *data* rather than *executable program code* forming part of the *application program* or system *software*.

data set A device which connects a *data processing* machine to a telephone or telegraph communication line. For example, a *telephone data set* converts *digital* signals to tones for transmission over a speech quality circuit.

data sink In the process of collecting and distributing *data* through *communications channels* (⍧ *data communications*), that part of a *network* which receives data. Contrasted with *data source*, which originates data.

data source In the process of collecting and distributing *data* through *communications channels* (⍧ *data communications*), that part of a *network* which originates data. Contrasted with *data sink*, which receives data.

data statements *Statements* written as part of a *source program* to identify and specify the format of data items used in the program.

data station A unit which incorporates data processing *input* and *output devices* and which is connected to a telephone or telegraph circuit by a *data set* to permit direct communication with a central computer.

data station console   A *console* situated at a distant *data terminal* to control the operation of the various *input* and *output devices* located there, and to control communication between the *data station* and a central computer. Generally includes a *data set* to connect the station to a communications channel, and circuits to handle automatic detection and correction of transmission errors.

data storage   The use of any medium for storing data; but implying a capability to store large volumes of data, immediately *on-line* to a *central processor* as in a *magnetic disk* store.

data stream   A sequence of *data elements* being transmitted in a continuous flow along a *communications channel*.

data terminal   A remote station employed to transmit and receive data from a central computer. ◊ *data communication terminal*.

data transfer instructions   ◊ general article on *Instruction Classification*.

data transmission   Pertaining to the automatic transfer of data from one computer system to another, or to and from a central computer and distant *data collection* points. The data may be transferred by special equipment using either telegraph or telephone circuits, or by radio link. The speed of transmission is largely governed by the characteristics of the data transmission line or channels. (◊ general article on *Communication Devices*.)

data unit   A group of one or more characters which are related in such a way that they form a whole. Similar to (but not always synonymous with) *field*.

data word   Any unit of *data* stored in a single *word* of a storage medium.

DBMS   Abbreviation for *data base management systems*.

daughterboard   A *board* connected to and extending the capacity of, a motherboard or *backplane*.

DC amplifier   Abbreviation for *directly coupled amplifier* or *direct current amplifier*.

DDE   Abbreviation of *direct data entry*.

DDL   Abbreviation of *data description language*.

deadly embrace   A condition which arises when all processes active at the same time within a computer become suspended while competing for the same resources. The condition is such that no one process can be continued without external intervention to remove a process from the system, allowing others to be reactivated.

dead time   A period of time allowed between two related events in order to avoid overlap or mutual interference.

dead zone unit A device used on an *analog computer* to give a constant output signal over a predetermined range of an input variable.

debatable time A term used in the keeping of computer usage statistics. It is usual to consider machine time under various headings for purposes of evaluating performance of the machine room, and debatable time is time that cannot be directly attributed to some other classification; e.g., where time is lost and there is no information to indicate whether it is due to, say, a programming error or an operator fault.

deblocking To extract *records* from a *block* of data so that the individual records can be processed.

debugging Debugging is the technique of detecting, diagnosing and correcting errors (also known as bugs) which may occur in *programs* or systems (both *hardware* and *software*).

The two main types of program error that can occur are logic errors and syntax errors. The former are the result of incorrect appreciation of the problem, and the latter the result of incorrect *coding* of the program. An example of an error in logic would be the attempt to calculate average speed by dividing fuel consumption by time taken, instead of distance travelled by time taken. The calculation would be performed correctly by program, but the result would be incorrect. An example of a syntax error would be writing the *instruction* DOV TIME, DIST where DIV, referring to the operation 'divide', should have been written instead of DOV, which is meaningless and would not be operated on by the computer.

Errors are detected by observing that programs do not produce the results expected from them, or by the failure of a program written in a *symbolic language* to *compile* correctly. Detecting errors by means of observing results involves testing programs with samples of data which the program would expect to be presented with in normal running. The nature of this data would be predetermined and the results expected from the program calculated by the programmer or systems analyst concerned, and compared with the actual results obtained. Test data of this sort is presented to the program either directly in the form expected in normal running, or by means of simulated input conditions, for example, by storing data with the program and altering the data input instructions to *access* the data directly from *store* rather than from an *input device*. As well as testing programs by means of *test data*, testing of all conditions expected in normal running must also be carried out, for example, all conditions causing a program to print messages requiring operator action, such as loading paper on a *printer*, must be

133

simulated. Any failure of a program to achieve expected results, or any unexpected halt occurring within a program, will require error diagnosis, as described below.

Programs written in a symbolic language require *compilation*, or translation into the *machine language* understood by the processor. The process of compilation enables syntax errors involving incorrect handling of the symbolic language to be detected. Most compilers reject incorrectly used statements, and print some indication of the type of error. However, errors in logic cannot usually be detected by compilers: any correctly formed statement will be translated, even if the instruction will cause the program to carry out an illogical function or perform a calculation incorrectly.

Once an error has been detected, either through incorrect results from test data or simulated operating conditions, or through an unexpected halt, or through compilation errors, the cause of the error must be diagnosed. Various methods of error diagnosis may be used. A *dry run* may be performed on the program *flowchart* or compilation listing. This involves the programmer in performing each step of the program as if he were the computer, checking and recording the action of each instruction or flowchart step. Instead of performing the computer's actions himself, the programmer may use a trace or diagnostic routine which performs the program on the computer in the normal way, but at the same time provides a printed record of the action taken by each instruction. Simpler versions of such a routine provide printed information about selected types of instruction. Other aids to diagnosing the causes of errors include prints of portions of internal store at various stages during the operation of a program, enabling the programmer to check the progress of the program. Prints may also be obtained of the contents of *backing store*, e.g., *magnetic disks*.

Errors of syntax detected by compilers are usually recorded by the compiler, and the type of error identified. Normally programs which have caused compilation errors cannot be run, and the errors must be corrected before the program can be tested.

Once the cause of an error has been detected, a correction must be applied to the program. Correcting source codes may be done directly by removing incorrect *statements* and substituting correct ones by using source code maintenance routines. Another technique for correcting programs is to apply a *patch*. This consists of deleting the incorrect instruction and substituting a *branch* to a section of coding correcting the error. Corrections may also be applied to a program at *run* time by directly altering the program after it has been loaded into store. However in most cases the best method of correcting errors is by amending incorrect coding at source, at the same time ensuring that all documentation supporting the program is kept up to date.

Debugging is not confined solely to programs. The term is also applied to the process of testing the performance of hardware systems, and also to the testing of a complete data processing system. In the latter case the system may be tested for flaws by means of *pilot systems* or *parallel runs*. ⇨ general articles on *Documentation, Flowcharting, Remote Testing*.

debugging aid routine Any *routine* used by programmers when testing *programs*. For example, a *diagnostic routine* or any routine for producing a *memory print*, a *tape print*, etc.

Also known as checkout routine.

debug on-line 1. To test and correct errors in a *program*, using only certain sections of the *hardware* in a *multiprogramming* computer, thus allowing the *central processor* to continue to process other routines which may be *loaded* in *memory* at the same time. 2. To detect and correct errors on a program from a *remote console* in a *multi-access* system.

decade A group of ten storage *locations*. For example, a *magnetic drum* might consist of a number of storage *tracks* each consisting of 200 words, the tracks being divided into twenty decades as the minimum unit of *access*.

decay time The time taken for a voltage to decrease to one-tenth of its original value.

deceleration time Pertaining to a *storage device* which requires the storage medium to be physically moved for *reading* or *writing* to take place. For example, using *magnetic tape*, the time required from the completion of a reading or writing operation to the moment when the tape is stopped.

decentralized data processing The organization of data processing activity within an organization so that computing equipment is deployed at several widespread branches to serve the operational needs of individual management groups.

decibel One tenth of a bel; a unit of measurement of signal loss or gain in a transmission circuit. The unit is often used to express intensities of sound.

decimal An integer represented by a single character in the range

0–9. The term is also used when referring to a *bit pattern* representing such a character.

decimal, binary coded   ⬦ *binary coded decimal notation.*

decimal notation   The system of writing numbers in which successive digit positions are represented by successive powers of radix 10. In computers decimal numbers are usually represented by *binary digits* arranged in groups of four, each group corresponding to a digit of a decimal number. ⬦ *binary coded decimal notation.*

decimal notation, coded   ⬦ *binary coded decimal notation.*

decimal numeral   A number represented in *decimal notation*; i.e., one using the *decimal* digits from the range 0, 1, 2, 3, 4, 5, 6, 7, 8 and 9.

decimal point   The *radix point* used to separate the integral and fractional parts of a decimal number.

decimal representation, binary coded   ⬦ *binary coded decimal notation.*

decision   An operation performed by a computer to choose between alternative courses of action. Usually made by comparing the relative magnitude of two specified *operands*, a *branch instruction* being used to select the required path according to the result obtained.

decision box   A *flowchart symbol* used to represent a *decision* or *branch* in the sequence of *program instructions*. ⬦ general article on *Flowcharting.*

decision instruction   Any *instruction* which discriminates between the relative value of two specified *operands*. Usually a *branch instruction* which will branch conditionally; e.g., when one operand is greater than another.

decision plan   A method for making managerial decisions according to rules developed to cover certain specified events or conditions. Not necessarily involving the use of *data processing* equipment, but generally concerned with the *exception principle system* of reporting.

decision support system   A *management information system* designed to assist in the decision-making process usually fulfilling a selection or weeding-out function. Often called *expert* system although no expert knowledge is required.

decision table   A method for presenting the relationship between certain variables in order to specify the required action when various conditions are present. These tables may be used to assist in developing solutions to problems, or to display the relationship between various phenomena when documenting a *system* or *program*. Some programming *languages* have been written to make use of *decision tables* when a problem is specified. ⬦ general article on *Decision Tables.*

136

decision tables In the general articles on *Programming* and *Documentation – Programs*, the processes of problem description and problem solution are outlined, and in the general article on *Flowcharting* a method of problem analysis is shown. The documentation of programs before, during and after they have been written is often a combination of English narrative and program flowcharts, but these alone are not always complete, easy to understand or capable of being easily altered to allow for system changes. Another method of logic analysis and presentation – sometimes supplementary to narrative and flowcharts, sometimes able to replace them altogether – is the use of decision tables.

Ordinary tables are a familiar way of recording data in a standardized format; they are called decision tables when they are based on an 'if . . . then' presentation. For example, if I am at railway station A and I wish to go to station D, I might expect to scan two or three lists of destinations (A to B, A to C, etc.) until my eye lit on A to D, showing me which platform to go to. The choice and necessary action could be presented like this:

A to B	Yes	No	No	No
A to C	No	Yes	No	No
A to D	No	No	Yes	No
A to E	No	No	No	Yes
Go to Platform 1	X	–	–	–
Go to Platform 2	–	X	–	–
Go to Platform 3	–	–	X	–
Go to Platform 4	–	–	–	X

It will be seen that I must go to Platform 3 for the A to D train, and that the problem has been represented in a tabular form rather than as a continuous flowchart. Each condition is shown, together with the appropriate result. The table has been drawn as four main blocks.

1	2
3	4

Block 1 (known as the 'condition stub') answers the question 'What are the conditions?' Block 2 (known as the 'condition entry') answers the question 'What values do the conditions have?' Block 3 (known as the 'action stub') answers the question 'What actions occur when a condition is fulfilled?' Block 4 (known as the 'action entry') answers the question 'What values do these actions have?'

This structure is the basis for all decision tables, and even extremely complex problems can be reduced to this format. The condition entry and action entry together make a further element, the 'decision rule', which is illustrated in the example below. If we are outlining the credit control rules for a business, we might describe them as 'If the credit is good, approve an order; if previous payment history has been favourable, approve the order; if neither credit nor previous history is good, a special clearance must be obtained before the order is approved.

	Rule 1	Rule 2	Rule 3	Rule 4
Credit good	Y	–	N	N
Payment history good	–	Y	N	N
Special clearance obtained	–	–	Y	N
Approve order	X	X	X	–
Do not approve order	–	–	–	X

Otherwise, no approval is to be given to an order'. This credit control procedure is represented by a decision table with four decision rules, as shown above. In the condition entry, Y = yes, N = no, – = not significant. In the action entry X = perform this action, – = do not perform this action.

The table shown above is a simple example of a 'limited entry' decision table, where all questions can be answered Y, N or –. There are also 'extended entry' tables (where only part of the condition or action is shown in the appropriate stub, e.g., where a condition entry might be 'less than 50' rather than Yes or No) and 'mixed entry' tables (a combination of limited entry and mixed entry).

An example of a mixed entry table, showing also how control is passed from one table to another, is given on the following page.

	Rule 1	Rule 2	Rule 3
Security available	Y	N	N
Credit allowed	–	£100	£100
Special clearance	–	Y	N
Pass	X	X	–
Return to customer	–	–	X
Go to table no.	4	6	7

It will be seen that, as complex problems can be considered and solved by the use of these tables, they can be an extremely powerful tool for both *systems analyst* and *programmer*, particularly when it is remembered that pre-processor *languages* exist for converting decision tables to *source language* statements (e.g., COBOL) for the production of an *object program* via an ordinary *compiler*.

It is true that the use of decision tables sometimes tempts systems analysts and programmers to identify in too much detail all the possible eventualities and to cater for them individually (which makes large programs) instead of by a general action; but this is probably outweighed by the overall advantages of the use of decision tables, which may be summarized as follows: (i) they ensure that the user makes a clear and complete statement of the problem; (ii) they provide an efficient means of communication between management, systems analyst and programmer; (iii) they ensure that program descriptions are structured in modules for ease of programming; (iv) alterations and additions can easily be made (and, incidentally, the re-drawing of flowcharts by systems analysts is unnecessary since fair copies can be made by typists); (v) decision tables provide a standard format, and deviations from the standard are immediately apparent; (vi) computer programs can be automatically created from tables.

deck 1. A collection or *pack* of *punched cards* belonging to a specific card *file*. 2. Also used as an abbreviation for *magnetic tape deck*.

deck, tape ◊ *magnetic tape deck*.

declaration Synonymous with *declarative statement*.

declarative macroinstruction *Instructions* used as a part of an *assembly language* to instruct the *compiler* (or *assembly program*) to perform some action or take note of some condition. When a declarative macro is used it does not result in any subsequent action by the *object program*. Contrasted with *imperative macroinstructions* and *macroinstructions*, by which object program instructions are generated.

declarative statement An *instruction* written as part of a *source program* to specify for the *compiler* the format, size and nature of *data elements* and constants used as *operands* in the program.

Also known as declaration.

decode To alter data from one coded format back to an original format. To translate coded characters to a form more intelligible to human beings or for a further stage of processing.

decoder A device used to alter data from one coded form to another. A *matrix* of devices capable of selecting one or more *output* channels in response to a combination of *input* signals. Contrasted with *encoder*.

decollator A device used *off-line* in a computer system to separate multi-part sets of continuous stationery produced as output from a *printer*.

decrement A quantity or value used to decrease the magnitude of a variable.

defect A fault in *hardware* or *software* liable to cause processing *failures* in a computer system.

defective Describes a *hardware* or *software* unit which is in such condition that it is likely to cause processing *failures* in a computer system.

deferred addressing A form of *indirect addressing* in which several references are necessary before the desired address is found, the successive references being controlled by some pre-set *counter*.

degradation Referring to the operation of a computer system, to provide a lower level of service in the face of failures in certain areas of the equipment. ⟡ *graceful degradation*.

delay device, digit ⟡ *digit delay device* .

delayed updating A method of *updating* a *record* or set of records in which *fields* in the records are not amended until all alterations related to a specific transaction (or set of transactions) have been processed.

delay element, digit ⟡ *digit delay element*.

delay line A transmission line (or circuit) in which signals are deliberately delayed to achieve some specific purpose.

delay line, acoustic ⟡ *acoustic delay line*.

delay line, magneto-strictive acoustic ⟡ *magneto-strictive acoustic delay line*.

delay line, mercury ⟡ *mercury delay line*.

140

delay line, quartz ⬦ *quartz delay line.*

delay line register A *register* in which data is stored by continually re-circulating a signal.

delay line, sonic ⬦ *acoustic delay line.*

delay line store A device which stores information by continually regenerating a signal. The output from the device is transferred via a *delay line* and is re-input. Thus, data in the store is allowed to circulate without alteration until such time as it is no longer required, whereupon the regenerating loop is interrupted.

delay unit ⬦ *transport delay unit.*

delete 1. Any operation to eliminate a *record* or group of records from a *file*. 2. To remove a *program* from the *memory* of a computer, e.g., at the end of a *run*.

deleted representation Related to *paper tape codes*; the use of a code superimposed upon any other character code to delete the character concerned. An *ignore* character, for example, consists of all code holes and when recorded upon any other previously punched character it effectively deletes that character.

deletion record A *change record* which will cause one or more existing records on a *master file* to be deleted.

delimit To specify the bounds of a certain related group of *characters*, by means of special characters not otherwise members of the group.

delimiter 1. A symbol which marks the bounds of a programming *construct*. 2. A symbol used to *delimit*.

demand processing Refers to a system in which *data* is processed virtually as soon as it is received; i.e., it is not necessary to *store* large quantities of *raw data*.

Also known as in-line processing, immediate processing.

demand reading (or writing) A technique for performing *input* (or *output*) *operations* in which *blocks* of data are transferred to or from the *central processor* as required for processing. No specific arrangements are made for storing input or output data in *buffer areas* to enable operations to take place in parallel.

demand writing ⬦ *demand reading (or writing).*

demodifier An element of data used to reinstate a *basic instruction* to its original value. ⬦ *program modification.*

demodulator A terminal unit to a *data transmission* link: capable of receiving a modulated carrier wave and of recreating the signal originally transmitted by removing the carrier wave. ⬦ *modulation.*

denial, alternative ⬦ *not-and operation.*

denial, joint   ⟡ *nor operation*.

density   A measure of the compactness of recording for data storage.
⟡ *double density, single density*.

dependent   In a data structure, a data item, or set of data items, belonging to a nominal point or *node*, or said to be dependent upon that point.

deposit   To preserve the contents of an *area* of *memory* by *writing* to a *backing store*: ⟡ *dump*.

description   A significant *element* of data used to identify a *record* in which it appears.

designating device, independent sector   ⟡ *independent sector designating device*.

designation   1. Special punching in a specific *card column* of a *punched card*, to indicate that the card was of a certain type. 2. Coded information forming part of a computer *record* to indicate the class of record and thus to determine the processing to be applied to it.

designation holes   Synonymous with *control holes*.

desk checking   Synonymous with *dry running*.

destination file   A term sometimes used to refer to a *file* that receives *output* data from a particular *run*.

destination warning marker   Synonymous with *end of tape marker*.

destruction (of a node)   The removal of a nominated point (or *node*) in a data structure, from a *catalogue* describing that structure (when the catalogue is used to control the selection of individual data items or sets).

destructive addition   An operation in which two *operands*, *addend* and *augend*, are added to form a *sum* which appears in the *location* originally occupied by the augend.

destructive reading   An operation in which data is taken from a *location* to a specified destination in such a way that the data in the original location is lost or mutilated.

DETAB   A programming *language* which is based on *COBOL* but enables the user to specify problems in the form of *decision tables*.

detachable plugboard   A *plugboard* which could be removed by the operator and exchanged for another; thus enabling the set-up to be changed for each *run*, without *connexions* having to be unplugged.

detail file   Synonymous with *transaction file*.

detail flowchart   ⟡ general article on *Flowcharting*.

detected error   An error in a system which is detected, but not automatically corrected, before the output from the system is produced.

de-updating   Part of a *recovery procedure*. A method of re-creating an earlier version of a *file* by replacing *records* which have been recently updated by versions of those same records which have been preserved from an earlier stage.

device control character　A character used in *paper tape codes* to control the operation of *data processing* or telecommunications equipment. When transmitted, or incorporated in any way in a *record* or *message*, it did not form part of the information conveyed.

devices, input/output　◊ general articles on *Input Devices, Output Devices*.

DFG　Abbreviation of *diode function generator*.

diagnosis　Locating errors in *software*, or failures in *hardware*. ◊ general article on *Debugging*.

diagnostic check　Synonymous with *diagnostic test*.

diagnostic program　Synonymous with *diagnostic routine*.

diagnostic routine　A *program* written to trace errors in other programs or to locate the cause of a machine breakdown. Usually written as a *general purpose program*, and may be supplied to the computer user as part of the *software* available with the machine. ◊ general article on *Debugging*.

diagnostic test　The use of a special *program* in order to identify and isolate faults or sources of potential failure in the *hardware* of a computer.

Also known as diagnostic check. ◊ general article on *Debugging*.

diagram, logical　◊ *logic diagram*.

dichotomizing search　A method of searching a *table* of items in order to locate an item with a specific *key* value. The method relies upon the items in the table being in some known sequence; e.g., in ascending sequence by key value. The technique involves comparing the key required with a key midway in the table; one half of the table is then rejected according to whether the result shows the required key to be greater or lesser than the key selected from the table. This process is repeated, continually dividing the remainder of the table in half until the desired record is located.

Also known as binary search, binary chop.

dictionary　A translation table used to specify the size and format of *operands* in a *file*, each *record* type and *field* type being identified by a *data-name*. Used, for example, in standard *file-processing programs* to enable the user to specify the size and structure of any particular file to be processed.

Also known as directory.

dictionary, automatic　◊ *automatic dictionary*.

difference The result obtained in the arithmetic *operation* of *subtraction*.

difference, symmetric Synonymous with *exclusive-or* operation.

differential amplifier A circuit which will produce an output signal derived from the difference between two input signals.

differential analyser An *analog computer* which employs connected *integrators* to solve differential equations.

differential analyser, digital ⟳ *digital differential analyser*.

differential gear A device used in mechanical *analog computers* in which two input variables and one output variable are represented by angles of rotation of shafts. The output variable may be the *sum* or *difference* of the two input variables.

differentiating amplifier A *computing amplifier* used in electronic *analog computers*. ⟳ *differentiator*.

differentiator A device, used on *analog computers*, having one input variable and one output variable which is proportional to the differential of the input with respect to time.

digit A component of an item of data – a character position in an *operand* which may assume one of several values. For example, the number 991 comprises three digits but is composed of two types of character.

digital Referring to the use of discrete signals to represent data in the form of numbers or characters. Most forms of *digital representation* in *data processing* are based upon the use of *binary numbers*, sets of *binary digits* being grouped together to represent numbers in some other *radix* when required; e.g., ⟳ *binary coded decimal notation*. In a similar way sets of binary digits can be grouped to represent alphabetic characters and symbols in coded form. Contrasted with *analog*. ⟳ general article on *Digital Computers*.

digital adder ⟳ *adder*.

digital/analog converter A unit which converts *digital* signals into a continuous electrical signal suitable for input to an *analog computer*.

digital clock 1. A timing device which controls operations within a computer. 2. Also used to describe a clock which records physical conditions and routine events that must be logged as part of the computer's operation.

digital computers A digital computer is a machine capable of performing operations on data represented in digital or number form; i.e., the data is represented as a series of discrete elements arranged in a coded form to represent numbers. The devices used for recording or manipulating the numbers usually contain a series of individual *elements*[2], one for each position in the number, and each element is capable of adopting any one of a number of stable states according to the base of notation required in each position. In most electronic digital computers the method of number representation is based on the system of *binary notation* and each element in any series must be capable of representing either of the *bits* (*binary digits*) 0 or 1. Sometimes sets of bits are grouped to represent numerals in other scales of notation and such sets are referred to as *binary coded digits*.

The individual operations performed by a digital computer are very simple arithmetic or logical processes involving the manipulation of the bits in *words* or *characters* of information. The great power of any digital computer rests in the ability to *store* large volumes of data and to perform these various functions at extremely high speed; e.g., two ten-digit numbers can be added together in a few *nanoseconds*.

The binary notation system is most widely used because of the convenience in constructing logic circuits and *storage devices* capable of handling data in this form. For example, a magnetic *memory* unit consists of many thousand individual magnetic cells, each of which can be energized in either of two ways to represent the binary digits 0 or 1. If these cells are grouped to form words or binary coded characters, information can be stored for processing in units of specified size. In the same way, digital data can be recorded as a series of magnetized spots on, for example, *magnetic tape* or a *magnetic disk*.

Arithmetic and logic circuits for processing data in binary form are constructed from simple basic units designed to perform the operations of *Boolean algebra*: 'and', 'or', 'not', etc. These simple units are used as building blocks in constructing the complex logic and control circuits required.

It can be seen that the processes performed by a *digital* computer are essentially simple. These operations can be performed at extremely high speeds and with a high degree of coordination between the different functional units of the *hardware* system, and this ability means that digital computers can undertake highly complex tasks.

Although digital computers are sometimes constructed for specialized tasks, the term is almost universally applied to mean a *general purpose computer* in which the operations to be performed are specified by means of a stored *program*. The *instructions* are stored with *memory* as data, and can be modified under control of the program itself to perform different processes as required (⬦ *program modification*). Some of the earlier digital computing devices were developed from *punched card* machines and the program was set up by means of connexions on a *plugboard*; machines in this category are generally referred to as calculators, rather than computers.

An electronic digital computer generally consists of *input devices*; a *central processor* containing memory, arithmetic and logic units and a control section; *backing storage*; and *output devices*. ⊗ general articles entitled *Analog Computers* and *Hybrid Computers*.

digital differential analyser A digital computing device which has special circuits in-built to perform the mathematical process of integration.

digital divider A device used in *digital computers* which accepts signals representing a *dividend* and *divisor* and generates a *quotient* and *remainder*.

digital incremental plotter An *output device* which is capable of accepting signals transmitted from a computer and which can plot graphs to show statistical trends and other graphical solutions to problems. Digital signals from a *central processor* are employed to activate a plotting pen and a plotting drum which carries the paper. The plotting action results from step motions of the drum and/or pen, giving steps in the XY plane on the paper.

digital integrator An integrating device in which digital signals are used to represent increments in input variables x and y and an output variable z.

digital multiplier A device used in *digital computers* to perform *multiplication*. It accepts two signals representing the *multiplicand* and *multiplier* and generates the representation of their *product*.

digital representation The use of discrete impulses arranged in some coded format to represent data in the form of numbers of *characters*. To record a value or quantity by means of *digits*.

digital subtractor A device operating with digital *operands* to perform the function of *subtraction*; capable of accepting two input signals representing numbers, and of generating an output signal representing their *difference*.

digit compression Describing any system for condensing the size of items of data in order to reduce the size of a *file*. Special *programming* techniques may be used to *pack* data into a lesser number of characters or digits and to *unpack* the data for subsequent processing.

digit delay device A logic device for delaying digit signals; e.g., to achieve the effect of a *carry* from one digit position to another in arithmetic circuits.

digit delay element A *logic element* which accepts a single digital input signal, and which produces an output signal delayed by one *digit period*.

digit emitter On a *punched card tabulator* or *calculator*, a device to emit signals at various points in the time cycle of the machine. The pulses emitted were used to initiate specified actions at corresponding moments during the machine cycle.

digit emitter, selective ⟡ *selective digit emitter*.

digit filter A device used on *punched card* equipment to detect the presence of a particular *designation* in a specified *card column*.

digitize To convert an *analog* representation, e.g., a voltage, to a *digital* form of representation.

digitizer A device which can convert a physical quantity (i.e., an *analog* measurement) into coded character form.

digitizing pad A *tablet* used as an *input device*: freehand drawing is converted into digital signals with a resulting image being shown on a *visual display unit*.

digit period The time interval for each consecutive digital signal in a series, determined by the basic *pulse repetition frequency* of the particular computer.

digit place Synonymous with *digit position*.

digit plane The devices which make up the *memory* of a computer are usually assembled in the form of a three-dimensional array. The term digit plane refers to the plane containing elements for a particular *digit position*; i.e., the first digit of each *word* will appear in the same plane, the second digit in another and so on.

digit position In *positional notation* the particular position of each digit in a number. The digit positions are usually numbered from the lowest significant digit of the number. For example, in a system using twelve-bit *binary representation*, the individual positions will be referenced as follows:

$$11\ 10\ 9\ 8\ 7\ 6\ 5\ 4\ 3\ 2\ 1\ 0$$

Also known as digit place.

digit pulse A pulse used to drive a number of memory elements, all corresponding to a particular *digit position* in a number of *words*.

digit selector A selecting device on a *punched card* machine which could be activated by *designations* punched into the cards thus calling for a particular series of operations to be performed according to the card type.

digits, equivalent binary ⟡ *equivalent binary digits*.

147

digit time The time interval corresponding to a specific digit signal in a series.

DIL Acronym for *Dual In-Line package*. (*DIP* is a more usual acronym).

diminished radix complement A number derived by subtracting each digit of some specified number from one less than the equivalent *radix*. *Complements* are used in many data processing machines as a means of representing negative values. ⟡ *nines complement* and *ones complement*.

diode A device used to permit current flow in one direction only, and thus used as a switching device to control current flow in an associated circuit. Originally used to describe a thermionic valve with only two plates (cathode and anode); nowadays diodes are constructed of germanium or silicon crystals.

DIP Acronym for *Dual In-line Package*.

direct access storage A *backing store* device in which the *access time* to retrieve items of data is constant, relatively short and independent of the *location* previously *addressed*; i.e., a *device* in which the mode of access is not *serial* as it is with *magnetic tape*. A more detailed examination of direct access storage is given in the general article on *Storage Devices* and the principles of direct access up-dating are given in the general article on *Updating*.

direct address Synonymous with *absolute address*.

direct allocation Contrasted with *dynamic allocation*; a system in which the specific *peripheral units* and *storage locations* allocated to a *program* are defined at the time the program is written.

direct code Synonymous with *absolute code*.

direct coding Program *instructions* written using the actual instruction codes and *addresses* employed in the computer's *machine code*.

direct control Relating to a system in which one machine is controlled by another master machine; i.e., the master machine exerts direct control over the other.

direct current amplifier Synonymous with *directly coupled amplifier*.

direct data entry Preparing *data* in such a way that conversion from a key stroke to a *magnetic medium* takes place without the intermediate process of, for example, creating a *punched card*. ⟡ general article on *Data Preparation*.

direct display A *visual display unit* used to display data in graphical or character form direct from *memory*.

direct insert subroutine A term sometimes used when referring to a *subroutine* written as part of a *main program*.

direct instruction Any *instruction* which directly *addresses* an *operand* on which the specified *operation* is to be performed.

directive A statement written as part of a *source program* to instruct or direct the *compiler* in performing the translation to *machine code*. A directive is not usually translated into *object program* instructions.

Also known as *control statement*.

directly coupled amplifier An amplifier for magnifying direct voltages, usually employing some form of resistive coupling between stages.

Also known as direct current amplifier.

director An integral part of an *operating system* which has direct control over the allocation of internal resources of the computer, and is usually responsible for the *programs* within the system. For example, control over *virtual machines*.

directory Synonymous with *dictionary*.

direct serial file organization A method of *file* organization on a *direct access* device in which the individual *records* can be selected for processing by number, and *updated* in situ on the device without affecting other records.

dirigible linkage A system of mechanical connectors used in mechanical *analog computers* as part of multiplication and division units.

disable To override or suppress some *hardware* or *software* feature; e.g., to suppress an *interrupt* facility.

disc ◊ *magnetic disk*.

discounted cash flow Discounted cash flow (DCF) is a method for the financial analysis of capital projects. This name for the technique tends to be particularly applied to capital projects but the principle is essentially the same as underlies the calculation of redemption yields on gilt-edged stocks and the actuarial valuation of pension and life assurance funds.

The data required for DCF calculations are estimates of the amount and timing of all the various cash inflows and outflows associated with the project throughout its estimated life (not forgetting investment grants, tax charges and tax reliefs which the project will generate). No differentiation is made between capital and revenue items and no attention is paid to accounting artifices such as book depreciation or book profit. There are two main ways of applying DCF techniques to such data. In one version the operator, at a standard predetermined rate of interest, discounts each item of inflow and outflow to produce the equivalent flow at a convenient standard datum point of time such as the date at which the first sum of money is to be spent. From the sum of the total discounted values of the inflows, the operator subtracts the sum of the discounted values of the outflows, to obtain the 'net present value' (NPV) of the project. Only if the NPV turns out to be positive will the project earn its keep in the sense that the (varying) amount of cash tied up in it from time to time will be earning more than the rate of interest used for the discounting process.

In the other common version of DCF analysis, the above process is carried out at several rates of interest until, by trial and error and finally interpolating between two adjacent rates, a rate of interest is found at which the NPV is zero. This rate, known as the DCF yield, is the effective rate being earned on the varying amounts of money invested in the project throughout its life. In general, projects with high yields will be preferred to those with low yields but special considerations apply if one project is more risky than another or if the commission of one project excludes the possibility of carrying out another. In the latter case, the amounts of money invested and the time in which the money is invested at the DCF yield may be more important than that yield itself. It would be foolish to embark on a project yielding 15% for one year on £1,000 if by so doing one were prevented from carrying out another project which would yield 14% per annum for 10 years on £10,000, if alternative uses of money were only expected to earn 10%.

Subject to such special features, one may stipulate a cut-off rate of DCF yield, and accept or reject projects according to whether or not the DCF yield exceeds this rate. If the rate chosen were the same as the standard rate of interest used in the NPV version, the two variants would produce the same criterion. This assumes, as is generally the case, that the DCF yield is unique; an objection to DCF yield is that if the cash outflows interleave in time with the inflows, instead of falling exclusively after them, it may be possible for there to be either two DCF yield solutions or none. This phenomenon, which rarely occurs in practice, can be avoided by an extension of the method known as the 'extended yield' method.

The cut-off rate of yield, or standard rate of interest for discounting in the NPV version, should be chosen as representing the effective after-tax cost of capital. Ideally this should have regard to how far an individual project can be financed from debt, i.e., relatively cheaply, and how far it must rely on equity capital, either in the form of plough-back earnings or a new equity issue, which is more expensive since equity money has to be obtained in competition with the equity market in general, from which investors expect to receive over the years (by way of dividend and capital appreciation) considerably greater net-of-tax returns than fixed interest investors, to compensate for their added

150

risk. Rates of the order of 8-12% are typically considered appropriate, but the particular company's balance between debt and equity finance and special risk features of the industry or of the project should be taken into account.

With the aid of interest tables, which give the present value of £1 receivable or payable at any future year, for discounting the future cash flows back to the starting date, the various NPVs required for DCF analysis can be easily calculated by hand; alternatively they lend themselves well to computer operation, and this will be preferred where a large number of analyses are required. There has been considerable controversy on the respective merits of the DCF yield and the NPV at a standard rate of interest; if the former is calculated, the production of the latter involves little extra effort (or programming) and there is much to be said for producing both figures as a matter of routine.

A frequent objection to DCF analysis is that it demands forecasts of cash inflows and outflows many years ahead and that these may be in serious error. However, these uncertainties with regard to the future *are* inevitably reflected in the yield which will be obtained in the event, and it is indeed a virtue of the method, rather than a vice, that it focuses attention on the forecasting problem instead of pushing it under the carpet. By contrast, more commonly used methods such as the 'payback period' (under which the amount of profit expected after the investment has been recouped is completely ignored) or the 'accountants' return on capital' (the ratio of average book profit after depreciation to the initial or average capital invested) can give seriously misleading results, in particular because they ignore the increasingly important effect of different types of tax allowance and their timing.

discrimination instruction Synonymous with *branch instruction*.

disjunction Synonymous with *inclusive-or operation*.

disk ⟡ *magnetic disk*.

disk drive A *peripheral unit* capable of storing data in, and retrieving data from, *magnetic disks*.

diskette Synonymous with *floppy disk*.

disk file controller A *hardware* device which is concerned with addressing a number of *magnetic disk* units and controlling the transfer of data between these units and the *main store*.

disk store, magnetic ⟡ *magnetic disk*.

disperse To distribute *items* of data extracted from an *input record* to several *locations* in one or more *output records*.

dispersed intelligence Describes any system in which programmable processing units (perhaps operated by *microprograms*) are used to perform *application* or *system control* functions remote from the *main frame*. The remote units are connected to the main frame which performs the major central application functions.

dispersion Synonymous with *not-and operation*.

display Any operation in which a message or selected data is output to the operator/user for visual inspection. For example, data may be output as a printed report, or in graphical or character form on a screen.

display console A unit which can be used to interrogate *files* or *areas* of *memory* in order to display *data* being currently processed or stored in a computer. A display console may be equipped with a *cathode ray tube visual display unit* to enable data to be presented in graphical or character form. Such a unit may also be equipped with a *light pen* to enable the user to change the information displayed under *program control*.

display console, message ⬦ *message display console*.

display control An *interface* unit used to connect a number of *visual display units* to a *central processor*.

display, data analysis ⬦ *data analysis display unit*.

display, inquiry and subscriber ⬦ *inquiry and subscriber display*.

display tube ⬦ *cathode ray tube visual display unit*.

distance Synonymous with *exclusive-or operation*. ⬮ *signal distance*.

distance, Hamming ⬦ *signal distance*.

distributed computing The organization of processing in such a way that a number of independent computers or *intelligent terminals* can cooperate in exchanging data over a *network*. Local processing is carried out locally: the exchanged data affects the system as a whole.

Also known as *distributed processing*.

distributed processing Synonymous with *distributed computing*.

diversity Synonymous with *exclusive-or operation*.

dividend An *operand* used in *division*. The dividend is divided by the *divisor* to produce the *quotient* and *remainder*.

divider A device which performs the arithmetic function of *division*.

division An arithmetic operation in which one *operand*, the *dividend*, is divided by another, the *divisor*, to produce the *quotient* and a *remainder*.

division subroutine A *subroutine* written specifically to perform the arithmetic operation of *division*. Usually achieved by an *algorithm* which basically performs repetitive *subtraction*.

divisor An operand used in *division* – the divisor is divided into the *dividend* to produce the *quotient* and *remainder*.

document Any form or voucher containing details of some *transaction*.

documentation – programming A fully tested working computer *program* typically exists as a pattern of flux changes on a magnetic recording medium capable of being loaded into a computer store and obeyed. The program may be capable of successfully fulfilling the task it has been designed for, but it will be impossible to use it unless enough people understand the *input* necessary for the program, the types of processing it performs, the output it produces and the way in which the computer must be operated to meet the requirements of the *programmer*. Some form of documentation must accompany a program otherwise it is useless.

Apart from assisting the everyday running of a computer program, documentation serves the following purposes. It enables the work of one programmer to be continued by another if the first programmer leaves. It makes it easier to amend existing programs. It enables programs to be converted to a new machine. It serves as a record of work done and enables the relative performance of programmers to be assessed.

A somewhat idealized picture of the way in which programmers document their work during the production of a program is as follows. Having studied the specification of the program in terms of input data formats, *file formats* and *printout* formats, the programmer produces an outline *flowchart* which shows in general terms the work the program is to do. A flowchart consists of a number of symbols, representing processing stages, linked by arrows which show the flow of control. Once the general logic of the program has been mapped out in *decision tables* or the outline flowchart a more detailed flowchart is produced and here the processes indicated by the symbols cover fewer steps, perhaps only a few program *instructions*. Finally the program is written down, input, *compiled*, tested and incorporated in a working *library* of programs. Compilation will usually produce a listing of the *source program*, which is a valuable item of documentation, and the programmers themselves are responsible for the production of *operating instructions* for the live running of the program.

Documentation produced in this way, as a by-product of program development, is unlikely to be completely satisfactory. First of all the final program will rarely bear much resemblance to the programmer's first ideas on the subject since it is inevitable that errors will be found during program testing. Program testing is a particularly arduous time during program development and the programmer is unlikely to have the time or the inclination to update his preliminary flowcharts as each error is discovered. Here the source listing is much more important, since a new listing will be produced after each round of *debugging* and recompilation.

All the items of documentation mentioned above should be preserved in a special file, and it should not now be necessary to alter the program or its documentation until a system change requires a program change; since any change to the system should involve acceptance by all appropriate authorities (◊ *Documentation – Systems*) the program documentation should at all times represent precisely the program for a current, fully approved system. A great deal of time and money has been spent by people trying to work out what sort of program they had got on their hands after a year or two of 'minor', undocumented, alterations.

documentation – systems   There is no general standard for the documentation which must be produced by the systems analyst to mark the end of his task in explaining to the *programmer* what is to be programmed. Luckily, though, the job must be done in some form or other (unlike *program documentation*, which is sometimes forgotten) and there are certain things the programmer cannot do without. If possible, the systems analyst will try to think of the specification he produces as something which will do a good deal more than merely tell the programmer what to write, and for this reason the document is often called a *systems definition*: it contains information for those who commissioned the work (a brief outline of the system, with a note on the benefits to be obtained and an introduction schedule); it provides a handbook for those who are going to use the system when the programs are operational (detailed instructions on *paper flow*, coding required, how the output is to be filed), which will include points which may have already been discussed in detail but which need to be set out in a permanent record; and finally it gives the details of the programming requirements, including all expected outputs from the tests.

The analyst should remember that his systems definition will have failed if he has to discuss anything with the programmer once the definition has been handed over, and he will be wise to work to a check-list of the headings he may have to deal with. Various attempts have been made to devise standard forms on which the systems definition must be prepared, but, because space has to be found for so many things which may have no relevance for one system and yet be vital for another, none of these forms is entirely successful. The definition itself falls into two clear parts, however: the systems description in words (to be read by those who need to know the outlines, but who will probably not take very kindly to being presented with a few yards of flowchart); and the program specification in detail. Most systems will include something under each of the following chapter headings in these two parts:

(a) Authorization
Definition of terms
Aims of the system
Summary of the system
Benefits
Planning and introduction schedule
Equipment utilization
Change-over procedure
Clerical procedures

(b) *Source document* specification
Output specifications
File specifications
Decision tables
Systems test data
Program descriptions

Even though the two halves of the definition are quite distinct, they should never be issued separately, one half for the general reader and one for the programmer. In particular, no definition should ever be passed for programming before being officially accepted by the line managers involved in using the system and by the appropriate *audit* and accounting authorities.

documentation book A collection of all the *documentation* relevant to a particular *program* or *system*.

document, original ⟡ *source document*.

docuterm A *data-name* used to designate a *data element* and to indicate the content of that element. Specifically assigned to assist in subsequent *retrieval*.

do nothing instruction An *instruction* which performs no action during the operation of a *program*. Sometimes used to allow for future changes to the program but more often used to complete a set of instructions where the *machine code* system requires instructions to be written in complete groups.

Also known as dummy instruction, null instruction.

dope vector Associated with the processing of *array* structures, and used in mapping data stored in a linear medium on to a multidimensional structure; a collection of information used as parameters to an algorithm which provides this function.

dot printer An output *printer* in which individual characters are formed by a matrix of wires or styluses.

double buffering The use of two areas of *memory* as *buffer stores* during *input/output* operations involving a particular *peripheral unit*. For example, if data from an input unit is loaded first into one buffer and then into the other, the unit can be driven at its maximum input speed: while the input loads one buffer the *central processor* can process the data in the other.

double density The *recording density* for *data storage* on second generation *floppy disks*, allowing up to 200k *bytes* on 8-in diameter disks. ⟡ single density.

double-length number A number stored in two *words* in *memory* for use in *double-precision arithmetic*.

double-precision arithmetic Relating to arithmetic operations performed with *operands* which each occupy two *words*, allowing greater accuracy to be obtained in the result.

double-precision hardware Special arithmetic units designed to permit greater accuracy in arithmetic results, by allowing a *programmer* to perform arithmetic operations using *double-length numbers* as *operands*. Double-precision hardware may also allow *floating point arithmetic* to be undertaken.

double-precision number Synonymous with *double-length number*.

double-pulse reading A technique for recording *binary digits* in a *magnetic cell*, in which each cell incorporates two regions that can be magnetized in opposite directions. For example, a cell containing a negative followed by a positive region may be used to represent a digit 0, whereas a positive followed by a negative region may represent 1.

double punching A term used to describe the condition where two holes appeared in the same *card column* of a *punched card*.

double-sided Pertaining to a *floppy disk* which has data recorded on both disk surfaces. Contrasted with *single-sided*.

double tape mark A physical indicator consisting of two *tape marks* used to indicate the end of a *volume* or *file*.

down time Time when a machine is inoperable due to a machine fault.

DRAW Acronym of Direct Read After Write.

drift A change in the output of a circuit (e.g., an amplifier) which takes place very slowly. Usually caused by voltage fluctuations or change in environmental conditions. Circuits can be designed to include correction for drift and are used in *analog computers* to eliminate the errors which would otherwise arise.

drift-corrected amplifier A device used in *analog computers* – a type of amplifier that includes circuits designed to reduce *drift*.

drift error In *analog computers*, an error incurred in a computing device because of *drift*.

drive 1. A general term for any device which physically transports some recording medium, e.g., a *disk drive*. 2. Also applied to any circuit which generates pulses for operating some electro-magnetic device, e.g., a *print member*.

drive, data cell ⟡ *data cell drive*.

drive, magnetic tape ⟡ *tape transport*.

drive pulse In a *core store*, a pulse applied to a storage element to induce a corresponding magnetizing force.

driver A *program* dealing with low level operations of *peripheral units* in order to handle such devices as part of an *operating system*.

drive winding A coil of wire (known as drive wire) inductively coupled to a *magnetic cell*.

drive wire ⟡ *drive winding*.

drop dead halt A *halt* which may be deliberately *programmed* or may be the result of a logical error in programming (e.g., division by zero) but from which, in either case, there is no recovery.

Also known as a dead halt.

drop, false ⟡ *false retrieval*.

drop-in The accidental generation of unwanted *bits* during *reading* from or *writing* to a magnetic *storage device*. Contrasted with *drop-out*.

drop-out A failure when *reading* or *writing* to a magnetic *storage device*. A loss of digits due to some fault condition during a *reading* or *writing* operation. Contrasted with *drop-in*.

drum ⟡ *magnetic drum*.

drum mark A special *character* used to signify the termination of a group of characters on a recording *track* of a *magnetic drum*.

drum printer Synonymous with *barrel printer*.

dry running Checking the logic and coding of a *program* from a *flowchart* and written *instructions*, using paper to record the results of each step of the operation before actually running the program on the computer.

Also known as desk checking, walk through. ⟡ general article on *Debugging*.

dual in-line package An *integrated circuit* packaged so that external connexions can be made through two parallel rows of pins at right angles to the edges of the package.

dual operation A *Boolean operation* whose *truth table* can be obtained from another operation by reversing the value of each element in the table is said to be a dual operation to the other, e.g., the *or operation* is dual to the *and operation*. Contrasted with *complementary operation*.

dual recording In a system which is required to provide *security* and *resilience* to *failure*, two copies of *master files* may be made by updating them at the same time as transactions are received. This method is not to be confused with the method of copying master files at intervals in a job.

ducol punched card system A system in which numbers in the range 0 to 99 were punched as two holes in the *lower curtate* of a single *card column*. The absence of *overpunching* indicated that the higher value digit was the tens digit, whereas the presence of 10(Y) overpunching denoted that the lower value digit was the tens digit. An 11(X) overpunching was used to denote that a single hole was to be treated as two digits, e.g., 33, 22, 55, etc.

dummy Any feature included in a *routine* to satisfy some logical or structural requirement, but which in a particular circumstance is not used. For example, a *subroutine* may be incorporated in a routine to satisfy some general *software* requirement; in certain applications the programmer may not wish to use the facilities offered by this routine, and may need to write a dummy routine which, as soon as it is entered, will cause an *exit* to the programmer's *main program*.

dummy instruction Synonymous with *do-nothing instruction*.

dump To *write* an area of *memory* to a *peripheral unit*. ⟡ *dumping*.

dump and restart When a computer *run* has been terminated at a point earlier than its completion (because of a machine failure, for example) dump and restart techniques ensure that the run can be restarted without the need to go back to the beginning. Various techniques can be used to achieve this, but all conform to a basic pattern: at various points within the *programs* making up the run *dump points* will be present; when the program reaches a dump point, the state of the *memory* and the state of all *peripheral units* is *dumped*. This will involve *writing* memory onto a suitable peripheral, e.g., *magnetic disk* or *magnetic tape*, and printing or punching details of the point reached by all peripheral units. Normally the program will continue to run after recording the dump details until it reaches the next dump point, when the new state of the program is dumped.

If a program is terminated for any reason – because of machine failure or because the machine is required for other jobs – the operator records the last dump point reached and preserves the dump information produced at that point. When it is required to restart the program, the memory dump is read into *store*, returning it to the state it was in when the dump took place. The operator resets the peripheral units to the condition needed by the dump point (for example, replaces magnetic media that must be read again) and the program can be restarted at the point immediately after the last dump point occurring before the stoppage.

Manufacturers or users usually write special dump and restart routines which automatically record and restore the peripheral and store information. The technique is particularly useful for inclusion in long or complex jobs where much time might be wasted if the whole job had to be run from the beginning. The selection of suitable dump points is at the discretion of the *programmer* or *systems analyst*: these points may occur at fixed time intervals or at recognized points within a run, e.g., when it is necessary to change *reels* in *multi-reel file* working.

dump check   A check performed to verify the accuracy of a *dump*; e.g., by creating *control totals* and/or *hash totals* during *dumping* and to check these totals when the data is re-entered into *memory*.

dump cracking   Used to describe the job performance by programmers or engineers in diagnosing faults in *application programs* or in *systems management software*. The process entails visually scanning and analysing lists dumped by the computer at the time of the failure, and showing the internal contents of the computer at the time the process failed.

dumping   A technique used during the running of a *program* to ensure, in the event of a machine failure or some other interruption of the job, that the program can be resumed without the need to start again from the beginning. This precaution is particularly advisable for long runs using slow *input/output peripheral units*. The technique involves periodically *writing* the program and its data, with the contents of *work areas*, to a *backing store*. The program will incorporate *restart* procedures to enable the program to be resumed from the last *dump point* in the event of an interruption. ⇨ general article on *Dump and Restart*.

dump point   A point in a *program* at which it is advisable to *write* the program and its data to a *backing store*, as a safeguard against machine failure. Dump points may be chosen to effect dumping at specific time intervals (e.g., every twenty minutes) or at predetermined events in the running of the program.

Also known as check point. ⇨ *dumping* and general article on *Dump and Restart*.

dump, storage Synonymous with *memory dump*.

duodecimal number system A *number system* in which each digit position has a *radix* of twelve.

duplex A system which allows transmission in both directions simultaneously; compare with *simplex* and *half-duplex*.

duplex channel A *channel* allowing simultaneous transmission in both directions.

duplex computer system An *on-line* configuration in which two computer systems are employed, one acting as a standby to safeguard against the failure of the other.

duplex console In *on-line* computer systems, a *console* which can be switched to control two computers so that one or the other may be connected on line.

duplexing Any system of *data transmission* which permits simultaneous two-way transmission between terminals.

duplicate To copy data from one *location* within *store* to another, without losing or mutilating the data in its original form.

duplicated records *Records* which are exact copies of other records and which are retained to safeguard against the loss or mutilation of the original records. (But ⌗ *duplicate record*.)

duplicate record An unwanted *record* occurring in a *file* and having the same *key* as another record in the same file. (But ⌗ *duplicated records*.)

duplicating card punch Synonymous with *reproducer*.

duplication An exact copy of a *file* or group of *records*; e.g., a copy of a *magnetic disk* or *laser card*.

duplication check A check that requires a particular calculation to be performed twice, using a different method on each occasion, the two *results* being compared. A form of *arithmetic check*.

dyadic Boolean operation A *Boolean operation* where the result is determined by the *bit patterns* of two *operands* and the *truth table* of the *operator*.
Also known as binary Boolean operation.

dyadic operation An *operation* utilizing two *operands*. Also known as *binary operation*.

dynamic allocation 1. A method adopted on *multiprogramming* computers for assigning *main store* and *peripheral units* to a *program*. Usually performed under control of an *executive program*, and designed to permit complete flexibility in the *loading* of programs dependent upon the peripherals and storage available at any one time. As each program is compiled a series of statements, sometimes known as the *request slip*, is generated indicating the requirements of the particular program. Before the program is loaded the *executive program* reads the request slip and ascertains whether the program can be accepted. If it can, the executive program allocates the appropriate peripherals and main storage to the program. The essence of the system is that the *programmer* need not specify the particular peripherals he requires, but only the type of peripheral and thereafter he uses *symbolic names* to address the units in the program. At *run time* the executive program allocates specific units of the desired type to the program. 2. An extension of the allocation system described in 1 above, concerns the assigning of *magnetic tape files* to a program. Here, the programmer specifies, by means of the *header labels*, the particular tape files processed by his program. The operator can then load these files on to any of the available *tape decks* at run time. When a program requires to open a particular file the executive program searches all unallocated decks to find a tape with the appropriate label. When it does so, the deck is allocated to the program. ◊ *multiprogramming*.

dynamic allocation (of memory) The system used in *multiprogramming* whereby an *executive program* allocates areas of *memory* to a *program* as and when the program is loaded. In such a system several programs may be operating in memory at the same time. Before any program can be accepted into the system the executive program has to check that sufficient *main storage* is available for running the program. This mode of operation requires that all programs must be written using *symbolic addresses*, and *absolute addresses* are automatically generated only when a particular program has been accepted and is being loaded into *memory*. At any time during the operation of programs the executive program may re-assign areas of memory to achieve a more efficient utilization of storage *locations*; this activity will usually take place when one program is completed, whereupon the executive program will attempt to create the largest possible free area of contiguous storage locations. ◊ *multiprogramming*.

dynamic buffering A technique used in handling messages entering a system or process in which messages may be of variable length and frequency. The *storage* area allocated as a buffer to receive messages is extended or contracted by adding or removing units of storage while messages are arriving.

dynamic check A check performed on the operation of an *analog* device and on the *set-up* of a problem, by comparing results obtained in the *compute mode* with some previously computed values.

Also known as dynamic test.

dynamic dump   A *dump* carried out during the execution of a *program*.

dynamic error   An error incurred in a *analog* device resulting from an inadequate frequency response of the equipment.

dynamicizer   A *logic element* which converts a set of *digits* represented by the spatial arrangement of *bits* in *store* into a sequence of signals occurring in time. Contrasted with *staticizer*.

dynamic memory   A *regenerative store* in which information is retained by a continually circulating signal (◊ *delay line store*). Essentially a store in which information can be obtained at fixed intervals in a cycle.
   Also known as dynamic store.

dynamic memory relocation   Relating to a characteristic of *multi-programming* computers, in which *memory* areas are automatically allocated and re-allocated to *programs* as and when any program is *loaded* or deleted from memory. ◊ *dynamic allocation (of memory)*.

dynamic stop   The use of a *branch instruction* to create a *program loop* which is in turn used to signify an error condition.

dynamic storage allocation   ◊ *dynamic allocation (of memory)*.

dynamic store   1. Synonymous with *dynamic memory*. 2. Sometimes used to denote any form of storage using a moving magnetic medium.

dynamic subroutine   A *subroutine* which requires *parameters* to specify the particular action to be performed each time it is entered. Contrasted with *static subroutine*.

dynamic test   Synonymous with *dynamic check*.

E

E 13 B A type fount used for *character recognition machines*.

EAM Abbreviation of *electrical accounting machines*.

EAROM An acronym for *Electrically Alterable Read-Only Memory*, a class of *read-only memory* to which it is possible to write information at any time using special circuits. Of the existing contents of an EAROM only the specific *locations* designated to receive new information are affected by this action.

Despite the apparent flexibility of such devices they are not much used by circuit designers, as they require complicated circuitry and their contents tend to degrade slowly, being much less stable than a *PROM*, *ROM* or *EPROM*.

EBCDIC A *data communication* code in which 8 *information bits* are used to form 256 unique *character codes*. The term is an abbreviation for expanded binary coded decimal interchange code and is pronounced as ebbseedik. Compare with *ASCII*, an *ISO* code which uses 7 information bits plus a *parity bit*.

EBR Abbreviation of *electron beam recording*.

eccles jordan circuit Synonymous with *flip-flop*.

echo check A *check* on the accuracy of *data transmission* in which the data transmitted is returned to the point from which it was sent and compared with the original data.

ECL Abbreviation of *emitter-coupled logic*.

ECMA Acronym for European Computer Manufacturers' Association, a body which has influenced standards concerned with the use of computers and their ability to interchange information.

econometrics Applying the techniques of the empirical sciences in order to establish significant relationships in economic and statistical data, and to use these relationships as a basis for predictions. The use of computers in econometrics lies mainly in their ability to analyse large volumes of data, and also to construct and test economic and *mathematical models*.

edge, card leading ⇨ *leading edge*.

edge, card trailing ⇨ *trailing edge*.

edge-notched card A card containing holes in one or more edges used in a simple mechanical search technique: each hole position was given a coded significance and for particular cards the holes were turned into notches by the removal of the part of the card between hole and edge. Particular cards could then be mechanically selected by the insertion of a long needle in a hole position and the raising of the card *pack* to allow notched cards to remain unraised while unwanted cards remained in the main pack on the needle.

Also known as margin-notched card. Contrast with *margin-punched card*.

edge-punched card ⋋ *margin-punched card*.

edit To arrange data into the format required for subsequent processing. Editing may involve deletion of data not required, conversion of *fields* to a machine format (e.g., *value fields* converted to *binary*) and preparation of data for subsequent output, e.g., *zero suppression* ⋋ editor.

editor A computer *program* used to assist a human operator to prepare text or data for entry to (or output from) a computer system, or to retrieve and rearrange data previously stored in a computer *file*. In small computers such as a *microcomputer* or an *intelligent terminal*, the editor may be stored in a *firmware* device such as a *ROM*. A common example of an editor is one used to assist a programmer to enter and amend a *source language* computer program. A user is able to insert, delete or change lines of code without retyping whole sequences of the text, and facilities may exist within the editor to carry out a *syntax* check on language *statements* entered via the editor or stored in an edited file.

Editors used for preparing text in *word processing* systems are designed to offer complex text manipulation functions to the keyboard operator, including insertion and deletion of text with automatic justification and realignment within the text frame. An editor is activated by commands typed by the user on a *keyboard*.

EDP Acronym for *Electronic Data Processing*.

EDS Acronym for *Exchangeable Disk Store*.

EEPROM Acronym for Electrically Erasable Programmable Read-Only Memory. ⋋ *PROM*.

effective address An *address* actually used by the computer for executing an *instruction*, as opposed to the address written in the *program*.

effective address: post-index The *address* derived when an indexing operation takes place to derive an *effective address*, and in which the contents of an *index register* are added to a *base address* selected indirectly as the contents of another specified *location*; i.e., effective address = contents of base location + contents of index register. Thus the effective address can be influenced by the previous setting of the contents of the base location or the index register.

effective address: pre-index The *address* derived when an indexing operation takes place to derive an *effective address*, and in which the contents of an *index register* are added to the contents of a specified *memory location* to derive an address, and the contents of that derived location are taken as the effective address; i.e., effective address = contents of a location whose address is given by the contents of base location + contents of index register.

effective data-transfer rate Most communication circuits are rated according to their speed and the rate of *error* that can be expected. The effective rate for transmitting *data* is usually less than the nominal *transfer rate* because *error detection and correction* techniques require *redundant* information to be carried or *blocks* of data to be retransmitted. The effective rate is usually expressed as an average number of *bits* per time unit.

effective instruction The *instruction* performed as the result of altering a *basic instruction* during *program modification*.
Also known as actual instruction.

effective-memory address Any *memory address* which is computed by information provided in a *program instruction*; i.e., the computation has to take place before the instruction can be executed. An example occurs in *paged* memory systems, in which the effective address is derived by adding the current page number to the location number indicated by the address portion of a current instruction.

effective time Time during which a computer is being used for work which produces useful results. This includes *productive time*, *program development time* and time used for demonstrations, training, *housekeeping*, etc. (*incidentals time*). Does not include time spent on operating delays and *idle time*. Related to *serviceable time*, contrasted with *ineffective time.*

efficiency ⟡ *serviceability*.

eighty-column card A *punched card* with eighty vertical *card columns*.

either-or operation Synonymous with *inclusive-or operation*.

elapsed time The total apparent time taken by a process, as measured by the time between the apparent beginning and the apparent end of the process. This may well be longer than the actual time taken by the process itself. ⟡ *real-time clock*.

electrical accounting machine Any electro-mechanical device used in *data processing*, other than computer equipment. The term was used to include *tabulators*, *calculators*, *balancers*, etc.

electron beam recording A method of utilizing an electron beam to write computer-generated data direct to a recording surface.

electronic Related to the branch of science concerned with the behaviour of electrons. A device is termed electronic if it depends mainly for its operation on the use of thermionic valves, vacuum or gas tubes, or solid state devices such as transistors and integrated circuits.

electronic calculating punch A device which read data from a *punched card*, performed a sequence of arithmetic calculations on the data and punched the result into another punched card.

electronic data processing *Data processing* performed by *electronic* machines; the methods and techniques associated with such processing. ⟡ *automatic data processing*.

electronic data processing machine Any machine or device used in *data processing* which uses *electronic* circuitry either wholly or mainly in order to perform arithmetic and logical operations.

electronic differential analyser An *analog computer* designed for solving differential equations.

electronic mail Use of a *mailbox* facility for storing, forwarding and accessing messages electronically.

electronic office An integrated network of computing devices used to create an automated office in which there is no paper and people communicate by electronic means. The paperless office of this concept does not yet seem either practical or fully desirable, but its precursor, the less-paper office, is readily accepted.

electronic switch A *switch*[1] which makes use of an *electronic* circuit, enabling the switching action to take place at high speed.

electrostatic printer A printing device in which the parts of paper which are to be printed are electrostatically charged, and attract a fine dust which is then fused to the paper by the application of heat.

electrostatic storage A *storage device* which uses the presence of an electrostatic charge to represent data, e.g., the surface of a *cathode ray tube*.

element 1. A member of a collection of items which cannot itself be subdivided into any constituent parts which may themselves be considered as members of the collection, e.g., the elements of a computer *word* are *bits*, while the elements of a *record* may be *words*. 2. A circuit which can be considered as a single entity in so far as it performs a unique function, can be combined with other elements to perform more

complex functions, but cannot itself be divided into individual components. ⟡ *logic element*.

elementary item   A *COBOL* expression for an item of data which
contains no subsidiary items.

element, equivalent-to   ⟡ *equivalence element*.

element, logical   ⟡ *logic element*.

element, nand   ⟡ *not-and element*.

element, non-equivalence   ⟡ *exclusive-or element*.

element, non-equivalent-(to)   ⟡ *exclusive-or element*.

element, not   ⟡ *negator*.

eleven position   ⟡ *Y-position* and *X-position*.

eleven punch   ⟡ *Y-punch* and *X-punch*.

else rule   In a set of operations depending on certain specified
conditions being satisfied, the else rule defines the operations to be
carried out if none of the specifically described conditions occurs.

emitter   A device in *punched card* machines for generating signals in
order to simulate the presence of holes not actually punched.

emitter-coupled logic   A form of electronic *logic*, described as non
saturated logic, because the transistor components within the *integrated
circuits* are able to operate effectively without being switched fully on
or fully off. As a result of this quality they are used with very high
frequency signals and are capable of very fast speeds of operation. A
standard ECL device may operate at around 100 MHz while some
specialized ECL devices can operate at 1000 MHz.

emitter pulse   One of a set of *pulses* which, in *punched card equipment*,
defined a particular *row* within the *columns* of a card. ⟡ *selective digit
emitter*.

emitter, selective digit   ⟡ *selective digit emitter*.

empty medium   A *medium* which has been prepared to accept information by having some preliminary data recorded in it, e.g., *sector
boundaries* in *floppy disks*, *magnetic tape* with *header labels* already
written. Contrasted with *virgin medium*. ⟡ *data carrier*.

emulated executive   A form of *emulation* in which *software* is used to
represent an *executive program* of a different computer type.

emulation   The process of using a computer to operate on data and
code produced for a different computer type; special *hardware* and
software are used to represent the computer for which the work was
originally implemented. ⟡ *Transition*.

emulator   A *hardware* or *software* device designed as part of a
particular range of computers, but used to run jobs originally prepared
for another range of computers. For example, used as *bridging* from

one *generation* of computers to another generation, or to link computers normally operating with different *communication protocols*. ⬦ *Transition*.

enable-interrupt An *interrupt* is a process in which a *sequence* of *instructions* is performed as an unscheduled *event* caused by a device external to the computer. The event arises in such a way that it could not be predicted by the main *program* operating within the computer. The capacity of a computer to handle interrupts varies greatly with the size, power and complexity of the overall computer system. If only one interrupt can be handled at a time, the computer has to set a *disable-interrupt* mechanism until it has initialled or scheduled the interrupt process, after which the computer sets an enable-interrupt condition so that it can respond to further external events.

enable pulse A *digit pulse* which together with a *write pulse* is sufficiently strong to alter the state of a *storage element*, but which is not of sufficient strength to do so on its own.

enabling signal A *signal* which allows an *operation* aready set up to take place.

encode To represent data in digital form as a series of impulses denoting *characters* or *symbols*. To facilitate *automatic processing* by the arrangement of facts into a coded form suitable for subsequent processing.

encoder 1. A device which converts signals into a coded digital format suitable for a particular processing stage. Contrasted with *decoder*. 2. A *keyboard* operated machine for printing characters onto documents in the stylized form necessary for subsequent reading by *character recognition* equipment.

end-around carry A *carry* generated in the *most significant character* position which causes a carry into the *least significant character* position.

end-around shift Synonymous with *logical shift*.

end-directive A *statement* in an *assembly program* which simply informs the assembler that there are no further *instructions* to be assembled or *executed* in the program.

end mark A *code* used to signal that the end of an item of information has been reached.

end of data marker A *character* or *code* which indicates that the end of all data held on a particular *storage unit* (e.g., a *reel* of *magnetic tape*) has been reached. This should not be confused with *end of file marker*.

end of field marker An additional *data element* which indicates that the end of a *field* (usually a *variable length* field) has been reached. Also known as *flag*.

end of file indicator Synonymous with *end of file marker*.

end of file marker   A *marker* which can be recognized by *hardware* as well as *software*, which indicates that the end of a *file* has been reached.

   Also known as end of file indicator or end of file spot.

end of file routine   A *routine*, either provided by a *housekeeping package* or user-written, which provides the special processing required when the last *record* of a *file* of data has been reached. This may involve checking *control totals* and *counts*.

end of file spot   Synonymous with *end of file marker*.

end of first file section label   A *record* used to define the end of first *section* of a *serial file* stored on *magnetic tape*.

end-of-job card   A *punched card* (placed at the end of a *pack* of cards used as input to a *job*) which informs the *program* that the job has been completed and usually initiates some form of further action such as starting the next job.

end-of-message   A *character* or *code* which indicates that the end of a message has been reached.

end of record word   A *word* which terminates a *record*, usually in a special format so that the end of the record can be identified.

end of run   The completion of a *program* or programs forming a *run*, usually signalled by a *message* or *indicator*[2] from the program.

end of run routine   A *routine* provided by the programmer to deal with various *housekeeping* operations before a *run* is terminated, e.g., *rewinding* tapes, printing *control totals*.

end of tape marker   A *tape mark* which indicates the physical end of a *reel* of *magnetic tape*, usually by means of a strip of reflective material attached to the tape.

   Also known as destination warning marker.

end of tape routine   A *routine*, either provided by a *housekeeping package*, or written by a user, which provides the special processing required when the last *record* on a *reel* of *magnetic tape* has been reached.

end page   A page in a *free-structured data base* which contains information. Contrasted with *underpage*, a page which directs the user to information.

end printing   A type of *interpreting* of data on *punched cards* in which the printing occurred across the end of the card.

endwise feed   A *card feed* designed to accept *punched cards* placed in the *hopper* so that one of the ends of the card entered the *card track* first. Contrasted with *sideways feed*.

engineer's journal   A *file* designed to receive information from a computer system providing the maintenance staff with details of the use of the system, thus assisting in diagnosis of faults and analysis of computer utilization.

enquiry ◊ *inquiry.*

entry 1. The *address* of the first *instruction* in a *program* to be obeyed; also the first instruction of a *subroutine.* 2. A unit of information, either *input* or *output*; an item of data in a list or table.

Also used for *statement* in a *source language.*

entry block Part of *store* into which an *entry*[2] or unit of information is placed on *input.*

entry condition A condition which must be specified before a *program* or a *routine* is entered. Entry conditions may include *parameter*-specified values for the *operands* to be used by the routine, the setting of *switches* to the state expected of them when first tested, and in the case of *subroutines* will include the *link* information giving the *address* of the instruction in the main routine to which the subroutine is to *exit.*

Also known as initial condition.

entry instruction The *instruction* obeyed when *entry*[1] is first made to a *routine.* Some routines may have several *entry points*, and depending upon conditions at the time of entry one of these points will be entered.

entry, keyboard ◊ *keyboard entry and inquiry.*

entry point The first *instruction* in a *routine* or *program* to be obeyed. A routine or program may have several entry points corresponding to different *entry conditions* or operations to be performed.

enveloped file A *file* containing information established on one type of computer, but provided with special *labels* enabling it to be *catalogued* and handled on a different type of computer.

EOF Abbreviation of *end of file.*

EOR Abbreviation of *end of run.*

EPROM Acronym for Erasable Programmable Read-Only Memory. A type of *read-only memory* which can be re-used by removing it from a computer, erasing its contents, writing new information to it and then replacing it within the computer. The contents of an EPROM are stored indefinitely until altered by the process described above, and they can be read over and over again. ◊ *PROM, EAROM.*

equality circuit Synonymous with *equality unit.*

equality unit A device which can accept as *input* two numbers and generate an *output signal* of 1 if these numbers are equal and 0 if they are unequal.

equal zero indicator An *indicator* which is set if the result of a calculation or test is zero, and which can be tested by a *branch instruction.*

equate assembler directive   A *directive* used in an *assembly language* which provides an instruction to the assembler to substitute a particular number each time it finds a specified *label* used as a *mnemonic operand*: e.g., FILE EQU $22AC. Here the *hexadecimal* value 22AC is always to be substituted where the mnemonic FILE is found in an instruction.

equate directive   Any *command* written into a language system to provide a programmer with a facility to assign a value to a *symbolic name*.

equipment compatibility   ▷ *compatibility*. The situation in which *programs* and data are interchangeable between different types of equipment.

equipment, electronic data processing   ▷ *electronic data processing machine*.

equipment failure   Any *hardware* fault that prevents the completion of a job.

equipment, input   ▷ *Input Devices*.

equipment, on-line   ▷ *on-line*.

equipment, output   ▷ *Output Devices*.

equipment, peripheral   ▷ *peripheral units*.

equivalence   A logical relationship in which two statements are said to be equivalent if they are both true or both false. ▷ *logic*, also *Boolean algebra*.

equivalence element   A *logic element* in which the relationship between two *binary input signals* and a single binary *output signal* is defined by the *equivalence operation*. In effect, the element produces an output signal of 1 when the two input signals are the same and 0 when they differ.

Also known as equivalent-to element, coincidence element.

equivalence operation   A *Boolean operation* on two *operands* (p and q), the *result* (r) being given by the table below.

operands		result
p	q	r
1	1	1
1	0	0
0	1	0
0	0	1

This operation is also known as match, bi-conditional, if and only if operation.

equivalent binary digits   The number of *bits* necessary to represent each member of a set of characteristics by a unique *binary number*, e.g., in order to represent each letter of the alphabet (i.e., 26 elements) five bits are necessary, since 26 in binary notation is 11010.

equivalent-to element   Synonymous with *equivalence element*.

erasable storage   A medium of *store* which can be used repeatedly because new information *overwrites* or erases information previously occupying its *location*. Examples are *magnetic tape*, EEPROM.

erase   The replacing of *data* in a medium of *store* with some uniform code representing null data. This may be zeros or space characters, or some suitable code.

erase character   Synonymous with *ignore character*.

erase head   The device on a *tape transport* which erases data before new data is written (◊ *write*) to the tape.

error   Any condition in which the expected results of an operation are not achieved. Errors may be of two main types, *software* or *program* errors and *hardware* errors. The former are errors in the writing or specification of programs and system, and the latter are caused by the malfunctioning of equipment.

error character   Synonymous with *ignore character*.

error checking code   A general term for all *error detecting codes* and *error correcting codes*.

error code   The identification of a particular *error* by means of a *character* or *code*. The error code can be printed out as information that an error has occurred or can be associated with the erroneous item of data in *store* so that the data may be ignored or dealt with in a specific manner when subsequently processed.

error correcting code   An *error detecting code* designed so that it is in some cases possible to recognize not only that an error has occurred, but also what the correct code should have been. An example will be found under *Hamming code*.

error correction routine   A *routine* designed to detect and correct errors on *files* of data.

error detecting code   A *code* in which the representation of each *character* is constructed according to specific rules. Certain combinations of the elements out of which the set of characters is constructed will not conform to these rules; such combinations are known as *forbidden characters* and can be recognized and rejected as errors if they occur in a message.

Also known as self-checking code. An example will be found under *Hamming code*.

error detection routine A *routine* designed to check data items for validity and to detect errors. ⟡ *validity checking*.

error diagnostics The checking of *source language statements* for errors during *compilation* and the printing of error messages identifying the errors made.

error interrupts An *interrupt* which occurs as a result of a *program* or *hardware* error, e.g., causing the message to be printed indicating the error condition, and the *suspension* of the program in which the error has occurred.

error list A list produced by a *compiler* indicating incorrect or invalid *instructions* in a *source program*.

error message A *message* output by *program* indicating the incidence and type of *error* which has occurred.

error range The range of values for an item of data which will cause an *error* condition if the item falls within the range.

error rate In *data transmission*, the ratio of the total number of transmission *errors* to the total volume of data transmitted e.g., one *bit* in 10^7 bits.

error register A special *storage location* whose individual *bit* positions are set when an error condition arises. For example, an error register may be associated with *input/output channels*, separate bits being used to record the correct or incorrect transfer of information during *handshaking operations* on specific channels. The error register can be examined by a *program* to monitor the status of data transfer operations across the different input/output channels.

error report A list of error conditions generated during the execution of a particular *program*; e.g., errors caused by incorrect or unmatched data.

error reset An operation which takes place to reset an error *flag* in an *error register* after an error condition has been detected and corrected.

error routine A *routine* which is entered whenever an *error* is detected. An error routine may output an *error message*, attempt to correct the error, repeat the process which caused it or perform any other required action.

error status bit A *bit* position in a special *register*, which is set to indicate the current status of error conditions recorded in an *error register*. For example, if the error status bit is set to 1, a processing unit or operating system has to examine an error register to detect the nature of the error, whereas no action is required if the error status bit is set to 0.

error tape   A *magnetic tape* onto which *errors* are written for subsequent listing and analysis.

escape character   A *character* which indicates that the following character belongs to a different *character set* from the preceding characters. Used to extend the *range* of characters derived from a given set of *codes*.

evaluating a new system   The last step in the design of any new system should always be an attempt to evaluate it in comparison with the system it will be replacing, and management should ensure that no new system is implemented until such an evaluation has been made: too many systems have been introduced on a wave of enthusiasm and followed closely by a trough of depression as expense and effort rise to keep the system operating. The two systems should be compared under two main headings, cost and information availability.

In order to evaluate a system's cost it will be necessary to establish a breakdown, for each area affected by the system, of the wages and salaries, equipment, supplies and overheads. It should always be possible to do this fairly accurately both for the new system and the old one, and a comparison of the respective costs can then be made. Since likely savings in the future will be a key point (the introduction of new equipment probably being a heavy initial expense) it is often useful to indicate a date when the installation costs of the new system will have been covered by savings. It is also important to realize that the replacement of several low-paid staff by fewer but better-paid staff is not necessarily a saving.

In considering information availability and quality it is essential to relate it to the need for readily available and better quality information. An inexperienced systems analyst will always try to justify an expensive system on the grounds that it provides information that was never obtainable before and that this may result in a saving of thousands, but such claims should always be very carefully examined; above all it must be clear that a system which results in the handling of mountains of irrelevant data by highly-paid executives will probably result in a loss rather than a saving. Evaluation of a new system may well result in the eradication of unnecessary information rather than its proliferation. In any event it will have involved a careful assessment of the disadvantages of the system which will have been salutary for all concerned.

even parity check   A *parity check* in which the number of ones (or zeros) in a group of *binary digits* is expected to be even. Contrasted with *odd parity check*.

event 1. Any occurrence which affects an item on a *file* of data, e.g., a purchase, sale, issue, etc. 2. In *PERT* an event is a defined occurrence which terminates one *activity* and commences another. ⟡ general article on *Critical Path Method*. 3. A signal generated by *hardware* or *software* indicating to the *operating system* a recognizable condition, e.g., hardware failure or completion of an internal activity.

event counter A *logical* device which can monitor regular events occurring within a computer to maintain a count of such events. The event counter can be examined by a *program* and used for *control* purposes; e.g., *clock pulses* known to occur at fixed time intervals can be counted to generate precise timing intervals in a *control* program.

event sequence timing diagram A line diagram dealing with *signal* levels and *transitions* and used by *logic* designers to show the conceptual relationships between signals within a computer system.

except gate Synonymous with *exclusive-or element*.

exception principle system A computer system designed so that normally only situations deviating from expected standards are reported, while results falling within expected limits are not reported.

exception reporting Related to an *information system* in which the *exception principle system* is used.

excess fifty A *binary code* in which a number n is represented by the binary equivalent of n + 50.

excess-three code A *binary code* in which a number n is represented by the binary equivalent of n + 3.

exchange 1. In a *transaction processing* system, a message received by the *TP program* in the central processor and the response given by the program to the originating *terminal* constitute an exchange. An exchange may provoke further messages which in total constitute a complete *transaction*. 2. An item of equipment used to provide interconnexions between subscribers in a switched *telecommunications network* (e.g., *public switched telephone exchange*).

exchangeable disk store A *backing store* device in which *magnetic disks* are loaded into a *disk transport* mechanism as a unit; e.g., as a capsule containing say six disks. A capsule can be replaced by an operator during operation of the computer and individual capsules containing particular *files* can be retained in a *library* until required for use with a particular *program* or *suite* of programs.

exchange instruction An *instruction* found in some *assembly language* systems, used where it is required to interchange the *operands* of two *registers* (e.g., the contents of register X are placed in register Y and vice versa).

exchange, remote computing system ⟡ *remote computing system exchange*.

exclusive-or element A *logic element* in which the relationship between the two *binary* input signals and the single binary output signal is defined by the *exclusive-or operation*.

Also known as except gate.

exclusive-or operation A *logical operation* applied to two *operands*, which will produce a result depending on the *bit patterns* of the operands and according to the following rules for each bit position.

Operands		Result
p	q	r
0	0	0
1	0	1
0	1	1
1	1	0

For example, operating on the following 6-bit operands

$$p = 110110$$
$$q = 011010$$
$$\overline{}$$
$$r = 101100$$

⟡ *Boolean algebra*.

Also known as anticoincidence operation, distance, diversity, exjunction, non-equivalence operation, symmetric difference.

execute To perform the operations specified by a *routine* or *instruction*. Also to cause a specified instruction to be performed by some external action, e.g., setting a *switch* from a *console*. ⟡ *execution*.

execute cycle Synonymous with *execute phase*.

execute phase That part of a *control cycle* in which an *instruction*, having been *accessed*, is performed. Usually an instruction is handled in two *machine* cycles: the instruction is loaded into a special *register*, and it is then *executed*. ⟡ *fetch cycle*.

Also known as execute cycle, execution cycle.

176

execution   The *execution* of a *program* occurs when its compiled *object code* is run in the computer to perform its intended *application* function.

execution cycle   Synonymous with *execute phase*.

execution time   The time taken to complete the cycle of events required to perform an *instruction*.

executive program   An executive program, or executive system, usually consists of a number of complex *routines* which reside wholly or partly in the *main memory* of a computer in order to monitor and supervise certain basic control functions. In *time sharing* computers the executive program is usually considered as part of the computer's *hardware*, since the equipment cannot generally be operated without such a program. An executive program might for example be employed to control the following functions: to handle and interpret all control messages and signals received from, or transmitted to, the *operator's console*; monitor and supervise the *time sharing* system to ensure that *peripheral units* can be simultaneously operated in an *asynchronous* manner, thus permitting all parts of the *hardware* system to be employed with maximum efficiency; and to control the simultaneous operation of several programs within a *multiprogramming* environment, including automatically switching control between one program and another, according to specified priorities, and to permit automatic *interrupts* to service *peripheral* units and other events.

Within a multiprogramming system an executive program should also control the *dynamic allocation* of peripheral units and areas of memory to programs, including automatically reallocating programs during processing in order to optimize the availability of memory for further programs. Protection against interference between programs is another common feature of executive programs, and also the automatic logging of program times and console *events*.

In some systems the executive control functions extend to the automatic control of communications circuits to handle simultaneous *input* and *output signals* on many different lines. In large computer systems the executive functions also include provision for *graceful degradation* in the event of equipment failures.

Executive programs are also known as supervising systems, *monitor systems* and *operating systems*.

executive system   Synonymous with *executive program*.

exit   The last *instruction* in a *routine* or *program*, usually a *branch* from the routine into another part of the program or into a control routine.

exjunction Synonymous with *exclusive-or operation*. ⟐ *Boolean algebra*.

expert system A means of making available to non-experts a data base of expert knowledge as, for example, in initial diagnosis of medical ailments or comparison of legal precedent. Expert systems differ from *decision support systems* (pre-defined rules), *knowledge-based* systems (knowledge but no expertise), and artificial intelligence systems (using methods of reasoning similar to human thought).

exponent The power to which a quantity is raised; e.g., in the expression 2^{23} the exponent is 23. ⟐ *characteristic, floating point representation*.

expression The symbolic representation of a mathematical or logical statement, e.g., A+B, P/Q, OR(A AND B) (C AND D).

extended basic mode *Basic mode* is a class of *interactive* processing between a *terminal* and its *main frame* processor. Extended basic mode provides additional functions allowing the basic mode and the transfer of bulk data.

extended time scale Synonymous with *slow time scale*.

exterior label A written or typed identification on the outside of a *reel* of *magnetic tape* or *floppy disk*, contrasted with *tape label*.

external computer A computer connected to a public information source such as a *videotex* network to provide a particular service to a *closed user group* or the general public via a *gateway*.

external delays time In accounting for the effective utilization of a computer system one classifies time lost according to various factors. External delays time is time lost because of circumstances outside the reasonable control of the user or manufacturer, e.g., power failure.

external device A *peripheral unit* attached to a computer via an *input/output port* or a *communications channel*.

external logic Logic *circuits* which reside outside the boundary of a central computer system (e.g., a *minicomputer* or *microcomputer*) and are within an *external device*. The input/output central logic within the computer has to *interface* with the external logic to ensure the accurate transfer of data between the two devices.

external memory Synonymous with *external store*.

external store A *backing store* which is under the control of, but not necessarily permanently connected to, a *central processor*, and which can hold data or *programs* in a form acceptable to it, e.g., *magnetic tape* or *floppy disk*.

Also known as external memory.

external sync detection A method used to synchronize two devices for a *serial data transfer* operation over a *communications path*. The external logic inserts a *sync* control signal which is detected by the input/output logic of the receiving device in order to receive a synchronous data stream.

external system bus   Synonymous with *highway*.

extract   To remove a selected part from an item or set of items of information.

extract instruction   An *instruction* which will place selected parts of an item of information into a specified *location*. ⟳ *masking*.

extractor   Synonymous with *mask*.

extrapolation   Extrapolation is the name given to the process of deducing a value greater or less than all given values of a function or graph assuming that a projection of the function or graph would continue to satisfy the same relationships as the part whose values are known. In everyday life almost everyone extrapolates; at a very early age we answer such questions as 'If two eggs cost 15p how much do a dozen eggs cost?' Most of us will quite happily have given the answer of 90p although now in later life we might not be surprised to find that a shop might well sell eggs at two for 15p and 80p a dozen. Here an important point emerges; we have extrapolated assuming the same conditions to hold as held in the values given. There is no statistical evidence to justify this; it is made as a basic assumption to our manner of dealing with the problem.

One of the simplest, and possibly most commonly used, methods of extrapolating is by 'regression techniques'. Regression technique assumes that the relationship between a variable and one, or several, other variables is linear. In the former case it is called 'simple' regression, in the latter 'multiple' regression. In both cases the treatment is the same in that we take a set of 'points' on a graph and find the straight line which gives the best 'fit' to these points. This line is called the 'regression line'; further points may be read off from the line either in the interval for which points are known or before or after that interval.

There are various techniques for finding the best fit of a curve, but an adequate description of these is not possible here. The 'least squares' method is frequently used although there are differing ways of applying this.

In order to extrapolate from a set of observed values one must first ensure that to the best of one's knowledge one has chosen variables which are at least to some extent reasonably well related; it would be pointless trying to correlate time taken to sort a *file* of *magnetic tape records* to the number of records without first ensuring that the same number of *tape decks* were always being used, and that the record size was always constant. Having made sure that one's assumptions are, as far as one can tell, reasonable, one must also remember that results obtained are, at best, a guide to actual future observations, an indication of a trend which may assist in the forecast of a future result.

F

face 1. In *optical character recognition*, the term used to distinguish character sets with different relative dimensions. 2. Of a *punched card*, that side which bears the printing: synonymous with *card face*.

face down feed Describes the attitude in which a *punched card* was placed in a *hopper* and moved along a *card track*; the *card face* of a punched card was that side which bears the printing. Contrasted with *face up feed*.

face up feed Describes the attitude in which a *punched card* was placed in a *hopper* and moved along a *card track*; the *card face* of a punched card was that side which bears the printing. Contrasted with *face down feed*.

facsimile The process of scanning any fixed graphite material so that the image is converted into electric signals which are transmitted and used at a receiving station to produce a recorded likeness of the original. A much-used method of communicating pictorial material and exact copies of *text*.

  Also known as fax.

facsimile posting The process of transferring a line of information from one group of records to another, e.g., from a listing of transactions prepared on an accounting machine to a ledger.

facsimile telegraph A telegraph system for the transmission of pictures, maps, diagrams, etc.

factor A *data element* which is one of the *operands* in an *arithmetical operation*.

fail safe Relating to a system which is able to close itself down in a controlled manner in the event of a serious *failure*. A certain level of functionality remains to prevent loss of data. ⟨⟩ *fail soft*.

fail soft Synonymous with *fail safe*, but perhaps a more pertinent phrase in view of the characteristic way in which *fail soft* systems are able to mitigate the effects of serious *failure*. The object is to terminate the system or reduce it to a low level of activity without loss or disruption of data, until the failure can be corrected.

failure Any disruption of a computer system caused by a defect in the *hardware* or system *software*. Failures can be of several types and have different levels of seriousness.

failure logging   The automatic recording of those machine faults which can be detected by *program*, giving rise to corrective procedures, e.g., the repeating of attempts to *read* or *write magnetic tape*.

failure rate   A measure of the number of *failures* occurring in a specific period of time. The time period may be expressed as hours of serviceable time, or over a longer period of weeks or months of calendar time. To appreciate the significance of the failure rate, it is necessary to classify types of failure and the time period concerned.

failure recovery   The re-establishment of system service following a *failure*. It may imply correction of the failure, but perhaps allows the service to be resumed after the system has been *reconfigured* to avoid the faulty condition.

fallback facility   A capability provided in a system to ensure that, in spite of failure of a major component, it is still possible for certain or all of the functions required of the system to be performed. At a minimum level of functionality the fallback system should prevent the loss of data and preserve transactions and files so that recovery can take place later when full functionality is restored.

false drop   Synonymous with *false retrieval*.

false error   A condition arising when the system signals an *error* condition but no error in fact exists.

false retrieval   In *information retrieval*, an error in specifying the criteria for selection causing an unwanted item of data to be selected.
    Also known as false drop.

fan-in /fan-out   A major consideration in the interconnexion of *integrated circuit* devices is the input current needed by devices in order to drive them correctly, and the current generated by devices as output to drive other devices. Within a given family of logic devices each device has a specified current requirement at a given voltage level expressed as a fan-in/fan-out factor. If a device has a *fan-out* of four, this implies that it can drive four standard input devices each having a fan-in of one.

fast-access storage   *Store* with relatively rapid *access time*; whether or not a particular storage device is described as fast depends on the relative speeds of other devices in the system.

fast time scale   When the *time scale factor* in an *analog* computer is less than one, the operation is said to be on a fast time scale. Contrasted with *slow time scale*.

fault   The failure of any physical component (*hardware* or *software*) of a system to operate in an expected manner.

fault time   Synonymous with *down time*.

FDM   An abbreviation of *frequency division multiplexing*.

feasibility studies   A feasibility study is research into the possibility of developing a solution to a problem. In computer terms this may mean placing an order for the appropriate *configuration* and the research may be primarily an appraisal of the current situation of *hardware* and *software*, leading to the choice of equipment. It may also be an assessment of whether a particular area of a company's activities should utilize a computer already used by the company. Some comments on this type of study are given at the end of this article.

The *raison d'être* of the feasibility study should be that there is reasonable doubt whether the problem is capable of solution within an acceptable time-scale and budget, or at the very least whether solution A or B is the better one. Any study which begins on firmer ground is not a feasibility study, it is phase one of an actual project. Probably over ninety per cent of systems design is imitative and the feasibility of the proposals is self-evident; however, the economic benefits may be more apparent than real; the originator of a real feasibility study should be moved by a vision of Utopia, on the other hand he should place a limit on the time and resources that may be expended before a return on the investment must be achieved.

Nowadays it is customary for some form of feasibility study to be carried out for every large project which affects the national interest: for example a conversion to the metric system. Even though the estimates of cost and benefits are sometimes wide of the mark such studies are an essential feature of the democratic process, providing an opportunity for debate and allowing priorities to establish themselves. The computer has become an essential tool in conducting these feasibility studies, both through the analysis of survey data and through *simulation* techniques.

As indicated earlier, feasibility studies are also made to establish whether a computer should be used in solving some particular problem. It is very important that such a study be made as crisply and tidily as possible, and it often helps if the study is carried out within a formal framework. For example, a representative of the problem area should be formally appointed to work with the man (often a systems analyst) conducting the study, and terms of reference should include a statement of the nature and type of application to be studied, the objectives and expected duration of the study, and a clear identification of the areas to be investigated. Those conducting the study will generally examine permanent records within the problem area; interview staff handling

183

the work; observe and measure the work; summarize the facts to provide a broad statement of requirements of a new system; consider possible solutions; and provide an estimate of the cost of completing a full systems investigation. This information should provide those who called for the study with enough information to decide whether or not the project is feasible.

feed To cause data to be entered into a computer for processing; a device for so doing.

feedback The use of information produced at one stage in a series of operations as input at another stage. In *cybernetics* feedback is the method by which the result of a *controlling* operation is used as part of the data on which the next controlling operation is based, enabling a system to monitor its own actions and take self-correcting steps.

feed holes Holes punched in paper or card to enable it to be driven by sprockets. The holes had no significance in themselves but were also sometimes used for indexing in, for example, *paper tape* (where other driving techniques were used instead of the sprocket wheel).

Also known as *sprocket holes*.

feed pitch The distance between *feed holes*.

feed track That *track* of a *paper tape* which contains the *feed holes*.

femto- Prefix denoting one thousand million-millionth or 10^{-15}.

FEP An acronym for *Front-End Processor*.

ferrite core A small piece of ring-shaped magnetic material, capable of receiving and holding an electromagnetic charge, used in *core store*. Now obsolete, having been replaced by *silicon chips*.

fetch cycle Many computers perform *program instructions* in an *operation* consisting of two cycles. On the first cycle, an individual program instruction is fetched from *memory* and placed into a special *register* within the *central processing unit* or *microprocessor*. In the second cycle, the instruction is analysed and performed. These are generally known as the fetch cycle and the *execute cycle*.

fibre optical transmission *Glass fibres* provide a *transmission* medium for *data* in which extremely wide *bandwidths* are possible, thus allowing for very high speed transmission of data and for the *multiplexing* of thousands of separate data *channels* onto one single glass fibre of small diameter. The fibre system operates by guiding light waves at extremely high frequencies along the fibre. The individual fibres are constructed of frequencies which present an optically dense core of high refractive index surrounded by a cladding of low refractive index. This structure creates the effect that light is guided along the fibre and the intensity of the *signal* decays only gradually as, little by little, light rays escape through the cladding.

Fibre optic transmission requires that *digital* electrical signals are converted to light signals at the transmitting end and are reconverted at the receiving end of the link. Light signals can be detected by special light-sensitive *semi-conductor* devices. Fibre optic cables are of small physical size and so require little physical space in cableways and ducts. They do not carry electrical power, so they are safe and are free from electro-magnetic interference.

Fibonacci series A number series in which each number is equal to the sum of the two numbers which precede it, i.e., 1, 2, 3, 5, 8, 13, 21, 34. The technique is sometimes used in computing to group records into *sequence* by key number, and the technique can then be used for an efficient search of the record set by dichotomy.

field A subdivision of a *record* containing a unit of information. For example, a payroll record might have the following fields: clock number, gross pay, deductions, net pay.

field identification The method used to identify sub-elements of a unit of data when it is necessary to examine the data using software. For example, an *instruction* written in *assembly language* may have a *format* consisting of a *label, mnemonic function code, operand field*, and *comments*. The assembler program must search for space codes which *delimit* these fields, and check the contents of certain fields to ascertain that they are valid.

field length The size of a *field*, in terms of the units in which the *record* is composed, e.g., on a *magnetic tape* record the field length may be measured in *characters* or *words*.

field protection A technique used in *data entry* or *on-line data collection* systems to limit the positions on a *visual display unit* into which a user may enter data. Some fields may be headings or information provided for the guidance of users and require protection from inadvertent or incorrect entry.

FIFO An acronym for First-In-First-Out.

fifth generation Pertaining to work done to develop computers intended to be addressed in a natural language and exhibiting *artificial intelligence*. A fifth generation programme was initiated in the UK as the *Alvey* programme in the early 1980s.

file An organized collection of *records*. The relationship between records on a file may be that of common purpose, format or data source, and the records may or may not be *sequenced*. ⟡ *file structure*.

file activity ratio   A measure of the level of activity associated with a particular *file* of *records* and defined as the number of retrievals or transactions received in a given period to the total number of records in the file; e.g., 300 transactions per day in a file of 30,000 records gives a daily activity ratio of 1%. Such a ratio would suggest a relatively inefficient system and might lead to a redesign of the *file structure* to achieve greater efficiency.

file conversion   The process of converting *data files* from one format to another; e.g., manually kept records to files created on a magnetic medium, or files created on a magnetic medium, for use on one type of computer to files for use on a computer of a different type.

file extent   A contiguous group of *tracks* on a particular *file volume*; usually representing a *section* of a file.

file identification   A *code* devised to identify a *file*. The purpose of file identification is to ensure that no confusion arises between files containing different data, and to provide a means by which *programs reading* and *writing* files may check that the correct files are input and output. The method of file identification varies and depends on the type of file and medium of *store* being used. ◊ file label, tape label.

file label   A type of *file identification* in which a file has as its first *record* or *block* a set of *characters* unique to the file. Information in the file label may consist of a description of the file content, the file *generation number* and, if the file is on *magnetic tape*, the *reel number*, and date written to tape.

Also known as *header label*.

file layout   A description of the organization of the contents of a *file*, usually part of a *systems definition* or *program specification*.

file maintenance   Modifying the contents of a *file* by adding, deleting or correcting *records*. Maintenance is distinguished from *updating*: a file is *updated* in order to reflect real changes in the *events* recorded on the file; maintenance is performed in order to make sure that the file contents do in fact accurately record the required data.

file name   The set of *alphanumeric characters* used to identify and describe a *file* in a *file label*.

file, on-line central   ◊ *on-line central file*.

file organization   Relates to the way in which *data elements* and/or *records* are mapped on to the physical *storage* medium used for a particular *file*. The file organization method may impose a particular method of file access, e.g., *index sequential, serial* or *random access*. ◊ *file structure*.

file overflow   A condition which may arise in *updating* or extending a file in which the number of records assigned to the file exceeds the capacity allocated on the *disk* system for use by the file. In most disk *operating systems* the overflow records are written automatically to a special *overflow area* from which they can be retrieved automatically. However, warnings are usually provided to the system operator so that file reorganization can take place. If the warning is ignored, delays in processing will occur and eventually the overflow area itself may become full. ⊘ *overflow records*.

file packing-density A ratio which expresses the extent to which the *records* in a *file* have utilized the space set aside for it on a *disk*. A ratio of 3:1 implies that 1/3 of the available space assigned has been used to store records related to the file. It is usual to allow for free space when a file is set up, so that extensions to the file (i.e., new records) can be stored in such a way that new or existing records can be retrieved or updated efficiently. As the file approaches a high *packing-density*, it becomes increasingly necessary to use *overflow areas* set aside for the file and eventually the file area assigned may have to be expanded. ⊘ *file structure* and *file overflow*.

file print A *printout* of the contents of a *file* stored on some *storage device*, usually for the purpose of aiding *debugging*.

file processing File processing involves all operations connected with the creation and use of *files*. These operations include: *creation, validation, comparing, collating, sorting* and *merging*.

file protection The prevention of accidental *overwriting* of data *files* before they are released for use. File protection can be by *hardware*, e.g., through the use of *file protection rings* on *magnetic tape*, or by causing a *program* to check *file labels*.

file protection ring A detachable ring which can be fitted to the hub of a *magnetic reel* or *floppy disk* to indicate the status of the reel or disk. In some computer systems *write permit* rings are used; e.g., the computer *hardware* is designed so that data cannot be written to a tape *file* unless the ring is fitted. Alternatively the system may use *write-inhibit rings*, in which case data cannot be written to the tape if the ring is fitted. Thus the ring is used to protect a data file by ensuring that an operator does not load a file to a *tape deck* in a situation which will allow it to be overwritten.

file recovery A procedure which occurs following a system *failure* which has interrupted *file processing*. It implies that the content of the file is brought to an accurate condition consistent with the valid *transactions* received to date, and that the status of the file is such that processing can be resumed without loss of accuracy.

file reconstitution The process of recreating a *file* which has been corrupted or damaged, usually involving the *updating* of a previous *generation* of the file with a file of previous *transactions* which have been retained for the purpose.

file section A part of a *file* occupying certain consecutive physical locations on a *disk volume* or on *magnetic tape*.

file set A collection of *files* related to one another and stored consecutively on a *magnetic disk volume*.

files, shared ⬦ *shared files system*.

filestore In an *operating system* the *files* required in the total environment may be stored on *backing store* in an organized *library* under the management of the operating system. The backing store resources allocated for this purpose may include *exchangeable disk volumes*, *magnetic tapes*, etc. The files needed *on-line* at a particular time are held on disks and referred to as being a *high level filestore*. Files held on disk or tape but not on-line are in *low level filestore*.

file structure This term relates to the way that information is organized into *fields*, *records*, *blocks* and *files*, and to the way in which they are organized into the available *backing storage* medium, including structures created to assist in access to required units of information.

In early computers, records held on *magnetic tape* were stored *serially* one record after another. The records were sequenced according to the significance of data appearing in a key field; e.g., account number or name. Such a file is known as a *serial file*, and examples can be found in many computer installations. Indeed, *applications* which use magnetic tape or *cassette tape* as their principal backing storage medium are very often organized using serial files. The disadvantage with such files is that to find a particular record it is necessary to search the medium from start to finish, a process which can take from 1 to 60 minutes, depending upon file size and medium and position of the record in the file.

The use of *magnetic disk* files gives the *system* designer the opportunity to use more convenient file structures which give rapid access to specific records in milliseconds. Such structures are essential for *on-line* or *real time* systems, where it is common to require record retrieval and display in 1 or 2 seconds from entry of a request for a specific key.

Commercial systems, such as order processing systems or reservations systems, usually employ file structures suited to such retrieval, using either *random* file structures or *indexed sequential* file structures.

In random files, records may be stored anywhere on the storage disk. The location is determined by computing a disk address from the key number of the record. The computation is performed in exactly the same way each time it is required to *read* or *write* to a record, so the same disk address is always generated for a specific key. This system is efficient where the structure of the key is such that a unique disk address is always created, but sometimes different keys will create the same disk address, and then some records have to be stored in an *overflow area*, and only a *pointer* to this record is stored in the original generated address. Random file structures may therefore be inefficient in the time taken to retrieve records and in the utilization of disk space, but they are effective where the system designer has control over the keys in use and can create a suitable *algorithm* (known as a *hashing algorithm*) to compute a *track* and *sector* address from the key number in such a way that an efficient distribution of the records arises over the disk surface.

Indexed sequential files are usually created in such a way that areas of the disk are reserved for storing records from a particular key sequence (e.g., Account Nos. 150–200 are assigned to a specific block/track/sector address) known as a *bucket*. An index is set up to relate key numbers to bucket addresses. Records in a file are accessed by looking up the index, retrieving the bucket indicated, and searching for the record required within the bucket. Since records may arise randomly throughout the life of the system, it is not usual for the records in the bucket to be in strict sequence, but in general the records are stored sequentially, although the file may be stored over non-contiguous areas of the disk. It is also usual to assign an area of the disk sufficient to cope with the present file size plus an amount for expansion; the file is then reorganized periodically to cope with file growth. Some buckets will get filled before others and therefore overflow areas are used.

Both random and index sequential files are useful where an *application* requires access to structured records through a simple key choice, but whole classes of computer application require responses to be constructed to user requests which are based upon logical relationships; e.g., 'present all the records which relate to persons between the ages of 25 and 35, who have a degree in engineering, and have served in overseas locations, are not married and have not risen above the rank of branch manager'.

File structures designed for this type of inquiry often use *inverted* files, or *relational* files, and there is not a conventional record structure in which all fields related by specific keys are stored in one place. Instead, any data *element* classed as an attribute or characteristic (e.g., marital status, age range, job title) is stored as a list of all the items which have that characteristic. Records can then be constructed during processing by comparing lists to create sub-files of records which fulfil a particular set of attributes. ⟡ *file overflow, file packing-density*.

file tidying An operation carried out on a *filestore* by an *operating system*, to remove various minor inconsistencies which are derived from previous errors. The purpose is to avoid lengthy operations to *reconstitute* files which have been affected by such errors, and use is made of data stored temporarily after previous incidents. Also used to refer to the reorganization of files for better utilization of *disk* space.

film ⟡ *thin-film memory*.

film optical sensing device A device which converts data recorded on film into a form acceptable to a computer by optical scanning.

film reader Any device capable of transcribing data recorded on film into a form acceptable to a computer.

film recorder An *output device* which transcribes data from a computer onto a photographic file.

filter Synonymous with *mask*.

final result A result created at the completion of a *routine* or *subroutine*; essentially a result presented to the user at the completion of a major processing operation. Contrasted with *intermediate result*.

fine index A secondary *index* used to supplement a main index or *gross index* when the latter is not sufficiently detailed.

firmware In many computers, sections of *software* which are to be used repeatedly are provided as part of the *hardware*, built into *storage devices* such as *read-only memory* (ROM). Thus the user is provided with tried and proven routines, which perform certain standard tasks efficiently. The most common example is in *microcomputers* where the *operating system* is regularly provided in a ROM, which contains sections of code performing complex system management functions which can be activated by simple *commands* entered on the keyboard by a user. Other examples of firmware occur in large general purpose computers where *input/output* functions are often encoded into firmware. Firmware is said to be between hardware logic which cannot be changed without redesign of the system, and software which can be altered readily, provided appropriate *source* documentation is available.

first generation computer A computer which uses thermionic valves. Compare *second generation, third generation, fourth generation* and *fifth generation*.

first-in first-out The processing of items in a list in such a way that the earliest arrival is processed first and the latest arrival is processed last. Contrasted with *last-in first-out* (LIFO) which is used in *pushdown stacks*.

first-level address An *address* which gives the *location* of the item referenced directly, without modification.

first remove subroutine A *subroutine* which is entered directly from a main *program* and which *exits* back to that program.

five-level code A *data communications code* in which five signal elements are used to represent a single character. The signal elements representing each character are usually transmitted with framing *bits* to signify start and stop.

In computer based communication systems, it is usual to use a seven-level code or an eight-level code to provide a greater range of characters and to avoid the use of *escape characters*.

fixed block length *Blocks* of data have a constant number of *words* or *characters* in a system with a fixed block length requirement. This requirement may be due to the *hardware* limitations of a machine, or be determined by *program*. Contrasted with *variable block*.

fixed disk system Describes any *disk storage* system in which the magnetic recording surfaces are on disks which are sealed into the *disk drive*, and cannot be replaced by the operator or be taken to be stored *off-line*. Contrasted with *exchangeable disk store*.

fixed field The organization of *fields* in *records* so that the fields containing similar information in each record are located in the same relative position within the record and are the same length. Contrasted with *variable field*.

fixed form coding The coding of *source languages* in such a way that each part of the *instruction* (*label, operation code, operand, narrative*) appears in a *fixed field* on the medium used as the method of *input* for the instruction.

fixed length record *Records* whose size in *words* or *characters* is constant. This may be because of *hardware* requirements, or be due to specific *programming*. Contrasted with *variable length*.

fixed placement file A *file* which may be expanded or controlled, but which has been allocated a fixed location in the *filestore*. This is done to ensure its availability in *high level filestore*, and to prevent *roll out* to *low level filestore*.

fixed point arithmetic The performing of arithmetical calculations without regard to the position of the *radix point*, treating the numbers as integers for the purpose of calculation. The relative position of the point has to be controlled during calculations.

fixed point part In *floating point representation* a number is represented by the product of the fixed point part and the *index* raised to the power of the *exponent*.

Also known as fractional part, coefficient.

fixed point representation A method of *number representation* in which a number is represented by a single set of digits, the value of the number depending on the position of the digits. In the case of fractional numbers the position of the *radix point* (e.g., decimal point in the decimal system) is located at a fixed predetermined position. ⬦ *positional notation, floating point representation.*

fixed radix notation The representation of quantities where all positions have the same *radix* of notation.

fixed word length A system of organizing a *store* where each computer *word* is composed of a fixed number of *characters* or *bits*.

flag 1. A *bit* position in a *register* used to mark the occurrence of a specific *event*. 2. An additional piece of information added to a *data* item which gives information about the data item itself, e.g., an error flag will indicate that the data item has given rise to an error condition. The term is also used to refer to *end of field* and *end of data markers*.

flag event A condition occurring in a *program* which causes a *flag* to be set.

flag-status register In many *central processors*, a special *register* exists in which the individual *bit* positions are used as *flags* to indicate to the *programmer* the status of various activities within the system. For example, the following flags are set or unset according to *events* occurring in previous instruction *execution cycles*. (i) If the result is positive or negative. (ii) If there has been a *carry* or not. (iii) If there has been automatic *overflow* or not. (iv) If the result is equal to zero or not.

Flags may also be associated with other events such as *interrupts* arising external to the processor. The instruction set provided in the particular machine *language* or *assembly* system usually includes instructions which test these flags, and in some cases these instructions may deliberately set or unset the flags. They are frequently used in association with *branch instructions* to determine the logical sequence in which parts of a program are performed.

flip-flop A device or circuit which assumes one of two possible states (0 or 1); the nature of the state is reversed on receipt of an *input signal*.

Also known as one shot multivibrator, eccles jordan circuit.

float To add the *origin* to all *relative addresses* in a *program*, thus determining the area of *memory* occupied by the program.

float factor Synonymous with *origin*.

floating address Synonymous with *relative address*.

floating lines Signals within a computer are usually considered to be in one of two on states, e.g., high voltage = +5V and low voltage = +1V. Under certain conditions an off condition may prevail in which no signal is discernible to logical devices connected to the line concerned. Such signals are known as *floating signals* and the lines are referred to as floating lines.

floating point arithmetic Arithmetical calculations based on *floating point numbers*. In floating point arithmetic the position of the decimal point does not depend on the relative position of the digits in the numbers as in *fixed point arithmetic*, since the two parts of the floating point number determine the absolute value of the number. The use of floating point arithmetic means that numbers can be stored more economically and in wider ranges of magnitudes, and calculations can be performed to consistent relative degrees of accuracy.

floating point conversion In order to handle *floating point numbers* within a computer, some technique is required for encoding and storing the components of the number. The base could be assumed as *binary* and the *exponent* and the *mantissa* are then stored separately, e.g., 8 *bits* for the exponent, and 24 bits for the mantissa which would normally be a signed binary fraction. Decimal floating point numbers must be converted on input into the above form, and after numbers have been processed as binary floating point numbers they must be converted back to decimal floating point numbers for output.

floating point number A number expressed using *floating point representation*.

floating point package *Software* provided with a computer system to enable the computer to perform *floating point arithmetic*.

floating point radix In *floating point representation* a number n is represented by two numbers a and b where $n = a.r^b$. The radix is the particular value of r used in the representation.

floating point representation A method of *number representation* in which a number is represented by two sets of *digits*, known as the *fixed point part* and the *exponent* or *characteristic*. If a number n is represented by a fixed point part a and an exponent b, then $n=a.r^b$, where r is the *radix* or *base* of the number system, e.g., 10 for the decimal system, 2 for the *binary* system. Contrasted with *fixed point representation*.

floating signal ◊ *floating lines*.

floppy disk A *disk* used for the storage of data which is encoded by electro-magnetic means on to tracks on the disk surface. A floppy disk is made of flexible material, usually a kind of plastic which has magnetizable particles upon its surface. Floppy disks are supplied within special envelopes which have holes set in them for the *drive* shafts and *read/write heads* of the disk drives which are used to operate with the disks. The disks are designed to be handled within the envelope which protects the recording surface. A typical floppy disk is 5¼ inches or 8¼ inches in diameter. Floppy disks are used with *word processing* systems and with *personal computers*, and their popularity is related to the ease with which they can be handled and stored *off-line*. They are classed as *exchangeable disks* and can be contrasted to *fixed disk* systems, which often cannot be stored off-line, although such devices may operate at much higher speeds and have a much greater storage capacity than that of a floppy disk.

For *microcomputers*, floppy disks often represent the most secure and convenient method for storing information. Valuable files can easily be copied and stored off-line and multiple copies can be easily and cheaply made to protect the user against hardware failure or any other event which may cause damage to the disk surface.

Also known as diskette.

floppy disk controller *Hardware* and/or *software* used specifically to control the orderly transfer of data between a computer and a *floppy disk drive*, and which may or may not include *file management facilities* to control automatically the allocation and utilization of space on the disk surface, and allow for the various logical access methods such as *sequential* and *random* access.

floppy disk drive A device used to handle one or more *floppy disks* and which includes a drive shaft to rotate the disks at the required speed, and *read/write* heads and circuitry which enable data to be recorded upon and read from the disk surfaces. The disk drive also includes circuitry which acts as external logic to enable the device to act as a *peripheral unit* to a *microcomputer* system.

flow A sequence of *events*, usually represented by a *flowchart*.

flowchart The diagrammatic representation of a sequence of events, usually drawn with conventional symbols representing different types of events and their interconnexion. ⟡ *flowchart symbols, systems flowchart, program flowchart* and general article on *flowcharting*.

Also known as flow diagram.

flowcharting Flowcharting is a technique for representing a succession of events in symbolic form. The 'events' recorded in a flowchart may represent a variety of activities, but in general a particular flowchart will record the interconnexion between events of the same type. In *data processing*, flowcharts may be divided broadly into *systems flowcharts* and *program flowcharts*.

Systems Flowcharts: The object of systems flowcharts is to show diagrammatically the logical relationship between successive events in a data processing system. The main types of 'event' in a systems flowchart will be the clerical and manual procedures involved, *data collection* and *data preparation*, and the computer *runs* involved. The flowcharts will identify the various procedures involved, showing their interconnexion and the overall design of the system.

Program Flowcharts: The object of a program flowchart is to show diagrammatically the logical relationship between successive steps in a computer program. Flowcharting a computer program may involve a number of different levels of complexity, but at least two levels are usually prepared, outline flowcharts and detail flowcharts.

The purpose of an outline flowchart is: (i) to help the conversion of a program specification into a sequential statement of operations; (ii) to guide the further development of the program; (iii) to ensure that no *input* or *output* record is overlooked, and that all requirements of the program specification are met. In order to achieve this an outline flowchart must show: (i) all input and output functions; (ii) how each type of record will be processed; (iii) how the program will be divided into *segments* and *routines*; (iv) all *entry points* and *halts*.

The purpose of a detail flowchart is: (i) to interpret the detailed program specification; (ii) to define the programming techniques to be used; (iii) to provide clear directions for *coding*; (iv) to make the coded program more intelligible. A detailed flowchart will be used as the basis for coding the program, either in a *high level language* or in *machine code*. Thus the level of detail must be sufficient for unambiguous coding. This will vary according to the language to be used and the complexity of the program: the most detailed level of flowcharting will have a symbol representing each individually coded *instruction*. However, it is usually sufficient to represent a sequence of instructions forming a logical unit of the program by means of a single symbol.

Symbols: flowcharting symbols usually conform to some standard set in which each symbol has a specific meaning. Internationally and nationally accepted standards have been designed, such as the European Computer Manufacturers' Association standard and the American Standards Association standard, but local peculiarities prevail in almost any installation. For this reason great care (and often great resourcefulness) is needed in reading the flowcharts of anyone whose personal whims are not publicly accepted: considering that the flowchart is a major tool in the science of communication, it can sometimes be strangely uncommunicative. Among the symbols defined will be symbols representing the following functions:

Flowlines   Flowlines show the *transfer of control* from one operation to another

Process   A symbol to represent any kind of processing function.

Decision   A symbol which represents a decision or switching type of operation that determines which of a number of alternative paths is to be followed.

Connector   A symbol to represent an entry to or exit from another part of the flowchart. It is used to indicate a transfer of control that cannot be conveniently shown by a flowline (e.g., because the flowchart continues on another page).

Terminal   A symbol representing a terminal point in a flowchart (e.g., start, stop, halt or *interrupt*).

Other special symbols are used to represent subroutines, input/output functions and different types of *peripheral unit* and sources of input and types of output.

The techniques of flowcharting are often complementary to those of using *decision tables*, on which there is a general article.

flowchart symbols   Conventional diagrammatic representations of different events which are shown on a *flowchart*.

flow diagram   Synonymous with *flowchart*.

flow direction   The method adopted to distinguish between antecedent and successor event on a *flowchart*. This may be by means of arrows or by the convention that *flowlines* connecting antecedent to successor flow from top to bottom and left to right of a page.

flowline   A line drawn on a *flowchart* connecting an antecedent event to a successor event. ⟡ *flow direction*.

flow-process diagram   Synonymous with *systems flowchart*.

fluid logic   The simulating of logical operations by means of varying the flow and pressure in a fluid – either gas or liquid. Fluid logic is used to control the operations of *pneumatic computers*.

font   The shape and style and size of a particular typeface used by any machine which is capable of producing printed output. The font is determined by the construction of the print hammers in a mechanical printer, but on such devices as a *daisywheel printer* the operator can present different type styles, different character sizes, and varying character sets for particular jobs.

Machines designed to read printed material (e.g., *optical character readers*) will usually work with characters presented within a limited range of fonts. Also spelt as fount.

forbidden character code   An *error detecting code* in which certain combinations of *bits* are not permitted and known as forbidden characters.

force To intervene in the operation of a computer *program* by *executing* a *branch instruction* transferring control to another part of the *routine*. Forcing is usually carried out in order to bypass an error condition which has caused the program to come to a *halt*, or to terminate a *run* by forcing *entry* to the *end of run routine*.

forced checkpoint An operation instigated by an operator to cause the status of a job to be recorded on *backing store*, so that the job can be restarted at a later occasion. Usually done in an emergency situation to relieve the load on the computer so that corrective action can be taken. ◊ *checkpoint*.

forecasting The problem of planning for the future is met in many situations, and in endeavouring to make the best possible plan some assumption or forecast of future conditions has to be made. The best forecast will be based on the projection and analysis of past results viewed in the light of experience. There have developed, in recent years, several statistical methods of making forecasts mathematically based on past performance, and whereas no one can pretend that these methods will always give an exact forecast there can be little doubt that the correct use of such methods can greatly improve planning.

The use of the digital computer commercially has greatly increased the value of statistical forecasting methods, for when used together they enable many forecasts to be made very quickly, where once armies of statisticians would have been needed. Such methods are of great value in such areas as market planning, *inventory control*, personnel planning, etc., where often forecasts of many items have to be made.

There are so many variants of different forecasting methods that it is impossible to discuss them all here. Instead we shall mention their common principles and give a few examples. In any forecasting system our first concern must be to obtain consistently expressed past results. Having ensured that they are so expressed, we study our past results under three headings:

(i) Seasonal Variation: Is there any periodicity to the sales level? Is the seasonal pattern changing? Are there any variable seasonal effects which we can categorize explicitly, e.g., those due to holidays.

(ii) Trends: Is there evidence of a regular change between successive results? Does this appear to be a 'long' trend or a 'short' trend? Are there any symptoms which indicate that a new trend is likely?

(iii) How large is the effect of any random variation? If there is a

197

large random variation we must remember this when quoting our forecast.

One of the most widely used methods of forecasting, in one form or another, is that of exponential smoothing. In its simplest form exponential smoothing is a means of dealing with item (iii) by computing a moving average. In carrying out this operation the square of the sum of successive errors is minimized. By a little more sophistication we can extend exponential smoothing to calculate a linear trend as well, and also to calculate any seasonal effects. R. G. Brown has developed multiple exponential smoothing, which can be adapted to give forecasts where almost any type of trend is being experienced. The problem here is in monitoring such a system. The basic idea in exponential smoothing is that of taking a moving average by adding to our last forecast a fraction of the difference between our last forecast and the observed result. By successively applying this technique we are able to find an 'average of an average' which can be made to give a trend.

Another method in use at the present time is that of Box and Jenkins. Developed as a method of *process control*, it can be shown to be equivalent to exponential smoothing in its developed form. The forecast is made by taking this month's known result and adjusting it in the light of the difference of the last two forecast errors to date. Any seasonal effects must be removed before this calculation is applied, but the method requires very little storage of information and therefore lends itself to use where many events or objects are to be controlled.

Of course there is no definitive forecasting system. One method may be best for one application where another may perform better in a different application. Before any method can be used a study of past data has to be made so that the best values of weighting factors can be made. Any method has to be adapted to suit the peculiar requirements of a particular system. The accuracy required and the cost of achieving this accuracy must be considered, for inevitably the more sophisticated our forecasting method becomes the more it will cost. Very often the simple method will give good enough results for the purpose required, and the expense of introducing a more sophisticated method is not justified by the small increase in accuracy that would be obtained.

Finally, no forecast will give an exact answer except by chance. All our forecast can do is to show us a region where the true answer will lie. If this region is small we can make firm plans; if it is large we must make flexible ones. At least we shall be working with relevant knowledge rather than on inspired guesswork.

foregrounding ◊ *foreground processing*.

foreground processing 1. In a *multi-access system*, processing which is making use of *on-line facilities*. 2. High priority processing which takes precedence (as a result of *interrupts*) over *background processing*. 3. Low priority processing over which background processing takes precedence.

As definitions 2 and 3 are directly contradictory and definition 1 has a related but different meaning, this phrase should be used with caution. Definition 2 is most commonly used.

Also known as foregrounding.

foreground program A *program* which requires *foreground processing*.

form 1. A *document* which has prepared spaces into which entries may be made by a human operator or a computer *printer*. Continuous form *sets* can be produced for printing of such documents at high speed under computer *program* control. 2. The term has been extended to include a *page* or screenful of *information* as presented on a *visual display screen*. In particular the term refers to displays in which present *fields* exist for users to enter data under user control, and where parts of the screen are automatically protected to prevent unwanted user entries.

formal methods The means of describing systems and program requirements symbolically and thus leaving no room for doubt or misinterpretation.

format 1. The predetermined arrangement of data, e.g., the layout of a printed document, the arrangement of the parts of a computer *instruction*, the arrangement of data in a *record*. 2. A predetermined pattern for the presentation, *storage*, collection or *transmission* of data. ◊ *data format, record format, print format, card format*.

format effectors Synonymous with *layout characters*.

formatting The act of imposing a basic structure on a *virgin medium*, such as setting *sector boundaries* on a *magnetic disk*.

form feed The mechanical system of positioning *continuous stationery* in a printing device.

form feed character 1. A formatting *code* used as part of a *data communications* code. 2. A character punched in a *paper tape control loop* used on some printing devices for the control of *form feed*.

Forth A computer *language* originally designed for use by astronomers, but having characteristics which have encouraged its use in the writing of *system software* for *microcomputers*. A primary feature of the language is that the user is able to construct procedures which can be effectively included in a Forth system as though they were extensions of the language, either at the user program level or within the *compiler/interpretater*. It thus provides for an extensible language within a basic structure which is very efficient in execution.

FORTRAN   FORTRAN is an acronym for FORmula TRANslation. It is a *problem oriented high level programming language* for scientific and mathematical use, in which the *source program* is written using a combination of algebraic formulae and English statements of a standard but readable form.

A FORTRAN program consists of data items, executable statements and non-executable statements. The program is structured in *segments*, which consist of a master segment and optional function segments and *subroutines*.

Data items in FORTRAN are either variables or constants, and are assigned *alphanumeric* names by the programmer. Groups of similar items of data can be processed as *arrays*, or tables of data in which case the individual items are defined by their position or reference within the array by naming the array followed by one or more *subscripts*. Data items in FORTRAN may take the following forms:

Integer   A whole number value falling within a range determined by the capacity of the computer being used.

Real   A number expressed in *floating point representation* accurate to a number of significant digits, the range again dependent on the capabilities of the particular machine being used.

Complex   A complex number in which two real numbers are used to express the real and imaginary parts.

Logical   A quantity which can only take two values, true or false. (◊ article on *Boolean Algebra*).

Text   Character information, which is not used for mathematical operations.

The actual operations of the program are expressed by means of 'executable statements'. These can take two basic forms, 'assign statements' and 'control statements'. An assign statement takes the form Variable = Expression. The expression may be either arithmetic or logical. An arithmetic expression can include variables, elements, form arrays, constants and a variety of standard functions, which are combined by arithmetic operators, e.g., +, −, *(multiplication), / (division), ** (exponentiation). A logical expression is similar but can include the operations A N D, N O T, O R, the logical operators. An example of an arithmetic assignment statement would be:

$$ROOT = (-B + SQRT(B**2 - 4*A*C)) / (2*A)$$

In more usual mathematical notation this expression would be written

$$\frac{-b + \sqrt{b^2 - 4ac}}{2a}$$

The word ROOT, and the letters A, B, C represent variables, and SQRT the function provided for calculating square roots. The compiler recognizes these symbols and translates them into machine code.

An example of a logical assignment statement would be:

$$BOOL = A. OR. B$$

In this expression the variable BOOL would be given the value true or false according to the truth values of the variables A and B and the *truth table* defined by the Boolean operator OR.

Each statement can be preceded by a numeric label, permitting reference to the statement by means of control statements. Control statements enable the program to *branch* to other statements and enable *loops* to be constructed. Branches may also be constructed which are conditional on the results of arithmetic or logical operations. Examples of control statements are:

$$GO\ TO\ 25$$

This statement is an unconditional branch to statement number 25.

$$DO\ 24\ I = J, K, L$$

This statement calls for the repeated execution of succeeding statements up to and including that labelled 24. At the first repetition I is set to equal J, at the second to J + L, at the third to J + 2L, and so on until the next value would be greater than K, at which point the loop is terminated.

$$IF\ (A.L\ T.B\ AND\ C.\ G\ T.D)\ GO\ TO\ 19$$

This statement causes a branch to statement numbered 19 if A is less than B and C is greater than D.

While executable statements specify the operations the program is to perform, 'non-executable statements' merely provide the *compiler* with information. An example is

$$COMPLEX\ ROOT\ 1, ROOT\ 2, ANS$$

which indicates to the compiler that storage is required for three complex variables with labels as specified.

A FORTRAN program consists of one or more *segments*, of which there is one and only one master segment, and, optionally, function and subroutine segments.

A function segment is used where the same form of function is required several times in a program. The statements describing the operation required to calculate the result of using the function are named and written once, and whenever the function is required in the program it is only necessary to give the function name and a list of parameters to replace the 'dummy' variables used in the function segment.

A subroutine is similar to a function segment except that it may provide more than one result, and must be specifically called by a separate statement, in contrast to a function, which itself may form part of an expression. Input and output in a FORTRAN program is performed by means of statements which identify the peripheral unit to be used and the external format of the list of items to be input or output.

forward compatibility standards Standards adopted to ensure that *programs* developed for one range of equipment can be utilized on a further range of equipment which will replace the present installation. ◊ general article on *Transition*.

foundation virtual machine A *virtual machine* established in a *virtual machine environment* to initialize the system, i.e., to enable the system to be *loaded* or reloaded.

four address instruction A computer *instruction* whose *address* part consists of four addresses, usually two *operand* addresses, the address of the destination of the result of the operation and the address of the next instruction to be performed.

fourth generation Computers which use VLSI, very large scale integration.

fourth generation language Any *high level language* designed to enable users who are not trained programmers to develop *applications*. Often based on a non-procedural language with *relational data base* support.

four-wire channel A circuit capable of transmitting and receiving simultaneously by using two separate and distinct paths in each direction.

fractional part Synonymous with *fixed point part*.

fragmentation The use of any object or *resource* in which parts of the resource are allocated on a dynamic basis; perhaps resulting in a pattern of usage in which a particular task is obliged to use dispensed elements of the resource. For example, the *main memory* of any computer which has a *virtual storage* capability may be allocated to several *concurrent programs* in such a way that none or few of the programs are assigned contiguous areas of memory. Fragmentation can lead to inefficient operation, but the ability of an *operating system* to work in this environment and to reorganize memory allocation automatically to achieve more efficient use is an important attribute in a *virtual machine environment*.

frame   1. A transverse section of *magnetic tape* or *paper tape* consisting of one *bit* position for each tape *track*. For paper tape the term *row* was also used for frame. 2. A *unit* of information in *data communication*; e.g., a page of information prepared for presentation on a *visual display terminal*. Any unit of data transferred as a unit and bounded by *framing characters*.

framing   Units of data which mark the boundary of *fields* or characters for *data transmission*. For example, every character in an *asynchronous* transmission system is framed by a *start bit* and, say, two stop bits. In a *synchronous* data *stream*, groups of special *sync characters* are used to frame a *block* of data characters in data transmission.

framing error   If a receiving device is unable to detect appropriate framing codes as part of a received unit of data, then it will register and report a framing error, usually requiring automatic retransmission of the blocks concerned.

free field   The organization of data in a *storage* medium so that an item of data, or *field*, may be located anywhere within the medium as opposed to *fixed field* organization in which the relative position of a field determines the nature of its contents.

free-standing display   A *display* unit apart from the main operating *console*, intended to assist in the efficient operation of a computer system by providing *prompts* to operators handling *peripheral units*.

frequency   The rate of repetition of a periodically recurring signal, usually measured in cycles per second (cps) kilocycles per second (1kcs=1000cps) or megacycles per second (1mcs=1000kcs). ⟡ *Hertz*.

frequency band   The range within which the *frequency* of a signal may be allowed to vary.

frequency division multiplexing   A method used to transmit several signals along a single *data communications* circuit, in which each signal is modulated on to a separate carrier wave and many carriers, each of different frequency, are transmitted simultaneously along the same channel. The carrier frequencies are chosen so that the distance between signal frequencies ensures that there is no mutual interference.

Using coaxial cables, a *broadband* width facility is provided in which hundreds or thousands of signals may be sent along the same circuit. The technique is used for both speech and data transmission.

frequency shift keying A method of *frequency* modulation in which digit signals are represented by tones of specific duration and frequency transmitted to the line. The technique has been developed for the generation and transmission of dialling signals in a telephone network (i.e., distinctive tones used for each of the digits 0 to 9 plus special keys as available on a push-button telephone pad). In *data transmission*, *binary coded* information can be transmitted using just two tones to represent 0 and 1.

front-end processor A computer system attached to another main system in order to handle communications traffic, thus allowing the main system to be dedicated to file and data processing procedures. A typical configuration would be for a minicomputer to act as a front-end processor to a main frame system, but microprocessors are sometimes configured to provide the front-ending capability. The functions performed in a front-end processor include: line scanning, control over modems or network interface devices, error detection, and network management.

FSK An abbreviation of *frequency shift keying*.

full duplex Transmission circuits in which messages may be transmitted in both directions at the same time.

full text retrieval *Information retrieval* which handles files of text with any word retrievable (rather than just defined key words).

function 1. That part of a computer *instruction* which specifies the operation to be performed. 2. The expression in mathematical symbols of the relationship between variables, e.g., the expression a + b = c may be said to be a function of the variables, a, b, c.

functional design The detailed specification of the interrelationship between the working elements of a system, taking into account both *logic design* and the equipment used in the system.

functional diagram The diagrammatic representation of a *functional design* in which conventional symbols are used to represent the specific elements of *logic design* and equipment.

functional specification A specification produced in the early stages of the design of a computer *application* system which clearly specifies what the application is to do, but does not specify how it is to be implemented as a computer procedure. The document should be capable of being read, understood and approved by the person who has requested the project, and should be written in a language and terminology understood by those who work in the specific application field. The document must usually be formally approved by those responsible for using and implementing the system, and any alterations at a later date may result in necessary changes in development timescale and cost.

functional unit A series of *elements*[2] which together perform a single computer *operation*, e.g., multiplication or addition.

function code The part of a computer *instruction* that specifies the operation to be performed.

function generator A unit of an *analog computer* which can accept one or more input variables and which will provide an output variable based on some mathematical *function*.[2]

function holes Synonymous with *control holes*.

function key Any *key* on a *keyboard* or a *keypad* which causes a specific *operation* to take place other than the *entry* of a standard *character* from the set of characters available. For example, *carriage return* is a specific function. Some function keys can be associated with sections of *program code* so that a series of quite complex *logical* operatives may result from the depression of a single key. *Personal computers* often provide several function keys which can be associated with user defined program tasks in this way.

function polling A method of *polling* in which a device requiring to be serviced not only provides a signal indicating a need for service, but also signifies the type of service required.

function table In *table look-up* techniques, the function table consists of two or more sets of information arranged so that an item in one set provides a cross-reference to items in the other sets.

future labels *Labels* used in *instructions* in a *program* written in a programming language (◊ *languages*); they refer to *locations* to which a *compiler* or *assembly program* has not yet allocated *absolute addresses*.

fuzzy logic Logic used much in *artificial intelligence*, *expert systems* and *knowledge-based* systems, which allows multiple values in truth tables so that as well as true and false, the table can include such values as fairly true, more or less true, very false, almost false, etc. This allows knowledge and reasoning to be represented more like that of human beings while still capable of being processed by a computer.

G

gain The ratio of output signal from a circuit to the original input signal.

gallium arsenide A *semiconductor* made of the elements gallium and arsenic. Semiconductor devices using GaAs have characteristics of speed, heat tolerance and low-power switching which point to their use in optical devices.

game chip A microelectronic component intended for use in a *home computer*, and including a range of logical functions required for *games*.

games Computer *applications* intended for amusement or education in which the user exercises knowledge, skill, dexterity of hand or quickness of reaction in response to audio/visual *events* presented on a *visual display unit*. Games are generally associated with *home computers* and three main classes of game can be distinguished: (i) Games of strategy; e.g., chess. (ii) Games of adventure; e.g., simulation of a quest. (iii) Games for amusement; e.g., arcade games.

Games range in the degree of difficulty presented to users. Some are intended to be simple diversions, perhaps 'designed' to introduce a newcomer to certain features of a computer. Simulations and certain strategy games can take a great deal of thought and application, perhaps requiring hours of effort from the user. Home computers equipped for playing games often have special devices attached (e.g., joysticks or paddles). Games have also been associated with training activities in industry.

gang punch 1. A *punched card* machine which had a single *card track* incorporating a *reading station* and a *punching station*, each with a position for each *card column*. The machine was used to reproduce information from a single card at the beginning of a pack into all subsequent cards of the pack. Cards were fed one after another along the card track and information originally punched into the leading card was read at the reading station and transferred to the punching station for punching into the following card; and so on. 2. Used as a verb, meaning to punch the same information, e.g., a date, into a group of cards by pre-setting the information so that the punching was automatic.

gap digit A *digit* present in a *word* which does not form part of the information conveyed by the word, e.g., a *parity bit*.

gap scatter The deviation from correct alignment of the magnetic *read heads* for the several parallel *tracks* on a *magnetic tape*.

garbage Meaningless data present in any *storage device*. The data may be meaningless because of errors or it may be data left in store by a previous unrelated job.

gate In general, an electronic *switch*.[1] Used in *data processing* to refer to an electronic circuit which may have more than one *input signal* but only one *output* signal. In this sense synonymous with *logic element*.

gate, and Synonymous with *and element*.

gate, coincidence Synonymous with *and element*.

gate, nor Synonymous with *nor element*.

gate, one Synonymous with *or element*.

gate, or Synonymous with *or element*.

gateway A means of accessing an *external computer* on a *videotex network* by going through a central computer controlling the network.

gathering, data ◊ *data collection*.

gather write The ability to write a *block* of data composed of logical *records* from non-contiguous areas of *store*. ◊ *scatter read*.

general peripheral controller A *hardware* unit, containing a *processor* which controls the transfer of data to and from a range of *peripheral units* and *main store*; usually operates under the control of commands set up by the main *order code processor*.

general purpose computer A computer capable of operating on different *programs* for the solution of a wide variety of problems, as opposed to a *special purpose computer* specifically designed for solving problems of a particular type.

Also known as all-purpose computer.

general purpose function generator A *function generator* which is not specifically designed for a particular type of function, but which can be adapted to generate different functions.

Also known as arbitrary function generator.

general purpose program A *program* designed to perform some standard operation, e.g., *sorting* or one of the *file processing* functions. The specific requirements for any *run* of the programs are provided by means of *parameters* which describe the requirements of the run. A general purpose program is similar to a *generator*, but differs in that it normally requires parameters each time it is run, whereas a generator produces a specific program which can subsequently be used without parameters.

generate To use a *generator* to produce a specificized version of a *general purpose program*.

207

generated address An *address* developed by *instructions* within a *program* for subsequent use by that program.

Also known as *synthetic address*.

generating program Synonymous with *generator*.

generating routine Synonymous with *generator*.

generation number A number forming part of the *file label* on a *reel* of *magnetic tape* or a *magnetic disk* file, which serves to identify the age of the file. Each time amendment data is applied to a file an entirely new copy of the file is created containing all the valid amendments. This new reel will bear the same *file name* as the original that was amended; the two will however be different generations of the same file and as such will bear different generation numbers. ⋈ *grandfather tape*.

generator A *routine* which will produce a *program* to perform a specific version of some general operation by completing a predetermined framework with the details required for the particular application. A generator is similar to a *compiler* in that source *statements* are converted into a program, but differs from it in that only programs of a specific type are produced, e.g., *sort generator, report generator*.

Also known as program generator, generating routine, generating program. Compare with *general purpose program*.

generator, analytical function ⋄ *analytical function generator*.

generator, arbitrary function ⋄ *general purpose function generator*.

generator, diode function ⋄ *diode function generator*.

generator, general purpose function ⋄ *general purpose function generator*.

generator, manual word ⋄ *manual word unit*.

generator, natural function Synonymous with *analytical function generator*.

generator, natural law function Synonymous with *analytical function generator*.

generator, number ⋄ *number generation*.

generator, output routine ⋄ *output routine generator*.

generator, program ⋄ *generator*.

generator, random number ⋄ *random number generator*.

generator, report program ⋄ *report program generator*.

generator, sorting routine ⋄ *sort generator*.

generator, tapped potentiometer function ⋄ *tapped potentiometer function generator*.

gibberish total A total accumulated for control purposes when handling *records* by the addition of specific fields of each record, although the total itself has no particular intelligence or meaning. For example, an accumulation of indicative data such as customer's account number. ◊ *hash total*.

giga- A prefix denoting one thousand million or 10^9, synonymous with *billi*.

gigo Acronym for Garbage In, Garbage Out; the principle that the results produced from unreliable data are equally unreliable.

graceful degradation Related to machine breakdowns on computers; the ability to undergo graceful degradation ensures that failure of certain parts does not cause complete breakdown, but allows limited operation. ◊ *resilience*.

Also known as operating in crippled mode.

grandfather tape It is normal practice when updating a *magnetic tape file* to retain the original copy of the file thus enabling the file to be reconstituted in the event of any permanent loss or damage to the current file. It is usual to keep at least three generations of a tape file, referred to as 'grandfather', 'father' and 'son'. The generation is identified by means of the *generation number*.

graphic display A specialized *display* unit, used to present graphical information to a computer user.

graphic panel In *process control*, a device which displays the state of the process in the form of illuminated light, dials, etc.

graphics The use of images generated by *software* for output to a *graphic display*. ◊ *computer graphics*.

graphics, kernel system The concept of a visual input/output device with an area of visibility which can be viewed in whole or part by actual devices, thus allowing standardization.

graph plotter ◊ *plotter*.

graunch An unplanned error.

gray code A code in which the binary representation of the numbers 0–9 are given in the following table:

Decimal	Gray	Decimal	Gray
0	0000	5	0111
1	0001	6	0101
2	0011	7	0100
3	0010	8	1100
4	0110	9	1101

Also known as cyclic code.

grid In *optical character recognition*, a scale for measuring characters by means of a network of parallel lines at right angles to each other and a fixed distance apart.

gross index The first of a pair of indices used to locate *records* in *store*. The gross *index* is used to give a reference in the second or *fine index*, which acts as a supplement.

group 1. A specified sequence of storage *locations* used to contain a particular *record* (or records). 2. The data stored within such locations. 3. A set of records in a *sorted file* which have the same *key* value.

group code A *systematic error checking code* used to check the validity of a group of *characters* transferred between two *terminals*.

grouped records Several *records* contained in a single group in which the *key* of one record is used to identify the group.

group indication Relating to a practice commonly adopted when printing a *totals only* tabulation on a *punched card tabulator*. A special device was used to list descriptive information from the first card of each group; this information would normally be common to the whole group of cards and was therefore referred to as group indicative data.

Also known as *first item list*. The device used was known as an independent sector designating device on some machines.

group mark A special *character* used to indicate the end of a *group* of characters in *store*, the group itself usually being a logical record to be *addressed* and processed as a unit of data.

Also known as group marker.

group marker Synonymous with *group mark*.

group polling A method of *polling* which enables a number of devices within a given set to respond to a single inquiry.

group printing In a *report program*, the information printed out for a *group* of *records* when a *key change* occurs.

guard band A frequency band left unused between two *channels* of a *data transmission* device, usually to prevent interference between channels.

guard signal A signal used to permit the output signals from a *digitizer* to be read only at moments when the signals are not susceptible to *ambiguity error*.

guide edge The edge of *paper tape* used when the tape was lined up for automatic handling by a *paper tape reader* or *paper tape punch*.

guide margin The distance measured between the *guide edge* of a *paper tape* and the centre line of the first *track* of holes punched parallel to this edge.

gulp A group of *binary digits* consisting of several *bytes*.

H

hacker Originally any individual programmer who communicated with others on a network. The word has since assumed the pejorative sense of one who invades a network's privacy.

half adder A device forming part of an *adder* capable of receiving two inputs, i.e., *augend* plus either *addend* or *carry*, and of delivering two outputs, *sum* and *carry*.

half adder, binary ◊ *binary half adder.*

half-duplex A system (e.g., telegraph) capable of working in either direction but not in both directions simultaneously.

half-duplex channel A *channel* providing for transmission in both directions but not simultaneously.

half subtracter A device forming part of a *subtracter* capable of receiving two inputs, i.e., *minuend* and *subtrahend* or *carry*, and of delivering two outputs, *difference* and a digit to be borrowed.

Also known as *one-digit subtracter.*

halt The situation which occurs when the sequence of operations in a *program* comes to a stop. This can be due to a *halt instruction* being encountered or due to some *unexpected halt* or *interrupt*. The program can usually continue after a halt unless it is a *drop dead halt.*

halt, dead ◊ *drop dead halt.*

halt, drop dead ◊ *drop dead halt.*

halt instruction A machine *instruction* to stop a *program*.

Also known as stop code, stop instruction.

Hamming code An *error checking code* (named after its inventor) in which each character has a minimum Hamming distance (◊ *signal distance*) from every other *character* in the code. An example of a Hamming code using four ternary digits with minimum distance of 3 would be:

    0000 0112 0221 1011 1120 1202 2022 2101 2210

It should be noted that this particular example is an *error correcting code* as well as an *error detecting code*. For example, the combination 0120 is detected as an error since it does not obey the rule for construction, and may be corrected to 1120 as it differs from this in only one respect.

Hamming distance Synonymous with *signal distance*.

hand coding Programming is usually achieved with the aid of a language system which supports the programmer in the process known as *program assembly* or *compilation*. In this process, *statements* written in the language form are converted by *software* to *hexadecimal code*, and finally into *binary machine code*. In some small *microprocessor* based computer systems, a rudimentary *operating system* or *monitor* may exist and the transition of code from the assembly language form to the hexadecimal form has to be done by the programmer. This process is referred to as hand coding.

hand feed punch Synonymous with *hand punch*.

hand punch 1. A device which caused holes to be punched in *punched cards* as a direct result of pressure on a key of a *keyboard*; it had no automatic facilities. Contrasted with *automatic punch*. 2. As for 1, but related to *paper tape* not punched cards.

handshaking A procedure which is used to coordinate activities between two logical devices which must communicate with one another. For example, the *input/output logic circuits* in a computer have to send and receive information to a *peripheral unit* which contains external logic. The purpose of these logic circuits is to ensure an accurate transfer of data, and to coordinate the precise timing of pulses which represent data across the *input/output interface*. During the process of data transfer there are exchanges of control information so that, for example, fresh data is not transferred into an input/output port until the previous set of data has been accepted by the receiving device. The handshaking procedure controls and monitors this interface and deals with timing errors which might arise.

hang-up Synonymous with *unexpected halt*.

hard copy Information output on to paper, often produced at the same time that information is output in machine-readable form or produced as a *transient* display on a *visual display unit*. Contrasted with *soft copy*.

hard disk A *magnetic disk* which is rigid, in contrast to *floppy disk*.

hard dump Synonymous with *automatic hardware dump*.

hardware The physical units making up a computer system – the apparatus as opposed to the *programs*. Contrasted with *software*.

hardware availability ratio A ratio used to measure the availability of a computer system to provide productive work. The availability ratio is normally expressed as the ratio of difference between *accountable* *time* and *down time* to accountable time. Down time usually includes *corrective maintenance* and *recovery time*.

Also known as hardware serviceability ratio.

hardware check   A *check* which is performed by *hardware* in order to detect errors in the transmission of data within a computer, e.g., *parity check* performed by hardware.

Also known as built-in check, automatic check. Contrasted with *programmed check*.

hardware dump area   An area of *storage* used to record the internal state of an *order code processor* after the occurrence of a system *failure* (e.g., *parity error*) which cannot be automatically corrected.

hardware recovery   Relating to the ability of a system to recover automatically from a *failure* and re-establish the current workload to enable processing to continue in a controlled manner.

hardware serviceability ratio   Synonymous with *hardware availability ratio*.

hard-wired logic   An implementation in which particular functions required in the operation of a system are provided by soldered connexions on *printed circuits*, and where the functions cannot be readily changed by *software* or *firmware*.

hash   Meaningless or unwanted information present, for example, in *store*, or written to *magnetic tape* in order to comply with *hardware* requirements on minimum *block length*. ⟡ *hash total*.

hashed random file organization   A method of *file organization* on a *direct access device*, in which the *address* used to select or *write records* to a file is determined by applying an *algorithm* to the record *key*. ◊ general article on *Updating and File Maintenance*.

hashing algorithm   An arithmetical function used to derive an *address* for the storage or retrieval of a *record* in a *hashed random file*. The function operates on a *data element* (a *key*) contained in the record to generate a more or less unique address for the location of the record in a table or on a *magnetic disk*.

hash total   An addition of values in a particular *field* or area of a *file* where the total has no indicative significance but is used for control purposes, e.g., a total of staff personnel numbers. Also known as check sum. Associated with *batch total, gibberish total*.

HASP   Acronym for Hansten Automatic Spooling Processor and referring to a communications *protocol* for handling *remote job entry* functions with IBM 360 and 370 computers.

HDLC   Abbreviation of *high-level data link control*.

head   An electromagnet used to read, record or erase polarized spots on a magnetic medium such as *magnetic tape, magnetic disk* or *magnetic drum*. Examples are *read head, write head, read/write head*.

header A set of data placed at the head of one or more sets of data, e.g., a *record* at the beginning of a *file*, and containing an *identifier* for the following sets. Sometimes the header will contain *control data* or data common to the following sets.

header label A *block* of data at the beginning of a *magnetic tape file* containing descriptive information to identify the file. Examples of data on a header label are: *file name, reel number, file generation number, retention period*, and the date when the data was written to tape. When a file is *opened* this data is checked by the *program* to ensure that the correct file is being processed; and also, if the tape is to be used for writing, to check that the *retention period* has been exceeded.

Also known as file label.

head gap The distance between a *read* or *write head* and the surface of the recording medium (*magnetic tape, magnetic drum, magnetic disk*, etc.).

head, playback ◇ *read head*.

head, reading ◇ *read head*.

head, record ◇ *write head*.

head, writing ◇ *write head*.

height balanced tree Synonymous with *AVL tree*.

help function A feature of a system designed to assist a user in understanding and operating the system. It might, for example, consist of a *data base* of self-teaching material which can be displayed to the user whenever he requests assistance in performing a function.

Hertz A unit used in the definition of frequency: e.g., 10 Hertz = 10 cycles per second. Named after Heinrich Hertz and usually abbreviated as Hz.

[kHz (kilohertz) = One thousand cycles per second; MHz (megahertz) = One million cycles per second; GHz (gigahertz) = One billion cycles per second.]

hesitation A short automatic suspension of a main *program* in order to carry out all or part of another operation, e.g., a fast transfer of data to or from a *peripheral unit*.

heuristic approach An exploratory approach to a problem which uses successive evaluations of trial and error to arrive at a final result. Contrasted with *algorithmic approach*.

heuristic program A *program* which solves a problem by a method of trial and error in which the success of each attempt at solution is assessed and used to improve the subsequent attempts until a solution acceptable within defined limits is reached.

heuristics The methodology of solving a problem by trial and error, evaluating each step towards a final result.

hexadecimal coding In many computer *language* systems used for programming computers, it is possible to represent computer *instructions* by means of *hexadecimal notation*. These numbers are more convenient for people to recognize and interpret than the long strings of *binary* numbers recognized within the logic of the computer. Although most commercial programming is done using a *high-level* or *low-level language*, there are some classes of work where there is a need to write and interpret hexadecimal codes. The following instruction illustrates the relevance of hexadecimal coding:

Instruction in English: load the Accumulator A with the contents of memory location 3151
Instruction in Hexadecimal code: 3A30F2
Instruction in binary code: 001110100011000011110010.

Hexadecimal coding is used when it is otherwise necessary to interpret long binary numbers.

hexadecimal notation A notation of numbers to the base or *radix* of sixteen. The ten decimal digits 0 to 9 are used, and in addition six more digits, usually A, B, C, D, E and F, to represent ten, eleven, twelve, thirteen, fourteen and fifteen as single characters.

high-going transition An event in timing sequences which have been implemented as electronic logic. A transition is a change of voltage level, e.g., from low to high to represent a change from 0 to 1 as in *binary* representation. A change from a lower voltage to a higher voltage is known as a high-going transition, whereas a change from a high to a low is known as a *low-going transition*.

high-level data link control A *communications* control procedure for checking the accuracy of data transfer operations between remote devices, in which data is transferred in units known as *frames*, and in which procedures exist for checking the sequence of frames, and for detecting errors due to *bits* being lost or inverted during transfer operations. There are also functions which control the set-up and termination of the data link. Usually referred to by the abbreviation HDLC.

high level filestore A type of *filestore* used in an *operating system* to hold *physical files* needed *on-line*. The medium typically used is *magnetic disk* or *magnetic drum*.

high level language   A *language* in which each *instruction or statement* corresponds to several *machine code* instructions. High level languages allow users to write in a notation with which they are familiar (e.g., FORTRAN in a mathematical notation, COBOL in English) rather than a language oriented to the machine code of a computer. Contrasted with *low level language*. ◊ *Languages*.

high level recovery   *Recovery* from a *hardware/software failure* by use of resources and information not directly associated with the cause of failure; e.g., use of a *back up file* to effect recovery rather than use of further attempts to execute a *block transfer* from a device.

high order   The more significant figure or figures in a number expressed in positional notation, e.g., in the numeric representation of sixteen as 16, the 1 is of a higher order than the 6, since it represents tens rather than units. In describing a *binary word*, therefore, reference can be made to the high order *bits*.

high performance equipment   Equipment which produced output signals of sufficiently high quality to permit these signals to be transmitted on telephone or teleprinter circuits. The phrase no longer has this connotation and is to be found in advertising copy, with a less specific meaning.

high-speed carry   A *carry* into a column which results in a carry out of that column, bypassing the normal adding circuit when the new carry is generated.

Also known as a ripple-through carry or, where appropriate, *standing-on-nines carry*. When, in contrast, the normal adding circuit is used in such a case, it is called a cascaded carry.

highway   A channel along which signals travel from one of several sources to one of several destinations.

Also known as trunk or bus.

highway width   Relates to the capacity of a *highway* to transfer data simultaneously, the greater the width the faster the throughput. For example, a highway which is four *bytes* wide, has the capacity to transfer four bytes at a time.

hit   A *record* which satisfies specified identifying criteria; e.g., in an *information retrieval* system; or, during *updating*, a *change record* which corresponds with a *master record*.

hit-on-the-fly printer   Synonymous with *on-the-fly printer*.

hit on the line   An error condition caused by a momentary open circuit on a communications channel.

hold   To preserve data in one *storage device* after transferring it to

216

another storage device or another *location* in the same device. Contrasted with *clear*.

hold facility A method of interrupting the operation of an *analog computer* without altering the values of the variables at the time of interruption, so that the computation can continue when the interruption ceases.

holding beam A continuous spray of electrons used for regenerating: electrons which have dissipated after being stored on the surface of a *cathode ray tube*.

holding gun The source of a stream of electrons which make a *holding beam*.

hold mode The operating mode for an *analog computer* in which the *hold facility* is used. Contrasted with *compute mode*.

holes, designation ⬦ *control holes*.

holes, function ⬦ *control holes*.

hole site Each specific area on a *punched card* or *paper tape* in which a hole could be punched, e.g., on an 80-*column*, 12-*row card* there were 960 hole sites.

holes, sprocket ⬦ *feed holes*.

Hollerith card A *punched card* in which information was punched using the *Hollerith code*.

Hollerith code A *punched card code* invented by Dr Herman Hollerith in 1888 in which the top three positions in a *card column* had a *zoning* significance so that a combination of a hole in the top position (known as *Y-position*) plus a hole in the fourth position would have a different significance from a combination of a hole punched in the second position (known as *X-position*) plus a hole in the fourth position. The third position (known as 0) gave another zone and it was thus possible to code all twenty-six alphabetic characters and the ten numerals 0-9 in the twelve *punching positions* of a card.

homeostasis The state of a system where input and output are exactly balanced, producing no change; steadiness.

home computer A *personal computer* with limited capability, largely constrained to use for computer games.

home record The first *record* in a *file* in which the *chained record* system of file organization is used.

hoot stop A *closed loop* producing an audible signal, generally used to indicate an error or for operating convenience.

hopper A device which held *punched cards* and presented them to a feed mechanism for reading or punching.

horizontal feed Where a *punched card* was placed in a *hopper*, entered and traversed the *card track*, all in a horizontal position. Contrasted with *vertical feed*.

horizontal flowcharting A technique for recording the movement of paper in an organization; distinguished from ordinary *flowcharting* by the fact that the movement of a recording medium is charted rather than the information it records. One line is used for each form or other medium, and the movement of each type (shown by standardized symbols for e.g., 'data added', 'handled' and 'filed') is recorded from the time it is first used to the time it is destroyed.

host computer Any central computer which provides data, information, and computing facilities to a distributed population of terminals. The terminals may be connected to the host by permanent fixed circuits or by dial-up lines. Sometimes the host computer also controls the commands and protocols concerned with the process of communication, but often the terminals are interfaced to the host by a *front-end processor* or communications controller.

housekeeping *Routines* within a *program* which are not directly concerned with the solution of the problem. Housekeeping functions include the setting of *entry conditions, clearing* areas of *store* if the program expects these to be set to some initial condition, performing any standard preliminary operations required by *input* or *output devices* (e.g., writing *header labels* to *magnetic tape*), performing standard *input/output routines*, e.g., the *blocking* of *records* on to magnetic tape.

housekeeping operation An operation performed by a computer in connexion with *housekeeping* requirements.

housekeeping run A *run* to maintain the structure of a *file* (or files), e.g., to add new *records* and to delete or amend existing records.

hub 1. The hole in the middle of a *reel* of *magnetic tape* or *floppy disk*, which fits over the *capstan* when the reel is mounted on a *tape deck*. 2. The socket on a *plugboard* into which a *plug* was inserted.

hunting An unstable condition resulting from a continuous attempt by an automatically controlled *closed loop*[2] to find a state of equilibrium. The system will usually include a method of measuring deviation from a predetermined standard and a method of ensuring that the difference between the standard and the measured state tends to zero except for 'hunting' oscillations.

hybrid ◊ general article on *Hybrid Computers*.

hybrid computers The term hybrid computer is frequently used to refer to any mixed computer system in which *analog* and *digital* computing devices are combined. A more strict definition requires that a digital and analog computer be interconnected via a *hybrid interface*, or that analog units be integrated as part of the *central processor* of a digital computer and have direct input/output facilities. Hybrid machines are in fact designed to perform specific tasks and it is probably for this reason that many forms exist. The basic objective of any such system is to obtain for the user the best properties of the two computing philosophies.

In analog systems data is handled in continuous form (e.g., input can be a continuous voltage lying in a specified range) and this permits true *real time* operation. Such systems can perform mathematical operations such as integration with speed and ease, and have great potential for tackling *on-line simulation* exercises, *model building* and *forecasting*. On the other hand they are not as accurate as digital computers, and have a very limited form of *memory* and less developed logical processes than digital computers. Analog machines are programmed by using a plugboard to interconnect various *hardware* devices, and this type of arrangement is inherently less flexible than the digital machine, which has the advantage of having both *program* and data recorded in the same memory medium.

The digital computer scores on account of its large memory capacity and the ease with which logical procedures can be set up, but whereas it is more accurate than the analog machine, it can perform the more complex mathematical functions by iterative routines only (see *iteration*).

In a hybrid system the digital and analog computers are interconnected in such a way that data can be transferred between them via *analog-to-digital converters*, and *digital-to-analog converters*. The digital unit is able to exert control over the analog computer by means of *instructions* stored in the digital memory. These instructions can control the operation mode of the hardware units in the analog section, while the analog machine can interrupt the digital computer to initiate input/output operations. This type of system combines the properties of the true analog system with the accuracy, reliability, memory capacity and programming flexibility of the digital system.

Hybrid machines are generally used in scientific applications or in controlling industrial processes; in both situations the user is able to exploit the machine's ability to process both discrete and continuous data, using accurate digital *subroutines* where necessary and the analog machine's fast integration functions.

hybrid interface A channel for connecting a *digital computer* to an *analog computer*. Digital signals are transmitted in serial mode by the digital machine and have to be converted and transmitted to the various operating units in the analog machine as simultaneous signals. On the other hand data collected as a set of simultaneous readings from the analog units must be digitized and transmitted in serial mode to the digital computer. Both control signals and data may be transferred through the interface system. ◊ general article on *Hybrid Computers*.

Hz Abbreviation of *Hertz*.

IAL Abbreviation of *international algebraic language*, which developed into *ALGOL*.

IC Abbreviation of *integrated circuit*.

icon A symbol displayed for a user by a *program* or *operating system*, to represent an event or object which might otherwise require a lengthy textual description. Systems based on this concept often include a pointing device such as a *mouse*, *touch sensitive screen* or a *light pen* which enables the user to point directly at one of a group of such icons and thus determine the action to be taken by a program. This technique has been used in the design of user-friendly interfaces for *work stations*.

identification A label consisting of a coded name that serves to identify any unit of data; e.g., a *file name*. ⊳ *file identification*.

identification division One of the four divisions of a *COBOL program*. In the identification division the programmer provides descriptive information that identifies the program being *compiled*. ⊳ general article on *COBOL*.

identifier A *label* which identifies a *file* of data held on an *input* or *output device*, or identifies a particular *location* in *store*. ⊳ *file identification*.

identifier octet An *identifier* of eight contiguous *bits*.

identity element A logical element, operating with *binary* signals, which provides one output signal from two input signals. The output signals will be 1 if, and only if, the two input signals are alike; i.e., both inputs are 1 or both 0. ⊳ *Boolean algebra*.

identity unit A device with several *binary input signals* and a single *binary output signal* which has the value 1 if all the input signals are identical, and 0 if they differ. An identity unit with only two input signals is also known as an *equivalence element*.

idle time The time during which a data processing machine remains inactive even though switched on and otherwise in an operable condition.

IDP Acronym of *Integrated Data Processing*.

if and only if operation Synonymous with *equivalence operation*.

if-then operation   Synonymous with *conditional implication operation*.

ignore   Synonymous with *ignore character*.

ignore character   A *character* used to cause some action to be inhibited, or a character that is itself ignored.

Also known as erase character and error character.

IKBS   Abbreviation of *intelligent knowledge-based system*.

illegal character   A group of *bits*, holes or other units used to represent any of the symbols in the *character set* of the system. ⊗ *forbidden character code*.

image   An exact copy of an area of *store* located in another part of store or in a different storage medium. ⊗ *binary image, card image*.

IMIS   Acronym of *Integrated Management Information System*.

immediate access   Pertaining to a *store* in which information can be retrieved without significant delay; e.g., retrieval of information from a storage device by directly *addressing* the unit of data required.

immediate access store   A *storage device* in which the access to data can be achieved without significant delay. Originally used to emphasize the advantages of *main memory* stores as against other magnetic storage devices in which the medium has to be physically moved past a *read head* to obtain data. The *access time* in the former case might be measured in *microseconds* whereas in the second it might be measured in *milliseconds*. Now commonly called *main memory* or *store*. ⊗ general article on *Storage Devices*.

immediate address   The *address* in an *instruction* which operates on its own address component.

Also known as zero-level address.

immediate data   Unit of data included in an *instruction statement* so that it appears immediately after the *operation code* of the instruction in *memory*.

Also known as *literal operand*.

immediate processing   Synonymous with *demand processing*.

imperative macroinstructions   Macroinstructions which result in the creation of *object program* instructions; as distinct from *declarative macroinstructions*, which tell the *compiler* to perform some particular action.

imperative statements   *Instructions*, in a *source language program*, which are converted into the actual *machine language* instructions of an *object program*.

implementation   1. Of a system – the process of conducting a systems project including the initial investigation and design followed by *programming*, *program testing*, *pilot running*, *parallel running*, live operation and review of the live system. 2. Also the implementation of a computer installation, including choosing the *hardware* and *applications* to be tackled, preparing the site and accommodation, selecting and training staff, as well as the activities mentioned in 1 above for each systems project.

implication   Synonymous with *conditional implication operation*.

implication, material   Synonymous with *conditional implication operation*.

implication operation, conditional   ▷ *conditional implication operation*.

implied address   A *program instruction* usually contains one or more *addresses* which define the *memory locations* that contain the *data elements* to be affected by the operation specified at that instruction step. Sometimes a location is defined implicitly without requiring the programmer to nominate an address or an *index register* containing the address. For example, it is not necessary to define an address for instructions which automatically increment the contents of a register; the address is then said to be implied.

impulse   An electrical signal the duration of which is short compared with the time scale under consideration.

incident   A *failure* which requires activity by an operator to correct or remove the jobs concerned.

incidentals time   Time during which a computer is being used effectively, but not for productive *runs* or *program* development. Incidentals time could be spent on demonstrations, training, etc. ▷ *effective time*, *serviceable time*.

inclusion   Synonymous with *conditional implication operation*.

inclusive-or operation   A *logical operation* applied to two *operands* which will produce a result depending on the *bit patterns* of the operands and according to the following rules for each *bit position*:

Operands		Result
p	q	r
0	0	0
1	0	1
0	1	1
1	1	1

For example, operating on the following 6-bit operands,

223

$$p = 110110$$
$$q = 011010$$
$$r = 111110$$

Also known as disjunction, logical sum, or operation. ⟨⟩ *Boolean algebra*.

incomplete program A *program* which consists of a basic framework of *instructions* designed to perform some general type of operation, but which cannot be run until the specific requirements of a particular version of the operation are supplied to the program either by *parameters* or by *own coding*.

incomplete routine Synonymous with *incomplete program*.

inconsistency A data condition detected by *software*, in which the data concerned is found to contain contradictory statements.

increment A quantity which is added to another quantity.

incremental computer A computer designed to process changes in variables; for example a *digital differential analyser*. Contrasted with *absolute value computer*.

incremental display Synonymous with *cathode ray tube visual display unit*; a device employed to convert *digital data* into character or graphical form.

incremental dump A method of *dumping* in which data is preserved for *security* purposes, by regularly *writing* away small amounts of data at frequent intervals. For example, used to preserve the contents of *filestore*.

incremental plotter A unit providing output from a computer in the form of continuous curves or points plotted, along with information in character form, under control of a *program*.

incremental representation A method of representing variables used in *incremental computers*, in which changes in variables rather than the variables themselves are represented.

incremental representation, binary ⟨⟩ *binary incremental representation*.

incremental representation, ternary ⟨⟩ *ternary incremental representation*.

increment/decrement instruction In many *programs* it is necessary, or useful, to perform certain *routines* a set number of times and then *branch* to perform a new process. It is customary to set up a data counter to maintain a running record of the number of times the program *loop* has been performed. Automatic increment instructions are provided in the instruction set of most computers, to enable a data counter to be incremented automatically (or decremented automatically).

increment/decrement register A *register* used to maintain a data counter which may be automatically incremented (or decremented) when a relevant *increment/decrement instruction* is performed.

independent sector designating device A device used for *group indication*.

index 1. A table of references, held in *memory* in some *key* sequence, which may be *addressed* to obtain the addresses of other items of data, for example items in a *file* on some *backing store*. 2. A number used to select a particular item from an *array* of items in *memory*. ⟨⟩ *indexing*.

indexed address An *address modified* by the contents of an *index word*.

Also known as variable address.

indexing 1. A method used to retrieve information from a *table* in *memory* or a *file* on a *direct access store*. For example, on a direct access device a file may be organized in such a way that one part contains an *index* which serves to locate items in other parts of the file. 2. The *modification* of an *instruction* by the contents of an *index word*.

index page A *page* in a *free-structured data base* which directs the user to an *end page*. ⟨⟩ *route*[2].

Also known as routing page.

index point A reference point during the cycle of operation of any *punched card machine* in which cards were transported by the action of rotating shafts.

index positions Synonymous with *punching positions*.

index register In some computers *program modification* is performed automatically and indeed it may be always used to *address* certain *locations* within *memory*. In such machines there will be at least one index register which will contain a *modifier* to enable data to be indirectly addressed. Each program *instruction* must therefore refer to an index register when addressing locations in store. Sometimes known as a *modifier register*.

index sequential access method The technique of *accessing records* held on a *file* in *index sequential file organization*.

index sequential file A *file* in which *records* are subject to *index sequential file organization*.

index sequential file organization A type of *file structure* for *files* on a *direct access storage* device in which the *address* of a *record* on a *physical file* is identified by reference to an *index* [1] which contains the record *key*.

index word During *program modification* an index word may be used to contain a *modifier* which will be added to a *basic instruction* when it is executed. An index word may, for example, be used to *address* data stored in a *table* in *memory*. ⟡ *index register*.

indicator 1. A lamp or display device on a *peripheral unit* or a *console*. 2. A device which can be set when a specified condition occurs (e.g., when a calculation has produced a negative result) and which may be tested by *program* to initiate an appropriate course of action. Related to *alteration switch*.

indicator chart A chart used by a programmer during the *logical design* and *coding* of a *program* to record details about the use of *indicators* in the program. Part of program *documentation*.

indicator, end of file ⟡ *end of file marker*.

indicator, sign check ⟡ *sign check indicator*.

indirect addressing A *programming* technique in which the *address* part of an *instruction* refers to another *location* which contains another address. This further address may specify an *operand* or yet another address.

 Also known as multi-level addressing.

indirect control The relationship between two units in which one controls the other by some sequence of events involving manual intervention. The unit being controlled is *off-line* to the controlling unit.

inductive potential divider An auto-transformer with a toroidal winding and one, or more, adjustable sliders.

industrial data processing *Data processing* concerned with or controlling some industrial process, as distinct from *commercial data processing* or *scientific data processing*.

ineffective time Time during which a machine is serviceable (⟡ *serviceable time*) but effective use of the machine is not made, due to *operating delays* or *idle time*. Contrasted with *effective time*.

infix notation A notation for representing *logical operations* in which the *operator* is written between the *operands*, e.g., A&B where & represents the operation 'and'. Contrasted with *prefix notation*.

informatics The science or art of processing *data* to provide *information*.

information Sometimes the following distinction is made between *information* and *data*: information results from the processing of data, i.e., information is derived from the assembly, analysis or summarizing of data into a meaningful form.

information bits   In a signal carried in coded form, information bits are *characters* or *digits* which are *data* and which can be processed to provide *information* subsequently; the term does not include digits which may be required for *control* purposes by *hardware* or *software*.

information channel   The *hardware* used in a *data transmission* link between two terminals. Including *modulator, demodulator* and any *error detection* equipment required. A channel may involve transmission by telegraph or telephone lines or by a radio link.

information–feedback system   A control system used in message transmission, in which information received at a terminal is re-transmitted to the sending terminal for automatic checking.

information flow analysis   The study of an organization or system in which analytical techniques are used to ascertain information about the origin and routing of documentation and to ascertain the requirements and uses of the *data elements* at each stage.

information, loss of   Synonymous with *walk-down*.

information processing   The processing of data to derive meaningful results as *information*. Generally used as a synonym for *data processing*.

information requirements   The results required from any series of data processing operations; e.g., the information required by management as output from a system.

information retrieval   A branch of computing technology related to the storage and categorization of large quantities of information and the automatic retrieval of specific items from the *files* and indexes maintained. Essentially incorporating the ability to retrieve items with relatively short *access time* and the ability to add additional information to the files as it arises. Usually requiring a *direct access store* with *on-line interrogation units*. ⊘ general article *Information Retrieval Techniques*.

information retrieval techniques   Information Retrieval is the phrase used generally to describe the problems of recovering, from collections of data, those particular items of information which are required at a particular time for a particular purpose. Information retrieval is basically a problem of communication: communication between the originator of information and the individual requiring to use the information. What is required is a method for providing the closest possible coincidence between the description of the subject by the user and the description of the information produced by the originator. Thus a third element appears in the line of communication between these two: the process of classifying or indexing the information. A common information retrieval system is a library. The user *accesses* the individual books he requires via a catalogue organized in such a way that he can formulate a request, find a reference to the book and then locate the book on the library shelves.

Information retrieval involves basically the following sequence of events: (i) Information coming into the system is analysed and given some form of classification. (ii) The information is stored in an ordered manner (not necessarily corresponding to the classification made at stage (i)). (iii) The user translates his requirement for information into a classification by a process analogous to that made for original information. (iv) A search of the store is made for an item with a classification corresponding to that made by the user. This step may be divided into two, the first stage being a search through an index to the classifications, which will give a reference to the location of the item in the store. (v) When a match or *hit* is obtained, the item of information is extracted from the store.

It can be seen from this general outline that the events correspond generally to normal experience of searching for information, for example in libraries, catalogues of merchandise, office filing systems, trade directories, reference book indexes. These techniques have been adopted and extended, utilizing the great speeds and storage facilities of computers to provide rapid access to increasingly large and diverse collections of information. There are an almost infinite number of possible approaches to the problems of information retrieval: this article can only attempt to describe in general terms some of the approaches made to solving the problems posed by each of the steps described above.

The problem of information retrieval starts, in fact, with that of storing information. Two possibilities are open: either the information entering the system can be stored separately from the index used to reference it (as happens in a library) or the index and the information can be stored together (as happens in an office filing system). In computer applications, the choice depends on the amount and type of computer *storage devices* available and the type of information being dealt with. A computer system used, for example, to provide an information retrieval system for accessing technical literature would normally be of the first type, the actual information items being stored apart from the index. A system of personnel records, however, might be of the second type, a complete computer record being created and stored for each individual together with identifying and classifying information. The development of storage devices with differing capacities and *access time* means that in some systems the information may be held on one type of device while the index to be searched is on another. Other developments, particularly in the field of miniaturization of original documents through microfilming, enable physical copies of the documents to be stored with some form of coded representation of reference information. *Punched card* systems were developed by which microfilmed documents could be inserted within a card on which reference information was punched. By using mechanical devices, selected cards could be retrieved and the associated document obtained. Extensions of this principle to computers involve associating microfilms with magnetic recording surfaces – either tape or cards – which can be coded and read by computers. Other developments are the recording of televised images of original documents on video tape or video disk, and associating the video image with identifying information which can be read by the computer. A different approach is the development of devices which can read printed documents automatically, and convert them into computer format.

Indexing information within a system makes possible the correlation of requests for information with relevant items of information stored by the system. There are many possible indexing schemes, but basically there are two types of approach to the problem. Each item of information may be given an identifying *key*, which in the case of systems separating the information from the index will act as the cross-reference from the index to the item. As well as this key, selected attributes possessed by the information will be coded in some form and associated with the identifying key. For example, in a system of personnel records, the identifying information may be a staff number, followed by a series of codes isolating such attributes as experience, qualifications, marital status, occupation code. In addition, if the system is one which incorporates information together with reference tables, there may be non-coded details such as the individual's name and address, job title, etc. An alternative approach is that of inverse filing. In this system each individual item is again given an identification code. Selected attributes are chosen, and a list of all possible combinations of attributes is made. Against each combination of attributes is placed the identifying key of all items of information having that combination. This system is used, for example, in assisting police forces to identify criminals from fingerprints. Any fingerprint may have several different attributes. Lists are made of all combinations of these attributes, and any known criminal having any combination of attributes is listed against the combination. Thus by studying any fingerprint, identifying its attributes and comparing them with the files, the police can find a list

229

of all criminals whose prints have the same combination of attributes. The more precise this classification can be the smaller will be the short-list obtained; ideally, the coding of attributes should be sufficiently detailed to identify a single individual.

The choice of which system to adopt depends again on the type of information being considered, and also on the sort of questions expected. Inverse filing can only be used if the type of inquiry will always be limited precisely to a given combination of attributes, since adding new attributes or revising the codes used is a difficult and complex activity. The alternative system is more generally used when flexibility of approach is required, since any combination of different attributes can be specified, and extension of attributes merely involves adding another code to each item of information without necessarily altering any of the codes already used.

Most storage devices are used in information retrieval systems, both for storing of indexes and for storing information. The type of device chosen will depend on the type of file organization adopted (*inverted files* or *serial files*) and on the amount of data to be stored. *Magnetic tape* is usually used for serial files, which require each record to be examined in turn when any search for information is made. If, however, the description of required attributes can be used to generate an *address* where the corresponding information is required, as for example in an inverted file, then *direct access* storage devices may be chosen. The great capacities of direct access devices may also be utilized for files which contain large quantities of information. These files may be held serially, and individual items located by first searching a magnetic tape containing index information only, the relevant items being accessed directly from the storage device by means of an address found on the index tape. Another factor relevant to the choice between types of storage device is the expected usage of the system. The time taken to read through a long magnetic tape file may not be justified if the normal expected 'hit rate' (the ratio of items satisfying the given inquiry to the total of items examined) is low.

Performance characteristics of an information retrieval system can be measured in terms of completeness, relevance, specificity and response time. 'Completeness' refers to the number of items which could be relevant to the user's inquiry that are in fact retrieved by the system. This will normally depend on the accuracy and efficiency of the coding and indexing system adopted. 'Relevance' is the inverse of completeness: it is a measure of the number of items retrieved by the system which do in fact conform to the needs of the user. 'Specificity' is a term which refers to the degree of generality of the information retrieved. These first three characteristics depend on the system design. The fourth item, 'response time', is a measure of the time taken to retrieve an item of information from store, and depends also on the *hardware* involved.

One of the major items of applications *software* provided by most manufacturers is software concerned with aspects of information retrieval. This software can assist a user at all the stages of setting up and using such a system. Indexing can be assisted by means of such routines as KWIC (key word in context) indexes, which provide lists of items of information sequenced by specific words or codes, each word or code appearing in the sequence in its appropriate location. Files of information can be subjected to statistical analysis to determine the frequency of occurrence of attributes, thus isolating factors for further identification. Routines can assist in setting up and maintaining files on tape and direct access devices. On the problem of specifying requests to a computer file, software exists which enables a user to relate different combinations of attributes by means of Boolean operators (AND, OR) and logical relations (equal to, greater than, less than, etc.). More specialized software may be provided for specific information retrieval problems, such as library cataloguing, indexing of technical literature and full text retrieval systems.

information separator An *indicator* which is used to separate *fields* or items of information within a *record*, particularly a *variable length record*.

information system A general term to denote all the operations and procedures involved in a *data processing* system.

information technology A portmanteau phrase to cover all aspects of the art or science of processing *data* to produce information.

information theory The theory concerned with the rate of information transmission over a communications network; related to the type of transmission channel employed. The theory was a result of the study of the ways of sending messages, particularly telephony, and relates to the least number of decisions necessary to identify any message in a given set of messages. ◊ *Probability Theory*.

information word A collection of *characters* representing information from a *store*, and handled by *hardware* or *software* as a complete unit. ◊ *word*.

inherent store A *store* forming part of the *hardware* of a computer system. Contrasted with *data carrier store*.

inherited error 1. An error in a result or intermediate result, attributed to some previous stage of processing. For example, in *single-step operation*, an error carried through from a previous step. 2. An error arising initially from the inability to measure values with sufficient *accuracy*.

inhibit To prevent a particular signal from occurring, or to prevent a particular operation from being performed.

inhibiting signal A signal which prevents an operation from being performed.

inhibit pulse A *pulse* applied to a *ferrite core* to oppose a corresponding *write pulse* and thus prevent the cell from assuming a set condition.

in-house software *Software* developed by a computer department for its own use, as contrasted with a software *package*, brought in from a software house or computer manufacturer.

initial condition Synonymous with *entry condition*.

initial condition mode Synonymous with *reset mode*.

initial instructions A *routine* stored within a computer to facilitate the *loading* of *programs*.

Also known as initial orders.

initialization A process performed at the beginning of a *program* or *subroutine* to ensure that all *indicators* and *constants* are set to prescribed conditions and values before the routine is obeyed.

initialize ⟡ *initialization*.

initial orders Synonymous with *initial instructions*.

initiate Synonymous with *trigger*.[2]

ink bleed The flow of ink by capillary action beyond the prescribed area of characters when characters are being printed for *optical character recognition*. Such action can prevent the character from being recognized when it is subsequently *read*.

ink jet printer A *printer* which uses a technique of projecting droplets of ink at paper to form the required image.

ink ribbon A continuous ribbon of ink, used, for example, when printing from a computer *line printer* or a *punched card tabulator*.

ink smudge The condition in which ink appears outside the prescribed area of a printed character. In *optical character recognition* this condition can prevent the character from being recognized during reading.

ink squeezeout The displacement of ink from the centre of a character when characters are printed for *optical character recognition*.

in-line coding A collection of *program instructions* written as part of the *main path* of a *routine*.

in-line processing Synonymous with *demand processing*.

in-line subroutine A *subroutine* the *coding* of which must be repeated each time it is required, in contrast to a subroutine which can be entered from the main *program* each time it is required.

in-plant Abbreviation of inside plant; a term used in *data transmission* to denote a communication system operating within a central office or factory. ⬦ *local area network*.

in-plant system Relating to a communications system for handling data automatically within a particular building or group of buildings, e.g., a factory. ⬦ *input station, local area network*.

input The process of transferring *data*, or *program instructions*, into *memory* from some *peripheral unit*. Sometimes used to denote the data itself, sometimes to denote the signal applied to a circuit or device.

Also used as a verb.

input area An area within *memory* reserved for data input from a *peripheral unit* or *backing store*. The data once received may be *edited* and distributed to *work areas* for processing.

Also known as input block.

input block Synonymous with *input area*.

input buffer ⬦ *input/output buffers*.

input devices Within the *central processor* of any computer, information can be processed at very high speeds, but before the central processor can be set to work, the data and *programs* must be entered into the computer *memory*. This is done by means of input devices which provide a vehicle for communication between the computer and the people who are concerned with its operation.

Some form of intermediate coding is required to bridge the gap between the language of human beings and the internal *machine code* language of the computer: human beings are able to recognize and understand the relationships between numerals, characters and symbols, whereas within the internal store of a computer the various electronic circuits are able to respond to patterns of electrical impulses. There are often various stages of translation between the original character representation used by human beings and the internal code of the computer, *punched cards* being an early example of an intermediate medium. Initially, during the course of a commercial procedure, a clerk might enter details of a transaction on to an original document (e.g., an order form). A copy of this form would be dispatched to the *data preparation* centre where an operator using an *automatic key-punch* would punch the information into a card in accordance with a standard punching code. This card might then be checked by a further operator using a *punched card verifier*, and in this way the initial stages were completed and an item of data was represented as holes punched into a card. The cards representing a particular series of transactions would eventually be *batched* together and input to the computer via a *card reader*, which would read the cards and translate the information into a series of coded impulses which could be transferred to the central processor and be stored in the computer memory. Card readers generally consisted of a *card hopper* into which the cards were initially loaded, and a card track which transported the cards past a *reading head*. The reading head was often a photo-electric sensing device which was able to detect the holes in each *card column* and generate appropriate coded signals. After a card had been read it was deposited in a *stacker*. (Some card readers had two or more stackers to permit cards to be outsorted according to whether they were read successfully or not.) The speed of card reading varies from one machine to another but an average would be in the region of 1000 cards per minute.

Paper tape was an input medium similar to punched cards and generally involved all the stages described above. First the data was punched into paper tape by means of a keyboard-operated tape punch, then it might be verified, and finally it was read into memory by a paper tape reader which might operate at about 1000 characters per second.

Paper tape readers and card readers were fairly reliable devices and were designed to input large batches of data, but although, as mechanical devices, it can be said that they operated at high speed, they nevertheless limited the operation of computer routines in which processing is carried out at electronic speeds.

They were largely replaced, therefore, by devices such as *key-to-disk units*, which allowed data to be written direct from data station keyboards to a magnetic medium without the need for the intermediate process of producing punched cards or paper tape, which are now little used.

There are various programming and systems techniques which can be used to mitigate the limitations of these input devices, including the use of *input buffers* which permit peripheral units to be operated continuously at high speed, and also the use of *time-sharing* techniques to enable the computer to perform other functions whilst waiting for input from a slow peripheral. With the development of *on-line* storage systems and *multiprogramming* a further range of input devices comes to the fore; these are devices which are permanently connected to the computer but which are situated at distant terminals to record transactions as they occur. Here it is not so much the speed of the device which counts, but the fact that the complete system is able to deal with the transactions as they arise, and it is then mainly a question of considering the economics of the number and type of input devices required in order to deal with the volume of transactions to be handled at each transaction point.

Another characteristic of these on-line input devices is that they frequently incorporate features to permit two-way communication; for example, *intelligent terminals* with *visual display units* can be connected via communications circuits to a computer. These connexions may be over long distances or may be part of an *in-plant* system. Here the operator may enter data directly into the system by typing on a keyboard and the computer may reply by causing a message to be printed directly at the inquiry terminal. One of the limiting factors here is that the operator may make mistakes in keying in the inquiry or data, and usually a comprehensive set of *validity checks* must be performed by the computer to detect such errors. Since such a system deals essentially with transactions as they arise errors are often detected immediately in the natural course of performing the transaction.

Where there is a danger that incorrect data may be input, much of the descriptive information relevant to any transaction can be input by means of some medium which allows certain elements of data to be prerecorded. For example, in some in-plant systems, operatives may be given magnetic cards in the form of plastic tickets which contain standard information such as job number, or employee number. Various simple card-reading devices can be located in the plant to record events that occur, and it is only necessary for the operative to insert the card and supply the variable data required for each transaction. The input devices will read this prerecorded data directly into the computer system and the operative can at the same time set up variable data by means of a keyboard, a dial, or a series of switches. Items such as date and time can often be generated automatically as each event is recorded.

Character recognition systems provide similar features; here it is often a question of prerecording data as characters on documents for *optical character recognition* or *magnetic ink character recognition*. These documents may be issued to be returned eventually to the system with the variable data added. For example, in electricity billing, documents may be printed with optical characters giving descriptive data for each customer. They are given to meter readers who add marks indicating details of electricity consumed since the last reading. The documents are eventually batched and an optical character reader is used to read

235

the information on the documents directly into the computer system. Bank cheques preprinted with magnetic-ink characters are a further example of this type of system. Although these character recognition systems do not provide a direct on-line input to the computer they do allow data to be captured more accurately, speedily and economically than other more conventional systems.

To return to on-line input/output systems, it is important to note that *visual display units* have many applications as input devices in *real time* systems. These units, which can be used for remote in-plant inquiry stations, usually have keyboards to enable transactions or inquiries to be input directly into the central computer, and have *cathode ray tube display* units to enable results to be presented to the inquirer.

Most of the input systems described above are designed to reduce the time required to get data into the computer for processing and to try to eliminate many of the stages necessary in more conventional systems. Graphic display units probably provide more potential than the other systems, and particularly noteworthy are the developments being made in the use of *light pens* (devices which enable data to be input into memory directly as drawings or graphs). The initial input of data is still a comparative limitation in most computing systems and it is to be expected that considerable efforts will be made to develop improved techniques.

input instruction code An *instruction set* forming part of some automatic input *language* designed to simplify the programmer's task in writing an *input routine*.

input limited Pertaining to a *program* in which the overall processing time is limited by the speed of an input unit; i.e., during the course of the program processing is delayed to await the input of further items for processing. ⟡ *output limited* and *processor limited*.

input loading The electrical load placed on units supplying a signal to the input of a device.

input log 1. A manual record prepared by an *operator* of all data input to a computer. 2. Within an *operating system* a *file* containing a record of all *messages* input to a system with the objective of allowing a *restart* to identify incompleted messages. ⟡ *log*².

input magazine Synonymous with *card hopper*.

input/output buffers Areas of *memory* assigned to receive data transmitted to or from a *peripheral unit*. The use of buffer areas enables a number of peripheral units to be activated simultaneously at full speed while data is processed within the *central processor*. On earlier machines, areas of storage were often allocated permanently for this purpose, but it is now usual to permit the programmer to specify the *locations* required according to the characteristics of his *program*.

input/output channel   A *communication channel* for transmitting data to and from a central computer.

input/output control   The *hardware/software* system which controls the interaction between a *central processor* and its *peripheral units*. Usually different modes of control are available according to the type of peripheral unit and the speed of transfer.

input/output control systems   *Software*, usually supplied by the computer manufacturer, designed to control the performance of *input* and *output operations*, including such activities as error checking, *record* batching, writing of *labels*, etc.

input/output devices   ◊ general articles on *Input Devices, Output Devices*.

input/output instruction   *Instructions* forming part of the repertoire or *instruction set* of a *programming language*, and designed to give the programmer control over the reception and transmission of data between a *central processor* (and thence *main memory*) of a computer and the various *peripheral units* which may be connected to a computer. An input/output instruction must usually specify these three entities: (i) Is the instruction concerned with reception or transmission of data? (ii) What memory locations in the computer are to receive or transmit the data? (iii) Through which *input/output ports* is the transfer to occur?

input/output interrupt   A break in processing during which a *central processor* may transmit or receive a unit of data to or from a *peripheral unit*. ◊ *interrupt*.

input/output interrupt identification   The act of ascertaining the cause of an *input/output interrupt*, including identifying the *channel*[1] and type of *peripheral unit* causing the interrupt, and the status of the peripheral unit.

input/output interrupt indicators   *Indicators* which are set when an *input/output interrupt* occurs.

input/output library   A collection of *programs* or *routines*, usually developed by computer manufacturers for users of their equipment. Part of a library of standard routines but denoting specifically those designed to control the operation of *peripheral units*. Such routines relieve the programmer of the task of writing standard routines common to a whole range of problems.

input/output limited   Pertaining to a *program* in which the overall processing time is governed by the speed of *input/output peripheral* units; i.e., processing is delayed from time to time during the program whilst data is transferred to or from the *central processor*. Contrasted with *processor limited*.

input/output ports   An access point for a computer through which data can be received from, or transferred to, an external *peripheral unit*. It incorporates connexion pins which are attached via a cable to the external device, and an *input/output buffer* in which data is stored. The buffer usually connects to the *data highway* or *bus* within the computer and thus offers a path between *main memory locations* or *registers* and an external device.

Input/output ports may allocate either serial or parallel paths of transmission to the external device. ◊ *parallel input/output* and *serial input/output*.

input/output processor   A device used to control input/output operations, concerned with the transfer of data to and from external *peripheral units* and the internal *data highway* of a computer. An input/output processor will normally contain its own processor, with its own set of executable *operation codes*. The purpose of such devices is to relieve the main *central processor* of the computer from the task of handling the input/output load. The input/output processor and the main processor may communicate through a *shared memory* system.

input/output, programmed   ◊ programmed input/output.

input/output referencing   A method by which specific *input* or *output devices* can be referenced by means of a symbolic name within a *program*, the actual device allocated to the program being determined at *run* time.

input/output routines   *Routines* specifically designed to simplify the *programming* of standard operations involving *input/output* equipment, e.g., the *blocking* of *records*, use of *input/output buffers*.

input/output switching   Relating to a technique in which *peripheral units* are allocated more than one *channel*[1] for communicating with a *central processor*. Thus if access to a peripheral is required the connexion may be made through any available channel, so that during the course of one *program* several channels may be used to service a particular peripheral.

input/output traffic control   This term is sometimes used to denote the *hardware/software* facilities which coordinate the activities of a *central processor* and its *peripheral units*. The function of this controlling feature is to permit the simultaneous operation of several *input/output devices* while data is being processed in the central processor.

input/output trunks   *Interface* channels between a *processor* and its *peripheral units.* The number of peripherals connected to a processor depends on the number of trunks available.

input/output unit   ◊ *input device, output device.*

input program   Synonymous with *input routine.*

input record   1. A *record* read into *memory* from an *input device* during a *run.* 2. The current record stored in an *input area* ready for processing.

input register   A *register* designed to accept data from a *peripheral unit* at relatively slow speed and to supply this data to the *central processor* at higher speed as a series of units.

input routine   That part of a *program* which controls and monitors the transfer of data from some external medium to an *input area* in *memory.*

input section   1. That section of a *program* which controls the *input* of data from external devices to *memory.* 2. The area of a *store* reserved for the receipt of input data.

input stacker   A *magazine* fitted to a *punched card* machine in which cards were placed prior to reading or punching. Note: the term *stacker* was also used in some cases to refer to the receptacle in which cards are automatically stacked after reading or punching.

input station   In an *in-plant* communications system input stations may be situated at various locations within a building to enable personnel to *input data* directly into the systems as *transactions* or events occur. This enables files to be immediately updated, and if necessary exception reports (◊ *exception principle system*) can be generated immediately for management.

input storage   An area of *memory* assigned to the task of holding *data* input from a *peripheral unit.*

Also known as *input area*, input block.

input unit   Any *peripheral unit* which provides input to the *central processor* of a computer, e.g., a terminal. ◊ general article on *Input Devices.*

input unit, manual   ◊ *manual input unit.*

inquiry and communications systems   Pertaining to computer systems in which central files are maintained from data input from various sources using *data transmission* equipment or *local area* networks. Inquiries may be *addressed* into the system from remote stations, immediately producing response from the central system.

inquiry and subscriber display   A *visual display unit* designed for operation as a remote *interrogation unit* for a *real time* data processing system. Capable of displaying information requested by the subscriber who keys in his inquiry on a *keyboard.*

239

inquiry display terminal A device which consists of a *keyboard* and a *cathode ray tube* display unit. Inquiries are specified to the computer by means of messages typed on the keyboard, and results are displayed on the cathode ray tube.

inquiry, remote ⬦ *remote inquiry, real time.*

inquiry station A terminal from which a *remote inquiry* may be transmitted to a central computing system.

inquiry unit Any device used to transmit an inquiry into a central computing system.

inscribe To rewrite data on a document in a form capable of being read by a *character recognition* device, e.g., the printing of the amount of a cheque in *magnetic ink* characters on the original cheque.

inside-plant ⬦ *in-plant system.*

installation 1. The installation of a computer including the preparation of the site and all services required; ⬦ general article on *Installation of Computers.* 2. A place where there is a computer.

installation of computers It would be wrong to consider the process of installing a computer as the installation of the equipment alone; more properly one should consider the development of all the resources necessary for the *data processing centre* as a whole, including the *hardware*, *software*, the buildings, air conditioning equipment, office furniture and specialized cabinets and furniture for storing and handling *input/output media*. The recruitment and training of new staff and the education of existing personnel must also be an integral part of any installation plan, and careful thought must be given to the timing of these activities. In this present article consideration is given mainly to those aspects referred to as the 'environment'.

If it is a *main frame* or *large minicomputer* the computer will be housed in an air-conditioned area which must include an engineer's room, and a room or area set aside for storing magnetic media – e.g., *magnetic tapes* and *magnetic disks*. Adjacent to the computer room there should be an area for *terminals work assembly*, an output dispatch area, and possibly further storage areas for non-magnetic materials such as stationery. There must be general office accommodation for computer operations staff and also for programmers, systems analysts, etc., but these latter need not be adjacent to the computer room.

The computer site plan should always be developed in consultation with the computer manufacturer's staff. It is most important to provide sufficient space and to site units in such a way that space is available to meet operating and servicing requirements. The floor of the computer room must be designed to bear the weight of the equipment, and generally a false floor is required to house cables and perhaps air conditioning ducts. The ceiling must be constructed to house air conditioning ducts and the height should permit a suitable air flow. The whole fabric of the computer room should be designed to minimize dust and to reduce the general noise level. The power requirements are important for the whole installation, and one of the first steps must be to test the main power supply to see if it meets the requirements specified for the equipment; for example a voltage regulator might be needed. Lighting within the computer room should be bright and evenly distributed.

The humidity and temperature of the computer room must be controlled strictly within limits laid down for the equipment. The air-conditioning plant installed for this purpose must also include an air-infiltration system to ensure that particles are removed from the air to a specified efficiency.

Computers are not potential fire risks in themselves, but there is a vital need to provide equipment for automatic fire detection, alarm systems and fire extinguishing equipment in the installation. Particular regard should be given to special furniture for the protection of magnetic recording media containing data files.

The cost of constructing these environmental conditions is often considerable, particularly where new structures have to be built to house the computer. It is therefore important to ensure that there is plenty of capacity for later expansion, not merely in terms of physical space required, but also in such expensive facilities as the air-conditioning plant.

The whole process of installation must be scheduled so that the various activities can be dovetailed to meet the final delivery date for the computer hardware, and to meet the various intermediate dates for the arrival of staff and ancilliary equipment.

installation processing control   A system for automatically scheduling the handling and processing of *jobs* within a computer installation in order to reduce time spent in setting up jobs and to deal automatically with job priorities.

installation tape number   A unique reference number given to a *reel* of *magnetic tape* to identify it. Differentiated from the tape manufacturer's reference number.

installation time   Time during which a computer is being installed, commissioned and tested before being handed over to a customer. ◊ general article on *Installation of Computers*.

instruction   That part of a computer *program* which tells the computer what function to perform at that *stage*. Instructions are usually examined by a special unit, sometimes known as a *program controller*, which interprets each instruction and initiates the actions specified. An instruction consists of a series of characters subdivided into groups which represent coded commands to the computer. An *operation* such as add or subtract may be specified, along with one or more *addresses* which specify the *locations* of operands to be used at that step; for a more detailed description of this, ◊ *Instruction Format*.

Also known as command, order. ◊ general article on *Programming*.

instruction, actual ◊ *effective instruction*.

instruction address The *address* of a *location* containing an *instruction*.

instruction address register A *register* which forms part of the *program controller*, and which stores the *addresses* of *instructions* in order to control the retrieval of the instructions from *memory* during the operation of a program.

instruction area The area of *memory* used to store *program instructions*.

instruction, arithmetic ◊ *arithmetical instructions*.

instruction classification Most computers can perform a wide range of *instructions* and these are defined by the processor used. The instructions can generally be classed as belonging to one of five major groups as follows: (i) *Data transfer instructions*: These are concerned with operations which entail the movement of data between *registers* in the processor, and between registers and *main memory locations*. (ii) *Data Manipulation Instructions*: These instructions result in the data contained in locations being altered, by arithmetic or logical processes. For example, ADD A, B creates a sum of the operands in registers A and B. A logical operation such as an *exclusive – or operation* falls within this classification but may sometimes be referred to by the sub-classification logic instruction or logical instruction. (iii) *Transfer of Control Instructions*: Any one of the instructions which causes an *unconditional* or *conditional branch* to take place in a program, e.g., a *branch*, *jump*, *call*, or *return* instruction. (iv) *Input/Output Instructions*: These result in the transfer of data between external *peripheral units* and registers or main memory locations within the computer. Such instructions cause data to be passed via the *input/output ports*, e.g., OUT 03 causes the contents of the A register to be transferred to a peripheral unit attached to Input/Output port 3. (v) *Machine Control Instructions*: These instructions affect the operation of the processor itself and include, for example, instructions concerned with enabling and disabling *interrupts* and resolving priorities.

instruction code   The set of symbols and characters forming the rules of a particular computer code or *programming language*.

Also known as order code, *machine code, instruction set, function code, operation code*.

instruction, conditional branch   ◇ *conditional branch*.

instruction, conditional stop   ◇ *conditional stop instruction*.

instruction, control transfer   Synonymous with *branch instruction*.

instruction counter   A device that indicates the *location* of the next *instruction* to be obeyed in a *program*. Usually part of, or associated with, the *program controller*.

instruction cycle   The complete sequence of events concerned with the *execution* of a single step in a computer *program* and usually entailing two major sequences: *instruction fetch*, which is concerned with the reading of an instruction from memory into the central processor where it is interpreted; and *instruction execute*, which entails the completion of the operations defined within the instruction itself.

instruction decoder   That part of a *central processor* which interprets the meaning of each *program instruction* and prepares the central processor to *execute* the instructions. The action of decoding or interpreting an instruction takes place on the *instruction fetch* cycle and the implied actions are performed on the *instruction execute* cycle.

instruction, discrimination   Synonymous with *branch instruction*.

instruction, dummy   Synonymous with *do nothing instruction*.

instruction execute   The cycle of events which cause the *central processor* to carry out the specific events indicated in an *instruction statement*. ◇ *instruction fetch*.

instruction execution time   The overall time taken to *fetch* and *execute* a specific *instruction* (usually measured in microseconds). The time taken depends on the specific activities defined in the instruction and the method of addressing used.

Also known as instruction time.

instruction fetch   In most digital computers, a single instruction is performed as two distinct cycles. First, the instruction is retrieved from *main memory* and stored in an *instruction register* and the contents of the register are examined automatically to set up the *central processor* to execute the instruction. Next, the instruction is *executed* as a sequence of events involving the memory *locations* and *registers* nominated in the instruction itself and in accordance with the operation code specified. These are known as fetch and execute cycles, and the first is an instruction fetch. After the second, a new instruction is performed.

instruction format Different types of *program instruction* may be prepared in different formats. To illustrate the term, a *word oriented* machine will be considered first. An instruction is usually required to fit within the basic *word-length* of the computer, allowing instructions to be processed as individual units. An instruction consists of a series of digits subdivided into groups, each group having a certain functional significance within the *machine code* system of the particular computer, and the way in which the various digits are allocated to represent specific functions is referred to as the instruction format. As a minimum an instruction must contain digits to represent the *function* to be performed, and two other groups to represent the *addresses* of *operands*. Thus for example, a machine having a word-length of 24 *binary digits* might have an instruction format as follows:

4 bits	10 bits	10 bits
Function Code	Operand 1	Operand 2

This simple example would only allow up to 16 unique *bit* combinations to represent different function codes (e.g., *add*, *subtract*, *logical shift*, etc.) and would permit operations capable of addressing operands stored in *memory locations* up to word number 1023 only.

This type of system is referred to as a two-address format, and the implication is that the result of any *arithmetic operation* will always replace one of the original operands. To avoid this a three-address format could have been adopted by specifying a third location address to be used for the result, but in general this practice is not adopted since it requires the machine to have a long basic word-length. As an alternative, a format known as the one-and-a-half address format is often adopted. In this situation one of the operands must always be moved to one of a series of special *registers* before being subject to any arithmetic process, thus the program instruction specifies a function code, a memory address for one operand and a register address for the other operand. The result is usually formed in the specified register. Thus the registers are used as *work areas* and are not required to store any particular operand for more than a few program steps, and the original operands are retained in memory if required. As only 8 or 12 registers may be required, a few digits only are needed to represent the register address in the instruction format. Some instruction formats also enable the programmer to specify an *index word* which may contain a *modifier* for the memory address specified in the instruction. On a computer with this facility the technique of *program modification* is much simplified from the programmer's point of view, and also the machine code system can address memory locations far in excess of the maximum number given by the operand field of the instruction (◇ *indirect addressing*).

A sample of an instruction format incorporating the features mentioned is given below:

7 bits	3 bits	12 bits	2 bits
Function code	Register	Operand	Index register
Can specify any of over 120 separate functions	Can address any one of 8 registers	Can address locations up to word 4095	Can address one of three index registers for indirect addressing

Another format is the four-address instruction in which the programmer is able to specify two operand addresses, the address of the result and the address of the next instruction to be performed.

So far only word machines have been mentioned, but the same principles apply to *character oriented* machines, except that groups of characters are used to represent functional elements rather than binary digits as in the example above. One of the features of character machines is the ability to specify *variable length* operands; for example, it is possible to specify an operand of one character only, or any number of characters up to the full size of the memory unit. The usual practice in the character machine is to specify the address of the first and last character locations of the required operand, or else the address of the first location and the number of characters in the operand.

Some instructions perform operations upon one operand and these will specify one address only. However, it is often necessary to include additional information in the instruction format; for example, a *shift instruction* requires an indication of the number of places to be shifted, a *conditional branch instruction* may require an indication of the tests to be applied to an operand. A brief study of the *instruction set* of any particular machine will reveal other examples.

To summarize: the instruction format is part of the basic machine code of the computer, and it specifies the way in which the digits or characters are allocated to represent the functional codes of the computer's instruction set.

instruction format, one-plus-one ⬦ *one-plus-one address.*

instruction format, zero address ⬦ *zero address instruction format.*

instruction, machine code ⬦ *machine code.*

instruction mix Pertaining to the composition of a specific set of *instructions* in a given *routine* or *program*. The mix of instructions may be chosen to achieve an objective, such as a test of the efficiency of a computer or microprocessor in handling problems of a given type.

instruction modification Changing the value of some parts of an *instruction*, so that the next time the modified instruction is obeyed it will perform a different *operation*. Since an instruction is held within the computer as a set of digits, *modification* is performed by treating the instruction as though it were an item of *data* and performing an appropriate *arithmetic* or *logical operation* on it. ⬦ *address modification* and general articles on *Programming* and *Program Modification.*

instruction, multiple address ⬦ *multiple address.*

instruction, no-op ⬦ *no-operation instruction.*

instruction, null Synonymous with *do nothing instruction.*

instruction register A control unit register in which the address of the current instruction is stored. Any data in an instruction register is always treated as an instruction.

Also known as *control register* and program address counter.

instruction repertoire Synonymous with *instruction set.*

instruction set The repertoire of commands available as the *language* of a particular computer or *programming* system.

Also known as *instruction code*, *machine code* and *order code.*

instruction statement A single line in a *source program* which forms a step in a computer program and defines the operation to be performed at that step and the items of data and/or *memory addresses* to be affected by the operation.

instruction, table look-up ⬦ *table look-up instruction.*

instruction time The time taken to *staticize* an *instruction* within the *instruction registers* of a computer, plus the time required to execute the instruction.

instruction, unconditional branch ⬦ *unconditional branch instruction.*

instruction, unconditional control transfer   Synonymous with *unconditional branch instruction*.

instruction, unconditional jump   Synonymous with *unconditional branch instruction*.

instruction, waste   Synonymous with *do nothing instruction*.

instruction word   A computer *word* containing an *instruction*. An *instruction format* is usually designed to fit within the basic *word length* of a computer. Thus instructions may be moved and manipulated like any other items of data stored in *memory*.

integer   A whole number, i.e., one that does not contain a fractional component.

integral   Pertaining to that part of a *mixed number* which is to the left of the decimal point.

integrated circuit   A circuit in which all the components are chemically formed upon a single piece of semiconductor material. Computers using integrated circuits are said to be *third generation*, as contrasted with *first generation* machines using thermionic valves and *second generation* machines using transistors. Fourth generation machines use VLSI, *very large scale integration*.

integrated data processing   A concept which implies that all systems within an organization are considered as sub-systems of a larger system which embraces all *data processing* requirements within that organization. In this way the systems are dovetailed to achieve, as far as possible, continuous and automatic processing with the elimination of unnecessary duplications, particularly seeking to reduce the number of entry points for *raw data*.

integrated management information system   ⬦ *management information system*.

integrator   1. ⬦ *integrator (computing unit)*. 2. Synonymous with *digital integrator*. 3. A person or organization performing the function of arranging text, images, indexes and retrieval software for optical storage devices such as *CD Rom*.

integrator (computing unit)   1. A device which has two *input* variables (x and y) and one *output* variable (z), the value of z being proportional to the integral of y with respect to x. 2. A device with one input and one output variable, the value of the output variable being proportional to the integral of the input variable with respect to elapsed time.

integrity   An attribute of a set of *data* signifying that the data is self-consistent (e.g., a *hash total* check has proved *valid*) and consistent with the information system the data is representing (e.g., a *validity check* has proved valid).

intelligence The ability of a system or device to improve its capability by repeated performance of a particular problem.

intelligence, artificial ◊ *artificial intelligence*.

intelligent controller A device which acts as a *node* in a communication sub-system, and has the function of controlling a group of *terminals* and providing an interface between them and a central computer or a *network*. The intelligent controller may also provide the terminals with logical processing capability to carry out tasks such as *editing*, *input validation*, and *point-of-sale* processing.

intelligent copier A photo-copier with computing capability, allowing the selection of page size, type size, type styles, etc.

intelligent knowledge-based system A *knowledge-based system* with elements of *artificial intelligence* which allow it to learn from reaction to its own responses, and thus build up an increasing *data base* of knowledge.

intelligent terminal A *terminal* which within its *hardware* contains logic circuits capable of retaining a *program* enabling the terminal to undertake some *processing* of data independently of the *processor* to which the terminal is connected.

intelligent work station A development of the *intelligent terminal*, in which a user is equipped with a variety of methods for addressing the terminal including *keyboard*, *light pen*, *graphics tablet*, or *touch sensitive screen*. Such a work station would also contain extensive processing facilities and may be capable of displaying and manipulating data, text, graphical information, voice, and photographic images. It may also be equipped with communication facilities to interface to a number of different networks or host computers.

interactive batch job A *background job* run under an *operating system* in *batch mode*, which is initiated and monitored from a *terminal*.

interactive debugger A *software* system built into a computing system in order to identify logical errors (*bugs*) in *programs*, and to provide facilities for the correction of them. This software can be used while programs are being operated to provide information concerning processes as they occur. An interactive debugger may include *commands* to display contents of *memory* and *index registers*, and to insert values into *locations*, and cause *routines* to be executed while displaying relevant data to assist in fault diagnosis.

interactive display Any *display* which allows the user to *input* data in response to the information displayed.

interactive mode Synonymous with *conversational mode*.

interactive system Any computer system in which the user is directly connected to a central computer in such a way that *transactions* are performed directly in response to the *commands* made by the user. The success, or otherwise, of the transaction sequence is immediately evident by the way in which the computer system responds and each complete entry by the user results in a reply culminating in a clean termination of the transaction sequence.

interblock A *hardware* device or *software* feature which will prevent interference between one part of a computing system and another. For example; in *multiprogramming*, to prevent one *program* from violating the *memory* area allocated to another.

interblock gap The distance between *blocks* of *records* on *magnetic tape*. The gap is originally created during the period in which the tape is slowing down at the end of a *write* operation. During subsequent passes of the *reel* during *reading* from the tape, the tape may be stopped and accelerated to full speed in this distance. Two gap lengths commonly in use are 0.75 inches and 0.56 inches.

Also known as interblock space.

interblock space Synonymous with *interblock gap*.

intercepting channel A *communications channel* specifically used to pick up calls which would otherwise fail to bring about a connexion. For example, when a subscriber number is changed, calls to the old number may be automatically switched to an operator.

interchangeable type bar Relating to a certain type of *punched card tabulator* in which special *type bars* could be exchanged by the operator to permit the printing of *special characters* or *symbols* for any particular job.

intercomputer communication With the growth of computing in organizations, it has become a common practice to employ several *host computers* in a single enterprise. Often the different hosts are dedicated to specific *applications* and *terminal* users are routed to specific hosts over a *network* according to the services selected by them. There is sometimes, however, a need to transfer information between computers in order to maintain updated records at different points in the *distributed network*, or sometimes to take copies of information from one location to another to provide for *file security*. High speed networks may be provided for this purpose, so that large volumes of data can be transferred at short intervals. Sometimes public data networks are used for the purpose, but also *broadband local area networks* are used.

intercycle A cycle of operation, on a *punched card tabulator*, in which card feeding was suspended and *control totals* were created and printed.

interface This term is used to refer to the *channels* and associated control circuitry providing the connexion between a *central processor* and its *peripheral units*. It may be used more generally to refer to the connexion between any two units. ⟡ *standard interface*.

interface channel ⟡ *interface*.

interface methods Interfaces may be considered in distinct categories, which can be observed in the designs made for computers or electronic machines such as those used in telecommunications or office automation. Communication often takes place with one device placing information on to a communications channel, or on the internal *data highway* of a computer, for reception by another device. Three methods are encountered, as follows: (i) *Master/slave interface*: in this category, one device has control over one or more devices, which may require to transmit or receive information from the controlling or master device. Transmission is controlled entirely by the master device which detects when slave units are in a condition to send or receive, and issues *instructions* to them individually to involve transfers at a time which is convenient to the master device. This may be controlled by a program in the master system which is running in the central processor. (ii) *Direct memory access*: some computer systems are designed to allow external *peripheral units* to place data directly on to the internal bus of the computer without requiring the attention of the processor. The DMA device is really a substitute for the processor for handling input/output operations. It in effect loads data directly onto the *highway* so that the data can pass efficiently between *main memory* and the peripheral devices. It does not require the action to be controlled by a program running in the main processor, but does momentarily suppress the action of the processor so that the data highway can be controlled by the DMA device. (iii) *Interrupt interface*: with this method an external device sends a signal to the main device, to request an interruption of the processor so that a special program can be called to handle data transfers. The processor has to suspend its current action and temporarily store the contents of its *registers* to deal with the interrupt program. ⟡ *interrupt input/output*.

interface routines Linking *routines* between one system and another.

interface specification A written definition of the way in which two units, or two *software programs*, are to work in conjunction with one another. The purpose of the specification is to provide a clear understanding between two people on two development teams so that development work may continue more or less independently on the separate units, while minimizing the risk of creating incompatible elements. The specification will normally consider the electrical and mechanical connexions between hardware devices as well as the objectives and underlying logical concepts of any software.

interface standards In order that computer products made by different manufacturers may work together, standards authorities in different countries have produced recommended methods of interconnexion which cover mechanical, electrical, and functional characteristics required in the *interface* between devices. For example, a common interface standard for communication between a computer and its *peripheral units* is one known as RS-232-C which is published by the EIA (Electronic Industries Association, Washington DC, USA). This standard embraces certain other standards produced by other organizations including: (i) A function for passing data in *serial* form between a computer and a *modem* as published by CCITT under their recommendation known as V24. (ii) Another associated CCITT standard known as V28, which recommends the electrical characteristics of these signals. (iii) A standard for mechanical connexions as published by *ISO* in standard 2110 for a plug known as a D type.

In short, RS-232-C defines a standard for passing data between two devices in serial form, including the timing pulses and control signals required through a standard plug connexion in which the significance of each pin is defined.

interference The presence of unwanted signals in a communications circuit.

interfix A method used in *information retrieval* systems to describe the relation between *key words* in *records*, in such a way that inquiries are satisfied without ambiguity.

interior label A *label* written to the beginning of a *magnetic tape* in order to identify its contents. Contrasted with *exterior label*, which refers to a written or typed identifying label placed on the outside of a *reel* of magnetic tape.

interlace A method of assigning *addresses* to memory *locations* so that locations in separated physical positions can be *accessed* with reduced average *access time*.

interleaved carbon set A *stationery* set, used for printing results from a computer, in which additional copies of the *output* are obtained by means of carbon sheets interleaved among the stationery.

interleaving A technique sometimes used in *multiprogramming*, in which *segments* of one *program* are inserted in another program to allow the effective execution of both programs simultaneously.

interlude A *routine* or *program* designed to perform minor preliminary operations, usually of a *housekeeping* type, before the main routine is entered. The area occupied by the interlude may be *overwritten* after it has performed its operations.

intermediate control   A level of control established when *intermediate totals* were produced on a *punched card tabulator* (as distinct from major totals and minor totals).   ⋄ *comparing control change*.

intermediate control change   A change in the value of an *intermediate control* initiating some predetermined action.

intermediate control data   ⋄ *control data*.

intermediate result   The *result* of an *operation* obtained in the course of a *program* or *subroutine* which is itself used again as an *operand* in further operation before the *final result* is obtained.

intermediate storage   A medium of *store* used for holding working figures or for storing totals temporarily until required.

   Also known as *work area*.

intermediate total   A total produced at an *intermediate control change*, i.e., resulting from a change of control data at neither the most nor the least significant level.

internally stored program   A *routine* stored within a computer *memory* rather than on a *backing store* or some other external medium.

internal memory   Synonymous with *internal store*.

internal store   A term used generally as a synonym for *immediate access store*; specifically a store forming part of the *main memory* of a computer as distinct from a *backing store*.

internal timer   An electronic *timer* which provides the facility of monitoring or logging events at predetermined intervals.

international algebraic language   An early form of the language which developed into *A L G O L*.

interpolator   Synonymous with *collator*.

interpret   To print information by means of a *punched card interpreter* on to a *punched card* from the *code* punched in the card.

interpreter   1. ⋄ *punched card interpreter*. 2. Synonymous with *interpretive routine*.

interpreter, punched card   ⋄ *punched card interpreter*.

interpreter, transfer   ⋄ *transfer interpreter* and *punched card interpreter*.

interpretive code   A form of *pseudocode* for use with an *interpretive routine*.

interpretive programming   The writing of *programs* in a *source language* which is subsequently *executed* by means of an *interpretive routine*.

interpretive routine A *routine* which translates *pseudocode instructions* into *machine code instructions* during the live operation of the routine; i.e., the pseudo-instructions are translated by sub-routines into machine code instructions which are immediately used to process data.

interpretive trace program A *trace program* which is also an *interpretive program*, i.e., translates each *symbolic instruction* into its equivalent *machine code* before executing it and recording its result.

interrecord gap The distance between *records* on a *magnetic tape*, where records have been written singly as *blocks*. In such a case, synonymous with *interblock gap*.

interrogating typewriter A typewriter connected to a *central processor* for the purpose of communicating with a *program* in *main memory*; e.g., capable of inserting data into the program or of receiving output from the program. Contrasted with *console typewriter*.

interrupt A break in a *program* or *routine* caused by an external source, which requires that control should pass temporarily to another routine; e.g., to monitor an *event* which may be proceeding in parallel to take action as a direct result of an event which has taken place. The interrupt is made so that the original routine can be resumed from the point at which the break occurred.

interrupt address vector An *address* associated with a specific *interrupt* request, and being the address of the first *instruction* in a *program* or *subroutine* which is to be executed as a consequence of the interrupt. In most minicomputers or general purpose computers, the techniques for associating the interrupt with a required address vector are dynamic, whereas many microcomputers have simpler procedures in which a fixed address is associated with each interrupt, leading therefore to the execution of a very specific procedure.

interrupt event An *event*[1] which causes immediate entry into a predetermined *procedure*.

interrupt handling Most digital computers have the ability to recognize several external requests from devices which need attention or service. These devices request attention by sending an *interrupt* signal to the *central processor*. Where several such requests may occur simultaneously, a computer must be equipped with the necessary logic to enable the processor to allocate and resolve priorities. It is sometimes possible to allocate priorities to the different devices, and once a high priority device has initiated an interrupt procedure other interrupts are not recognized until higher priority interrupts have been acknowledged and dealt with. Devices requiring attention will normally contrive to request attention until their interrupt request is acknowledged and serviced. ⟡ *interrupt input/output, interrupt address vector, interrupt service routine* and *interrupt priority levels*.

interrupt input/output A method of organizing and controlling the transfer of data between a central computer and its *peripheral units*, in which control signals from external devices signify that the devices require attention. It is usually arranged that the *central processor* is diverted from its current task to service the particular device requesting an interrupt. ⟡ *interrupt priority*.

interruption ⟡ *interrupt*.

interrupt mask A method of ignoring an *interrupt* when it occurs and postponing action required until some later point in time.

interrupt mode Synonymous with *hold mode*.

interrupt priority levels In dealing with *interrupts*, it is necessary to allocate priorities according to the significance of the events which may give rise to the interrupts. The highest priority is usually reserved for dealing with serious conditions which require immediate attention (e.g., an alarm/emergency condition signified by an external device). Interrupts will be initiated as they arise in accordance with the established priority, but a low priority interrupt may be suspended to allow a higher priority interrupt to be initiated. Priority levels are assigned by the programmer.

interrupt service routine A *program* which is *executed* when an *interrupt* occurs; the purpose of this program is to preserve (and later restore) the contents and status of *registers*, so that an interrupted program can be resumed after the interrupt request has been handled.

interrupt signal The *signal* which is generated in order to cause an *interrupt* to occur.

interrupt trap A *switch*[1] under *program* control which prevents or allows a corresponding *interrupt* according to its setting.

intersection Synonymous with *and operation*.

interstage punching Punching which took place between the normal *punching positions* on a *punched card*. Used in a punched card system in which each *card column* contained the equivalent of two columns of information. The equipment processing such cards *sensed* in the normal stages and the interstage positions of each column, and treated these positions as separate columns; thus, an 80-column card would contain 160 columns of information.

intersystem communications The ability of two or more computer systems to share *peripheral units* and to intercommunicate by means of common *input* and *output channels* or by direct linking of *central processors*.

inventory control   In most industries it is the practice to hold stocks to meet demands, for there are few occasions where demand and supply are matched closely enough to make this unnecessary. Even when stocks are held, temporary shortages are often experienced, due perhaps to a sudden rise in demand or delay in production.

The theory of inventory control, or 'stock control' as it is often called, is applicable to all types of stockholding and aims to strike a balance between costs of turnover, shortages, stockholding and administration. The earliest developments in this field were shortly after the 1914–18 war, and in the 1950s this was expanded into a powerful science. General commercial use of the computer means that stocks, shortages, etc., can be recorded accurately and many savings thereby obtained. Although many systems using a computer are operational, providing a variety of output including orders, invoices and shortage reports, most of them which use cost-optimal control rules have the control levels fed in as data rather than being computed by the machine.

There are four main costs associated with an inventory control system: (i) the value of stock turnover; (ii) the cost of shortages; (iii) the cost of stockholding; (iv) the cost of operating the system.

The value of stock throughput is the total value of material received by a stores system. Although the control of stock throughput can be achieved to some extent by pricing and quality decisions, it is not readily controlled by an inventory control system which regards throughput as dependent on needs which arise from outside the system.

The cost of shortages is often difficult to estimate, since it involves such intangibles as loss of future sales, etc. Often the approach used is to opt for a particular service level which is decided as a matter of policy, often based on forecast costs of maintaining that level.

The cost of stockholding is the cost of storage space plus the cost of tied-up capital, and can also include the cost of deterioration and scrapping. Stockholding affects shortages directly; the more stock held, the fewer the shortages.

The operating costs of the system cover the cost of ordering and receiving material and keeping records, and exclude the cost of shortages and stockholding.

The role of an inventory control system is to measure the effect of reprovisioning decisions in terms of physical effects (number of shortages, volume of stock) and to translate this into cost effects. By suitably manipulating the provisioning *model* to give lower total costs the optimum provisioning policy can be obtained. There have been two main streams of approach here. The first concentrates on a study of mathematical methods of optimizing total system costs, while the second studies methods of predicting demand (⬦ *forecasting*). The full inventory control system should aim to forecast demand and from this forecast calculate those quantities which will give best results in terms of total costs. Such calculations would include optimum order quantities, buffer stocks, etc., relevant to service levels and stock holdings.

inversion 1. The process of creating an *inverted file* from a *file* organized in some different way. 2. Synonymous with *negation*.

inverted file A form of *file organization* in which each separate characteristic which may apply to a particular item has attached to it an identifying *key* indicating each item having that characteristic. For example, if one of the characteristics in a personnel record file is 'salary in the range £9000–£9250' this item would be followed by the identifying key of all personnel having this characteristic. Inverted files are used mainly for *information retrieval*.

inverter A *logic element* having one *binary* input signal and performing the logical function of *negation*.

inverting amplifier Synonymous with *sign-reversing amplifier*.

invigilator A device which checks the performance of a *control unit* and generates a signal if the response to control action does not conform to specified limits.

invisible failure A *failure* of either *hardware* or *software* which has no noticeable effect on the operation of a system.

I/O Abbreviation of *input/output*, as in I/O routine.

IPOT Acronym of *Inductive POTential divider*.

irreversible magnetic process A change of magnetic flux within a magnetic material which persists after the magnetic field causing the change has been removed. Contrasted with *reversible magnetic process*.

irreversible process Synonymous with *irreversible magnetic process*.

ISAM Acronym for *Index Sequential Access Method*.

ISO Abbreviation of International Standards Organization.

isolated locations *Locations* of *store* which are protected by some *hardware* device which prevents them from being *addressed* by the user's *program* and safeguards their contents from accidental mutilation.

ISO reference model ⬦ *seven layer reference model*.

isosynchronous serial input/output A form of *serial transmission* in which data is transferred in *asynchronous character* format, including start/stop *bits*, but as part of a synchronous data stream bounded by *sync characters*.

IT Abbreviation of *information technology*.

item advance A method for operating successively upon a group of items in *memory*.

item design The designing of a *record* or *file* in order to achieve efficient processing or efficient *input/output* operations. For example, the *packing* of several items into one *word* may significantly reduce the overall time for a *program* by reducing the input/output time, but this might be offset by the need to unpack the items into individual words for internal processing. Similar considerations may apply when items are stored in, say, *character* or *binary* form.

item of data Any data treated as a unit within a program or process, e.g., a single *operand* or an entry in a *table*.

item size The number of *characters* or *digits* in an *item of data*.

iteration A single cycle of operations from an *iterative routine*. Iterative methods of obtaining approximate solutions to various types of equation are most suitable for use by digital computer. If an iterative process can be set up, the computer, by virtue of its ability to perform simple calculations quickly, can produce an answer of any desired accuracy. The prerequisites for an iterative process are: (i) a starting point or a guess. (ii) an iterative step.

Suppose, for instance, we want to find the square root of a number, then if we take as our starting point the integer which gives the nearest answer, and define our iterative process to be:

$$x_n = \frac{x^2_{n-1} + a}{2x_{n-1}},$$

where a is the number whose square root is required, we will successively get better and better answers (i.e., we will produce a series of numbers which converge to $\sqrt{a}$. Take for instance the square root of 2.

If we start with $x_1 = 1$ we get:

$$x_2 = 1.5$$
$$x_3 = 1.417$$
$$x_4 = 1.414$$

So that with only three steps we have reached a very good approximation. Of course we need not have started as close to the answer as 1. Suppose we had started with $x_1 = 50$, then we would get:

$$x_2 = 50$$
$$x_3 = 25.02$$
$$x_4 = 12.54$$
$$x_5 = 6.36$$
$$x_6 = 3.34$$
$$x_7 = 1.97$$
$$x_8 = 1.499$$
$$x_9 = 1.418$$
$$x_{10} = 1.414$$

As we might have expected then, the better guess one takes as a starting point the less steps one has to make. Usually a compromise has to be made between making a good guess and having a large number of steps. If we wanted to find the square root of a number which we knew lay between 0 and 10,000 we might well take 50 as a starting point rather than search for a closer one.

The iterative process may be continued until any desired accuracy is reached. In terms of a *program* this merely requires the insertion of a test routine to test how much more accurate each step is making the solution. If the value of our *x* changes only by one part in 1000 at a particular step, then our solution will be within at least one part in 100 of the exact solution.

A very simple iterative process has been cited here: there are many extremely useful and sometimes sophisticated iterative processes for solving various types of equation. The example was, in fact, an application of Newton's Method, which may be applied to many types of equation.

It would be wrong to suggest that all equations can be solved by iterative methods. Where such methods can be used, however, the digital computer proves invaluable in removing the tedium of repetitive calculation.

iterative process A process for calculating a result by performing a series of steps repeatedly, and in which successive approximations are made until the desired result is obtained. ⋄ *Iteration*.

iterative routine A *program* which achieves a result by repeatedly performing a series of operations until some specified condition is obtained. ⋄ *Iteration*.

jack A connecting device used for terminating the wiring of a circuit, to which access is obtained by inserting a *plug*. Otherwise known as *socket*, or, in *punched card* machines, *hub*.[2]

jack panel Synonymous with *plugboard*.

jam A machine fault which prevents *punched cards* from feeding through a machine and causes a piling up of cards on the *card track*.

Also known as wreck.

JCL Abbreviation of *job control language*.

jitter Instability of a signal for a brief period; applied particularly to signals on a *cathode ray tube*.

job A unit of work for a computer, usually consisting of several *runs*.

job control language A *language* associated with an *operating system* which enables the user to express to the system the requirements for the control of the *jobs* within the system. ⇨ *job control program*, *control language*.

job control program A *program* which accepts *statements* written in a *job control language* and interprets these into *instructions* that control the course of a *job* in an *operating system*, e.g., *programs* to be *run*, *files* to be *loaded*.

job control, stacked ⇨ *sequential-stacked job control*.

job flow control Control over the sequence of *jobs* being *processed* on a computer, in order to maximize the efficient use of *peripheral units* and *central processor* time. Job flow control may be performed manually, e.g., by a work controller, or by means of an *operating system*.

job oriented terminal A data terminal designed to allow data to be transmitted to a computer directly from the data source, e.g., a cash register designed to collect data on a *cassette* tape which can be fed directly to a computer.

job restart ⇨ *restart*.

job stream A group of *jobs* run consecutively in a processing system, generally under the control of a *scheduling* system.

joggle Before a *pack* of *punched cards* was placed in a *hopper* the cards had to be aligned to help trouble-free feeding. The agitating of the cards was called joggling.

join   Synonymous with *inclusive-or operation*.

joint denial   Synonymous with *nor operation*.

JOVIAL   A *programming language* based on *IAL*.

journal   A *file* containing *messages* within an *operating system* so that information is available both for *restarts* and for historical analysis of the functioning of the system.

Josephson junction   A device which can act as a fast switch with low power dissipation, based on a junction between two metals, which, at *cryogenic* temperatures, exhibits elective tunnelling and superconductivity.

joystick   Synonymous with *paddle*.

jump   Synonymous with *branch*.

jump, conditional   Synonymous with *conditional branch*.

jumper   A length of electrical conductor used temporarily to complete a circuit or to bypass an existing circuit.

jump instruction   Synonymous with *branch instruction*.

jump, unconditional   Synonymous with *unconditional branch instruction*.

justification   ⟡ *justify*.

justify   1. To adjust the positions of words arranged for printing so that either left-hand or right-hand margins or both are regular. 2. By extension of 1, to shift an item in a *register* so that the most or least significant digit is at the corresponding end of the register.

K

k An abbreviation for *kilo*, used to denote a thousand. Also commonly used to denote 1024 or 2^{10}, so that a 4k *byte memory* contains 4096 bytes of storage.

KCS An abbreviation standing for a thousand *characters* per second.

kernel 1. In a *virtual machine* a set of *procedures* controlling real *resources*. ⊗ *graphics kernel system*. 2. The message handling facility of a control system.

key 1. A digit or digits used to locate or identify a *record*, but not necessarily attached to the record. ⊗ *argument*, *subscript*. 2. A marked lever or button on a *keyboard* depressed manually and used for entering a *character*.

keyboard A device for encoding *characters* by the depression of *keys*.[2] This causes the selected code to be generated by, for example, the punching of holes in a *punched card*.

keyboard computer A computer which received *input* directly (and only) from a *keyboard*.

keyboard entry and inquiry The use by an operator of a *keyboard* to provide a computer with information and to establish what is stored in any specified *location*.

keyboard lockout An interlock on a *keyboard* on a *data transmission* circuit which prevents data from being transmitted while the transmitter of another station on the same circuit is in operation.

keyboard punch Synonymous with *key punch*.

key change When a *file* of *records* which have been *sorted* into a sequence defined by *keys* is being read, e.g., by a *report program*, a key change occurs when an *input record* has a key different from its immediate predecessor. ⊗ *control break*.

key-driven Pertaining to devices which require operators to depress a *key*[2] in order to translate a character into a form which a machine can recognize; e.g., a *terminal*.

keying-error rate The ratio of incorrectly keyed signals to the total number of signals keyed. The term is usually (but not necessarily) used in a *data transmission* context.

key, load ◊ *load key*.

keypad A form of *keyboard*, usually free-standing rather than attached to a *terminal*, with a reduced *character set*, often restricted to numerals and *function keys*.

key punch A *keyboard*-operated machine used for punching data manually into *punched cards* or *paper tape*. ◊ *card punch, tape punch*.

key-to-disk unit A *data preparation* device which allows data to be written direct from a punch station keyboard to a *magnetic disk*.

key verify To use a *punched card verifier*. ◊ *card verifying*.

keyword In *information retrieval* systems, the significant word in a phrase: used for the significant word in a title which describes a document. For example, in the title 'The Practice of Philately' the word 'philately' is the keyword, the other three having no significance on their own. ◊ *full text retrieval*.

KHz Abbreviation of kilohertz. ◊ Hertz.

kilo A prefix signifying one thousand.

kilobaud A measure of *data transmission* speed; a thousand *bits* per second.

kilocycle A thousand cycles, especially a thousand cycles a second (◊ *megacycle, gigacycle* and *teracycle*).

kilomega A prefix with a significance of 10^9. Synonymous with *billi* and *giga*.

kilomegacycle 10^9 cycles per second.

Also known as gigacycle, billicycle.

knowledge-based system A means of making available a set of accumulated rules and knowledge, so that it can be used by those not familiar with the subject. Differs from an *expert system* in that it does not contain experience-related data or opinions. ◊ *artificial intelligence, intelligent knowledge-based system*.

L

label 1. A group of *characters* used as a *symbol* to identify an item of data, an *area* of *memory*, a *record* or a *file* (◊ *header label*). 2. A label assigned to a particular *instruction* step in a *source program* to identify that step as an *entry point* in the coding or to enable that step to be used as a reference point for entry to the *routine* or *subroutine* in which it appears.

label field One of the *fields* used in the *source* format of an *instruction* written in *assembly language*. This field is the first in each assembly language statement (i.e., the left-hand column of the source listing).

It is not essential to have an entry in this field for each instruction. An entry here is treated as a name, which can be used to identify the specific line of the program (and hence its *memory address*). Usually *labels* are used as addresses within *branch* or *jump* instructions to cause control to pass to an instruction bearing a specific label.

label group A collection of *labels*[1] held in an *operating system*, usually of the same type.

label identifier A set of *characters* held within a *label*[1] used to identify the type of item labelled.

label (magnetic tape) ◊ *header label*.

label record A *record* used to identify a *file* recorded on some magnetic storage medium such as *magnetic tape*. ◊ *header label*.

label set A collection of *labels*[1] with the same *label identifier*.

label, tape ◊ *header label*.

laced card A *punched card* in which all, or nearly all, *card* columns were punched and wherein several holes appeared in each column.

LAN Acronym for Local Area Network.

language, programming ◊ *languages*.

languages In order to communicate with each other, men use language; in the same way, 'languages' of one sort or another are used in order to communicate instructions and commands to a computer. The unique feature which distinguishes a computer from other man-made tools and devices is its versatility in dealing with vastly different problems. This means that some very versatile method of communicating these enormously varied problems has to be devised. This article describes in outline the development and use of the concept of computer languages.

A computer performs its various functions by means of a *program* of *instructions*. In the form in which they are actually operated on by the computer's *central processor* these instructions consist of a series of numbers or a coded pattern of digits. The general article on *Instruction Format* describes in detail the various types of representation used for instructions in the form they take when present in the computer's central processor. In this form, the instructions are said to be in *machine code*. When computers were in an early stage of development, all programs had to be written in this basic machine code. This was the only 'language' of communication available for the programmer.

However, machine code as a means of communication has many drawbacks. The various numeric operation codes have no obvious relationship to their function. *Addresses* of *store locations* used by the programmer have to be carefully noted and their numeric values used when the area is referred to. Similarly, the programmer has to keep careful note of the numeric addresses of each program instruction, so that *branches* and *loops* may address the correct branch points. If the programmer has to make any alteration in his program which alters the numeric addresses of any locations, all other references to these locations must be checked and changed. This complexity and need for constant checking means that a machine code program, particularly a long and complicated one, is difficult to write and prone to many errors.

It became obvious that a great deal of the work involved in checking and cross-checking when writing a machine code program was purely mechanical. The first step in the development of computer languages came when it was realized that much of the detailed checking of addresses, locations, branches and so on can be done by a computer program. Languages were devised in which numeric operation codes were replaced with mnemonic codes, such as ADD, SUB, MPY. Store locations are referred to by *labels* or alphanumeric codes, which can be remembered more readily than numbers. A program called an *assembler* or *compiler* is used to convert the program as written by the programmer into a machine code equivalent known as the *object program*. Since the assembler program allocates actual numeric values to addresses referred to by labels in the original or *source program*, the programmer is relieved of the burden of remembering the actual address of locations or instructions. Further, if he alters his program in its 'source' form, when it is assembled again addresses will be automatically adjusted wherever they occur.

These basic languages, where the program as written by the programmer is similar to the machine code version, when each instruction has a corresponding machine code equivalent but the use of mnemonics and labels relieves the programmer of 'clerical' effort, are known as *low level* or *basic* programming languages or *autocodes*. Such languages have been refined, and many sophistications added, such as facilities for creating and using *macro instructions*, the incorporation of *library subroutines* at *compilation time*, the use of *packages* to handle *input* and *output routines*. However, all such basic languages are closely allied to the machine code into which the source program can alternatively be converted. While they are relatively easy to use, their use has drawbacks. Programs written in a basic language can normally only be used on a particular machine or range of machines (a restriction which applies even more to machine code programs themselves). Further, since the languages are closely linked to machine code, a program is not related in any way to the problem it is designed to solve, so that anyone looking at a program will have little indication of what the program is trying to do.

The first problem, that of intercommunication between different types of machines, was brought into prominence by the US Department of Defense, which found itself faced with massive investment in a large number of different types of computer. In order to overcome this problem, a language was devised for which all suppliers of equipment had to provide compilers rendering programs written in this language capable of being run on any computer. This language was designed to make the writing of commercial programs simpler, and was called *COBOL* (Common Business Oriented Language). Other *high level languages* which have been developed for scientific and mathematical purposes include *ALGOL, FORTRAN* and languages for real-time applications such as *PASCAL* and *Ada*. *BASIC* is particularly useful for interactive computing. Features which high level languages have in common are the fact that they are *problem oriented* rather than machine oriented (that is, designed not with a particular machine code in mind but rather so as to make the solving of a specific type of problem simpler) and also the fact that compilers exist for converting the languages into the machine code of different types of machine.

Higher level languages differ from lower level languages in that the *instructions* in a high level language take the form of fairly complex *statements*. On compilation a high level statement will generally be translated into several machine code instructions. With low level languages, each instruction generally is equivalent to a single machine code instruction. The object program produced from a high level language is thus normally rather more cumbersome and hence longer than that produced from a low level language, since the programmer has less detailed control over the specific machine code instructions his program generates and less control over the organization of the object program as it appears in store.

Generally, a program written in a high level language makes some sort of 'sense' and can be read and understood by someone who has not 'learned' the language. In the case of a commercial language, the program resembles a highly artificial but still recognizable English; in the case of a scientific language, the resemblance will be to mathematical notation.

However, the fact that these languages have this generality which enables them to be understood by people does not mean that they are automatically capable of being understood by all computers. It is still necessary for a compiler to be written for each machine on which the program is to be run. Thus high level languages only become general if manufacturers can agree on their features and provide the appropriate compilers.

The fact that generality of use of high level languages is only as good as the compilers supplied by manufacturers has led to the situation where large numbers of 'dialects' of the various common high level languages have emerged. It is usually the case that when a compiler for a specific machine is being written, certain features of the language have to be omitted or modified because of the difficulty of translating them into a specific machine code. Thus although in theory a general language is common to all machines, in practice only some subset of the language will apply to all machines. In fact, with the development of more powerful computers, the efficiency and capacity of compilers has improved, so that this common 'subset' is increasing for most languages.

However, the ideal situation in which a universal language would allow complete communication between all machines is still hardly nearer realization than in the ordinary world of human communication. The problem still remains to devise a language which is sufficiently general for all purposes, but which can be 'understood' by anybody, and be sufficiently simple for the production of compilers for identical versions on all types of machine. An attempt to achieve generality was made in the development of the language *PL/1*, which combines features from commercial languages (COBOL) and mathematical languages (FORTRAN). The problem of producing standard compilers and avoiding different 'subsets' was met in PL/1 by making the language *modular*. The language was defined in a series of units, each specifying a related but independent set of features. Thus the user needed only use the particular set of features needed for his program, and a compiler provided for as many of these modules or units as required. However, any language which attempts to do everything inevitably has its critics, and criticism of PL/1 was made on the grounds that it was cumbersome, and that it was difficult to produce compilers which would create efficient object programs.

Another approach to the problem of generality and intercommunication between computers is the attempt to develop a common machine code. The object of this is to standardize the internal instruction formats for all machines. Thus, any object program could run on any machine. Compilers would still be needed to translate high level languages into this machine code, but, since compilers themselves would be written in the common machine code, a single compiler would suffice for each language, thus making the problems of 'dialects' disappear.

All these solutions have been based on the assumption that the ideal state to aim at is for all programmers to be able to write all programs in the same language, which can then be compiled and run on all machines. Another approach, however, is to develop problem oriented languages even further. This means that, for example, in order to write payroll programs, a special 'payroll language' is devised; similarly an 'inventory control' language, 'structural analysis' languages or 'matrix analysis' languages can be developed. Each such highly specialized language requires a compiler, and special high level languages have been developed specifically for the production of compilers: a language for producing other languages.

In fact, high level problem oriented languages approach the field of applications software: e.g., applying *parameters* to a highly sophisticated application such as a PERT package could be said to be writing a program in a high level language designed to perform network analysis programs.

Languages are the medium by which man communicates problems to the computer and the easier this communication can be made the wider will be the application of computers; the problem of ideal communication has still to be solved, although much progress has been made.

Throughout the 1960s and 1970s great interest was created in *structured programming*. Some large programs consist of tens of thousands of source statements, and structured programming could enable such large programs to be subdivided and treated as many small programs each of which can be written, tested and debugged separately before eventual integration. Languages such as *Pascal* were developed with the object of creating a disciplined approach to programming.

A new attempt to create a language which combines attributes suitable for mathematical, scientific and business applications has been inspired by the US Department of Defense. This language, known as *Ada*, has been specified to meet these objectives.

In a general article it is not possible to describe in detail all the various types of language and the details of the methods used to translate languages into the machine code understood by the computer. Details of the languages ALGOL, BASIC, COBOL, FORTRAN and PL/I will be found under those headings. The reader will also find useful information under *Programming, compiler, assembler, Instruction Format formal methods*.

The following notes describe in outline some of the common features of languages and the processes of converting them into machine code.

A program written in any language other than machine code requires conversion to machine code before it can be run. This applies equally to basic languages and higher level languages. Programs used to convert programs written in a high level language (known as source programs) into a lower level language (known as the object program) are known variously as assemblers, compilers and *generators*. The term generator is used specifically for the conversion of highly problem-oriented languages used for producing such programs as *reports* and *sorts*. Assembler and compiler are often used synonymously, although assembler usually refers to the process of converting basic languages into machine code, where each language instruction has a corresponding single machine code equivalent. A compiler is a program which converts higher level languages into a lower level language – either machine code or a basic language. A compiler will normally generate several low level instructions for each source language statement. Assemblers and compilers, as well as providing a method for communicating the instructions which form the program, also allow the programmer to perform additional functions. Storage areas used by the program can be defined and allocated, and the programmer can define and store any *constants* needed by his program. In addition, compilers enable the programmer to incorporate *subroutines* from a *program library* held on *backing store*, and enable the programmer to define and use macro instructions. Compilers usually allow the programmer to incorporate statements which direct the compiler to take some action but have no effect on the program (e.g., directives to include *trace* routines within the program). Compilers and assemblers will usually print out their actions on a *printer*, giving the programmer a listing of the source program together with details of the generated object program. Such listing may, at the programmer's option, include comments or *narrative* to explain what the program is doing: these statements have no effect on the object program.

large scale integration   Refers to the number of logic *gates* constructed on a micro-electronic device or *chip*. LSI usually implies a level of density for *integrated circuits* in which somewhere between 1000 and 10,000 components exist on a single chip. Above 10,000 components the term, very large scale integration is used. Below 1000, the term medium scale integration is used.

laser   Acronym for Light Amplification by Stimulated Emission of Radiation. The physical properties of lasers allow for the very precise positioning of a narrow beam of light, transferring a high energy source to a very small area. This property is used to control printing (laser *printers*) to read information from *bar codes* and to *read* and *write* information in optical storage devices.

Last-In-First-Out   A procedure used to control an activity in which queues must be formed to control *sequential* processes. For example, in a *program*, a hierarchy of processes may exist, in which a series of *subroutines* are called one from another. Eventually control has to be returned to the highest level routine. An area of *memory* known as a *stack* is reserved to store *operands* and *return instructions*. Each subroutine will place such operands on to the stack which are then recovered on a last-in-first-out basis, to facilitate an orderly return to the highest level routine. Contrasted with (*FIFO*).

latch   A circuit which maintains a stable condition until it is specifically energized to adopt an alternative condition.

latency   The time delay required for an event to be initiated from the moment when the event is called. For example, to transfer a unit of information from a *disk drive* into the *main memory* of a computer two operations must be considered: (i) The time required for the disk *drive* to rotate to a position where the desired *sector* of the disk is beneath the *read/write head* of the disk drive. (ii) The time required to read the sector into main memory. The first of these time movements is the latency.

Also known as waiting time.

lattice file   A *file* within an *operating system* within which individual *records* can have more than one *owner*, and also themselves are *owners* of more than one record.

law and computers Early fears of the inadmissibility of evidence based on magnetically recorded data have proved groundless. Any loss of data by *overwriting* or other electronic hazards would have no greater significance in law than the loss of documents in a fire. Also the need to print out records held on a magnetic medium may be compared with the translation of evidence gathered in a foreign country. Although a computer system may dispense with intermediate records, the validity of its *output* can be established by circumstantial evidence obtained by a re-run of the *programs* with proven *input* data. In a vital case it may also be desirable to call an expert witness to give evidence that the installation is efficiently conducted and that the information it provides can be relied on in a commercial environment.

There is, however, some danger from actions in tort. The directors of a company should ensure, when they delegate responsibility for customer relations to an unthinking computer, that fail-safe *exception reporting* has been incorporated in the programs and procedures. Thus, in Burnett *v*. Westminster Bank Limited (1965) the bank was held liable for damages when its computer system (which relied on the *magnetic ink character recognition* encoding on cheques) failed to detect that the customer had altered the account details in manuscript.

A company providing computing services for others might also be liable for damages, for example, in the event of an incorrect engineering calculation resulting in the collapse of a structure. On the other hand, negligence could be held against a company which failed to employ a computer in a situation where similar enterprises had established their value in maintaining safety limits.

Whatever litigation may arise, a company's interests will be protected best when a meticulous control is maintained over its data processing operations, through the enforcement of proper *data processing standards*. All activities should be logged immediately and accurately, recording *batch* sequence numbers, the total number of items processed, *control totals* and other matters relevant to data security. *Operating systems* should be operator-proof. There should be automatic checks on the *validity* of data, e.g., correct codes, logical situations, quantitative limits. A reliable *dump and restart* procedure should be used. Output should be identified by program-generated *header* and *trailer labels* giving time and date, description, page numbers, data record count and control or *hash totals*. Environmental records should be equally thorough in respect of atmospheric conditions, maintenance schedules, the logging of *down time*, fault reports, and operators' duty rosters. There should always be two people on duty when operational jobs are being run. All these precautions will substantiate the evidence of an 'expert witness' if the need should arise.

layer   Synonymous with level[2].

layout character   A special character appearing amongst data for the purpose of controlling the way in which the data is printed or otherwise treated in some subsequent processing operation.

Also known as format effector.

leader   1. A length of unpunched paper that preceded the data recorded on a reel of *paper tape*. Usually containing *feed holes* only. 2. A *record* that precedes a group of records and which identifies the group or provides data common to the group.

leading edge   Pertaining to a *punched card* – the edge that first entered the *card track* of a punched card machine. Contrasted with *trailing edge*.

leading end   The end of a piece of *paper tape* that first entered a *paper tape reader*; i.e., the end at which the first character of a message appeared.

leapfrog test   A test performed by a *program* which is in *memory* and which performs tests on different *locations* and then transfers itself to another *memory area* to continue the tests on other locations.

leased line   A communications circuit reserved permanently for a particular user; i.e., not a switched circuit for servicing different users.

least frequently used memory   Areas in which *memory* is *allocated dynamically* in response to work load. The *operating system* maintains a record of those areas of memory which are being used least often by the current job mix, and when demands arise to read in new data or program files from the *backing store*, the contents of the least used area are written temporarily away to disk to accommodate the new demand for memory space.

Scheduling algorithms perform the necessary calculations to manage memory space. An alternative system is one in which memory is selected simply on the basis of the length of time since last used. This is referred to as least recently used memory.

least recently used memory   ◊ *least frequently used memory*.

least significant character   The character in the extreme right-hand position of a group of *significant characters* in *positional notation*.

LED   Acronym for *Light Emitting Diode*.

left justified   Descriptive of any item of data which is stored in such a way that it occupies consecutive *locations* starting at the left-hand end of the area allocated to it. Thus empty locations may appear consecutively at the right-hand end if the item requires less positions than have been allowed.

left shift　A *shift* operation in which the digits of a *word* are displaced to the left. In an *arithmetical* shift this has the effect of multiplication.

leg　A *path* in a *routine* or *subroutine*.

length　The numbers of *bits* or *characters* forming any *word*, *record* or other unit of data.

length, fixed　◊ *fixed length record*.

length, variable　◊ *variable field*.

letter　A character of the alphabet. Contrasted with *symbol* in a *character set*.

level　The position of an object within a physical or conceptual model.
1. ◊ For example, *high level language* contrasts with *low level language*.
2. Another use occurs in describing *software architectures* in which a software system may be constructed in levels and where each level has a specific function. ◊ seven layer reference model for *Open Systems*. In this case, the lower levels of control relate to the structures necessary to establish communication links and transfer data successfully between communicating systems, whereas the higher levels are concerned with the presentation of data and the logical processes which form specific applications.
　Also known as layer.

librarian　1. The person who controls the library in which all *magnetic files* and *programs* are kept, issues *data files* and maintains records of tape usage, including details of current *file generations* and their associated *reel numbers*. May also assemble tapes ready for running a job and issue all associated materials and *operating instructions*. 2. A synonym for *librarian program*.

librarian program　A *program* forming a part of the *operating system* of a particular computer. The program maintains a complete library of all the *routines* and *subroutines* required by the user including programs developed for the user's applications, *compilers*, *service routines*, and any special *packages* or subroutines developed by the user or the computer manufacturer. Programs can be deleted, added or modified by the librarian program under the user's control. The complete library is stored on a *backing store* (e.g., a *disk file*) so that required routines can be called into *memory* as necessary.

library facilities　The facilities provided by a *program library*, but more specifically relating to the library of *routines* developed by computer manufacturers for users of their equipment. These routines and *subroutines* are generally available on a *backing store* and can be directly compiled into the user's *object program* by the *instructions* written in the user's *source program*.

library program A program available in the *program library*.

library routine A *routine* in the *program library*.

library software All *programs* and *routines* forming part of the *library facilities* of a computer system.

library subroutine A *subroutine* in the *program library*.

library tape A *magnetic tape* containing the *library software* of a computer system.

library, tape ⋄ *magnetic tape library*.

LIFO An acronym for *Last-In-First-Out*.

light emitting diode (LED) A device which can be energized to emit light and thus indicate the status or operating condition of a circuit within an electronic machine. Such devices are usually positioned on the panel of a machine.

light pen A highly sensitive photo-electric device used as an adjunct to a *cathode ray tube* display unit. The operator can pass the pen over the surface of the cathode ray tube screen to detect images displayed on the screen. The light pen can also be used to activate a computer to change or modify images it has caused to be displayed, in accordance with movements made by the operator and under *program* control.

limited integrator An *integrator*[1] in which two input signals are integrated as long as the corresponding output signal does not exceed specified limits. ⋄ *integrator (computing unit)*.

limiter A device used to limit the power of an electrical signal to some predetermined maximum value.

line Term used for a channel in a *telecommunications* system.

linear equation An equation in which both sides are linear functions of the variables. The equation may be expressed in the form $1(a, b, c, \ldots) = k$, where 1 is a linear function and k is a constant.

linear optimization Synonymous with *linear programming*.

linear program A mathematical technique used in *operational research* to solve problems in which it is required to find an optimum solution involving the combination of many variables; a procedure for ascertaining the minimum or maximum linear function of variables subject to constraints in the form of linear inequalities. ⋄ general article on *Linear Programming*.

linear programming Linear programming is a section of mathematical programming which has proved extremely valuable in many fields, particularly that of allocation problems (⋄ *Allocation*).

Linear programming problems are those in which: (i) the objective can be expressed as the maximization or minimization of a linear function of the variables, i.e., the variables have fixed costs, profits, etc., per unit of the items; and (ii) the objective function described in (i) is restricted by a set of constraints which may also be expressed as linear functions of the variables. Putting this less formally, linear programming enables us to maximize or minimize a function which is the sum of multiples of several variables subject to constraints upon these variables; these constraints can themselves be written as sums of multiples of the variables.

To illustrate the use of linear programming we shall consider a very simple example, for clarity. Suppose we wish to make a diet for pigs, and we want the diet to cost as little as possible, but to contain definite minimum quantities of various vitamins, using certain basic foods. We consider one unit by weight of this food, say one pound. We want to minimize the total cost so we need to know the cost of each food per ounce. Our constraints are that the diet must contain certain minimal quantities of various vitamins, and since the vitamin content of each food will depend on its weight this can be expressed linearly. Thus we will need to know: (i) the cost of each food per ounce; (ii) the vitamin content per ounce of each food. We can then write:

Total cost=a×(cost of first food)+b×(cost of second food), etc.
Content of vitamin 1=a×(vitamin 1 content of first food)+b×(vitamin 1 content of second food), etc.
Content of vitamin 2=a×(vitamin 2 content of first food)+b×(vitamin 2 content of second food), etc.
Total weight=16 ounces=a+b+c, etc.
where a, b, c, etc. are the amounts of each food.

Use of linear programming will then find for us the values of a, b, c, etc., which will give us the minimum vitamin content defined and minimize the total cost.

Perhaps linear programming has become so popular because its results can be readily shown to be economically valuable and that it can be very easily used with a digital computer.

There are several techniques for the solution of linear programming problems, perhaps the most common of which is the simplex technique.

linear unit　A unit used in an *analog computer* in which the change in output, due to any change in one of two or more input variables, is proportional only to the change in that input and is not dependent upon the values of the other prevailing inputs.

line-at-a-time printer　Synonymous with *line printer*.

line-feed code   A control character which is used to specify the number of lines of paper to be passed through a *printer* between each line of print.

line (in display)   A horizontal row of *character* positions forming part of a *display* on a *visual display unit*.

line, magneto-strictive delay   ⋄ *magneto-strictive acoustic delay line*.

line, mercury delay   ⋄ *mercury delay line*.

line, nickel delay   ⋄ *nickel delay line*.

line noise   *Noise²* generated in a *data transmission* line.

line printer   A *printer* which prints out results from a computer one line at a time (⋄ general article on *Output Devices*).

line, quartz delay   ⋄ *quartz delay line*.

line, sonic delay   ⋄ *acoustic delay line*.

link   A *branch instruction*, or an *address* in such an instruction, that is used specifically to *exit* from a *subroutine* in order to return to some desired point in a *main program*.

linkage   A connexion between mechanical members used in a mechanical *analog computer* to perform some arithmetic function. For example mechanical multiplication units can be made based on the geometry of similar triangles.

linked subroutine   A *subroutine* which is not stored in the *main path* of a *program*, but which is entered via a *branch instruction* from the *main routine* and which executes a branch instruction to return control subsequently to the main routine.

link register   A *register*, often of single *bit* capacity, which provides for the joining of two *operands* together as in a *logical shift instruction*.

LISP   Acronym for LISt Processing. A *programming language* designed for manipulating non-numeric data, particularly used in *artificial intelligence* applications.

list   1. Any printing operation in which a series of *records* on a *file*, or in *memory*, are printed one after another. 2. When processing *punched cards* on a *tabulator*, to print details from every card being processed rather than *totals only*.

literal operands   *Operands*, usually in *source language instruction*, which specify precisely the value of a *constant* rather than an *address* in which the constant is stored. This technique enables the coding to be written more concisely than if the constant had been allocated a *dataname*.

liveware   A word deliberately coined to contrast with *hardware* and *software* meaning the personnel associated with all aspects of a computer, e.g., *operators*, *programmers*, *systems analysts*.

load 1. To load a data medium on to an *input unit*; e.g., a *reel* of *magnetic tape* on to a *tape deck* or *punched cards* into the *hopper* of a *card reader*. 2. To read data or *program instructions* into *memory*.

load-and-go Descriptive of a type of automatic coding in which the user's *source program* is automatically translated into *machine code* and stored in the *central processor* ready to be performed. Thus it is never necessary to create the *object program* on any external medium.

loader Synonymous with *loading routine*.

loading routine A *routine* existing permanently in *memory* to enable any *program* to be loaded into memory from an external medium.

Also known as loader, loading program, load program.

load instruction An *instruction* in a *program* which moves *data* to an *accumulator* or other *register* from a *memory location*. Contrasted with *store instruction*.

load key A hand-operated switch used on earlier computers to activate circuits for reading data or a *program* into *memory*.

load point A physical marker at the beginning of a *reel* of *magnetic tape*, which is detected by *hardware* to ensure that the reel is correctly positioned when the tape is first *loaded*, or after it has been rewound.

load program Synonymous with *loading routine*.

local area network A *network* designed to provide facilities for inter-user communication within a single geographical location. It does not use public facilities or standards. Contrasted with *wide area network*.

local system library A *program library* containing standard *software* available to a particular computer system.

location Any place in a computer *store* capable of containing a unit of information. Usually expressed in terms of the basic unit of storage employed in a particular computer system; e.g., a *word* is a location in a *word oriented* storage unit, and a *character* in a *character oriented* machine. The position of a location in store is identified by its *address*[2].

location counter A value used within a *subroutine* for *addressing* a series of *locations*; the value being modified by *program* to address a separate location on each occasion the subroutine is used.

lock In an *operating system* a method by which a *process* is given exclusive use of a *resource*.

locked down A condition in which an *area* of *virtual store* remains in a fixed position in *main store*.

locking of files A process by which different *virtual machines* are prevented from simultaneously *accessing* a *file*.

lock-out 1. To inhibit the activation of a *hardware* unit or a *routine*;

e.g., where the action would otherwise have coincided with some uncompleted operation utilizing the same areas of *memory*. 2. A device used to safeguard against an attempted reference to a routine or area of equipment currently in use. 3. The status of a *process* which is waiting to obtain a *lock* in order to give exclusive use of a *resource*.

log 1. To record a series of events. 2. A record of a particular series of events; e.g., a maintenance engineer's log, operator's log, console log.

logger Any device which records events over a period of time.

logic The science dealing with the formal principles of reasoning; in electronic data processing, the principles observed in the design of a computer system or of any particular unit. Pertaining to the relationships between elements in the unit concerned, without consideration of the *hardware* necessary to implement this design. ⟡ *fuzzy logic*.

logical A term used in the context of *operating systems* to describe entities (*files*, *resources*) as they appear to a *user*, in contrast to *physical* files etc., which are the actual entities as they exist. Logical entities are derived from physical entities by means of operating system software. Associated with *virtual machine environment*.

logical comparison The operation performed when two *operands* or *keys* are examined to decide whether they are equal in value or to ascertain their relative size one to another.

logical connectives The words that connect statements and which enable the truth or falsity of the statements thus created to be ascertained from the individual statements and the logical meanings of the connectives. ⟡ *logical operator* and *Boolean algebra*.

logical decision A choice between alternatives made by reference to some specified conditions. For example, alternative paths might be available in a *routine* and the selection of the required path might be made according to whether an *intermediate result* were, say, negative or positive.

logical design ◊ *logic design*.

logical diagram ◊ *logic diagram*.

logical element ◊ *logic element*.

logical flowchart ◊ *logic flowchart*.

logical instruction Any *instruction* which specifies one of the *logical operations* (e.g., an *and* instruction). Used in the widest sense to embrace those instructions that are not *arithmetical instructions*, e.g., *comparing*, *shifting* or *branching* instructions.

logical multiply A *logical operation* involving the use of the *logical operator* known as *and operator*. ⟡ *Boolean algebra*.

logical operation 1. Any operation involving the use of the *logical*

277

operators 'and', 'not', 'or', 'nand', etc. 2. In a computer, any operation in which the result in each digit position is dependent only upon the values of the corresponding digit positions in the *operand* or operands concerned, i.e., no *carries* take place. 3. Sometimes used to refer to any processing operation not involving arithmetic, e.g., *shifting*.

logical operator A word or symbol representing some logical function to be applied to one or more associated *operands*. It may appear in front of the operand, as in the *monadic* operation known as *negation*, but in *dyadic* operations it appears between operands and is often known as a *logical connective*. ⟡ *Boolean algebra*.

logical product Synonymous with *and operation*.

logical record A *record* containing all the *fields* necessary to represent some transaction or to present some specific collection of facts. The length and structure of the record is expressed in regard to the information that it must convey, rather than to satisfy any limitations imposed by the medium of *store*.

logical shift A *shift operation* in which *digits* in a *word* are moved left or right in circular fashion, so that digits pushed out at one end of the word are re-introduced at the other.

Also known as circular shift, end-around shift and non-arithmetic shift. Contrasted with *arithmetical shift*.

logical sum Synonymous with *inclusive-or operation*.

logical symbol A symbol used to represent one of the *logical operators* such as 'and', 'or', 'not', 'nand', etc.

logical track A group of *physical tracks* which can be *addressed* as a single entity.

logical unit Of data, a group of *characters*, *digits* or *fields* which, as a group, represent some *transaction* or any other unit of information.

logic chart ⟡ *logic flowchart*.

logic design A description of the working of a computer or any associated unit, in which the functional parts of the system are represented by *logical symbols*. A specification of the mode of operation without consideration of the physical components required.

Also known as logical design.

logic diagram A representation of the design of any device or system in which graphic symbols are used to represent the *logic elements* and their relationships.

Also known as logical diagram.

logic element A device used to perform some specific *logical operation*; e.g., an *and element*, *or element*, *not element*, etc. A small unit, part of a system consisting of several logic elements each performing some logical function such as 'and', 'or', 'not', 'nor', 'nand', etc. ◊ general article on *Boolean algebra*.

Also known as *gate*, logical element.

logic flowchart   1. A chart representing a system of *logical elements* and their relationships within the overall design of a system or *hardware* unit. 2. The representation of the various logical steps in any *program* or *routine* by means of a standard set of symbols. A *flowchart* produced before detailed *coding* for the solution of a particular problem. ◊ *flowcharting*.

Also known as logical flowchart.

logic instruction   An instruction using the logical operations of 'or', 'and', 'nor', etc. A subset of the group of instructions concerned with data manipulation; ◊ general article on Instruction classification.

logic shift   ◊ *logical shift*.

login   Synonymous with *logon*.

logon   To identify to a system; the process of authenticating, perhaps by a password. Contrasted with logoff.

longitudinal check   A type of *parity check* performed on a group of *characters* or *bits*. For example where a number of characters are transmitted as a *block*, a parity check is usually performed on each character, but in addition it is often desirable to treat each bit position within the successive characters of the group as being a further unit for checking purposes. To this end, a *parity character* is generated and transmitted as the last character of the group, thus achieving either *odd* or *even parity* for each longitudinal bit formation.

longitudinal-mode delay line   A *magneto-strictive delay line* in which the mode of operation depends on longitudinal vibrations in some magneto-strictive material.

long word   This expression refers to an arrangement of the *storage elements* in a computer, in which an extraordinary number of *bytes* are taken as a unit for processing in a particular operation. For example, a computer organized with 16-bit *main memory words* may occasionally process *operands* as 32-bit words.

look-up   A programming technique enabling an item of data to be selected from an *array* or *table* in which the item is identified by a *key*.

look-up table   An *array* of data so organized that it can be searched by a *routine* to retrieve information related to specified *keys*.

loop   1. A series of *instructions* which are performed repeatedly until some specified condition is satisfied, whereupon a *branch instruction* is obeyed to exit from the loop. ◊ general article on *Programming*. 2. Sometimes also used as a synonym for *control tape* or *control loop*.

loop checking A method sometimes used to check the accuracy of *data* transmitted over a *data-link*; signals received at one terminal are returned to the transmitting terminal for comparison with the original information.

loop network ⟡ *network architecture*.

loop stop A *loop* that is entered to stop a *program*, usually when some specific condition occurs requiring action by the operator.

loosely coupled twin A system in which two *processors* are used with *switches* to enable them to use common *peripheral units*; each processor has its own *operating system* and it is not possible for them to operate simultaneously sharing *data* and *code*. Such a system provides switching to aid in system *resilience* in the event of *hardware failure*.

loss Synonymous with *attenuation*.

loss of information Synonymous with *walk down*.

lower curtate Certain *punching positions* of a *card column* (usually those without *zone* significance) grouped at the bottom of a *punched card*. Contrasted with *upper curtate*.

low-going transition Signals within digital machines usually consist of voltages at different states used to represent *binary digits* 0 and 1. For example, 1 is a higher voltage than 0. Thus a change from low voltage to high voltage is described as a *high-going transition* and from high to low voltage as a low-going transition.

low level filestore A type of *filestore* used in an *operating system* to hold *physical files* not needed *on line*. Typically the medium used is *magnetic tape*, and the user cannot access such files directly.

low level language A *language* in which each *instruction* has a single corresponding *machine code* equivalent.

Also known as basic language. Contrasted with *high level language*.

low order Descriptive of the significance attached to certain *characters* or *digits* in a number. For example, the two low order positions of the decimal number 38654 are those occupied by the numerals 5 and 4.

low-order position The right-hand or least significant position of a number or *word*.

LP Abbreviation of *linear programming*.

LPM Abbreviation of lines per minute, as used to describe the output speed of a *line printer* (e.g., 1000 l.p.m.).

LSB Abbreviation of least significant *bit*. ⟡ *least significant character*.

LSI Abbreviation of *large scale integration*.

M

MAC Acronym for Multi-Access Computing. ⟨⟩ *MAC mode.*

MAC background job A *background job* run under an *operating system* in *batch mode*, either as an *interactive batch job* or as an ordinary *batch job* (in which the status of the job is determined through a terminal). ⟨⟩ *MAC mode.*

machine address Synonymous with *absolute address.*

machine code The coding system adopted in the design of a computer to represent the *instruction repertoire* of the computer. The various operations that can be performed are represented by numeric *function codes* and all *store locations* are allocated numbers to enable the *data* stored in such locations to be *addressed.*

Also known as computer code, *instruction code, instruction set,* order code.

machine cycle Pertaining generally to a machine in which operations are performed during a complete cycle. Applicable to any machine in which a cyclic pattern of events exists.

machine error An error in the results of automatic processing which can be attributed to a machine malfunction rather than to a *software* or operating fault.

machine independent Used to describe a *program* or procedure which is expressed without regard to any particular *machine coding* system. The procedure is designed in terms of the logical requirements of the problem.

machine instruction An *instruction* written in terms of a computer's *machine code*; i.e., one which can be obeyed directly by the machine without translation.

machine instruction code Synonymous with *machine code.*

machine interruption A break in the processing of a *program* caused by some event detected by the computer *hardware.* For example, some automatic checking operation may reveal a *parity error.*

machine language In its strictest sense refers to *instructions* written in *machine code* which can be immediately obeyed by a computer without translation. Used more loosely to refer to any *symbolic instructions* which are written for execution by a computer system.

machine language code ⟡ *machine code.*

machine learning The ability of a machine to improve its performance with repeated experience of particular problems; i.e., *artificial intelligence.*

machine logic The design of a computer in respect of the way in which its various elements are interactive. Relating to the methods employed in the machine to solve problems rather than to the actual components used or any circuit values.

machine operation A predetermined group of activities which a machine is built to perform, e.g., *addition.*

machine operator The person who loads *programs* and data into a computer or who manipulates the *console* controls to achieve the running of a program or *suite* of programs.

machine processible form Describing any data arranged in some medium which can be accepted and processed by an *automatic data processing* machine.

machine run A complete *routine*, or set of interlinked routines, which would normally be executed on a computer without major intervention. Sometimes an operator may have to take specific action in the event of certain error conditions but otherwise a run would not require any additional set-up procedures following the initial *loading* operations for the job.

machine script Any data represented in *machine code* form.

machines, electrical accounting ⟡ *electrical accounting machines.*

machine sensible Related to data recorded in such a way that it can be sensed or read by an *automatic data processing* machine.

machine-spoilt work time Time spent in processing data where the results contain *errors* because of a machine fault. Essentially, wasted time where the results are useless and in which all or part of the job will need to be re-run.

machine word A physical location in *memory*, which may be *addressed* as a single unit but which will contain a predetermined standard number of *characters* or *digit positions*. The *word* is a standard unit of transfer for computers having *fixed word-length*, and usually operations are performed in *parallel mode* when performing any specified function; i.e., all digit positions are processed simultaneously. This method may be contrasted with that of *character oriented* computers in which operands can be of *variable length* and can consist of a *string* of characters as specified by the programmer for any particular *instruction*.

In this latter method most processes are performed in *serial mode* on one character after another. In most *personal computers*, the unit of transfer is a *byte* consisting of 8 *bits* or two bytes of 16 bits.

MAC mode A method of using an *operating system* in which *jobs* are submitted from *remote terminals* and are then carried out in *conversational mode*. MAC is an acronym for *multi-access* computing.

macro 1. An abbreviation for *macroinstruction*. 2. In an *operating system*, used for the name of a set of operating system *control language* statements which can be activated collectively by giving the macro name.

macro assembly program An *assembly program* in which concise *instruction* statements are used to generate procedures containing several *machine code* instructions for each source statement. Such an assembler may also permit the *segmentation* of large programs and facilities for tracing programming errors.

macro code Synonymous with *macroinstruction*.

macro-coding The use of *macroinstructions* in the writing of a program. Contrasted with *micro-coding*.

macro flowchart A chart used in designing the logic of a particular routine, in which the various *segments* and *subroutines* of a program are represented by blocks. No attempt is made in such a chart to specify detailed programming tactics, this being the province of the programmer.

macroinstruction A single *instruction* written as part of a *source language*, which when compiled into a *machine code* program will generate several machine code instructions.

Also known as programmed instruction, macro, macro code.

macrologic Certain logical devices known as chip slices hold *microprograms* which perform basic *instructions* as required in a microprocessor. A microprogram has to be written by the system designer to link these basic processes together to create a coherent set of microprocessor responses. Macrologic is the term given to these basic building blocks.

macroprogram A macroprogram consists of a series of *macroinstructions* (*statements* in *assembly language*), each of which invokes a series of *microinstructions* stored within a microprocessor control unit. A macroinstruction generates a series of microinstruction codes which represent the standard response of a microprocessor to a given assembly language statement. A series of macroinstructions is referred to as a macroprogram, or conventionally simply as a program. A macroprogram operates upon data stored in *RAM* or *ROM*. Contrasted with micro-program.

macroprogramming The *programming* of a problem in which all statements are written in terms of *macroinstructions*; usually where some *assembly system* or *package* is available to perform translation of the macroinstructions into *machine code*.

MAC sub-system Part of an *operating system* which controls work submitted in *MAC mode*.

magazine 1. An input *hopper* which holds documents or cards and presents them to a feed mechanism for reading or punching. 2. A device forming part of a *magnetic card file* which holds *magnetic cards* and presents them for reading or selection.

magnetic card A card having a magnetizable surface upon which data is recorded by the energizing of certain parts of the surface, thus providing a storage medium.

magnetic card file A *direct access storage device* in which individual *buckets* of data are stored upon *magnetic cards* held in one or more *magazines*². The cards, once addressed, are selected from the magazine and transported at high speed past a *read/write head*.

magnetic cell A storage *cell* in which the two possible values of one *binary digit* are represented by different magnetic flux patterns. A magnetic cell may consist of one or more storage *cores*, or of a small part of a larger piece of perforated ferromagnetic material known as an aperture plate.

Also known as a static magnetic cell because the means of setting and sensing the contents are stationary with respect to the magnetic material.

magnetic cell, static Synonymous with *magnetic cell*.

magnetic character ◊ *magnetized ink character*.

magnetic core A small ring of ferromagnetic material which could be polarized by electric currents applied to wires wrapped around it. The magnetic core was thus capable of assuming two states and could be used as a switching device, or as a storage medium. These devices were used extensively for the *memory* of computers; e.g., a single magnetic core being used to represent a single *binary digit* of some item of information represented in a numerical code.

magnetic core storage A large array of *magnetic cores* arranged in *matrices* to form the *memory* of a computer. Each individual core was capable of assuming two states and some cores could be assigned as storage *locations* for information to be held in *binary coded form*, whereas others could perform *switching* or *gating* functions.

magnetic disk   A storage device consisting of a number of flat circular plates each coated on both surfaces with some magnetizable material. A number of *tracks*[1] are available on each surface and data is read from or written to these tracks by means of *read/write heads*. There may be several heads to each surface, a particular head being allocated a specific area (or *sector*) on the disk. Disks, including *floppy disks* are described more fully in the general article on *Storage Devices*. ⊳ *random access*.

magnetic disk file   A *file* of data held on a *magnetic disk*.

magnetic drum   A storage device consisting of a cylinder coated with magnetizable material; the cylinder is continuously rotated past a series of *read/write heads* which are arranged to coincide with recording *tracks* on the surface of the cylinder. *Binary coded* data can be recorded serially upon any track as the drum rotates, and data can be read from or written to any one of the tracks by switching from one *read/write head* to another.

magnetic film store   ⊳ *thin-film memory*.

magnetic head   An electromagnet used to read, record or erase polarized spots on a magnetic medium such as *magnetic tape*, *magnetic disk* or *magnetic drum*. Examples are *read head*, *write head* and *read/write head*.

magnetic ink   Ink containing particles of magnetizable material, which can be energized to facilitate automatic reading of printed characters. ⊳ *magnetic ink character recognition*.

magnetic ink character reader   A *character reader* which reads characters printed in magnetized metallic ink by using *magnetic ink character recognition* techniques.

magnetic ink character recognition   The technology related to the recording of information on documents by means of *magnetized ink characters* and the automatic recognition of such characters by means of machines. ⊳ *magnetic ink document sorter/reader* and *Character Recognition*.

magnetic ink document reader   A device which reads specified fields of *magnetized ink characters* from documents and translates the information read into a coded format, usually for direct insertion into an *input area* of a computer's *core storage*.

magnetic ink document sorter/reader   A machine capable of reading information from documents containing *magnetized ink characters* and of sorting the documents into order according to the digits recorded in a specified *field*.

285

magnetic memory Pertaining to any *storage device* which operates using principles of electro-magnetism.

magnetic store Synonymous with *magnetic memory*.

magnetic tape Magnetic tape is a very common form of *backing store* used for computers. It is usually in the form of a continuous strip of plastic material which is coated with a magnetic oxide on which data may be recorded as a series of magnetized spots. The general dimensions of the tape vary somewhat from one system to another, but ½ in. tape is probably most common and is ½ in. wide and may be approximately 2400 feet in length.

A *magnetic tape deck* must be used in order to record data on to a reel of magnetic tape. A deck consists basically of a drive mechanism capable of driving two tape reels at very high speed so that tape is wound from one reel on to another. As the tape is transported between the two reels it passes a *read/write head* which is used either to read from the tape or to write to it.

With ½ in. tape data is recorded in seven *channels* which run lengthwise along the tape, and seven *bits* are therefore available across the width of the tape. Of these seven bits, six are used to form a coded *character*, whilst the other is used as a *parity* bit. In this way data is recorded as a series of sequential tape characters which are grouped to form the basic *records* of information required.

These records may be written singly as *blocks* of data on tape, but generally it is more efficient to group a predetermined number of records into each block. A block is a physical unit of data written to or read from tape as a single operation. Each block is separated by an *interblock gap* which is a small area of unrecorded tape about ½ in. in length.

Although data is recorded in most systems as a series of tape characters this does not necessarily imply that all data must be recorded in character form. *Binary numbers* may be recorded directly on magnetic tape by the technique of regarding any number of sequential 6-bit tape characters as a contiguous set of binary digits.

The capacity of a reel of magnetic tape is initially dependent on the density of the recorded signals on the tape. A number of *recording densities* are currently in use, and generally the higher the density, in terms of tape characters per inch, the higher the cost of the magnetic tape system. A typical recording density is 556 characters per inch, and it will be seen that at this density the speed for transferring data between a reel of tape and *memory* can be very high. This in turn depends on the speed of the tape drive mechanism, but for example with a density of

556 characters per inch and a tape speed of 75 inches per second the rate of transfer is 41,700 characters per second.

The actual capacity of any particular reel is dependent on the way in which blocks of data are organized: the shorter the tape blocks the more interblock gaps are incurred. A full reel containing blocks 400 characters in length would, at 556 characters per inch, permit a total capacity of 7.84 million characters.

The physical beginning and end of tape are distinguished by strips of reflective material which are automatically detected by hardware.

The important thing to note about magnetic tape is that it is a serial medium, i.e., all data must be organized into sequential files. To update the information on a tape file it is necessary to read records from the file as a series of blocks and place them in turn in memory. Amendment records in the same sequence are read into memory at the same time as a series of blocks, so that amendments can be applied consecutively to the records from the original file. An entirely new file is created on another reel of magnetic tape, still in the original sequence, but this time containing all details relevant to the latest amendments. Thus at least two *generations* of the same file may exist but only one will be current at any particular time.

The operations controlling magnetic tape are initiated by instructions executed in the *central processor*. The main instructions are those which write to tape, read from tape or rewind tape. A read or write instruction is required for each block of data read from or written to the tape. A rewind instruction may be called at any time to wind the tape back to the *load point*. Other operations available in some tape systems include: read reverse, which enables a tape to be read backwards; write *tape mark*, which causes a special character to be written to tape; skip to next tape mark, which enables the tape to be moved without reading until a special tape mark character is detected; and backspace tape, which causes the tape to be moved backwards one block.

The use of the parity bits previously mentioned enables the computer to detect any errors that may arise when reading or writing. When a character is written to tape a parity bit is generated to complete the 7-bit character as it is recorded. The parity bit is computed automatically to make the number of 1 bits in the character equal to an even number (in some systems odd parity is used: ◊ *parity checking*). When the tape is read on some subsequent occasion a check is again performed on each character to ensure that the parity is even.

In many systems the tape decks are equipped with recording heads that enable the computer to read each character immediately it has been written. It is then possible to check not only that the correct parity has been maintained but also to check that the actual *bit pattern* detected for that character on the tape is the same as the original bit pattern in memory.

Whenever an error is detected during a write operation the computer automatically rewrites the block concerned; during a read operation the computer will try again to read the block. Where the error is caused by some transient condition this will often prove successful and the job may be continued. Persistent errors will usually mean that the reel of tape is damaged or that there is a tape deck malfunction. It is always necessary to safeguard against tape failure by retaining a previous generation of every master file plus the associated amendment records so that the current generation can be re-created if necessary.

Tape failure can be caused by dust particles or by damage to the oxide coating. A proper system of air conditioning is required in the machine room, and also in any *magnetic tape library*, so that dust and dirt are avoided. Proper maintenance of the tape decks and correct handling of tape reels by operators are also necessary. All this might lead one to suspect that magnetic tape is a very sensitive medium for storing data but in any well-run installation tape failures are comparatively rare.

It is clear from the foregoing that considerable care is taken by computer equipment manufacturers and by computer users to safeguard the physical condition of reels of magnetic tape. It is also necessary to safeguard the information forming data files on the magnetic tapes to ensure that the data is not inadvertently *overwritten*. To this purpose each tape file starts with a *header label* which identifies the file name, generation number and the retention period. The *tape serial number* is also recorded as part of this label as well as the reel number, the latter being important where more than one reel is necessary for a particular file. When a tape file is opened to be read the header label is checked by program to ensure that the correct file has been loaded; on the other hand when a reel is opened as a write tape the retention period is checked to make sure that important data is not being overwritten.

In a program which processes tape files there are many operations that are common to any tape processing job. In order to simplify matters for users it is customary for computer manufacturers to supply *housekeeping packages*, which are designed to perform many of the routine functions concerned with magnetic tape processing. The user is able to write his tape processing requirements using *macroinstructions*

288

which will call into operation standard routines perhaps consisting of many instructions.

An indication of the relative advantages and disadvantages of direct access equipment compared with magnetic tape is given under *Direct Access Storage*.

magnetic tape deck A complete *tape transport* and its associated *read/write heads*, capable of either reading from or writing to a *magnetic tape file*.

Also known as deck[2], *tape deck* and magnetic tape unit.

magnetic tape drive Synonymous with *tape transport*.

magnetic tape file Used in the strictest sense to refer to a *reel* of *magnetic tape* containing *records* of information arranged in an ordered sequence; loosely used to refer to any *scratch tape* or *work tape* used in some intermediate processing.

magnetic tape group A set of *magnetic tape decks* built into a single cabinet, each deck capable of independent operation but sometimes arranged to share one or more *interface channels* for communication with a *central processor*.

Also known as cluster or tape cluster.

magnetic tape head That part of a *magnetic tape deck* which reads or writes information to the tape. Some tape decks have a single *read/write head* but others have separate heads for reading and writing; these are known as two gap heads. The heads are positioned so that reading takes place immediately after writing thus enabling a *parity check* to be made after the data has been recorded on the tape. If a machine malfunction causes the data to be incorrectly recorded this will be detected and the *block* will be rewritten.

magnetic tape librarian The person who stores *magnetic tape files* ready for use on a computer; he is usually responsible for maintaining clerical or mechanical records showing the use and availability of tape reels[3] and is responsible for issuing correct files to operators. In some installations the tape usage records may themselves be maintained on a tape file by a special *program*.

magnetic tape library The physical location in which *magnetic tape files* are stored, or the tapes themselves including all necessary clerical or mechanical records maintained to administrate the allocation and handling of tape reels[3]. ⟐ *magnetic tape librarian*.

magnetic tape parity An automatic checking technique used when *reading* or *writing* data to *magnetic tape*. As each tape *character* is transferred to the tape a *parity bit* is generated and added to the character. Each character written is read back, to check that the writing operation for that character has been correctly executed. In addition a complete parity character is written to the end of each tape *block* and this is used to check parity for the whole block. A *parity check* guards against the loss of *information bits* during the transfer of information from tape to *memory* and vice versa.

magnetic tape plotting system A system in which data recorded on *magnetic tape* is used to develop an X–Y plot for the purpose of controlling a *digital incremental plotter*.

magnetic tape reader A device for sensing data recorded as a series of magnetized spots on *magnetic tape*. ⟡ general article on *Magnetic Tape*.

magnetic tape streamer A *magnetic tape deck* used to back up a *magnetic disk*.

magnetic tape unit Synonymous with *magnetic tape deck*.

magnetic thin film ⟡ *thin-film memory*.

magnetic wire store A storage device in which data is recorded on a thin moving wire by an electro-magnetic *read/write head*.

magnetized ink character A character printed on a document by means of ink which is impregnated with a magnetizable material. The characters are in a stylized format to allow automatic recognition by machines (*magnetic ink character recognition*), while at the same time remaining readable by human beings. Machines which recognize such characters are usually fitted with a head which magnetizes the ink before the characters are presented to the reading head.

magneto-strictive acoustic delay line An *acoustic delay line* in which certain materials exhibiting the *magneto-strictive effect* are used to convert electrical signals to sonic waves and vice versa.

magneto-strictive effect An effect observed in certain materials when they are magnetized; certain physical strains are apparent, the mechanical stresses being approximately proportional to the square of the applied magnetic field. Such materials have applications where electrical signals are to be converted into sonic waves.

magnitude Of a number, the absolute value of the number irrespective of its sign.

mailbox 1. A computer application designed to offer a *messaging* service between members for a *closed user group*. 2. A process, perhaps in an *operating system*, used to exchange data between co-operating processes.

main frame Originally implied the main framework of a central processing unit on which the arithmetic unit and associated logic circuits were mounted, but now used colloquially to refer to the *central processor* itself and used to distinguish large computers from *minicomputers* and *microcomputers*.

main memory   The internal *memory* of a computer, i.e., the *immediate access store*, as distinct from any *backing store* that may be available as part of the computer system.

main path   The main course followed during the execution of a *routine* as distinct from the various alternative routes that may be entered according to conditions occurring during execution of the routine, perhaps dependent on the data being processed.

main program   The central part of a *program* which usually transfers control to other *subroutines* according to the nature of the data being processed or dependent on conditions arising during the operation of the program. The central framework on which the various sections or subroutines are mounted.

main routine   Synonymous with *main program*.

main storage   The *store* from which *instructions* are executed; usually the fastest store of a computer.

Also known as primary storage.

main store   The principal fast or *immediate access store* of a machine.

main store quota   In an *operating system* the area of *main store* made available by the *scheduling system* to a process when it is *rolled in*.

maintenance   The efficiency of any computer installation is dependent on the effective maintenance of both *hardware* and *software*. Various categories of maintenance of hardware may be recognized, all aimed at reducing *down time* and maximizing the serviceable time for running of *programs; preventive maintenance, routine maintenance* and *scheduled maintenance* are terms used to imply work performed to prevent failures, undertaken according to a pre-arranged timetable, whereas *corrective maintenance* is work required to correct a machine fault. These and other categories are useful classifications for collecting statistics about the efficiency of a particular computer or *peripheral* device. Software maintenance is the work required to keep *programs* up to date, e.g., to make them more efficient or otherwise amend them in accordance with changing circumstances affecting the user. It is usually necessary to see that programming effort is clearly scheduled for this task separately from any time scheduled for the development of new programs.

maintenance contract   Many computer manufacturers have a standard contract which allows the user the benefit of a resident service engineer or of periodic visits from a member of the manufacturer's service staff. The contract usually guarantees the user certain hours of *preventive* *maintenance* work throughout the duration of the contract, and may also specify a timetable for this work during which time the user must allow access to the equipment.

maintenance, file   ◊ *file maintenance.*

maintenance of programs   ◊ *maintenance.*

maintenance routine   A *routine* specifically designed to assist a service engineer in performing routine *preventive maintenance.*

maintenance, scheduled   ◊ *routine maintenance.*

major   Describing the relative significance of a *key* or *control data*[1] stored in a computer *record* or in a *punched card.*

major control change   On a *punched card tabulator*, the action of suspending *card feeding* and initiating *major control cycles* as a result of detecting a difference in major *control data* between one card and the next. ◊ *comparing control change.*

major control cycles   On a *punched card tabulator*, a series of control cycles that were automatically initiated during the processing of a file of punched cards as a result of detecting a change of major *control data.*

major control data   ◊ *control data.*

major cycle   1. The time between the recurrence of a given digit in a *cyclic store*. 2. One of the *control cycles* initiated in a *punched card tabulator* on a change of major *control data*. 3. A complete revolution of the storage medium in a *dynamic store.*

majority element   A *logic element* which has several *input* signals and which can be switched to provide an *output* signal only if a majority of the *weighted input signals* are present. ◊ *threshold element.*

malfunction routine   A *routine* designed to trace a fault in a computer's *hardware* or to assist in diagnosing an error in a *program.*

management information system   A system which may perform routine commercial processing functions, but which is designed so that such processing will also produce information that will be presented to management, including top management, to assist in decision making. The implication is that the results will be produced speedily, perhaps requiring *real time* processing, to enable management to ascertain the progress of the organization in terms of satisfying its major objectives.

manipulated variable   An *operand* which may be altered by *program* in order to control the operation of a *routine* in which the operand is used as a *parameter.*

mantissa   Strictly the fractional part of a logarithm; but also used to refer to the *fixed point part* of any *floating point* number (◊ *floating point arithmetic*). It can be misleading to use this word in the latter context and the term fixed point part is usually preferred.

manual control   Relating to a *program* or system in which some aspect of the work is controlled by the computer operator from the computer *console*.

manual input   The entry of data into a system or *program* directly, by the use of a *keyboard* device.

manual input unit   Any device which allows an operator to inject data into a system directly without the use of some intermediate medium such as *punched cards* or *paper tape*. For example, the entry of data into *memory* by means of a *console typewriter*.

manual operation   Any *data processing* operation performed without the use of automatic equipment; e.g., the pulling of documents or *punched cards* from a file.

manual (operations)   The status of a *peripheral unit* when it is *off-line* and hence cannot be controlled by an *operating system*.

manual word generator   A device by means of which an operator can set up a *word* of information for direct entry into *memory*.

Also known as manual word unit.

manual word unit   Synonymous with *manual word generator*.

marginal checking   ◊ *marginal testing*.

marginal cost   The amount by which the cost of any operation is altered as a result of a change in the number of units handled or processed.

marginal testing   A test performed on equipment to diagnose some intermittent fault or to see whether the equipment is able to operate within specified operating tolerances. For example, the output of a power unit may be restricted to ascertain the effect on circuits of a reduction in power supply.

Also known as marginal checking. ◊ *bias testing*.

margin-notched card   Synonymous with *edge-notched card*.

margin-punched card   A card which was punched with holes in a comparatively narrow strip along one edge of the card, leaving the centre free for written information. The punching *code* often resembled the type of punching used in 5, 6 or 7 *track paper tape*.

Also known as edge-punched card, border-punched card, verge-perforated card. Contrasted with *edge-notched card*.

mark   1. A *character* used to identify the end of a set of data, e.g., *tape mark*, *group marks*. Also known as marker. 2. In *telegraphic communication*, a positive pulse representing an element in a *character code*.

mark, control   ◊ *tape mark*[1].

marker   Synonymous with *mark*.

mark hold   In telegraphic circuits, a steady signal transmitted to signify that no information is being transferred. The first element of any message would be a *space signal* of opposite polarity to the mark; thereafter the characters transferred would consist of a coded series of marks and spaces each of comparatively short duration.

marking In *serial data signals*, such as those used internally within a computer, the data signal line may be held with a high voltage when data is next being transmitted on the line. This is referred to as marking.

mark reading Synonymous with *mark scanning*. ⊗ *Character Recognition*.

mark scanning A process in which marks made in predetermined positions on documents are read optically and interpreted as *digits* or *characters* for direct entry into a computer, or for punching into some other medium. The documents are preprinted to enable entries to be made in specified locations; the layout of the documents can be designed to enable the user to code information in a required manner. The marks may be made with any material provided there is a clear optical contrast with the paper. Contrasted with *mark sensing*.

Also known as mark reading. ⊗ *Character Recognition*.

mark scanning document A document specially printed with reference columns to enable marks to be made for subsequent reading by a *mark scanning* device.

mark sense cards *Punched cards* divided into *card columns* to facilitate *mark sensing*. Mark sense columns are usually the width of two or three normal punching columns.

mark sensing The automatic sensing of marks made with some conductive material on predetermined positions of a *punched card*. The marks were made, usually with a graphite pencil lead, in columns to represent digits, in much the same way as holes in *card columns* represent digits. These marks were sensed electrically and as a result holes were punched in corresponding *punching positions* of predetermined card columns, either on the same, or another, card. ⊗ *mark sensing*.

mark-space multiplier A *multiplier*[2] used in *analog computers* wherein an input voltage is used to regulate the *mark-to-space ratio* of a square wave. Another input voltage controls the amplitude of the wave, and the output signal is then operated upon by a smoothing circuit to develop a product which is represented as an average value of the signal.

mark-to-space ratio A ratio of the duration of the positive and negative cycles of a square wave. A mark is a positive cycle and a space is a negative cycle.

mask A pattern of *characters* or *bits* devised so as to alter or isolate specific *bit positions* present in another *bit pattern*. A mask is usually one of the *operands* in a *Boolean operation*.

Also known as extractor, filter. ⟡ *masking*.

masking The technique of using a *mask* to operate on the *bit pattern* of some other *operand*, in order to alter or isolate certain *bit positions*. Usually involves the use of one or more Boolean operations such as *and operation, or operation*.

mask register A *register* used specifically for *masking*; i.e., to determine which portions of *operands* are to be tested under the aegis of some *logical operation*.

mass data Data in such volume that it cannot be stored in *memory* at one time, e.g., data stored on a *magnetic disk file*.

mass storage Some *backing storage* medium of large capacity directly *on-line* to a *central processor*. For example, a large *magnetic disk file*.

Also known as bulk storage.

master card A *punched card* holding any fixed information about a group of cards or a whole card file, usually appearing as the first or last card of the group.

master clock A device which generates clocking signals to synchronize the operation of a machine. In an electronic computer, a device which generates clock pulses to maintain the basic time frequency of the electronic circuits.

master control routine 1. A *routine* which forms part of a *program* consisting of a series of subroutines. The master control routine controls the linking of the other subroutines and may call the various *segments* of the program into *memory* as required. 2. Also used to describe a program which controls the operation of a *hardware system*, for example assigning *peripheral units* and controlling operator activities; but ⟡ *executive program*.

master console A *console* exercising overall control over a computer system.

master data Those *data elements* of a *record* which seldom change; e.g., descriptive data such as personnel number, stock item number.

master file A *file* of reference data which is changed relatively infrequently but which is used to provide data for a system on a routine basis; e.g., a cross reference index. 2. A current, fully updated file to which *change records* of new transactions are applied.

master instruction tape A *magnetic tape* which maintains all the *routines* required for a particular *suite* of *programs*.

master library tape A *reel* of *magnetic tape* which contains all the *programs* and major *subroutines* required in a particular data processing centre. During operation of the computer this tape may remain permanently *loaded* on a *magnetic tape deck*: at the beginning of any *run* the computer operator calls into *memory* the particular program required.

Also known as master program file.

master operating station An *operating station* which contains a *console* by means of which overall control of a computer system can be exercised.

master program file Synonymous with *master library tape*.

master record In a *magnetic tape* system, the latest version of any particular *record* carried forward to the next processing *run*. Contrasted with *change record*.

master/slave system A system in which a large central computer is connected to one or more *satellite processors*. The central or master computer has control over the other machines, usually via direct control over the input and output operations. The computers in the system may be assigned special tasks under control of the master computer such as the transmission and receipt of data to or from some external source, the assembly and editing of data for processing or the processing of data to obtain desired results.

master tape A *magnetic tape* containing data that must not be *overwritten*; for example a tape containing a *master file*, or current transaction data.

match Synonymous with *equivalence operation*.

matching The technique of comparing the *keys* of two *records* to select items for a particular stage of processing or to reject invalid records.

material implication Synonymous with *conditional implication operation*.

mathematical analysis The study of the relationship between numbers and the operations performed on them, including the concepts of algebra and arithmetic.

mathematical check A check performed to verify a result achieved by some arithmetic operation. The use of alternative methods to obtain results using given *operands*; e.g., $(A \times B) \div C = (B \div C) A$.

mathematical logic The use of mathematical concepts, including the adoption of a symbolic notation, in order to represent valid argument without the attendent inaccuracy and ambiguity of ordinary language.

mathematical model A representation of some process or problem in mathematical form in which equations are used to simulate the behaviour of the process or system represented. Usually enables a range of alternative actions to be simulated in order to ascertain the optimum conditions under which the system would be operated to achieve, or most nearly achieve, its objectives. ⟡ general article on *Model Building*.

mathematical subroutine A *subroutine* written to perform some mathematical function; e.g., square root, sine, tangent, etc.

matrix 1. A rectangular array of numbers that may be operated on using prescribed rules involving mathematical operations such as addition, multiplication, etc. The term has become more loosely applied in data processing to any table of items. 2. Sometimes used to refer to an array of circuit elements; e.g., diodes in a conversion matrix for generating one set of coded signals from another.

matrix printer Synonymous with *needle printer*.

matrix store A *store* in which a particular *location* or circuit element is addressed by the use of coordinates.

Also known as coordinate store.

mean repair time In a given time period, the ratio of time spent in *corrective maintenance* of a unit to the number of unit *failures*.

mean time between failures In a given time period, the ratio of the total time in the period to the number of *failures* in the period.

mean time to repair Synonymous with *mean repair time*.

medium As, for example, in input medium, the particular material in which data is recorded for the purpose of input to *memory*. Examples of input media are *punched cards*, *paper tape*, *magnetic tape*, *magnetic ink* documents or documents bearing characters for *optical character recognition*.

medium scale integration An imprecise term referring to a level of microelectronic technology in which up to a 1000 *logic gates* may exist on a single *chip*. The term *large scale integration* (LSI) refers to more than 1000 gates per chip, and the term *very large scale integration* (VLSI) refers to more than 10,000 gates per chip.

meet operation Synonymous with *and operation*.

mega- A million; as in 10 megacycles per second, meaning 10 million cycles per second.

megabit Pertaining to a *store*, a million *binary digits*.

megabyte A million *bytes*.

memory This term is usually reserved for describing the *internal store* of a computer, i.e., the *immediate access store*. In its strictest sense it refers to the storage *locations* that can be immediately addressed by the *program controller* of the *central processor*, rather than to any *backing store* medium such as *magnetic tape*, *magnetic disk* or *magnetic drum* *storage*. However, these backing stores are sometimes referred to as *memory units*, as in *disk-file memory*, in which case the internal storage would be referred to as *main memory*.

Also known as immediate access storage, *store*, *core store*, main store.

memory, acoustic ◊ *acoustic store*.

memory address A *binary* numeric code given to a *memory location* in order that the location can be selected for *reading* or *writing* under program control. For example, a microcomputer with 64,000 *words* of memory would be required to carry an internal *address highway* capable of handling a binary address of 16 *bits*. An addressing system of this dimension will yield a sufficient range of numbers to address 64,000 separate memory locations uniquely. To help the programmer to avoid handling 16-bit binary address codes, a computer is normally provided with a programming *language* system which allows *hexadecimal* numbers or *symbolic* addresses to be used.

memory address register A *register* used in the addressing of *operands* in other *locations* of *store*. The *address* component of each *instruction* is stored in a memory address register while the instruction is executed.

memory, associative ◊ *associative store*.

memory buffer register A special *register* through which all data entering or leaving *memory* must pass. Thus the register acts as a *buffer store* to facilitate transfers of data to and from the memory and *peripheral units*.

memory capacity The number of units of data that can be stored in *memory*, expressed in terms of the number of *locations* available; examples are 32,000 24-bit *words*, 1 million *binary digits*, 120,000 6-bit *characters*, 1 *megabyte*.

memory core ◊ *ferrite core*.

memory cycle 1. The complete sequence of operations required to insert or extract a unit of data from *memory*. 2. The time taken to perform a complete sequence of operations. ◊ *fetch* and *execute*.

memory dump An operation to output the contents of all or some of the *locations* in *memory* by printing out or writing to some *backing store medium*. Printing out is usually adopted when a *program* is being tested or an attempt is being made to diagnose some *software* error, but memory dumps are also made as a precaution against machine malfunction.

Also known as storage dump. ◊ general articles on *Dump and Restart* and *Debugging*.

memory, dynamic ◊ *dynamic store*.

memory, external ◊ *external store*.

memory fill A technique used to bring to notice the fact that a *program* is trying to derive *instructions* from forbidden *locations* or *registers*. The registers concerned are filled with predetermined characters which signal an error condition if addressed.

memory guard A *hardware* or *software* device which prevents a program from *addressing* specified *locations* in *internal store*.

memory, internal Synonymous with *internal store*. ⟡ *memory*.

memory module In designing internal *memory* systems for computers, it is not always efficient or practical to create a memory system of required capacity from a single memory *chip*. In most cases, a number of chips have to be arranged to support the required capacity. A group of chips arranged for this purpose is referred to as a memory module.

memory overlays The utilization of *memory* by various sections or *segments* of a *program*; e.g., where the program is of such size that it cannot conveniently be held in its entirety in *main memory* at any one time. Thus at any instant the memory locations will be occupied by segments which in turn may be *overwritten* by other segments as the functions performed by these segments are required.

memory parity bit An extra *bit* attached to each *memory storage location*, in order to allow *error detection* (and perhaps *error correction*) when monitoring internal data transfers within a computer. Computer *architectures* for *mainframe* and *minicomputers* invariably use this parity checking system, but some microcomputers do not. ⟡ *parity bit* and *parity check*.

memory, permanent ⟡ *non-volatile memory*.

memory power The efficiency of a particular *memory* design in respect of its rate of processing; e.g., a *store* may be said to have a cycle speed of 30 *nanoseconds* one *microsecond*.

memory print The output of the contents of *memory locations* to a *printer*. ⟡ *memory dump*.

memory protect A feature of *multiprogramming* computers, in which a *hardware* device is used to protect each *program*, and its data, from being mutilated by any other program that may be operating in the system at the same time.

memory, random access Synonymous with *direct access storage*.

memory, rapid-access ⟡ *rapid-access loop*.

memory, thin-film ⟡ *thin-film store*.

memory unit Synonymous with *backing store*. ⟡ *memory*.

menu selection A method of using a *terminal* to *display* a list of optional facilities which can be chosen by the *user* in order to carry out different functions in a system.

mercury delay line An *acoustic delay line* in which mercury is used to recirculate sonic signals.

mercury memory A storage device in which information is retained by recirculating signals in a *mercury delay line*.

merge An operation performed on two, or more, ordered sets of *records* to create a single set or *file*. The two original sets must first be arranged into the same sequence by *sorting* on a common *key*. This operation may be performed on *punched cards* by a *collator*, or on any ordered file of records held in *memory* or on a *backing store* medium.

mesh network ◊ *network architecture*.

message 1. Any combination of *characters* and *symbols* designed to communicate information from one point to another. For example, a set of *records* transmitted over a *data link* between one computer and another, or an *error message* displayed on a computer *console* to draw the operator's attention to some specific machine or *program* error. 2. *Data* input to a *transaction processing* system through a *terminal* for processing. A message together with the *reply* it generates constitutes an *exchange*. A set of *exchanges* constitute a *transaction*.

message display console A *console* unit fitted with a *visual display tube* to permit data to be displayed in character form. When this is fitted to a *central processor*, data stored in *memory* can be selected and displayed as a page. For example, 20 lines each of 80 character positions might be displayed, using a full *character repertoire* of 64 characters.

message exchange A *hardware* device forming part of a *data link*, which performs certain routine switching functions to relieve the computer of these tasks.

message queuing In a *data communications* system, a technique for controlling the way in which messages are handled. Messages may be accepted by a central computer and be temporarily stored until they are processed or routed to some further destination.

message routing A function performed by *hardware* or *software* in a *data communications* system: messages received in a central computer are examined and routed to the destination required.

message switching system A *data communications* system in which a central computer is used to service several distant terminals, receiving *messages* from them and storing them until they can be retransmitted to some desired destination.

messaging service A form of *electronic mail* designed to enable users to exchange short messages, and not intended for the interchange of lengthy documents.

method study The use of certain techniques for recording and examining existing and proposed methods of working in order to improve them. ⟡ *time study*.

MHz Abbreviation of megahertz. ⟡ *Hertz*.

MICR Acronym for *Magnetic Ink Character Recognition*.

micro- A prefix denoting one millionth (10^{-6}), as in *microsecond*.

micro code Synonymous with *microinstruction*.

micro-coding The process of simulating a program *instruction* not normally part of an *instruction set* by means of a series of simple program steps. A section of micro-coding forms a *macroinstruction*. Contrasted with *macro-coding*.

microcomputer A term used to define the first small desk-top computers which were based upon an 8-*bit microprocessor*, with up to 64,000 *words* or *bytes* of *memory* (*ROM* and *RAM*), and *input/output ports* for connecting *peripheral units*.

The electronic logic of a microcomputer is often housed on a single *printed circuit board*, which is stored in a case and provided with a *keyboard* for *data entry* and a *visual display unit*. The input/output logic may support a range of peripheral units such as a *line printer*, *modem* for telecommunications, *floppy* or *hard disk*, a *mouse*, or a *joystick*. Such devices will attach to plug connexions on the rear panel of the microcomputer.

The first microcomputers were intended for single users only, and this clearly distinguished them from *minicomputers*; however, the later 16-bit microcomputers and 32-bit microcomputers have *operating systems* and peripheral connectivity to support many simultaneous users, and there is no clear distinction between them and so-called minicomputers.

All computers of this type are best considered as general purpose computers which may be distinguished by their architectural attributes and operating system facilities which allow them to support a type of workload (e.g., number of peripherals, number of simultaneous users, of main memory and disk capacity). ⟡ *microprocessor*.

microinstruction An *instruction* at *machine code* level which directly controls the functioning of *hardware* independently of *operating system* or *application software*. Also known as micro code.

microprocessor An electronic device which can perform a range of basic logical functions (such as and, or, add, sub) upon given input signals. The device also contains *memory* and features which enable it to be programmed to perform sequences of such functions, and thus a complete *instruction set* for a central processing unit can be created in this single logical device.

A typical microprocessor will consist of a series of *registers* into which *binary data* is stored and processed. The *order code set* is provided by a *microprogram*, stored in the control unit of the microprocessor, which invokes sequences of logical operations to make up the individual instructions of the order code. Thus a microprocessor is described as a *microprogrammed device*, where the microprogram offers machine code and even *assembly* code *languages*. Usually the microprogram is built into the microprocessor and cannot be altered by the designers who build such components into computer products. However, some microprocessors are provided in such a way that their microprograms can be amended – these are then defined as *microprogrammable devices*, which allow an application specific order code to be created.

The first microprocessors appeared at the beginning of the 1970s and prior to this all processor functions within computers were built of discrete logical devices by computer designers working for the main computer manufacturers. Today a wide variety of microprocessors are available from a number of component manufacturers. These are supplied as standard components to manufacturers to be incorporated into computer systems. The first microprocessors were relatively slow devices which could operate only upon 8-*bit words*, but today devices handling 16-bit and 32-bit words are also available. The first 8-bit microprocessors were extensively used in small personal microcomputers, as well as in the control of processes such as heating and lighting systems. Today microprocessors are used as processors for most general purpose computers, and broadly in all forms of control engineering.

microprogram A *program* stored within the *control unit* of a *microprocessor*, and usually created by the designer of the microprocessor and not normally alterable by users. A microprogram consists of a series of *binary* codes which carry out the specific actions requested by *assembly language* statements. These actions provide the underlying logic of the microprocessor as represented to users by the assembly language, although in reality each assembly statement may give rise to five or six or more *microinstructions*.

A microprogram is stored entirely within the microprocessor in a special internal data area associated with the *registers*. Unlike a *macroprogram* it may not use *ROM* and *RAM* as *memory*. ✑ macroprogram.

microprogrammable device A *microprocessor* which has been specifically designed to allow users to create or modify *microprograms* stored within the *control unit*.

microprogrammed device All *microprocessors* contain *microprograms* which impart the basic logic given by their *instruction set*. They are said to be microprogrammed. Some microprocessors allow users to create or amend the microprogram and they are then in a special class known as *microprogrammable devices*.

microsecond One millionth of a second.

microwave Pertaining to *data communications* systems in which ultra high-frequency waveforms are used to transmit voice or data messages.

middleware Computer manufacturer's *software* which has been tailored to the particular needs of an installation.

milli- A prefix meaning one thousandth (10^{-3}), as in *millivolt, millisecond*, etc.

millisecond One thousandth of a second.

millivolt One thousandth of a volt.

minicomputer An inexact term distinguishing computers which tend not to need a special environment and highly specialized operators from *main frame* computers. Also contrasted with *personal computers*.

minimum access code A coding system which minimizes the time needed to retrieve any required unit of data from a *storage device*.

Also known as minimum latency code, minimum delay code, optimum code.

minimum access coding The technique of *programming* computers so as to reduce *access time* to a minimum. ◊ *minimum access code*.

Also known as minimum delay coding, optimum coding.

minimum delay code Synonymous with *minimum access code*.

minimum delay coding Synonymous with *minimum access coding*.

minimum latency code Synonymous with *minimum access codes*.

minor control change On a *punched card tabulator* the action of suspending card feeding and initiating *minor cycles* as a result of detecting the difference in minor *control data* between one card and the rest. ◊ *comparing control change*.

minor cycle 1. On a *punched card tabulator*, a cycle of machine operations occurring during a *minor control change*. 2. In any *storage device*, the interval between corresponding positions of successive *words*.

minuend One of the *operands* used in subtraction, the quantity from which another quantity is subtracted.

minus zone The *character* or *digit position* displaying the algebraic sign of an *operand*.

misfeed A failure to feed a document from the *hopper* of a document handling device.

mixed base notation   The representation of quantities where any two or more adjacent *digit positions* have a different *radix* of notation.

Also known as mixed radix notation.

mixed number   A number consisting of an *integral* part and a *fractional* part; e.g., 10.52 is a decimal mixed number.

mixed radix notation   ◊ *mixed base notation*.

mnemonic   A *label* chosen so as to be associated in some way with the item to which it refers, e.g., the *fields* in a payroll *record* might be given labels GROSS, NET, TAX, etc. ◊ *mnemonic operation codes*.

mnemonic operation codes   In *symbolic programming languages*, the *operation code* forming part of each *instruction* is represented by some symbolic code easier for the programmer to remember than the numeric code forming part of the basic *machine code*. For example, the operation *multiplication* might be represented as MULT.

mode   A particular method of operation for a *hardware* or *software* device; for example, a particular unit might be capable of operating in, say, *binary mode* or *character mode*. For further examples, ◊ *burst mode, byte mode, conversational mode*.

model   A representation of a system, device or process in a mathematical form ◊ *mathematical model, model building*.

model building   Many computer systems, and most *operational research*, can be regarded as comprising the formulation and studying of models of real life situations. In this sense a model is a representation of a situation. Loosely the model may be many things, from a profit and loss account representing a business situation to a weather chart representing the meteorological situation. More strictly we use the word 'model' in the operational research sense to mean a model expressed in terms which can be analysed, usually by mathematical methods, or, if not analysed directly, can be studied by *simulation* techniques.

The aim of building a model is to include in it only those features of the situation which are important to it. The model builder must consider, at the formulation stage, what features he is to include. It is easier to investigate the model than the situation it represents (which may not even exist), although generally speaking, the more features that are included the more difficult the subsequent analysis will be. The amount of detail included should give both meaningful results and ease of analysis.

The simplest models will yield results directly, the more complicated will need complex techniques to handle them. In the simple case the analyst may find he has only to solve a series of simultaneous equations, or optimize some variables, perhaps by *linear programming* techniques. In the more complex he may have to resort to sampling theory, using perhaps Monte Carlo Methods, or operational gaming. The engineer (and others) may often find that the *analog computers* can be of help.

A *digital computer* is often essential in analysing a model. Simulation studies are made much more easily, allowing larger samples to be taken. Particularly when the analysis has to be repeated regularly (e.g., in reflecting market demand for a product) the digital computer achieves something that would be impossible without it. However the use of a computer can present its own problems. The *programming* of a computer for simulation studies is not an easy task, although the introduction of new *languages* is making this easier. Also the ability of a computer to handle large samples does not replace the necessity for the model builder to provide a model which corresponds closely to the real situation. Sampling errors are, of course, unavoidable, but there are many techniques for detecting and measuring them.

The construction of a mathematical model of a situation is nearly always worthwhile, since it can only add to the understanding of that situation; it must be remembered, however, that a model is literally only a model, and the more detailed the model becomes the more difficult will become subsequent analysis.

modem An acronym for M Odulator/D EModulator. A device which enables *data* to be transmitted over long distances without error. ⬦ *modulation* and general article on *Communication Devices*.

modification The technique of altering *instructions* and *addresses* in a *program* by treating them as data and applying *arithmetical* and *logical operations* to them. ⬦ *program modification*.

modifier An item of data used to alter a *program instruction* so that the instruction, sometimes referred to as a *basic instruction*, can be used repetitively to execute a different operation on each occasion, e.g., the *operand address* may be modified to operate upon successive items in an *array* of data. ⬦ *program modification, address modification*.

modifier register A *register* into which a *modifier* can be loaded in order to effect the *modification* of a *basic instruction*.

Also known as *index register*.

modify To apply the technique of *modification*. ⬦ general article on *Program Modification*.

modular A method of constructing a *hardware* or *software* system using standard compatible units. In this way a wide range of *configurations* can be built up with combinations of the standard units.

modularity The condition exhibited by any *hardware* or *software* system that permits the subsequent expansion of the system by the addition of standard *modular* units.

modular programming   Modular programming is a technique used in *programming* which simplifies the tasks of developing and maintaining large *suites* of programs. The objective of modular programming methods is to achieve two main goals: speed and efficiency of *debugging* and ease of *maintenance* of the programs in a suite.

The basis of modular programming techniques is to divide each program at the planning stage into a number of logical parts or *modules*[2]. Each module corresponds to a particular program function and can be treated as a separate entity. A number of different programs may in practice share certain common modules. Each individual module is relatively simple to specify, write and test. Changing requirements can be met by simply changing existing modules or adding new modules to the system.

Modular programming techniques have been powerfully extended by means of modular program testing software, sometimes known as a *testbed*. A testbed is a software system which allows the user to test individual modules independently of the overall context of the program of which they are subdivisions. *Test data* needed for the program is supplied to the testbed and fed automatically to modules being tested. Where modules require to pass data to or from other modules not yet developed, the testbed can simulate the presence of these modules for testing purposes. A testing system for program modules may also have available other programming aids such as keeping records of the progress of testing, providing detailed diagnostic information, automatic generation of test data. A further feature is the ability of the user to choose different *languages* for different modules, for example mixing *COBOL, FORTRAN* and possibly a *low level language* within a single program. The testbed software would co-ordinate the *object code* generated for the complete program regardless of the *source code* used for each module.

Also known as structured programming.

modulation   A technique used in radio, telegraphic and telephonic communication systems, in which data signals are used to modify either the amplitude, phase or frequency of a carrier wave by means of *modems* (modulator/demodulators). The carrier wave is of a suitable frequency for transmitting over a specified channel, and therefore carries with it the data signals which normally would not be capable of transmission over the circuit concerned.

modulation code   A coded signal used to modulate the frequency or *amplitude* of a carrier wave. ⟡ *modulation, modem.*

modulator   A device which superimposes a data signal on a carrier wave according to a predetermined method. ⟡ *modulation.*

modulator/demodulator   ⟡ *modem* and *modulation.*

module   1. A *hardware* device or *software* item which, as a standard unit, forms part of a *modular system.* 2. The term is used more specifically for a self-contained subset of a *program* and in this sense is related to *segment.* ⟡ general article on *Modular Programming.* 3. In an *operating system,* the unit of a *process,* consisting of a number of *areas* including *code* areas and *data* areas, which can be held as a single entity in a *filestore.*

module key   A *key* used to identify and access an area in a *module* in *filestore.*

modulo   An *arithmetical operation* in which the *result* is the *remainder* after the first *operand* is divided by the second, e.g., 27 modulo 4=3.

modulo *n* check   A method for checking the validity of a numeric *operand,* in which the number is divided by *n* to produce a remainder (⟡ *modulo*). The remainder then accompanies the result as a *check digit* and subsequently the number may again be divided by *n* and the remainder is compared with the previously calculated check digit. When *n*=9, known as *casting-out-nines.*

modulo 2 sum   Synonymous with *inclusive-or operation.*

monadic operation   A processing operation performed upon one *operand.*

monitor   Any device which examines the status of a system to indicate any deviation from prescribed operational conditions. For example, a device which examines a signal in a communications channel.

monitor display   A *display* on a *terminal* which is for information only and is not an *interactive display.*

monitor routine   1. Any *routine* which observes the progress of work in a computer system. 2. More specifically, a routine designed to supervise and control the operation of *programs* in the computer, performing the functions of an *executive program.* 3. A routine used to provide diagnostic information on the progress of a program for the purpose of *debugging.*

monitor system   A collection of *routines* stored permanently in *memory* which control the operation of users' *programs* and coordinate the various *hardware* and *software* activities. Synonymous with *executive program.* Such a system controls the allocation of *store* and *peripheral* *units* to programs, the loading and scheduling of programs, *time sharing* of *input/output* operations, and *multi programming*.

monostable device A device which has only one stable state. For example, a monostable trigger can be activated to assume momentarily an unstable condition but it will immediately resume its stable state.

most significant character The character in the extreme left-hand position of a group of significant *characters* in *positional representation*.

motherboard Synonymous with *backplane*. Sometimes used to mean a stand-alone unit with all functional elements of a *microcomputer*, accepting further elements as *daughterboards*.

mouse A device whose movements on a flat surface are reflected by *cursor* movements on a *visual display unit*, thus obviating the need for a keyboard. See also *icon*.

MSX A *microcomputer operating system*.

MTBF Abbreviation of *mean time between failures*.

MTTR Abbreviation of *mean time to repair*. ◊ *mean repair time*.

multi-access A multi-access system is one that allows a number of people to perform the interactive role usually associated with an *operator's console*. The access points (which may be a few only or hundreds in number) are generally linked to the *central processor* by switched *data transmission* lines rather than by direct cabling as with most types of *on-line peripheral unit*. The remote terminals may range from simple devices like cash registers, perhaps with an automatic input mechanism for reading pre-coded data, through *console typewriters* and *visual display units* to complete *satellite processors*. There are two main categories of multi-access system: one operates with a single complex of *programs* and the other allows the processing of as many diverse programs as there are terminals.

Systems which employ multi-access terminals in support of a common series of tasks are mainly *real time* applications, such as airline seat reservation, banking, stock exchange dealing, crime detection and weather forecasting. Essentially, multi-access is used to facilitate communications. The remote stations transmit data to the central processor for *updating* large central files held on *direct access storage devices*; and the same network is used to send back status reports to the terminals, such as the number of seats available on a given flight or the name and address registered under a vehicle licence number.

Multi-access, *multiprogramming* systems have been installed by many universities and research institutes to make a powerful computing facility available to the greatest possible number of students and researchers. The technique provides the benefit of *open shop* problem-solving without consequent dispersal of the budget for *hardware*. Numerous terminals can be used simultaneously, each programmer conducting his work in *conversational mode* so that his experiment can be completed in one sitting, avoiding the difficulty of scheduling *debugging time*. A *response time* of a few seconds can be given to each terminal because human intervention is an inherently slow process. This level of service is sufficient to make each user feel that he has the machine to himself.

Both types of multi-access system rely on the art of *time sharing*. A different degree of sophistication is required for different applications, for example a critical real time system should be *modular* to permit *graceful degradation* rather than catastrophic failure, and a multi-user system must incorporate *memory protection*. It may be necessary to charge users pro rata for the service, requiring adequate logging of time and peripheral usage by the central *operating system*.

Considerable developments are taking place in multi-access and time sharing systems, leading to the establishment of *data banks* for various spheres of activity. Thus insurance brokers, travel agents, doctors and lawyers may be able to share systems which will provide background information and do their clerical work, with access by telephone circuits. *Videotex* systems have greatly stimulated such use.

multi-address instruction An *instruction* which specifies the *address* of more than one *operand*. ⇨ *Instruction Format*.

multi-aspect search A search conducted on a series of items using various logical combinations of the elements within each item to identify and select the items required. ⇨ *Information Retrieval*.

multi-cycle feeding A system used on *punched card tabulators* in which several lines of print could be obtained from a single card. The card was *read* repeatedly on several consecutive machine cycles and on each occasion certain specified *fields* (e.g., name, street, town, etc.) were read until all the lines required had been printed. Synonymous with multi-read feeding.

multi-drop network ⇨ *network architecture*.

multi-length arithmetic ⇨ *multiple-length arithmetic*.

multi-level addressing Synonymous with *indirect addressing*.

multiple address Pertaining to *instructions* which specify the *addresses* of more than one *store location*. For example, some computers have *instruction formats* which enable two or three *operands* to be specified as part of one instruction.

multi-address code Pertaining to an *instruction format* that requires the programmer to specify the *address* of more than one *operand* at any one *instruction*.

multiple connector A symbol used in *flowcharting* to indicate the confluence of several *flowlines*.

multiple-length arithmetic Arithmetic performed using two or more machine *words* to *store* each *operand*, usually to achieve greater precision in the result, e.g., by storing a decimal function in two words, one holding the *integer* and another the fractional part. Arithmetic involving the generation of a result which requires to be stored in two or more words.

Also known as multi-length arithmetic. ⋄ *double-precision arithmetic* and *triple-length working*.

multiple-length number In a *word oriented memory*, any *operand* which exceeds the capacity of one word.

multiple-length working Any processing in which two or more *words* are used to *store* a number.

multiple punching In *punched card* practice, the punching of more than two holes in any single *card column*.

multiple recording Where more than one copy of a *file* is maintained, and *updated* simultaneously *on-line* to a processor. The objective of multiple recording is to minimize the chances of losing a current file. ⋄ *redundancy*[4].

multiplex 1. A multiplex system involves the transfer of data from several comparatively slow-speed *storage devices* over a series of channels to a fast central storage device which continually scans and accepts data from each channel in turn. The fast storage device is able to service the channels without any part of the system being delayed. 2. To transmit a number of messages concurrently over the same circuit.

multiplex data terminal A terminal unit at which two or more *input/output* devices may be stationed and which acts as a modulator/demodulator (⋄ *modem*) to accept and transfer signals between the input/output units and a data channel.

multiplexer ⋄ *multiplexor*.

multiplexing 1. The simultaneous transmission of several messages over a single communications channel, usually by modulating a carrier wave in such a way that separate signals are transmitted using particular frequencies within the full bandwidth of the channel. 2. Pertaining to any system in which a single device is used for many purposes.

multiplexor A communications control device which enables a *central processor* to be connected to a large number of different communications *channels*, any or all of which may be transferring data to or from the processor. The multiplexor operates at high speed to service each channel in turn *character* by character, and interrupts the processor to place each character into *memory*. Control data is transferred to and from the central processor to identify each character, and this allows input messages to be assembled in memory for processing or retransmission.

multiplexor channel A *channel* allowing the interleaving of many simultaneous transmissions in both directions.

multiplexor-channel time sharing A system whereby a number of terminal units may be connected to the same communications *channel* so that effectively a number of independent channels exist over the same circuit. Each unit is able to transmit data *characters* over the circuit accompanied by identifying characters, and by the use of *time sharing* techniques the terminal units can all use the channel concurrently.

multiplexor, data channel ⇨ *data channel multiplexor*.

multiplicand One of the factors used in *multiplication*: a quantity which is multiplied by another.

multiplication The arithmetic process in which a result (the *product*) is obtained from two factors, the *multiplicand* and the *multiplier*. In most digital computers the result is obtained as an accumulation of the *multiplicand* repeated according to the value of the *multiplier*; but this basic method is usually adapted to reduce the number of steps involved. ⇨ *multiplication table*.

multiplication table In some computers the process of multiplication is performed indirectly by looking up values in a table stored permanently within the *memory*. The table is referred to as the multiplication table.

multiplication time The time required to multiply a specified pair of *operands*.

multiplier 1. One of the factors used in *multiplication*; that number which is used to multiply another. 2. A *hardware* unit capable of performing multiplication.

multiplier register A *register* used to hold the *multiplier* while *multiplication* is being performed.

multi-precision arithmetic The use of two or more *words* for any *operand* in an arithmetic process, where undesired inaccuracy would have resulted if a single word had been used.

multiprocessor A *central processor* containing two or more independent arithmetic units and their associated *control logic*.

multiprocessor interleaving A technique for allocating *memory* areas to the different processors within a *multiprocessor system*. The *store* is subdivided into *modules* which are referenced as even or odd, and the *addressing* structure for the *locations* within any module remains as in the standard *machine code*. In this way a number of modules are allocated to each processor to avoid interaction between *programs* being run simultaneously.

multiprocessor system Two or more *processors* capable of driving the same *applications* and providing extra processing power and/or *resilience* in the total system. In a fully effective multiprocessor system the *main store* (i.e., *data* and *code*) must be shareable between processors and no one processor inherently has a dominant relationship to the others. All processors operate under the control of one *operating system*, which automatically switches work from any processor which is faulty, and will ensure that work is distributed to ensure rational loading of the processor. ⟨⟩ *loosely coupled twin* and *tightly coupled twin*. Contrasted with *multiprogramming* system, in which a single processing unit is used on a *time sharing* basis to operate several *programs* independently.

multiprogramming There is an extreme difference in the speeds at which a computer handles its internal operations (performing calculations on data in its *central processor*) and the speeds at which even the fastest *peripheral units* used for input and output of data operate. In the time taken to print one line on a *printer* working at 1200 lines per minute, a processor could perform many thousand additions. Few *programs* would in fact perform many operations between printing successive lines of print, or performing any other peripheral operation, and this means that during the operation of a program which makes fairly frequent use of a peripheral device there will be long periods of time (long, that is, in relation to the internal speeds of the computer, something like several thousandths of a second) during which the processor is idle, waiting for a peripheral transfer to finish before it can continue by performing the next set of internal operations.

To help redress the balance, *time sharing* techniques have been developed which enable a single program using more than one peripheral unit to continue processing while several of the units under its control continue their respective actions. However, there will still be periods of time when the processor remains idle, and in any event peripheral units not used by the program during time sharing cannot be used at all, since they need a program to 'drive' them.

Multiprogramming is a technique developed in order to utilize a computer more efficiently by enabling the processor to spend a greater proportion of its time in action and by making more use of all available peripheral units. The basic principle of multiprogramming is that more than one program can be present in *memory* at the same time, and share the available processor time and peripheral units. Each program is written as a completely independent unit, as if it were being produced for a single-program machine, and each program uses peripheral units allotted to it for the duration of a *run*. With several programs sharing the computer the best use is made of the central processor time, whilst all the programs concerned also make more practical and extensive use of the available peripheral units. For example, a program to read data from magnetic disk and rewrite to *magnetic tape* will only require the use of the central processor for a very small fraction of the program running time, the remainder representing peripheral transfer time during which other programs in the system can use the central processor. Benefits to be gained from this concept of multiprogramming include the elimination of *off-line* equipment to transcribe data on to a faster medium for input since while this activity is proceeding, using limited numbers of peripheral units and little processing time, other more productive programs can use the remaining peripherals and processor time.

In order to achieve multiprogramming, several problems must be overcome. Obviously, if more than one program is present in memory at the same time, there must be no danger of one program interfering with another. Interference could involve *overwriting* another program's *area*, or attempting to use a peripheral unit at the same time as another program. In order to achieve optimum utilization of processor time and of peripheral units, some method of allotting priorities between the programs sharing the computer must be made. Further, in order to enable programs of different sizes to be *loaded* into the computer at different times, as and when store space becomes available because of programs finishing, the method of loading programs and sharing memory between them must be as flexible as possible. These various objectives are achieved by a combination of *hardware* and *software*. Different multiprogramming systems adopt different combinations of these two methods; in a short article it is not possible to describe all types of system. One typical approach combines a system of hardware checks to prevent one program from interfering with another's area, and an *executive program* to control peripheral sharing and the operations concerned with loading and communicating with programs.

The method by which the executive program controls the sharing of processor time between programs and the operation of peripheral transfers can be described in outline as follows. When a program requires a peripheral transfer to be carried out, it obeys an instruction which transfers control to the executive program. The executive program then initiates the transfer, and returns control to the program just left. This program may proceed until it requires to use the information being read in by the transfer or the area from which data is being transferred. At this point the program will obey an instruction which suspends the program from further operation until the peripheral transfer is completed. Control is then transferred to the executive program. At this stage the order of priorities allotted to the programs present in the computer is consulted by the executive program, which looks for the program of highest priority that can now proceed because it is not held up for a peripheral unit. This program is entered to make use of processor time which would otherwise be wasted. When the transfer relating to the first program is complete an automatic *interrupt* occurs, and, assuming that the first program had higher priority, the executive program suspends the current one and re-enters the first one. As a general principle, programs that are *peripheral limited* (i.e., those which use very little processor time compared to the time they spend on peripheral transfers) will be given a higher priority than those which are *processor limited* (i.e., those which use a relatively large amount of processor time). Written at the beginning of each program is descriptive data which includes the program's priority number. This number is entered by the programmer, but to allow flexibility when several programs are being run simultaneously, it is also possible for the operator to alter the priority at any time during the run. Another technique used to achieve multiprogramming is *interleaving*. In this method, *segmented* programs are used, and segments of one program are inserted between segments of another program so that control is constantly switched from one program to another as each segment is completed. Using this technique the programmer will segment his program in such a way that processing and peripheral transfers occur in different segments; he must also know with which programs interleaving is to take place, so that as control alternates between segments, one program is performing a peripheral transfer while a processing segment of another program is being executed.

A further refinement of multiprogramming systems is the use of sophisticated *operating systems*, in which the functions of an executive program are extended to cover more comprehensive control over the scheduling of many programs and associated data files through the system.

multi-read feeding A system for reading cards on a *punched card tabulator*, in which the card passed a *sensing station*, and consecutive machine cycles took place to enable different data to be read on each occasion, e.g., name, street, town, etc., each held in a different *field*.

Also known as *multi-cycle feeding*.

multi-reel file   A *file* of data stored on *magnetic tape* which exceeds the capacity of one *reel* of magnetic tape and is therefore stored on two or more reels.

multistation   Relating to any communications *network* in which several data terminals are involved. ⟡ *data transmission*.

multivibrator   A type of oscillator which is used to generate non-sinusoidal waveforms.

MUX   Abbreviation of multiplexor.

mylar   A trade name used for polyester film which is often coated with magnetizable particles for use as a magnetic storage medium.

315

N

NAK Acronym for *Negative ACKnowledgement*.

name A term used by a *programmer* to identify any item such as a specific *instruction*, *data element*, resource, device, or function. Names must generally be used according to conventions established as standards for the development and maintenance of the project or system.

nano- Prefix denoting one thousand-millionth or 10^{-9}.

NAPLPS Abbreviation of North American presentation level protocol standard, a standard for *alphageometric* display in *videotex* systems.

narrative Statements included in the *coding* of a *program* to serve as explanatory documentation of the coded procedures. Such statements are not translated into program *instructions*, but serve as useful aids during the *debugging* or amending of a program.

Also known as *comment, remark*.

native language A computer *language* which has been specifically designed or implemented for a class of computer or *operating system*. This implies that the language system has been correctly integrated with the range of *software* available within the computer *system*.

natural function generator Synonymous with *analytical function generator*.

natural law function generator Synonymous with *analytical function generator*.

needle printer A printing device in which characters are formed by activating pins to strike paper and on to ribbon. A print head consisting of a matrix of pins is passed along the paper and appropriate pins are energized to strike the paper as required in each print position.

Also known as a matrix printer, dot matrix printer.

negation An operation performed upon a single *operand* in which the result produced has reverse significance in each *digit position*;

e.g., a *bit pattern p*: 010110

would appear as *r*: 101001

Also known as Boolean complementation, inversion, not operation.

negative acknowledgement An indication in a *network* that a *message*

316

has been incorrectly received and must be retransmitted. ⟨⟩ acknowledgement.

Negative BCD A number stored in *binary coded decimal* form but having a negative sign. The sign of a BCD number is often stored in a separate control word which must be associated with the BCD number.

negative indication Relating to the practice of specifying negative *fields* on a *punched card*, e.g., by an *overpunching* in the most significant *card column* of the *field*. It is not essential to use a position within the field itself and any column of the card could be assigned to receive a negative indication.

negator A *logic element* which has one *binary* input signal and which provides a single binary output signal of reverse significance. That is, if a 1 *bit* is used as input, a zero bit is produced as output, and vice versa.

Also known as *not element*.

neither-nor operation Synonymous with *nor operation*.

nesting Pertaining to a *routine* or *subroutine* which contains a structure similar to itself. For example, a *loop* of *instructions* which may contain another loop and so on perhaps down through several levels.

nesting loops A programming technique in which a *loop* of *instructions* contains another loop, which may in turn contain another, and so on.

nesting store A *store* comprising several *locations* only one of which may receive data from or transmit data to the associated equipment. Thus data entering the store is pushed down from location to location as though moving through several levels.

nesting subroutines A series of *subroutines* arranged at different levels, i.e., one written within another. Thus, *entry*[1] to a lower level subroutine can be achieved via any of the other high-level subroutines, and in each case facilities are incorporated to generate an appropriate *branch* to *exit* back to the *calling* subroutine.

network A series of interconnected elements which form an overall system or structure. Examples of the use of this term include: (i) Network *database*: a database structure in which *elements* are not organized in set *records* on *files*, but one in which related data elements are linked by *pointers*. Thus any desired record or file can be created by following pointers and assembling records to contain relevant data elements. (ii) Communications network: a system of computer devices (*nodes*) interconnected by communications circuits to permit files, transactions and data to be interchanged to fulfil the information and data processing needs of a community or business organization. (iii) Event network: in *critical path analysis*, a computer model or diagram which represents the relationship between various activities which must be completed to fulfil a given task.

network architecture In a communications *network*, the arrangement of *nodes* and their interconnecting communications circuits, to represent the structure of the network and the significance of nodes in network control.

Examples include: (i) Star network: this is typically a network in which there is one central coordinating node, and distant devices are connected along communications lines which radiate as spokes from the central node. (ii) Multi-drop network: a network in which several nodes are connected at a distance along a single communications line – one node is usually dominant in controlling the network and instructs other nodes to transmit/receive. (iii) Loop network: the nodes are arranged at intervals around a circuit which is depicted as a circle or loop. Nodes may intercommunicate by transmitting to the loop, and signals are propagated throughout the loop. A protocol will exist to govern which nodes may transmit or receive at any instant, but usually there is no central controlling node. (iv) Tree network: a form of star network in which there is a hierarchical structure of control represented by an inverted tree structure. The node at the apex controls nodes at the next level, and so on down through the required number of levels in the network. (v) Mesh network: a network in which every node is connected to every other, so that communication takes place over dedicated circuits between nodes. In practice, networks may consist of combinations of the archetype versions described above.

Also known as network topology.

network analog An *analog* device for studying *networks*, in which electrical circuits are used to represent the physical phenomena under study.

network analyser A *simulator* designed to study *networks*.

network analysis ◊ general article on *Critical Path Method*.

network diagram Any diagram which depicts the overall structure of a *network*, the key *nodes* or stations, and the possible paths between them. It could therefore represent a communications *network*, but the term equally refers to a diagram used to depict key events in the management of a project with the critical paths which represent the best routes to sequence activities. ◊ *critical path method*.

network interface unit A device which performs a function similar to that of a *modem*; i.e., it connects a data *terminal* to a circuit, forming part of a communications *network*. This term is preferred to the term modem in situations in which connexions are to be made to a digital network rather than to an analog network. The function of a network interface unit is to convert the digital signals passing between the terminal and the network, to ensure compatibility in terms of format and speed of transmission.

network level   In the ISO *seven layer reference model* for *communications protocols* the third level is the network level, defining the *packet switching service* standards to be adopted.

network management   The set of policies, functions and procedures used to control a *communications network* and to maintain its efficiency and integrity. The procedures and functions are usually implemented as a computerized management system under the control of human operators. The network management includes the maintenance of a directory of authorized users and their addresses within the network; the existence of various communications paths through the network and the control procedures associated with availability, obligation, testing and maintenance of these paths; the collection of data and the maintenance of files, as well as processing, billing, accounting, traffic analysis and network performance.

Fault detection and management procedures associated with avoidance and correction of fault paths through the network are also part of the network management system. *Configuration* control – including the ability to switch circuits or *nodes* into or out of operation – is also part of this function and allows a communications network to be expanded and developed to meet the demands of an expanding user community.

network topology   The arrangement of *nodes* in a *communications network.* ◊ *network architecture.*

network user identifier   An identification code given to a user of a communications service; the code by which that user is identified within the system and from which *routing* procedures are able to identify the physical location of a subscriber or his *terminal.* The NUI may also be used as a basis for the collection of statistical or accountancy information, allowing the use of the system to be monitored and bills to be raised.

nexus   A point in a system at which interconnexions occur.

nibble   Some computers are able to process units of data comprising four *bits*; i.e., two such units constitute an 8-bit *byte.* A 4-bit unit is known as a nibble.

nickel delay line   An *acoustic delay line* in which nickel is used to recirculate sonic signals.

nine-edge leading   The manner in which cards were placed in the feed *hopper* of some *punched card* machines. The cards were fed broadside so that the *row* of 9-digits was read first then the row of 8-digits and so on through to the *X-position*. Contrasted with, for example, *column 1 leading*.

nines complement Related to a method used in some computers and *accounting machines* to represent negative values. The number itself is represented by the result obtained when subtracting each digit from a digit one less than the *radix*. For example, the five-digit decimal number − 18,764 would be represented as 81235

i.e., 99999

   − 18764

   81235

Some type of sign indicator is used when this technique is adopted, in order to distinguish between complements and positive numbers. Complements are converted to the correct representation before output. In a *binary notation* a *ones-complement* could be used to achieve the same effect.

ninety-column card A *punched card* which has 90 columnar positions in any of which holes may be punched to represent a character.

NMC Abbreviation of network management centre. ◊ general article on *Network Management*.

no-address instruction An *instruction* that does not require to specify an *address* in *memory*.

node A point on a junction of paths in a *network*. In communications systems, this term refers to any exchange or *switching centre* at which routings may take place to link subscribers to one another or to a central service. In modern communications systems, nodes are invariably computer processors equipped to perform specific functions. ◊ *address*, *rout*, *switch*, *message query*.

The exact purpose of a node depends upon the type of network, and the position and role ascribed to the node within the network. In networks concerned with circuit switching, the main purpose of a node is to provide connexions which physically link paths between subscribers, i.e., no transmissions can take place until a point to point circuit exists. In *packet switching* or *message switching systems*, the emphasis can be on accepting and storing messages, until such time as a circuit can be provided to route messages to their desired destinations.

noise 1. Any disturbance affecting the characteristics of a signal, e.g., random variations in voltage, current or frequency. 2. Errors in data generated by disturbance in a circuit, particularly in a *data transmission* circuit.

noise digit A digit, usually zero, generated during the *normalizing*[2] of a *floating point number*, and inserted during a *left shift* operation into the *fixed point part*.

noisy mode The method of operation adopted when *normalizing* a *floating point number*, in which digits, other than zero, are generated as part of the *fixed point part*.

non-accountable time Time during which a system is not available to the *user*, either because it is switched off or is unavailable for reasons beyond the user's or the supplier's control, e.g., in a power failure.

non-arithmetic shift Synonymous with logical shift.

non-destructive cursor A *cursor* which can be moved around a screen to point at required locations or characters, without corrupting or affecting the information currently displayed.

non-destructive read Reading information from a *location* or *register* in *memory* in such a way that the data is retained undamaged in the source *location*.

non-equivalence operation Synonymous with *exclusive-or operation*.

non-erasable store Any medium of *store* of which the contents cannot be erased during processing, e.g., *ROM*, *paper tape*, a photographic store.

non-numeric character Any *character* that is not a numeral, e.g., alphabetic characters or symbols.

non-print code Relating to telegraphic communications: a code which will initiate functions on a teleprinter without printing taking place.

non-reproducing codes In relation to *paper tape*, special codes punched into the tape to cause a *hardware* unit to perform specific functions when the tape was read. The codes were not punched into any resultant output tape.

non-resident routine Any *routine* which does not reside permanently in *memory*. Contrasted with *resident routine*.

non-return to zero A method for encoding and interpreting a serial *binary* data signal, in which a low level signal is treated as 0, and a high level signal as 1. There is no automatic return to a zero level after each binary digit, thus, for example, the signal will be held at a high level for any consecutive series of 1 digits. The individual digits are identified by clock signals which signify the instants at which the signal must be interpreted. Contrasted with *non-return to zero inverted*.

non-return to zero inverted A method for the encoding and interpretation of serial binary data signals, in which a 1 digit is represented by a signal level change, either *high-going* or *low-going*, and a 0 digit is represented by a continuation of a previous signal level. Thus any consecutive series of 1 digits will be represented as a series of changes in signal level. Contrasted with *non-return to zero*.

non-volatile memory A *memory* device which does not lose its magnetic charge when electrical power is removed. *Bubble memories* and *magnetic core memories* are examples of non-volatile devices. Most *semiconductor memories* are volatile (i.e., do not retain their charge), but *read-only-memories* (ROM) can be constructed of semiconductor components in such a way that binary data can be permanently retained. However, the data in ROM has to be fixed during manufacture and cannot be amended during normal operation. ⟨⟩ *static memory*.

non-von Neumann architecture Any computer *architecture* which departs rapidly from the *von Neumann* model; in particular *data flow*, *parallel processing* computers.

no-operation instruction Synonymous with *do nothing instruction*.

nor circuit A digital circuit which produces an output signal only when two corresponding input signals are absent.

nor element A *logic element* operating with *binary digits* which provides an output signal according to the following rules applied to two input signals:

Input	Output
1	0	0
1	1	0
0	1	0
0	0	1

Thus a 1 digit is obtained as an output only if neither of the two input signals is 1.

Also known as nor gate.

normalize 1. In mathematics, to multiply a quantity within an expression by a numeric coefficient so that an associated quantity can be made equal to a specified value. 2. In programming, using *floating point numbers* to adjust the *fixed point part* of a number so that the fixed point part is within a prescribed range.

normal mode (stack operation) Some computers have more than one *stack*, and it is sometimes the case that one stack is used by the system *software* provided by the manufacturer, whereas another stack is used by users' *application* software. The application stack is said to operate in normal mode, whereas the system stack may operate in privilege mode, including the use of privileged instructions which are not allowed in normal mode.

normal range   A prescribed range of values established for the results obtained from a system or routine. Any results falling outside the limits of this range are presented to management or are subject to further analysis.

normal stage punching   Relating to a *punched card* system in which *interstage punching* was used, and describing the data punched as holes in the usual *punching positions* of a card.

nor operation   A *logical operation* applied to two *operands* which will produce a result depending on the *bit pattern* of the operands according to the following rules:

Operands		Result
p	q	r
1	0	0
0	1	0
1	1	0
0	0	1

For example, operating on the following 6-bit operands:

$$p = 110110$$
$$q = 011010$$

$$r = 000001$$

Also known as dagger operation, joint denial. ⟡ *Boolean algebra*.

not   A *logical operator* with the property that if a condition p is true, then the not of p is false, and if p is false then the not of p is true. ⟡ *Boolean algebra*.

not-and   A *logical operation* with the property that if p is a statement, q is a statement and r is a statement, then p.q.r . . . is true if at least one statement is false; and p.q.r . . . is false if all the statements are true. ⟡ *Boolean algebra*.

not-and element   A *logic element* operating with binary signals which will produce an output signal representing 1 when any of its corresponding input signals represent zero.

not-and operation   A *logical operation* applied to at least two *operands* which will produce a result according to the *bit patterns* of the operands, thus:

Operands		Result
p	q	r
0	1	1
1	0	1
1	1	0
0	0	1

For example, operating on the two following 6-bit operands:

$$p = 110110$$
$$q = 011010$$
$$\overline{}$$
$$r = 101101$$

Also known as nand operation, not-both operation, alternative denial, dispersion. ⟡ *Boolean algebra*.

notation, binary   ⟡ *binary notation*.

notation, binary-coded decimal   ⟡ *binary-coded decimal notation*.

notation, coded decimal   ⟡ *binary-coded decimal notation*.

notation, mixed radix   ⟡ *mixed base notation*.

not-both operation   Synonymous with *not-and operation*.

not circuit   A circuit which provides an output signal of reverse phase or polarity from the original input signal.

not element   Synonymous with *negator*.

not operation   Synonymous with *negation*.

nought output signal   The signal obtained when a *read* pulse is applied to a *magnetic cell* which is in the condition representing zero.

noughts complement   Synonymous with *radix complement*.

nought state   Synonymous with *zero condition*.

n-plus-one address instruction   An *instruction* containing an *address* plus one address which specifies the *location* of the next instruction to be obeyed.

NRZ   Abbreviation of *non-return to zero*.

NRZI   Abbreviation of *non-return to zero inverted*.

NUI   Abbreviation of *network user identifier*.

null instruction   Synonymous with *do nothing instruction*.

number cruncher   A name given to machines with great computational power, where the accent is on the ability to handle large figures rather than to process large amounts of data.

number generator   Used as a synonym for *manual word generator*; a device which could be set by a computer operator to cause a *parameter* or *constant* to be entered into a predetermined *memory location*. This sort of device has been superseded by *console typewriters* and other keyboard *input units*.

number representation   1. Any method in which symbols are used to represent numbers, e.g., the use of digits 0 and 1 arranged in groups to represent *binary* numbers. 2. The use of coded impulses, or other signals, to represent numeric data.

number system   Any system for representing numeric values or quantities. For example, the decimal system utilizes ten digits, 0 to 9; these digits may be arranged in groups, the contribution of each digit being made according to the value of the digit and the significance of its position in the group.

numeral   One of a set of digits that may be used in a particular system of *number representation*.

numerical analysis   The study of mathematical methods for solving problems numerically and ascertaining the bounds of errors in the results.

numerical control   ⬦ *numeric control*.

numerical tape   A tape containing punched holes to represent numbers; usually made of paper, or sometimes of plastic, and used to input instructions to a numerically controlled (N/C) machine (e.g., to control an automatic milling and drilling machine). (⬦ *numeric control*.) These tapes may be generated automatically by means of a computer *program*, which significantly reduces the time spent by planning engineers in developing the detailed instructions required to set up the numerically controlled machine.

numeric character   Any character used as a digit in the representation of numbers; e.g., in decimal notation one of the characters 0–9.

numeric coding   Any system of coding which uses numerals only.

numeric control   Pertaining to the control of machinery, particularly machine tools, by means of numerical instructions. Computers have been used extensively in this field to provide programming *languages* for automatically generating numerical lists. These lists are *compiled* from simple *source language statements* written by planning and production engineering staff.

Also known as numerical control.

numeric data Any *field* of characters which contains numeric digits only.

numeric punching On a *punched card*, data represented by the punching of single holes in each *column* of a *field*. *Alphabetic* characters and other symbols might be punched, for example, as two holes per column.

O

O and M ◊ *organization and methods*.

object computer The computer on which an *object program* is designed to be run, as opposed to the computer used to *compile* the program. ◊ *compiler*.

object configuration The system *configuration* necessary for running an *object program*, which may be applied on a different configuration.

object language The *language* or set of coded *instructions* into which a *source language* is translated by means of a *compiler*. The object language is usually but not necessarily a *machine language* directly understandable by a computer; some *high level languages* are translated initially into a lower level object language which requires further translation before it is converted into machine language.

object machine Synonymous with *object computer*.

object program A program in *object language* produced by translating the program written in the *source language* through the use of a *compiler*. The object program will normally be in a *machine code* capable of being directly understood by the computer and thus in the form required for running. When some *high level languages* are in use the object program may itself need further translation before it is in a form understandable by the computer.

observation matrix ◊ *data matrix*.

OCR Abbreviation of *optical character recognition*.

octal digit A *digit* in the *octal notation* system, i.e. one of the digits 0, 1, 2, 3, 4, 5, 6, 7.

octal notation The *number system* using 8 as a base or *radix*. The octal system uses the digits, 0, 1, 2, 3, 4, 5, 6, 7, and each digit position represents a power of eight, thus the octal number 107 represents $1.8^2 + 0.8^1 + 7.8^0 = 71$ in decimal. Octal notation is sometimes used as a shorthand way of representing a *string* of bits. For example, the string 001000111 can be considered as being formed by the three *binary coded* octal numbers 001 000 111, i.e., 1 0 7. Thus the string 001000111 can be represented as 'octal' 107, sometimes indicated merely as #107.

odd couple Synonymous with *twisted pair*.

odd-even check   A form of *parity check* in which an extra *bit* is added to a *word* or *character*; this bit has the value 1 or 0 depending on whether the number of 1 bits in the word or character is odd or even. The value of the parity bit is recalculated whenever the data is transferred, and compared with the value of the original bit as a check on the accuracy of the transfer. In the case of odd parity, the parity bit is 1 if the number of 1 bits is even, 0 if odd; in the case of even parity the parity bit is 0 if the number of 1 bits is even, 1 if odd.

odd parity check   A *parity check* in which the number of ones (or zeros) in a group of *binary digits* is expected to be odd. Contrasted with *even parity check*.

office automation   ⋄ *electronic office*.

off-line   A part of a computer system is off-line if it is not under the control of the *central processor*. ⋄ *off-line processing*.

off-line equipment   Devices which are used in conjunction with a computer system but which are at no time connected to the *central processor*.

off-line processing   Performing some part of a data processing system on equipment not directly connected to the *central processor*, and thus not under *program* control. For example, *punched cards* may be transcribed to *paper tape* by means of an off-line *card-to-tape*[1] machine and the tape subsequently processed *on-line* by the computer.

off-line storage   A *storage device* not under the direct control of a central processor. A *reel* of *magnetic tape* not *on-line* but placed in a *library* may be considered an example of off-line storage.

off-line unit   Synonymous with *off-line equipment*.

off-line working   Synonymous with *off-line processing*.

off punch   To punch a *punched card* in such a way that the holes are not aligned with the *punching positions*. This means that when the card is subsequently *read* the reading mechanism may not be able to sense the presence of the holes.

one address instruction   An *instruction format* which makes use of one *address part* involving one *location* of *store* only.

one condition   The state of a unit of *store* when it is representing the value 1.

one digit adder   Synonymous with *half adder*.

one digit subtracter   Synonymous with *half subtracter*.

one element   Synonymous with *or element*.

one-for-one   A form of *compiler* in which one *machine code instruction* is generated for each *source instruction*.

one gate   Synonymous with *or element*.

one level address   Synonymous with *absolute address*.

one level code   Synonymous with *absolute code*.

one level store   A concept used in a *virtual machine environment* to describe a storage system which appears to the user as a single directly accessible *store* while in fact being made up of a number of different *hardware* devices, e.g., *memory, disk*.

one level subroutine   A *subroutine* which is complete in itself, i.e., does not use any other subroutines during its operation.

one output signal   The form of signal produced by a unit of *store* in a *one condition* when a *read pulse* is applied to it.

one-over-one address format   Synonymous with *one-plus-one address instruction format*.

one-plus-one address   An *address format* in which each *instruction* includes one *operation* and two addresses, one showing the *location* containing the data to be operated on and the other showing the location containing the next instruction. (The purpose of the second address is indicated by the phrase *plus-one*: a two-plus-one address, for example, has three addresses, one containing the location of the next instruction.)

ones complement   The term used to describe the *radix minus one complement* applied to *binary notation*. ◊ *complement, nines complement*.

one shot circuit   Synonymous with *single shot circuit*.

one shot multivibrator   Synonymous with *flip-flop*.

one shot operation   Synonymous with *single step operation*.

one state   Synonymous with *one condition*.

one to one assembler   An *assembly program* which translates each *source language statement* onto a single *machine language instruction*. Also known as one to one translator.

one to one translator   Synonymous with *one to one assembler*.

one to zero ratio   The ratio of the magnitude or amplitude at a particular instant of time of a *one output signal* to a *zero output signal*.

on-line   A part of a *computer system* is on-line if it is directly under the control of the *central processor*. Contrasted with *off-line*.

on-line central file   A *file* of data present on a *storage device* which is *on-line*, and can be used in *real time* or *direct access* applications as a continually available data source.

on-line data reduction   The processing of information as soon as it is transmitted from source to a computer system. ◊ *real time*.

on-line equipment   Those devices which form part of a computer system and which may be placed under the direct control of a *central processor*.

on-line processing *Data processing* in which all operations are performed by equipment directly under the control of a central *processor*. Contrasted with *off-line processing*.

on-line programming A method of *programming* by which the programmer inputs program *statements* directly to the computer by means of a *terminal*. Program statements are checked for validity as they are input, and the programmer controls the *compilation* and *execution* of the program by means of commands from the terminal. ⬧ *BASIC*, *conversational mode*.

on-line real time operation (OLRT) ⬧ *real time*.

on-line storage A *store* under the direct control of a *central processor*.

on-line typewriter An *input/output* typewriter under the control of a *central processor* and thus under *program* control. An on-line typewriter may be used as a form of *peripheral unit*, as an *interrogating typewriter* or as a *console typewriter*.

on-line unit ⬧ *on-line equipment*.

on-line working ⬧ *on-line processing*.

on-the-fly printer A type of high-speed *line printer* in which all the characters in the *character set* are engraved on the surface of a rapidly rotating *print barrel*, and are printed by means of hammers which strike the paper as the appropriate character position on the barrel is in position relative to the paper.
   Also known as hit-on-the-fly printer.

op code Abbreviation for *operation code*.

open ended A *program* or system so designed that it can be extended in scope or sophistication without alteration to those parts already in existence.

opening a file This process is performed by manufacturer's *software* and consists basically of identifying the *file* and checking the *header label* against details supplied in the user's *program* to ensure that the file can be used for the purpose defined by the program. For example, if a *magnetic tape file* is to be used as an output tape the *retention period* must be exceeded and a *write permit ring* must be present. To open a magnetic tape as an input file the correct file name and file *generation number* must be present.

open loop A control system in which corrective action is not automatic, but depends on external intervention as a result of displayed information.

open routine A *routine* inserted into a larger routine without the *calling sequence* and *link* associated with a *subroutine*.

open shop   The organization of a *data processing* installation so that any suitably qualified individual has access to the machines. Contrasted with *closed shop* in which only specialist staff have access. In particular, open shop implies that *programmers* may test *programs* on a computer rather than by *remote testing*.

open subroutine   A *subroutine* which has to be reinserted into the main sequence of *instructions* each time it is required, rather than merely requiring a *link* to a sequence of instructions held in a separate part of the *program*. Contrasted with *closed subroutine*.

open system   A *network* which allows computer equipment from different manufacturers to communicate with each other. ◊ *seven layer reference model*.

operand   The item in an *operation* from which the *result* is obtained by means of defined actions.

operating delays   Time lost as a direct result of mistakes or inefficiency in operating a *data processing* installation, as contrasted with delays due to other causes such as *repair time, machine-spoilt work time, fault, program* errors, data errors.

operating instructions   A step-by-step description of the activities to be performed by an *operator* in running a particular *program* or *suite* of programs. Usually provided by a programmer or systems analyst as part of the program *documentation*.

operating ratio   A measure of the time that a particular system (usually a combination of *hardware* and *software*) is able to provide a service. The measure is derived as a percentage of the time available, excluding *down time*, to the total time that the machine is switched on. (Down time may include time lost due to *failure*, scheduled maintenance, unscheduled maintenance, time waiting for engineering staff.) The operating ratio may or may not include time required to establish the service once failures have been corrected. Thus it is necessary to specify whether the operating ratio includes *recovery time* or not.
    Also known as availability ratio.

operating station   A *console* or set of consoles which is used by an *operator*[2] to control all or part of a data processing system.

operating systems   An operating system can be properly defined as those procedures which control the *resources* within a *data processing* installation. Resources include *hardware, programs, data* and *operators*, and control is by manual procedures or *software*. Generally, however, an operating system is defined as a program which supervises the running of other programs. Operating systems were unknown in *first* *generation* computers, the programs standing alone within the computer. In about 1955–6 several large US companies began to develop operating systems to suit their individual requirements. These were on *second generation* machines and while effective to a certain extent they are more important in that the manufacturers realized this field required serious investigation. With *multiprogramming* being so much a part of *third generation* machines an operating system became almost a necessity and a lower level version of this type of program exists in the *executive program* of the third generation computers.

In practice the operating system supervises the programs, controlling the input and output functions of each program and passing control from one program to the next. Human action is still required for the physical loading of magnetic media on to the respective units but all human intervention or decision-making at the end of each program is by-passed. The operator loads as many programs and relative data files as the *configuration* will allow.

Control language instructions are fed in, often by use of the *console typewriter* and the machine is started by the operator. By referring to the control instructions the operating system selects the first program and data files to be processed. During processing the operator unloads each *peripheral unit* as it is released and loads further data files, etc. At the end of the processing of the first program all control information for that program is printed out, e.g., files used, record counts, time charged, etc., and control is given to the next program for processing. The main object is to keep the operator *loading* the units in advance of the program requiring them, using the processing time for one job as the set-up time for another. Before one series of programs and control instructions comes to an end the operator loads the programs, data, etc., for the next, thus avoiding, if possible, a machine halt. An important additional function of an operating system is job *scheduling*. Jobs are loaded and the time when a job must be completed is given to the operating system together with relevant data on the size of the files, etc. The time may vary between a few minutes and days. At intervals – say 10 seconds – the operating system interrupts the job being processed to review the timings on other jobs. It selects the job which is least advanced according to the time schedule and processes it until it is interrupted and the jobs are again reviewed. By continuing in this manner the jobs are produced when and as they are required and central processor time is fully utilized. Obviously jobs can be advanced or retarded by altering their scheduled time for completion. In ways like this an operating system can increase the efficiency of an installation, and such increases grow more and more necessary as computer users recognize the difficulties encountered by human operators in controlling the varying input and output requirements of a big machine which may be running, at the same time, a complex mix of *batch* and *on-line processing* as well as controlling a network of *communication devices* and the activity of a number of *remote processors*.

operation 1. A defined action by which a *result* is obtained from an *operand*. 2. An action defined by a single computer *instruction*. 3. An action defined by a single *logic element*.

operational amplifier Synonymous with *computing amplifier*.

operational research Operational Research first became recognized as a separate field of study just before the Second World War, and its use spread rapidly in the armed services. Since then operational research has become widely used in industry and commerce, where the adoption of quantitive techniques in management has been shown to be universally successful.

The aims of the operational research scientist are principally to quantify a problem in statistical or mathematical terms and to use these methods to find a solution, or a better solution, to the problem. In this respect operational research is the leading applied science. Since the aims of the systems analyst or programmer are at least in the first part identical to this, the two will often be found working together.

Fifty years ago the term 'management science' was unknown. Nowadays terms like economic re-order quantity are common and the art of decision making is becoming a science of interpreting data: it is here that operational research has an important role.

There are two main methods of analysis used by the operational research worker. The first is that of handling complex information in order to reach a decision, *linear programming* and *critical path method* (or *PERT*) being two examples of techniques using this analysis. The second deals with those problems where difficulty arises because of uncertainty; information is available as probability distributions or frequencies of past events. Here such techniques as *forecasting* and *simulation* have been developed.

Techniques in operational research often involve statistical and mathematical methods and are frequently viewed with suspicion by line management. Here lies one of the major problems of the day. Not until management science is fully accepted as an essential part of management can the full value of operational research, and with it often the value of a computer, be realized.

Some of the techniques of operational research are discussed under the following headings: *simulation, queuing theory, critical path method* (*PERT*), *linear programming, forecasting, extrapolation, iteration, allocation.*

operation, biconditional   ⬦ *equivalence operation.*

operation, binary (Boolean)   ⬦ *dyadic Boolean operation.*

operation code   The *code* which specifies the particular *operation* to be performed in an *instruction.*

operation cycle   The part of a *machine cycle* during which an *instruction* is executed.

operation, dagger   Synonymous with *nor operation.*

operation decoder   A circuit which interprets the *operation* part of an *instruction* and switches to the circuits required for its execution.

operation, dyadic Boolean   ⬦ *dyadic Boolean operation.*

operation, either-or   ⬦ *inclusive-or operation.*

operation, meet   ⬦ *and operation.*

operation, nand   ⬦ *not-and operation.*

operation, neither-nor   ⬦ *nor operation.*

operation, non-equivalence   ⬦ *exclusive-or operation.*

operation, not-both   ⬦ *not-and operation.*

operation, one shot   ⬦ *single step operation.*

operation, or   ⬦ *inclusive-or operation.*

operation part   The part of an *instruction* which contains the specification of the particular *operation*[2] to be performed. The *operation code* will be contained in the operation part of the instruction.

operation register   A *register* in which the *operation code* is stored during the *operation cycle.*

operation, single shot   Synonymous with *single step operation.*

operations research   ⬦ *operational research.*

operation, step by step   Synonymous with *single step operation.*

operation time   The time required to complete the *operation cycle* for a particular *operation.*

operation, unary   Synonymous with *monadic operation.*

operator   1. In an *operation,* an operator defines the action to be performed on the *operand* to obtain the *result.* ⬦ *operators.* 2. A person who operates a machine. ⬦ general article on *Computer Personnel.*

operator command   A *message* input to an *operating system* by an *operator*[2] at his own instigation in contrast to a message input in response to a message generated by the operating system itself.

operator name   In an *operating system,* the name used by an *operator*[2] to identify himself to the operating system through an *operating station,* thus enabling him to input *operator's control language* commands and receive *prompts*.

operator part The part of an *instruction* in which the *operator* is specified.

operators Characters which designate different operations, e.g., +, −, ×, etc.

operator's console A *console* used by the computer *operator* in order to control the operation of the *programs* and *peripheral units*, and to receive information about their functioning. The console may include a panel of switches and warning lights, and/or a *console typewriter*.

operator's control language *Control language* commands designed for use by an *operator*[2].

optical bar-code reader A device which reads by optical means information which has been coded *using bar codes*.

optical character reader A device which uses *optical character recognition* to read information into a computer system; a character reader which reads characters by analysis of their configuration.

optical character recognition The identification of printed characters by means of light sensing devices. ⟡ general articles on *Character Recognition* and *Input Devices*.

optical disk A disk using *optical storage* technology.

optical scanner A device which analyses the light patterns made by printed characters and converts the pattern into a signal which can be processed by a computer.

optical storage The use of a *laser* for recording digital data as microscopic 'pits' on concentric tracks. The data is read by photoelectric sensors which do not make active contact with the storage medium.

optical type fount A special fount designed for use with *optical character recognition* devices which is also easily read by people.

optimization The design or modification of a system or *program* in order to make it achieve maximum efficiency. The particular type of efficiency sought after in optimization depends on the requirement specified: examples are time, cost, storage capacity.

optimum coding Synonymous with *minimum access coding*.

optimum programming The production of optimized *programs*. ⟡ *optimization, minimum access code, linear programming*.

optional stop instruction An *instruction* which will halt the *program* if certain conditions are satisfied.

OR Abbreviation of *operational research*.

Oracle A *teletext* system provided by Independent Television in the UK.

order 1. Synonymous with *instruction*. 2. As a verb, synonymous with *sequence²*.

order code Synonymous with *instruction code*. ⟡ *order code processor*.

order code processor Part of a large computer system whose function is to select *low level language instructions* from *main store*, carry them out and return the results to main store. In addition the order code processor may initiate *input* and *output* instructions and respond to *interrupts*.

ordered serial file A *serial file* whose *records* have a *key* and which are *sorted* on that key so that the *physical* and *logical* sequences are the same.

orders, initial Synonymous with *initial instructions*.

order structure Synonymous with *instruction format*.

or element A logic element operating with *binary* digits, and providing an output signal according to the following rules applied to two input signals.

Input		Output
1	0	1
1	1	1
0	1	1
0	0	0

Thus a 1 digit is provided as an output if any one (or more) of the input signals are 1.

Also known as one gate, one element, or circuit, or gate. ⟡ *Boolean algebra*.

organization and methods The activities, often known as O & M, involved in a specialist view of the organization, management, methods of control and general procedures of any undertaking. A systematic review is carried out, as opposed to the general duties of any administrator with overall responsibilities for such procedures. Sometimes O and M staff are included in a *data processing* organization.

or gate Synonymous with *or element*.

origin The *absolute address* of the start of any area of *store* to which reference is made when *indirect addressing* techniques are used to locate items in the storage area. The term is also applied to the absolute address of the beginning of the *program* area in store. (This is not necessarily the first instruction to be processed.)

Also known as base address[1], float factor.

original document   Synonymous with *source document*.

OROM   Acronym for *Optical Read-Only Memory*.

OSI   Abbreviation of open system interconnexion. ⟡ *open system*.

outline flowchart   ⟡ general article on *Flowcharting*.

out of line coding   Part of the *instructions* of a *routine*, but stored in another part of the *program storage*. ⟡ *patch*, for example.

out of service time   Time during which a computer cannot be used for running *programs* for any reason. This may be due to the development of a fault in the machine or because the machine is undergoing *routine maintenance*, etc.

out-plant system   A *data processing* system which uses remote *data transmission* terminals for transmission of information to a central computer. Contrasted with *in-plant system*, *local area network*.

output   1. Results produced by a computer. 2. To transfer information from a *central processor* to an *output device*. Computer output may take many different forms, including *printout, magnetic disk, punched paper tape, visual display*.

output area   A part of *store* from which data is transferred to an *output device*.

Also known as output block, output section.

output block   Synonymous with *output area*.

output buffer   ⟡ *input/output buffers*.

output bus driver   A device for amplifying output signals.

output devices   All the data and *programs* within a computer are stored as electrical impulses in a coded form according to the *machine code* system of the particular computer. When data is held in this form it cannot be readily understood by human beings and therefore output units are employed to transcribe this data into information that can be used by human beings as and when they require it. There are various types of unit designed to present information in a particular manner or to deliver it at appropriate speed. For the most part output units will deliver information in *character* form to be examined visually by the user, but sometimes output data is required for subsequent entry to another data processing machine and is therefore output in some other coded medium (e.g., on *paper tape* or *magnetic tape*.)

The commonest types of output unit are *line printers*. These are generally electro-mechanical devices which print complete lines of print, up to 160 characters in width, at speeds from about 300 to 2000 lines per minute. There are also *page printers* which operate using *xerographic* printing techniques or the result of *electron beam recording*.

Of the electro-mechanical printers we can distinguish two classes, *barrel printers* and *chain printers*. Both rely on a similar principle – type characters are driven continuously at high speed, and print hammers are energized by electronic signals to strike the paper and an ink ribbon against the moving type at precise instants. The electronic circuitry in the line printer and the *central processor* is designed to transcribe the data in the output area of the internal store into a series of timing pulses which will activate the hammers.

Line printers of this type are used mainly to print out the results of calculations and they can be programmed to print on preprinted stationery, for example, to produce invoices or statements. The individual pages are part of a continuous sheet and are marked out by folds and perforations across the sheet at intervals according to the required form depth. The stationery is supplied as a pack and a complete set may consist of several sheets with interleaved carbon paper to produce additional copies. After being printed, these stationery sets can be split up into single sheets by means of *decollators* and *bursters*.

Most line printers have a repertoire of about 64 separate characters, any of which may be printed at any of the *print positions* across the page. This repertoire normally includes all twenty-six capital letters of the alphabet, the numerals 0–9, and a range of special symbols.

Punched card or paper tape output is achieved by *card punches* and *paper tape punches* designed to respond automatically by signals transmitted from the central processor. Speeds of output vary from about 100 to 400 cards per minute in the case of cards, and for paper tape from 25 to 110 characters per second. Output in this form is often used to record data which will be processed further by other equipment. Where output data is in relatively small quantities (e.g., *error reports* from programs) an output device of this type may be preferred, particularly where the alternative would tie up a line printer for a whole *run*.

Magnetic tape decks or *magnetic disk stores* may be used for input and output, but are not usually considered as either input or output units: rather as *backing stores*. ♢ *Storage Devices*.

Typewriters are often used as input/output units, particularly as *interrogating typewriters* to interrogate programs to ascertain conditions regarding the status of the programs or data being processed. They are also used specifically as *console typewriters* in which they satisfy the need for communication between the operator and a supervisory or *executive program*.

The operator is able to enter data (e.g., run *parameters*) or inquiries directly from the *keyboard* and may receive information typed automatically on the typewriter. Thus where a device such as a console typewriter is used, the output on the stationery forms a complete operating log for all the jobs that have been run.

Other types of output unit include *visual display units* which can present information in character form, but will also display data as drawings or graphs. These units incorporate either a *graph plotter* or a *cathode ray tube* and associated control electronics. For drawings shown on a cathode ray tube the computer has to calculate the coordinates of every spot forming the picture to be portrayed. Characters can be more simply formed by passing the cathode ray through a mask which creates the appropriate character shape and the beam is then deflected to display the character on the desired part of the screen. The more complex the output pattern, the more complex the program to control the cathode ray tube.

Some graphical display units incorporate facilities to input data. For example, some models have keyboards that enable queries to be input in coded form to a control program which will in turn select and display the required answer in a matter of microseconds. When such an input/output device is used in conjunction with a *direct access store*, inquiries can be satisfied from files on a random basis.

Some display units can be used as input units by means of a special stylus known as a *light pen*. In such a system graphs, shapes and other pictorial data can be entered into the *memory* of the computer by passing the light pen across the screen. The position of the pen is detected by light sensors which with associated circuitry instruct the computer to form a corresponding drawing in memory. Thus drawings can be created, displayed and amended. This type of input/output system, in conjunction with the keyboard input mentioned above, opens great potential for applications in the fields of science, education and engineering. Where large volumes of data are to be produced and distributed, use is often made of computer output microfilm with consequent savings in storage space and distribution costs.

output program A *program* written specifically for the transcription of data to an *output device*.

output punch 1. An *output device* which transcribes information on to *paper tape*. 2. An output device which transcribes information on to *punched cards*.

output record 1. A *record* written (⬦ *write*) to an *output device*. 2. The current record stored in the *output area* before being *output*[2].

output routine A *routine* which performs all the processing associated with the transcription of data to an *output device*. This processing may include placing the information in the *output area*, *editing*, converting information from internal format to external format and providing control information to the output device.

output routine generator   A *generator* which will produce an *output routine* to given specifications.

output section   Synonymous with *output area*.

output table   Synonymous with *plotting board*.

output unit   ◊ *output device*.

overall availability ratio   ◊ *operating ratio*.

overall serviceability ratio   ◊ *serviceability ratio*.

overflow   The generation of a quantity as a *result* of an arithmetic operation which is too large to be contained in the result *location*. The term is also used to describe the actual amount of the *excess*. Contrasted with *underflow*. ◊ *overflow records*.

overflow bucket   A *bucket* used to accommodate *overflow records* in a *direct access file*.

overflow records   *Records* which cannot be accommodated in assigned areas of a *direct access* file and which must be stored in another area from which they can be retrieved by means of a reference stored in place of the records in their original assigned area.

overlay   A technique in which, during the operation of a lengthy *program*, the same area of *store* is used to contain successively different parts of the program. Each part of the program that is to share the same overlay area is held on some form of *backing store* and read into the area by means of a control program. Communication between different overlays is usually through use of a *common area*. ◊ *programming*, *segment*.

overpunch   A hole punched in a *zone* position of a *punched card* used for *designation* purposes, e.g., to indicate whether a *field* was positive or negative.

overwrite   To place information in a *location* and destroy the information previously contained there.

own coding   The addition of user-written *coding* to a standard *software routine* in order to extend its capabilities to cover special conditions.

owner   A *user* or *process* which has overriding control over *resources* or *data*. ◊ *ownership*.

ownership   A relationship between the elements within an *operating system* indicating that the *owner* has overriding control over the object owned, e.g., a *process* owns a data item if it has the right to access and alter the data and to transfer this right to another process; a user owns a *resource* if he has overriding control over the resource.

P

pack   1. A collection of *punched cards* having something in common, e.g., a data pack or a *program* pack. Also known as deck[1]. 2. To place more than one item of information into a single unit of *store* in order to conserve storage space. In this sense, also known as crowd; contrasted with *unpack*.

package   A generalized *program* written for a major application in such a way that a user's particular problems of data or organization will not make the package any less useful. Examples might be a *production control* package, a payroll package, an *inventory management* package ◊ *software*

packet   In a *packet switching service*, the smallest unit of data which can be handled as a logical entity, conforming to the service protocol in regard to size, addressing and sequencing.

packet assembly   The process of forming a *message* into a *packet*.

packet disassembly   The process of extracting a *message* from a *packet*.

packet switching service   A method by which the data handling capacity of a *network* is measured, allowing the same circuits to handle data destined for many different users by subdividing information into a series of units, known as *packets*, each of which conforms to a *protocol*. It thus sets out the *address* of the *mode* to which the packet relates, and other standard information such as the packet sequence number.

packing density   A measure of the capacity of a *medium* of *store*, usually given as the number of storage units per unit length of recording surface. ◊ *file packing density*. ◊ *density*.

PAD   Acronym for *Packet Assembly and Disassembly*. A software *routine* within a *packet switching network*, which deals with the process of forming *messages* into packets and reconstituting messages from packets.

pad   A device for creating input by means of writing on a flat surface with a special pen. Data input may be text or graphics.
   Also known as tablet.

padding   The adding of blanks or non-significant characters to the end of a *record* or *block* in order to make it up to some fixed size. This technique is employed when *fixed length records* or *fixed blocks* are being used, to enable units which do not contain enough significant data to be processed.

paddle   An *input device* used in computer games for controlling the movement of images on a screen.

Also known as joystick.

page   1. A concept used in *virtual storage* to refer to the subdivisions of large sets of data into smaller units which can be more economically located within the *physical storage* available to a system. 2. A set of information treated as a logical unit in an information system; in particular, a term used to describe the organization of information in a *videotex* or *teletext* system, where a page is the unit of information transmitted to the user as a result of a request. ◊ *end page, index page.*

page-at-a-time printer   Synonymous with *page printer*.

paged segment   A *segment* occupying more than one *page*[1].

page printer   A *printer* for which the character pattern for a complete page is determined before printing. Contrasted with *line printer*.

Also known as page-at-a-time printer.

page turning   The process by which the *pages*[2] displayed on a *video* are successively replaced.

paging   The method in *virtual storage* whereby *physical storage* is allocated to the *pages*[1] which make up a set of data.

paint box   A menu of colours available for use in a *graphic display*.

Also known as palette.

pair, binary   Synonymous with *bistable circuit*.

pair, trigger   Synonymous with *bistable circuit*.

PAL   Abbreviation for phase alteration by line; a colour television standard adopted in the United Kingdom, West Germany and elsewhere with 625 picture lines and a 50Hz field frequency.

palette   Synonymous with *paint box*.

pan   A technique in image processing whereby an image appears to move across the screen; used to display detail from an image too large to display on a screen in its entirety.

panel, patch   Synonymous with *plugboard*.

paper advance mechanism   That part of a *printer* which moves the paper past the printing positions. The mechanism may be under computer control, enabling the number of lines advanced to be determined by *program*.

paper low condition   A warning condition indicating that the supply of *continuous stationery* on a *printer* is about to run out.

paper tape This general article describes a largely obsolete medium, very important in its time, but now referred to in the past tense.

Punched paper tape used as a key *input/output* medium during the earliest developments of electronic *digital computers*. To some extent it was used initially simply because 5-track paper tape was already in use to meet the requirements of the telegraph service, and *paper tape readers* and *paper tape punches* were adapted for use as input/output units. As an input medium it was rivalled only by *punched cards*.

Each *character* was recorded as a single *row* of holes across the width of the tape; a further hole, known as a *sprocket hole*, also appeared in each row and was used to feed the tape mechanically in slow speed readers, or, on high speed machines, to act as a *clock pulse* when the tape was read by a photo-electric head. Paper tape was normally in reels approximately 1000 ft in length and one inch in width, the individual character rows being punched into the tape 10 to the inch. Paper tape might have either 5, 6, 7 or 8 data holes in each row, and was referred to as 5-track tape, 6-track tape, 7-track tape or 8-track tape. Several different tape codes remained in use today but a great deal of work was undertaken to standardize the character sets and to specify the particular coding structure of 5, 6, 7 and 8-track codes. Bodies such as the British Standards Institute and the American Standards Association cooperated with the International Standards Organization and standard codes were recommended. For data processing purposes the 5-track code had little appeal, since there was not sufficient coding capacity for the full range of characters and special symbols needed. It was common practice to use an 8-track code, based upon ISO recommendations; this allowed each character to be represented by seven data *bits* plus one *parity bit*, the seven data bits providing sufficient unique code combinations to represent 128 alphanumeric characters and symbols.

Paper tape had the advantage that it was a compact medium, less bulky than punched cards. It was comparatively cheap to produce and easy to transport. It could be read at a speed of 1000 characters per second without difficulty, and could often be prepared as a by-product of some other machine operation; e.g., from a cash register or adding machine. The punching and verifying of punched tape from original documents was similar to the operation for cards, some details being given in the general article on *Data Preparation*.

There were some disadvantages in using paper tape but these were not really significant where the tape was used simply as an input medium for *raw data* or transactions. The most significant disadvantage lay in the fact that one *error character* in a tape might mean that the tape must be repunched, but provided that individual tapes were generated for batches of transactions with suitable batch *control total*, this problem did not represent a severe constraint. Input programs could be written to check and validate individual batches of transactions on paper tape; these batches could be presented to the computer in any sequence, and this allowed invalid batches to be rejected and re-input at a later stage. Typical validity checks at the input stage might include checking to see that *fields* conformed to specified maximum and minimum values, that decimal places were in correct positions, that specified fields contained alphabetic characters and other fields numeric only, and so on.

As a computer output medium paper tape was particularly useful for small volumes of data; e.g., summaries or error reports which could be printed *off-line* on a teleprinter or typewriter. Paper tape could also be produced for subsequent transmission over a *data link* or could also provide a numerical list for controlling an automatic machine tool. The speeds of paper tape output punches ranged from 25 to 300 characters per second.

Paper tapes usually had to be wound into reels so that they could be easily stored, handled and fed into *paper tape readers*. Some readers and punches were equipped with automatic winding attachments, although there was a possibility of damage to tapes if the units got out of adjustment; in any case they usually wound tapes directly fed from the machine, and therefore wound the *leading end* towards the centre of the spool. Manually operated winding devices were more popular and were surprisingly efficient in spooling paper tape. The usual practice was to allow the tape to fall into a bin until it was expended, whereupon the operator took the *trailing end* and wound the tape manually onto a spool.

Damaged tapes could be repaired by the use of simple tape *splicers* which could be employed to join independent lengths of paper tape or to insert corrections. The nature of error and the type of data governed the extent to which splicing was employed.

paper tape channel $\diamond$ *channel*[2].

paper tape code A *code* consisting of a pattern of holes punched across a strip of *paper tape*. Codes were determined by the number of *tracks*[2] on the paper tape, the most usual being 5-track, 7-track and 8-track codes.

paper tape loop Synonymous with *control loop*.

paper tape punch Synonymous with *tape punch*.

paper tape punching The punching of holes into *paper tape* whereby the pattern of holes formed a *code* for recording information. Once one of the basic methods of *data preparation* for *input* to a computer.

paper tape reader A device which translated the information punched in code on *paper tape* into *machine language* and transmitted the data into a *central processor*.

paper tape reproducer A device which could automatically produce a copy of a punched *paper tape*.

Also known as a reperforator.

paper tape verifier A machine once used for checking that the holes punched in *paper tape* represented the data on the original documents.
⟡ general article on *Data Preparation*.

paper throw Movement of paper through a *printer*, other than the advance of paper for printing, at a speed greater than that of single line spacing.

parallax The apparent distortion of an image viewed, for example, through the glass front of a *video screen*. Parallax errors occur when attempting to touch a point on the display with a *light pen* or when using a *touch sensitive screen*.

parallel Dealing with all the elements of an item of information simultaneously. Contrasted with *serial*.

parallel access Synonymous with *simultaneous access*.

parallel allocation A method of allocating *controlled files* in such a way that each file is allocated the same *tracks* in each *cylinder* of the *controlling file*.

parallel attribute A *videotex* and *teletext* standard, whereby an attribute defining the characteristics of a particular character cell is encoded as part of the character code and does not occupy a separate cell. ⟡ *serial attribute*.

parallel computer Synonymous with *simultaneous computer*.

parallel interface An *interface* in which parallel transfer of data occurs between *peripheral units* and *processor*. Contrasted with *serial interface*.
⟡ *ribbon cable*.

parallel processing Processing by a number of different *processors* simultaneously on one particular process, each processor dealing with a different slice of the process.

parallel running A method of testing new procedures by operating both the new system and the one it is designed to replace together for a period of time; the results produced by the new system can be compared for accuracy with those produced by the old.

parallel search storage Synonymous with *associative store*.

parallel storage A *storage device* in which the time required to *access* any item within the store is the same as the time required to access any other item in store.

parallel transfer   A method of data *transfer*[1] in which each element of a unit of data is transferred simultaneously.

parameter   A quantity or item of information which is used in a *subroutine, routine, program, adaptive control system* or mathematical calculation, and which can be given a different value each time the process is repeated.

Also known as *control data*[2].

parameter card   A *punched card* on which the value of a *parameter* required by a *program* was punched and subsequently read.

Also known as *control card*[2].

parameter word   A *word* of *store* in which the *parameter* for a *routine* is placed.

parity bit   1. A check *bit* whose value (0 or 1) depends on whether the sum of 1 bits in the word being checked is odd or even. If the total number of 1 bits, including the parity bit, is even, the word is known as having *even parity*; if the number is odd, it has *odd parity*. 2. A bit added to a group of bits to make the sum of bits (including the parity bit) always even or always odd, e.g., with a set of six bits 010110 a parity bit of 1 is needed to give the set even parity, and a bit of 0 is needed to give the set odd parity.

parity check   A check made when data is *transferred* which consists in adding up the *bits* in a unit of data, calculating the *parity bit* required and checking the calculated parity bit with the parity bit transferred with the data item. This form of check will normally be performed automatically by *hardware*.

parity check, even   ◊ *parity check*.

parity check, odd   ◊ *parity check*.

parity error   An *error* caused by incorrect parity detected as a result of a *parity check*.

partial carry   A technique used in *parallel* addition in which a *carry* is temporarily stored instead of being added in immediately. Contrasted with *complete carry*.

Pascal   A *high level language* developed in the late 1960s as a derivative of *A L G O L*. Pascal is a structured language with algorithmic features designed for fast execution of the resulting *program*. There are several versions of Pascal, of which the most widely used is *U C S D* Pascal.

pass   1. The passage of *magnetic tape* past the *read heads*. 2. A single execution of a *loop*.

password   A group of *characters* which on input to a computer from a *terminal* give the *user* access to information and allow the user defined control over the information. ⬦ general article on *Security*.

patch A group of *instructions* added to a *routine* to correct a mistake. The patch is usually placed as *out of line coding* and is entered by means of an *unconditional branch* from the part of the routine being altered.

patchboard Synonymous with *plugboard*.

patchcord A connector with a flexible part used to connect the sockets of a *plugboard*. In *punched card* usage, synonymous with *plug*.

Also known as patchplug, plugwire. Contrasted with *cordless plug*, where there is no flexible part.

patch panel Synonymous with *plugboard*.

patchplug Synonymous with *patchcord*.

path 1. The logical sequence of *instructions* in a computer *program*. (But ⬦ *critical path*.) 2. The complete set of stages through which a message packet passes during its transmission between two points. Paths may be linked by *switches*[3] to form a *switched circuit*. ⬦ *channel*[1].

pattern-sensitive fault A *fault* caused by the recognition of some specified pattern of data.

PCB Abbreviation of *printed circuit board*.

PCM Abbreviation of 1. *punched card* machine; 2. *pulse code modulation*.

PDI Abbreviation of *picture description instruction*.

PDN Abbreviation of *public data network*.

peak load The maximum traffic experienced by or planned for a *network*.

peak volume The number of simultaneous calls being handled by a *network* at its busiest period.

pecker The sensing device in a mechanical *paper tape reader*.

peek A *high level language* facility, for example in *BASIC*, which allows the *programmer* to read the contents of a specified *memory address*. Related to *poke*.

pel Acronym for *Picture ELement*.

pen A device used for operating handwritten input. A light pen may be used to write directly on a screen; other pen types are used with graphics pads.

perception data Information on factors which impact the way users perceive a computer system; in particular, features which make the system *user friendly*.

perforated tape Synonymous with *paper tape*.

perforation rate The rate at which holes can be punched into *paper tape* with a *tape punch*.

perforator   A hand-operated *tape punch* for punching *paper tape*. Also known as *keyboard* perforator.

perforator, keyboard   ⬦ *perforator*.

performance   A measure of the power of a computer system. Various performance criteria exist, including *throughput*, *access time*, and processing power in terms of mips (millions of instructions per second). Frequently a computer system is required to undergo a *benchmark* as a verification of performance targets.

performance monitoring journal   ⬦ *journal*.

period, scan   Synonymous with *regeneration period*.

peripheral   Used as a noun, for *peripheral unit*.

peripheral buffers   Small elements of *store* forming part of a *peripheral unit* used for storing data before transmission to a *central processor*, or receipt from the central processor before transcription to the *output medium*. ⬦ *input/output buffer*.

peripheral controller   That part of a system whose function is to control data transfer to or from *peripheral units* of different types.

peripheral control unit   A device which acts as the link between a *peripheral unit* and a *central processor* and which interprets and acts on instructions from the processor.

peripheral device   Synonymous with *peripheral unit*.

peripheral equipment   Synonymous with *peripheral units*.

peripheral interface channel   A *channel*[1] which provides the connecting path for information to flow between a *peripheral unit* and a *processor*. ⬧ *standard interface*.

peripheral limited   A system is known as peripheral limited when the overall processing time is dictated by the speed of the *peripheral units* rather than the speed of the *central processor*. Contrasted with *processor limited*.

peripheral manager interface   Part of a *kernel* which controls *input* and *output* requirements.

peripheral processor   In a *data processing* system making use of more than one *processor*, a peripheral processor is a processor operating under the control of another processor. Usually the peripheral processor will control all *input/output* functions of the system, providing a flow of data to and from the processor.

peripheral prompt   A *message* initiated by an *operating system* to inform the *operator* of the state of a particular *peripheral* unit, or the need to *load* a *file*. ⬧ *prompt*.

peripheral transfer   The transfer of a unit of data between a *peripheral unit* and a *central processor* or between peripheral units.

peripheral units   Machines which can be operated under computer control. Peripheral equipment consists of *input devices*, *output devices* and *storage devices*. For examples of peripheral equipment: ⬙ *tablet*, *floppy disk*, *magnetic disk*, *magnetic drum*, *magnetic tape*, *printer*, *video*. ⬙ general articles on *Input Devices*, *Output Devices* and *Storage Devices*.

permanent memory   Synonymous with *non-volatile memory*.

personal computer   A *microcomputer* with enough *memory* and processing performance to be used for business *applications* and *word processing*. Contrasted with *microcomputer* and *home computer*. The introduction of *spreadsheets* greatly accelerated the acceptance of personal computers.

personnel records   The recording of data concerning personnel is a common computer application. Personnel records may be kept both in order to produce a payroll and to provide a record of information about employees which can be used by management for a variety of planning and administrative functions. The type of information recorded and the method in which it is coded and stored depends largely on the ultimate use to which the data is to be put. The Data Protection Act, which gave the right of access to individuals, ensured that companies reviewed very carefully all data held about employees.

If records are kept purely for payroll purposes then information will be confined to the financial details relevant to each employee together with data necessary for payment, such as details of hours worked, absence, rates of pay, etc. Tax calculations in payroll applications are usually performed by means of *software packages* provided for the purpose by the manufacturer or user. The medium for storing personnel records used primarily for payroll purposes will normally be one suited to regular *sequential processing* in which each *record* is processed at every *run*.

Personnel records can provide a more detailed source of information about employees. Additional data about each person can include information on qualifications and experience, administrative details such as department, address, medical details, etc. The actual data recorded will depend on the applications envisaged for the information, but in all cases some system of coding information, so that retrieval and analysis may be simplified, must be devised. Where a file of personnel records is going to be used extensively for *information retrieval*, e.g., searching for personnel satisfying given conditions, the file organization will depend on the retrieval techniques to be adopted. If frequent interrogation of the file is expected, each interrogation producing a limited number of *hits*, a *direct access* storage device would normally be used, using random storage methods. The use of *inverted file* structures is used in some applications. e.g., in the recording of fingerprint details on criminal files.

Updating methods will depend on the particular application, but the *turn-round document* technique is particularly suited to updating personnel records of employees.

PERT Acronym for Project Evaluation and Review Technique ⋄ general article on *Critical Path Method*.

phase Voltage in alternating current varies over time, and phase is the measure over time of the variation between voltage peaks or amplitude of the current. ⋄ *phase modulation*.

phase alteration by line ⋄ *PAL*.

phase modulation A method of representing *binary* information in which the phase of a carrier signal is used to indicate 0 and 1.

philoxenic Synonymous with *user friendly*, from the Greek 'philos' (friend) and 'xenos' (stranger).

phosphor A material placed on the surface of a *cathode ray tube* which glows when excited by an *electron beam*. Coloured phosphors are used to create coloured images.

photographic An image created by means of light from an object concentrated optically on a light sensitive medium as, for example, with a television camera. Photographic images may be digitized and input into a computer system, for example, by means of run length encoding. ⋄ *alphaphotographic*, *videotex*.

photosensitive A material whose electrical properties vary with light intensity is said to be photosensitive.

physical A term used in the context of *operating systems* to describe actual existing entities (*files*, *resources*), in contrast to *logical*.

physical address ⋄ *address*.

physical level In the *ISO seven layer reference model* for *open systems architecture*, the control level which defines the physical interface between a *terminal* and the data circuit terminating equipment.

physical data independence Where a *file structure* or the *physical medium* on which a file is held, may be changed without affecting the *application program* using the data.

physical file In an *operating system* refers to a *file* contained on a specific physical *storage* medium, e.g., a specific *magnetic tape* or *disk*. A file in an operating system may be contained on a number of different physical files.

physical file copy   A copy of a *physical file* on the same or different *medium*.

physical file report   A list in readable form of the contents of a *physical file*.

physical interface   The specification of the electrical properties of the signals required to establish, maintain and clear the connexion between a *terminal* and data circuit terminating equipment.

physical track   The path along which a single *read/write head* on a *disk* or *drum* moves. Synonymous with *track*[1] and used in *operating systems*. ⟡ *logical track*.

pico-   Prefix denoting one million-millionth or 10^{-12}.

picture   A set of information which is available for *display* on a *video* or *terminal*. Because of the physical limitations of the screen on a specific device the picture may consist of a number of *pages*[2].

picture description instruction   Usually referred to by the abbreviation *PDI*. A form of code used to describe the formation of an image by means of a combination of elements such as dots, lines, polygons, arcs, etc. PDIs are used, for example, in *alphageometric videotex* coding standards.

picture element   In any *graphic display*, the smallest element of the image which can be individually *addressed* by the computer program. In a graphics system, the number of picture elements will depend on the resolution capability of the display.

  Also known as pel or pixel.

picture frequency   The frequency with which the complete set of lines which make up a television picture is displayed, measured in cycles per second (Hz). Typically, picture frequency in the USA is 30 Hz, and in Europe is 25 Hz.

pie chart   The graphical representation of information in the form of a 'pie', with each 'slice' showing the proportion contributed to the whole of a number of constituent elements.

pilot system   A method of testing new procedures by processing a representative sample of data from the operations to be covered by the new system, either by sampling historical data or taking a sample from current operations. ⟡ *parallel running*.

pin   The small 'legs' on a *chip* which correspond to matching holes on a *printed circuit board*, by which the chip is connected to the board.

pinboard   A form of *plugboard* in which the interconnexions are made by cordless *plugs* in the form of pins.

ping-pong   A programming technique for processing *multi-reel files* which uses two *magnetic tape* units, switching between them until the whole file is processed, the successive reels being placed on alternate units.

pipelining The overlapping of the *execution* of several *instructions* in an *order code processor* at the same time. Each instruction is usually executed as a number of cycles which must be performed in sequence. Pipelining enables several instructions to be performed by the execution of different cycles on different instructions simultaneously.

pixel Abbreviation for *picture element*.

PL/1 PL/1 (Programming Language 1) is a programming *language* developed with the intention of combining features of commercial languages (such as *COBOL*) and scientific languages (such as *ALGOL*). Commercial applications with their emphasis on efficient handling of large volumes of data have led to the development of languages with sophisticated *input/output* facilities; scientific problems with their emphasis on rapid definitions and description of complex problems have led to the development of highly sophisticated *algorithmic* languages while neglecting the data handling aspects. PL/1 aims at combining the problem-solving facility of scientific languages with the data-handling capabilities of commercial languages, in order to meet the needs of increasingly mathematical commercial analysis and increasingly large volumes of data being processed by scientific routines. Among the more important features of PL/1 are the following: (i) The language is *modular* in structure. This means that the user need only master the set of facilities necessary for his programming needs. More complex problems can use more extensive *subsets* of the language. (ii) The language has a 'default' feature by which every error or unspecified option is given a valid interpretation, thus minimizing the effects of programming errors. (iii) The language structure is 'free form'. No special documents are needed for *coding*, since the significance of each statement depends on its own format and not on its position within a fixed framework.

An example of PL/1 is given below; it is a routine designed to read the maximum and minimum temperatures for every day of the week, and calculate and print the average temperature for each day of the week.

```
WEATHER: PROCEDURE
DECLARE MAXDAY (7); MINDAY (7); AVERAGE (7);
READ LIST ((MAXDAY (I). MINDAY (I)) I=1 TO 7);
AVERAGE=(MAXDAY+MINDAY)/2; WRITE ((MAXDAY
```

(I), MINDAY (I), AVERAGE (II)) I=1 TO 7) (2F(5),F(8,1), SPACE); END WEATHER;

place In *positional notation*, a *digit position* within an ordered set of digits corresponding to a given power of the *radix* or *base* of the number system.

plant To place the *result* of an *operation* of a *routine* in a *location* where it will be used at a later stage in the *program*.

plasma display A visual *display* which creates an image by causing a series of gas filled cells to be illuminated by means of an electric current. Each cell represents a *picture element*. Plasma displays, an alternative to *cathode ray tube* displays, are flatter but have lower resolution.

platen A solid, usually cylindrical backing used in certain printing devices to form a base for a striking mechanism.

playback head Synonymous with *read head*.

plot To draw a line connecting the points on a graph.

plotter A device which automatically draws a graph.

plotter, digital incremental ◊ *digital incremental plotter*.

plotter, x–y Synonymous with *data plotter*.

plotting board A *plotter* which acts as an *output device* giving graphical representation to the results of computer operations.

Also known as plotting table, output table.

plotting table Synonymous with *plotting board*.

plug A device, usually consisting of a flexible cord with one or more metal pins at each end, used to connect the sockets of a *corrector*.

plugboard A device for controlling the operation of certain types of *data processing* machine by means of a removable board with terminals which might be connected in different patterns by the use of plugs fitting into sockets on the board. The specific action required for the machine was determined by the particular interconnexions made; these might be changed at any time to alter the functioning of the machine.

Also known as patch panel, patchboard, control panel[3], problem board, jack panel.

plug compatible Any *peripheral unit* which can be connected directly to a *host* by conforming to the necessary physical and electrical connexion standards and *protocols*. Plug compatible peripherals are frequently manufactured by organizations independent of the host's manufacturer.

plugging chart A printed chart representing the sockets on a *plugboard*. It was used for planning interconnexions of sockets which would enable a machine to perform its required function.

plug-in card A *printed circuit board* which is able to perform a discrete logical function in a computing system, and is inserted into the *host* system by connexion through a slot. ⟫ *daughter board*, *backplane*.

plug-in unit   A self-contained circuit assembly which forms part of a more complex whole but which can be removed and replaced as a unit.

plug-to-plug compatible   The original phrase used to denote connexion compatibility, superseded by *plug compatible*.

plugwire   Synonymous with *plug*.

pneumatic computer   A computer in which signals are transmitted and information stored by means of the flow and varying of pressure in a fluid – either gas or a liquid. ⟫ *fluid logic*.

pocket   Synonym for *stacker*, usually used in connexion with a *sorter*.

pointer   Any *location* used to hold the *address* of another location is said to act as a pointer to that location.

point, floating   ⟫ *floating point arithmetic*.

point mode display   A method of displaying data as dots plotted on the tube surface of a *cathode ray tube visual display unit*.

point-to-point connexion   A circuit connecting two (and only two) devices without any intervening device, for example, a *terminal* and a central computer, or two computers.

point-to-point network   A *network* in which the connexions between individual *nodes* is by means of *point-to-point connexions* without the necessity for any form of *switching*.

poke   An *instruction* in a *high level language* (usually *BASIC*) which allows a value expressed in *machine code* to be inserted in an *absolute address*. ⟫ *peek*.

Polish notation   A form of notation in *Boolean algebra* in which all the *operators* in a statement precede all the variables.

poll   A technique used in *data transmission* whereby several *terminals* share *communication channels*, the particular channel chosen for a given terminal being determined by testing each channel in order to find a free one available for transmission, or locate a channel on which incoming data is present. Also used for the technique of calling for transmissions from remote terminals by signal from a central terminal. Polling is a method used for avoiding *contention*.

POP-2   A programming language used in *artificial intelligence* applications.

port   1. Any socket in a computer system into which an *input/output device* may be plugged. 2. A single *channel* to which a user of a *network* may be connected.

portability   A characteristic of *code* or data which can be used on more than one system.

POS Abbreviation of point-of-sale.

positional notation A form of *number representation* in which a given number is represented by a set of digits in such a way that both the position, of the digit within the set as well as its value is of significance. The normal decimal system of number representation is an example of a positional notation in which each position in the set of digits represents an increase by a factor of ten on the preceding place. ⊘ *binary notation*.

positional representation Synonymous with *positional notation*.

post To update a *record* with information.

posting interpreter Synonymous with *transfer interpreter*. ⊘ *punched card interpreter*.

post-mortem dump A *dump* which takes place after a *program* has finished, usually to give information during *debugging*.

post-mortem program ⊘ *post-mortem routine*.

post-mortem routine A *routine* which is used to provide information about the functioning of a *program* after the program has finished. ⊘ *debugging, diagnostic routine*.

post-mortem time ⊘ *system recovery time*.

P-pulse Synonymous with *commutator pulse*.

preamble sequence A series of *bits* used to establish synchronization of messages transmitted within a *local area network* ⊘ *sync bytes*.

precision, double ⊘ *double-precision arithmetic*.

pre-edit The technique of having a preliminary *editing* run on *input* data before the data is used for further processing.

prefix notation A type of notation in which a complex *expression* consisting of several *operators* and associated *operands* is formed without the use of brackets, the scope of the operators being determined by their relative positions. ⊘ *Polish notation*.

pre-read head A *read head* placed in such a position near another read head that it may be used to read *records* before they pass under the second head.

presentation level The sixth level within the *seven layer reference model* for *communications protocols*, which defines the way data is displayed to the user.

preset parameter A *parameter* whose value is fixed before a *routine* is run. ⊘ *program parameter*.

presort 1. The first *pass*[1] of a *sort program*[2]. The sorting of data on *off-line equipment* before processing it on a computer.

Prestel The *videotex* system supplied as a public service by British Telecom. Prestel was the world's first operational videotex service, and it was launched in 1980 after extensive trials.

pre-store   The placing of data in a special part of *store* before entering a *routine* to process the data.

presumptive address   A quantity which appears in the *address part* of a *quasi instruction* and acts as an *origin* for subsequent *address modification*. ⊘ *base address*.

presumptive instruction   Synonymous with *basic instruction*.

preventive maintenance   *Maintenance* carried out with the intention of preventing the occurrence of faults, i.e., regular maintenance as opposed to 'fire-brigade' maintenance.

PRF   Abbreviation of pulse repetition frequency. ⊘ *pulse repetition rate*.

primary storage   Synonymous with *main storage*.

primitive file   In an *operating system* a term used for a set of *physical files*, possibly on different devices, which are handled as a single entity by the operating system.

print bar   A type of *print member*.

print barrel   A drum on the surface of which are engraved all the *characters* used by an *on-the-fly printer*. The barrel is rotated rapidly and characters are printed by hammers which strike the paper as the appropriate character is in position relative to the paper.

printed circuit   The technique of etching the details of a computing *circuit diagram* on the surface of a board, a process allowing for the exact replication of unlimited copies of the original circuit.

printed circuit board   A *board* on which a *printed circuit* is etched, and into which *chips* are inserted by means of *pins*.

Also known as pcb.

printer   An *output device* which converts data into printed form.

printer, dot matrix   ⊘ *needle printer*.

printer, hit-on-the-fly   Synonymous with *on-the-fly printer*.

printer, line-at-a-time   Synonymous with *line printer*.

printer, matrix   Synonymous with *needle printer*.

printer, wire   Synonymous with *stylus printer*.

printer, xerographic   ⊘ *xerographic printer*.

print format   A description of the way information is to be printed on a *printer*, usually provided as part of a *program specification*.

print hammer   The device on certain types of *printer* which is activated in order to force paper into contact with the *character* to be printed.

print member   The mechanism in a *printer* responsible for the form of the printed character.

printout   A general term for the output from a *printer*; printed pages produced by a printer.

printout, memory ◇ *memory print*.

print position The position on a *printer* at which a *character* may be printed. The positions are usually numbered 1–n (where n is the maximum number of characters which can be accommodated on a line) starting from the left-hand edge of the line.

print totals only To print totals pertaining to a batch of input data, as contrasted with *list²* which involves the printing of details from each individual record in the batch.

print wheel In a *wheel printer*, a wheel which has around its rim the type for the characters available for printing. The wheel is moved to bring the appropriate character into position for printing.

priority indicator In *data transmission*, a code used to indicate the relative importance of a message, and hence the order of transmission of the message.

priority processing A system used in *multiprogramming* for determining the sequence in which different *programs* are processed.

privacy The concept of restricted *access* to *data* and *information* held within a computer system. ◇ general article on *Security*.

private volume A category of *filestore* where the *user* has direct control over the placing of his *files* and can restrict the ability of other users to place files in his *volumes*.

privilege The rights of a *user* to make use of facilities within a system, e.g., the right to have *access* to certain *files*.

probability The assessment of probabilities of events is one of the spheres where the *digital computer* can prove to be an extremely useful tool. Probability calculations are often long and tedious and by their nature repetitive; such calculations may be performed with ease with the aid of a computer.

The term 'probability' is given a precise meaning. The probability of an event is defined to be the quotient formed by dividing the number of ways the event can happen by the number of possible happenings. If we take the simple example of tossing a coin, the probability of throwing a tail is ½, since a tail can be thrown in only one way, whereas there are two possible results of a throw, namely a head or a tail. Thus,

$$\text{Probability} = \frac{\text{Number of successful results}}{\text{Number of possible results}}$$

Many readers will be familiar with comparing 'odds' of events (usually connected with horses). The odds of an event may be obtained directly from the probability. In our previous example the odds of throwing a tail are 1:1 or evens; if the probability of an event is the quotient p/q

357

then the odds of that event are p:q − p; or, putting this another way, if the probability of an event is P the odds are 1:1/P − 1.

i.e., Odds = Number of successful results: Number of unsuccessful results.

The value of the probability as calculated above can lie between 0 and 1 corresponding to odds of 0:1 and 1:0. A probability of 0 represents the impossible; that of 1 the unavoidable. A probability of greater than ½ is more likely to happen than not; that of less than ½ is more likely not to happen.

In calculating probabilities care has to be taken to choose a 'random variable', and to distinguish between connected and unconnected events. The following two examples set out the differences:

(i)   A boy is chosen at random and found to come from a family with two children. What is the probability that the other is a boy?

Answer: ½. The other child can be either a boy or a girl, the fact that the first child was a boy does not affect this.

(ii) A certain family with two children is known to contain a boy. What is the probability that it contains two boys?

Answer: ⅓. Writing down all possible families with two children:

First child	Second child
Boy	Boy
Boy	Girl
Girl	Boy
Girl	Girl

Of these four possibilities, three satisfy our initial condition that the family shall contain a boy, and one that the family will consist of two boys. Thus the probability is ½.

Where an event consists of a combination of two independent events the probability of the compound event is calculated by multiplying together the two independent probabilities. Thus the probability that two consecutive throws of a coin will both be heads, for example, is obtained by multiplying the probability of a head by the probability of a head to give ½ × ½ = ¼. Note that this is the same as the probability of two tails, or head–tail, or tail–head, but that the probability of throwing one head and one tail (with no ordering condition) in two throws is ½.

Probability theory often turns up rather unexpected answers, and an assessment of probabilities is nearly always worth while when examining possible behaviour or comparing differing systems.

problem board Synonymous with *plugboard*.

problem definition A method of presenting a problem for computer solution in a formal and logical manner.

Also known as problem description. ◊ general articles on *Documentation* and *Programming*.

problem description Synonymous with *problem definition*.

problem oriented language A *program language* designed for handling problems in certain broad application types related to e.g., mathematical, scientific or engineering systems, or to business systems. Essentially a language which enables the user to write *statements* in a form with which he is familiar, say in mathematical notation or English. Examples of mathematical languages are *ALGOL*, *FORTRAN*, and of a business language, *COBOL*.

procedure 1. The sequence of steps required in order to solve a problem. 2. More specifically, used to describe a section of *code*[1] which acts as a *subroutine* within an *operating system*.

procedure analysis ◊ *systems analysis*.

procedure oriented language A *program language* designed to make the expression of problem-solving procedures simple to use.

process 1. A general term for any computer operation on data. 2. More specifically, is used in connection with an *operating system* to refer to a set of user *programs*, system *software* and *data* brought together by the operating system in order to carry out a specific job.

process chart Synonymous with *systems flowchart*.

process control The use of computers (usually *analog computers* or *hybrid computers*) for controlling directly the operation of physical processes, e.g., the use of computers in the automatic control of chemical and electrical plant.

process image Within an *operating system*, used for the totality formed by a particular *program* together with any system *software* utilized to carry out the program.

processing, automatic data ◊ *automatic data processing*.

processing, centralized data ◊ *centralized data processing*.

processing, conversational ◊ *conversational mode*.

processing, electronic data ◊ *electronic data processing*.

processing, in-line Synonymous with *demand processing*.

processing, integrated data   ⟡ *integrated data processing.*

process, irreversible   ⟡ *irreversible magnetic process.*

process limited   Synonymous with *processor limited.*

processor   A general term for any device capable of carrying out operations on data. Sometimes used as a synonym for *central processor.*

processor error interrupt   The interruption of a *program* because of the failure of a *parity check* in the transfer of information within the *central processor.*

processor limited   A system in which the overall processing time is dictated by the speed of the *central processor* rather than the speed of the *peripheral equipment.*

Also known as process limited. Contrasted with *peripheral limited.*

process, reversible   ⟡ *reversible magnetic process.*

process state   The state which a *process* has reached during the course of its *execution.*

product   The result of multiplying two *factors*, the *multiplicand* and the *multiplier.*

production control   The purpose of production control is to enable a manufacturing organization to meet all orders placed by customers within a reasonable time. Computerized production control will often increase business by means of an improvement in delivery dates. Other benefits are a reduction of capital tied up in stock, reduction in labour costs and improved utilization of plant.

The starting point for a production control cycle is a sales forecast. Typically a company will have firm orders for a short period in the future, tentative orders in the medium term and intelligent anticipation (perhaps based on *extrapolation* of past trends) will have to be used for the long term. The length of these time periods will be specific to particular industries and production problems. Given a sales forecast as *input*, a computer can break down the products demanded into their constituent main units, assemblies, sub-assemblies, etc., down to piece parts and raw materials. Processing of this information is in two stages: (a) calculation of gross requirement of each constituent element of each product; and (b) calculation of net requirements of each constituent element taking into account work-in-progress and stock levels.

Finally the net requirements must be converted into economic manufacturing batches and orders to outside suppliers.

It is obvious that an integral part of a production control system must be a system of *inventory control*, because without a knowledge of stock levels it is impossible to establish net requirements for parts and raw materials. The basic objective of inventory control is to maintain stocks at the lowest levels that are compatible with the economics of production. There are two conflicting requirements here. On the one hand the cost of stockholding increases with the quantity of stock held and, on the other, the lower the stock levels the longer the turn-round time on orders tends to be. The break-even point for each stock level is most likely to be achieved using a computer system.

Input to the computer will be details of items received into, returned to and issued from stores. These items will be used to keep up to date a master stock file which can be processed for reports and queries. The computer can also carry out automatic re-order point control on stock levels and signal unusual circumstances (for example, exceptional demand and non-moving stocks).

Breakdown and inventory control are reasonably straightforward applications to put on a computer. Having ascertained the production requirements in terms of components and raw materials reached, however, the next stage is to plan the flow of work on the factory floor. This is also amenable to computer control but is a more challenging project to design and implement.

The final output from the breakdown analysis is a list of manufacturing batches, which will be necessary to meet the required production. This information can be used to plan plant loading, showing the effect of the work load on production centres and enabling management to make decisions: for example, on the need for increased plant capacity and labour force or on the possibility of subcontracting. The role of the computer is to tabulate the load in hours for a given time period, on each production centre.

Computer analysis of plant loading can be made more sophisticated in various ways. For example, the computer can load demand against appropriate time periods, starting at the required completion date and working backwards, and printing out the potential overload/underload on each shop in each time period.

Once any imbalances between load and capacity have been smoothed, it becomes possible to plan the workload through machine and assembly shops so as to optimize use of plant. This procedure involves several operations, among them maintenance of a work-in-progress file which reflects the current state of all jobs, the printing of works documentation (such as route lists and departmental schedules) and progress control. Progress control is achieved by analysis of the work-in-progress file and the printout of details of jobs behind schedule.

production run A normal operational *run* of a system. Contrasted with *parallel run*, *pilot run*, *test run*.

productive time Time spent by a computer system in processing *production runs* during which no machine faults occur.

product, logical Synonymous with *and operation*.

program A set of *instructions* composed for solving a given problem by computer. ⋄ general article on *Programming*.

program address counter Synonymous with *instruction register*.

program cards *Punched cards* containing *program instructions*, either in *machine language* or *source language*, often with one card used for each instruction.

program compatibility The situation in which two different computers can accept and operate on the same *program* or programs written in the same *machine language* or *source language*.

program compilation ⋄ *compiler*.

program control Any device operating *on-line* to a *central processor* is said to be under program control.

program controller The unit in a *central processor* which controls the execution of the computer *instructions* and their sequence of operation. Also known as program control unit.

program control unit Synonymous with *program controller*.

program counter A *control unit register* in which the *address* of the next *instruction* to be performed is stored. Synonymous with *control register*.

program development time The total time taken to produce a working computer *program*. This will include time taken in *compilation*, *testing* and *debugging*.

program, diagnostic ⋄ *diagnostic routine*.

program documentation ⋄ general article on *Documentation*.

program file Synonymous with *program tape*.

program flowchart A *flowchart* using *flowchart symbols* to represent the functions performed by a particular routine. ⋄ general article on *Flowcharting*.

program, general ⋄ *general purpose program*.

program generator ⋄ *generator*.

program generator, report ⋄ *report program generator*.

program instruction ⋄ *instruction*.

program, internally stored ⋄ *internally stored program*.

program language A *language* used for writing computer *programs*. ⋄ *Programming*.

program library 1. A collection of proven *routines* or *subroutines* used in a particular installation and consisting usually of *programs* developed by the user concerned and also by the computer manufacturer. The programs may exist in various media (e.g., *floppy disk* or *cassette tape*) but are generally maintained on *magnetic tape* or a *direct access file*. 2. An indexed book or volume of papers describing the routines and programs in the *program library*[1] with instructions to enable users to employ them for their specific tasks.

programmable function key A *function key* whose function can be determined by *program*, and which may vary depending on the program being *executed*. For example, in computer *games*, the same key may be used to initiate a number of different actions when different games are played.

program maintenance The keeping of *programs* up to date both by correcting errors, and by altering programs according to changing requirements.

program, master control ♢ *master control routine.*

programme ♢ *program* for computer program.

programmed check A *check* performed by means of *program instructions*. Sometimes contrasted with an *automatic check* performed by *hardware*.

programmed dump A *memory dump* which occurs at specified points within a *program* as a result of instructions incorporated into the program. ♢ *debugging.*

programmed halt A *halt* in a *program* due to the program encountering a *halt instruction* or an *interrupt*.
    Also known as coded stop. Contrasted with *unexpected halt*.

programmed instruction Synonymous with *macroinstruction*.

programmed switch ♢ *switch*[3].

programmer 1. A person responsible for producing a working *program* from a *program specification*. ♢ *Programming.* 2. ♢ *Programmer unit.*

programmer defined macro A *macroinstruction* defined by a programmer for use in a specific *program*, in contrast with a predefined macroinstruction which may form part of the *instruction set* of a given *language*.

programmer unit A device which sets the correct conditions for programming a *PROM*, and thus allows a user to program a PROM.

programming Programming is the process by which a set of *instructions* is produced for a computer to make it perform a specified activity. The activity can be anything from the solution of a mathematical problem to the production of a company payroll. The instructions ultimately obeyed by the computer are the numerical codes significant to the computer's *central processor*. Since a computer cannot reason, but is entirely dependent on instructions supplied to it by its all too human users, it cannot be expected to perform any task adequately unless the problem it is required to solve has been specified correctly in every detail and the instructions it is asked to obey define in complete detail each step of the solution. The main steps which have to be covered before a program is completed are: (i) Understand the problem, and plan the solution. (ii) Prepare a *flowchart* or *decision table* of the problem. (iii) Prepare the instructions in coded form. (iv) Test the program until it is performing correctly. (v) Prepare detailed documentation of the program and instructions on its operation. The amount of time spent on each of these steps, their relative importance and the techniques used depend largely on the type and complexity of the problem being programmed: but some attempt to implement each of these stages must be made for nearly every program.

Understanding the problem is of fundamental importance. In most cases the programmer will work from a detailed program specification prepared by a systems analyst. A detailed program specification will include descriptions of all input to be processed by the program, the processing required and details of all output from the program. The programmer must satisfy himself that all possible conditions have been specifically catered for, or that any conditions not specifically detailed can be adequately handled. Having satisfied himself of the adequacy of the specification of the problem, the programmer has next to consider the 'strategy' to be adopted in writing the program. Depending on the complexity of the problem, the capacity of the computer and the type of *language* to be used, the program may be written as a single entity or divided into sections or *segments*, each one covering a logically distinct part of the problem. For example, a program might be divided into a *housekeeping* segment in which the program is set to its *entry conditions*, an input segment which deals with reading and validating data input to the program, a processing segment which operates on the input data and an output segment which presents the results of the processing in the required format. Each of these segments can be considered as separate programs, possibly written by different programmers. Further, if the whole program cannot fit into *store* certain segments can become *overlays*.

Flowcharting the problem is the next step to be performed. The general article on this topic gives details of the techniques involved and the general article on *decision tables* is also of relevance here. The object of flowcharting is to produce a diagram showing the logical relationship between the various parts of the program. It is particularly important to maintain an overall outline flowchart of the whole problem when segmentation takes place to ensure that all parts of the program specification are taken care of. A flowchart will normally be independent of the type of computer to be used or the language the program is to be written in, although these factors must be borne in mind. In some cases however the restrictions on the language to be used will determine the logic of the program and hence the flowcharting, e.g., in the case of report programs in which a *report generator* will be used as the program language.

Coding the program follows the completion of flowcharts. The logical steps described in the flowchart are translated into instructions to the computer. These instructions will either be in *machine code*, i.e., the basic code of instructions understood by the processor, or in some form of *symbolic language*. The nature of programming languages is described in the article on *Languages*. The choice of language will depend on the complexity of the problem and the capacity and resources of the computer to be used. The more sophisticated and easier to use a language is, the less control a programmer will have over the final form of the *object program* operated on by the computer, and thus some loss of efficiency in running time or increase in size of program may occur. These penalties are counterbalanced by the speed of writing a program in a higher level language and the fact that fewer mistakes are likely.

Whatever language is used to write a program, the programmer must achieve the same basic end: to reproduce the logic of the program as shown in the flowchart as simply, economically and efficiently as possible. In a brief article it is not possible to describe in detail all the techniques used by programmers to achieve these aims; more information will be found under the following headings: *instruction*, *loop*, *program modification*, *switch*, *subroutine*.

It is most unusual for a program to work correctly the first time it is tested. Errors in a program are known as *bugs*, and the process of correcting these errors is described in the article on *debugging*. Errors are of two main types: errors due to incorrect use of the programming language and errors due to incorrect logic in the solution of the problem. Programs are tested with samples of the data normally expected to be input to the program and the results obtained compared with calculated results obtained manually from this test data. When the results obtained by the program match up to the expected results, and the programmer or systems analyst is satisfied that all possible conditions that the program is expected to meet with in normal operating circumstances have been simulated, the program may be said to be working correctly. However, a correct program is of little use unless it is supported by full *documentation*, and it is the duty of a programmer to ensure that this is maintained and supplied to any user of the program.

Documentation of a program is designed to fulfil two functions: to enable a user to operate the program correctly, and to enable another person to understand the program so that it may if necessary be modified or corrected by someone other than the programmer who first wrote it. Operating instructions include the following elements: a program description; set-up; running procedure; output disposal. Program documentation will include details of the program specification, flowcharts, coding and any *compilation* listings, and test results: a description of these requirements will be found in the general article on *Documentation.*

programming, automatic   ◊ *automatic coding.*
programming, heuristic   ◊ *heuristic program.*
programming language   ◊ *language.*
programming, micro   ◊ *microcoding.*
program modification   1. The use of *modification* in a *program* by which *arithmetical* and *logical operations* are performed on *instructions* and *addresses* so as to alter their actions during the program. 2. To modify a program by re-writing it or adding a *patch* so as to change the function of the program.
program overlay   ◊ *overlay.*
program parameter   A *parameter* whose value is incorporated into a *routine* by means of *program instructions* after the *run* has commenced. Contrasted with *preset parameters*, which are incorporated into a routine before the run commences.
program register   Synonymous with *instruction register.*
program segment   ◊ *segment.*
program-sensitive fault   A *fault* which occurs as a result of some combination of *program instructions.*
program specification   A comprehensive description of procedures for which a computer *program* is required. The program specification is used by a programmer in order to prepare a program. ◊ *system definition*, and general articles on *Documentation* and *Programming.*
program step   A single element of a *program*, usually a single *instruction.*
program storage   The area of *store* in which a *program* is placed. On some systems this may be a specially reserved part of store, or may be specially protected to prevent accidental interference with the program.

program, supervisory ◊ general article on *Multiprogramming*.

program tape A *magnetic tape* or *paper tape* on which one or more *programs*, usually in *object program* format, are stored. When a particular program is required for running, it is read into the *main store* from the program tape.

Also known as program file.

program test A computer *run* designed to discover errors in the *program* being run. ◊ *Debugging*.

program testing Checking a *program* (in order to establish that it is performing expected operations correctly and that all errors have been discovered) by running the program on a computer, usually with *test data*. ◊ *Debugging, dry running, Remote Testing*.

program testing time Time spent on a computer in *program testing*. Progam testing time is part of the total *program development time*.

program, utility ◊ *service routines*.

PROM Acronym for Programmable *Read-Only Memory* (ROM). A form of ROM whose contents may be altered by the 'user' by means of a device known as a *PROM programmer* or *PROM* blower. *PROMs whose contents can be erased and reprogrammed are known as EPROMs; when the erasing procedure is electrical, they are known as EEPROMs* (electrically erasable PROMS); where the erasing process uses ultra-violet rays, they are known as *UVEPROMs*.

PROM blower Synonymous with *PROM programmer*.

PROM programmer A device (not an individual) which inserts code or data into a *PROM*. This activity is sometimes known as 'blowing' a PROM, and the device is thus also known as a PROM blower.

prompt Any *message* given to an *operator* by an *operating system*.

prompt identifier A code or number displayed with a *prompt* in order to identify it uniquely.

proof total A *control total* which can also be used, in combination with others, to check the consistency of a group of totals, e.g., if a group of control totals consists of a gross total, deductions total and net total, proof totals will check that gross less deductions equals net.

propagated error An error which occurs in an operation and whose influence extends to other operations.

propagation time The time taken by an electrical impulse to travel from one *node* of a *network* to another.

protected location A *location* of *store* whose contents cannot be altered without some special procedure, thus preventing unplanned *modification* of the location.

protected record (or field) A *record* or *field* displayed on a *video* which cannot be *overwritten* by the *operator* but can be changed only by data sent from the processor.

protection 1. The techniques of prevention of interference between units of *software* or areas of data within a *multiprocessing system*. 2. The technique of preventing or making difficult the unauthorized use of *software* or *data*, e.g., by the use of *passwords* or sophisticated *hardware* techniques.

protection mechanism Means of carrying out *protection*.

protocol A set of rules which determine the formats by which information may be exchanged between different systems. Protocols for data communication are formal and elaborate and are set by international bodies, such as *CCITT*, *ISO*.

provable system *Software* which is capable of meeting the requirements of a formal mathematical proof that its semantics meet its specification.

proving Testing a machine in order to find out whether it is free of *faults*, usually by running a *test program*.

proving time Time spent on a machine in *proving*.

pseudocode A *code* in which *program instructions* are written, making use of symbolic representations of *operation codes* and *addresses*, and requiring translation into *machine code* by means of a *compiler* before the program can be run. ⟡ *languages, programming*.

pseudo instruction An *instruction* composed of characters arranged in symbolic form, but not performed as an actual instruction in the running of the *program*, but used to control the conversion from *source language* to *object language*.

pseudo off-lining Synonymous with *spooling*.

pseudo operation An *operation* which is not performed by means of *hardware*. Such an operation may be performed by means of a *macroinstruction* or by means of special *software*.

pseudo-random sequence A set of numbers which is produced by a defined process but which can nevertheless be considered to be a set of *random numbers* for a given calculation.

PSS Abbreviation of *packet switching service*.

PSTN Abbreviation of *public switched telephone network*.

PTT Abbreviation of post, telephone, telecommunications (originally post, telephone, telegraph). The national communications authority in most countries, although in some (e.g., UK, USA), postal authorities and communications authorities are separated and are not nationalized.

public data network A *network* provided as a service, normally by a national body, allowing data to be transmitted on a national and international basis. Public data networks can be of several types, including digital line circuits, digital *switched circuits*, and *packet switching services*.

Public Switched Telephone Network (PSTN) The national voice telephone system. Increasingly the PSTN is used for the transmission of *data*, as an alternative to public data networks.

pulse A sudden and relatively short electrical disturbance.

pulse code The representation of *digits* by means of sets of *pulses*.

pulse, P- ⟡ *commutator pulse*.

pulse recording, double- ⟡ *double-pulse recording*.

pulse repetition frequency A *pulse repetition rate* which is independent of the time interval over which it is measured.

pulse repetition rate The average number of *pulses* occurring in a unit of time.

pulse train A sequence of *pulses*.

punch 1. To make a hole in a *punched card* or piece of *paper tape*. 2. A device for making such a hole. ⟡ *card punch*, *tape punch*.

punch, automatic feed ⟡ *automatic punch*.

punch, automatic tape ⟡ *automatic tape punch*.

punch card ⟡ *punched card*.

punch, duplicating card Synonymous with *reproducer*[1].

punched card This general article describes a largely obsolete medium and the machines which used it. Nostalgically, it is written in the historic present.

A punched card contains data represented in the form of punched holes which can be sensed by a variety of machines in order to carry out functions such as adding, subtracting, comparing, collating, printing. There are various shapes and sizes of card, the most common being an 80-column card which measures 7⅜ in. × 3¼ in. and may be .007 in. or .009 in. thick. The columns are numbered from 1 to 80 from left to right along the face of the card and each vertical column is divided into 12 *punching positions*. Each column of a card is used to contain a numeric digit (represented by a single hole in a card column) or an alphabetic character or special symbol (represented by two, or more, holes in a single column). Examples of other cards in use are 21-column, 40-column. 45-column, 65-column, 90-column, and the holes may be round or rectangular. The principles of all are much as described below, as are the machines which use them, although of course different manufacturers' equipment differs in detail.

Of the twelve positions in each card column, nine are used to represent the numeric digits 1, 2, 3, 4, 5, 6, 7, 8 and 9, and the other three, known as zone positions, are designated as 0, 11 and 10. The 11 position is sometimes referred to as the X-position and the 10 position is also known as Y or 12. More annoyingly, the 11 position is as often known as the Y-position, and the 10 position as the X-position, so communication on this subject is best handled with care.

Numeric digits are represented by punching in the appropriate position of each column from 0 to 9, whereas alphabetic characters or symbols are represented by punching a *zone* digit (0, 11 or 10) in combination with a numeric digit (1 to 9). By this means up to 48 individual characters can be encompassed within the card code. Some card codes permit three holes to be punched in the same card column in order to represent a further range of special symbols, e.g., to represent up to 64 individual characters.

Items of data are recorded by grouping consecutive card columns to form *fields*, the number of columns required depending upon the maximum length of the item concerned. Thus a numeric field consisting of four columns could be used to represent any decimal number up to the value 9999, the layout of a particular card being determined by the user according to the requirements of his application.

The holes are punched into the cards by a *keyboard* operated machine known as a *card punch*, sometimes referred to as a *key punch*, or *automatic key punch*. The operator simply depresses keys on the keyboard to cause holes to be punched column by column into the card. Two basic types of keyboard are available, a numeric keyboard or an alphabetic keyboard.

A numeric keyboard is operated with one hand; it has twelve keys corresponding to the *punching* positions of a card, plus a number of function keys, e.g., a space key. An alphabetic keyboard is very similar to a typewriter keyboard, except that on a punch the numerical keys are grouped to permit one-handed operation if required when entering numerical data.

A card punch usually consists of a hopper into which blank cards are placed, a *card track* along which the cards are fed column by column to be punched and a *stacker* into which the punched cards are finally ejected. The punch unit is positioned above the card track and is activated directly from the keyboard. Some card punches include facilities for automatically *gangpunching* information from one card to another, and some also include a simple print unit for printing characters along the top edge of the card.

When cards have been punched they must usually be checked to ensure that the punching operation has been completed correctly. A machine known as a *verifier* is used for this purpose. It is very similar to a card punch except that it has a reading unit instead of a punch unit and it has *comparator* circuits to compare entries made on the keyboard with information punched in corresponding card columns. The verifier operator therefore merely works from the original source documents repeating the keystrokes made by the original punch operator. If the comparator reveals a discrepancy the verifier operator checks again to see that she herself has not caused the error and if the original card is incorrect will reject it. All verified cards are usually notched automatically on one edge and may then be taken to further stages of processing. (⊘ *Data Preparation*.)

Punched cards can be used as direct input to a computer using a *card reader*, but there is also a wide range of punched card equipment available for processing data in punched card form. Some of these are described below.

Punched cards can be *sorted* into some desired sequence according to the information punched in specified fields; e.g., if a particular field of each card contains the employee number, the cards can be arranged into numerical sequence of employee number. A machine known as a *sorter* is used for this purpose. A sorter has twelve pockets which correspond to the twelve punching positions in a card column, plus a further pocket called a reject box which corresponds to a blank column. Each column of the required field is examined one column at a time, the cards being automatically sorted into the appropriate pockets according to the information appearing in the specified column. When sorting numerical fields one pass is required for each column of the field under examination. Alphabetic sorting however requires two examinations of each column. Sorters operate at speeds ranging from 400 to 1200 cards per minute.

When two independent card files have been sorted into sequence they can be merged, using a machine known as a *collator*. The card files must each have identical control fields, e.g., both be sorted into the same *key* sequence. The collator is also able to outsort unmatched cards while the merging operation takes place, and to check the sequence of each of the two files.

Sometimes a complete duplicate set of cards must be produced, in which case a *reproducer* is used to read the original cards and punch another copy automatically.

A *tabulator*, or *accounting machine* as it is also known, can be used to produce printed reports of information contained in punched cards. These reports may list every item from each card or certain fields from specified cards only. Tabulators have facilities to perform addition and subtraction using electro-mechanical counters, and therefore totals can be accumulated and printed at the end of specified card groups and sometimes a reproducer or a *gangpunch* can be linked to a tabulator to punch summary cards. Thus the tabulator produces the end product of any punched card data processing activity: reports or commercial documents on preprinted *continuous stationery* such as cheques, invoices, statements, bills, etc.

These and other ancillary machines provide a wide range of processing functions for punched cards. Punched card machines are sometimes referred to as *unit record* equipment since each transaction within a system is represented by an individual punched card. *Electronic calculators* were a development of the earlier punched card systems and themselves led to some of the developments of the first computers. Calculators were principally developed to perform multiplication and division upon *operands* punched into card fields. Sometimes the result was punched into the same card and sometimes into another card.

Most 80-column punched card machines were programmed by plugged connexions on a *plugboard*. These plugboards became quite complex and unwieldy on the larger tabulators and calculators. The major development work for this type of equipment ceased in the late 1950s and the computer with its internally stored program gradually superseded punched card unit record systems. However, many such systems continue to be in use and punched cards themselves still form an important input/output medium for computers.

punched card duplicating   Synonymous with gang punching. ⬦ *gang punch*.

punched card, edge-   Synonymous with *margin-punched card*.

punched card field   A *field* of information present in a *punched card*.

punched card interpreter   A machine capable of reading the holes punched in a *punched card* and causing the corresponding alphabetic and numeric characters to be printed on the same card or (on a *posting interpreter* or *transfer interpreter*) on the following card.

punched card system, ducol   ⬦ *ducol punched card system*.

punched card tabulator   A machine which automatically fed *punched cards*, reading data from them to be directly listed and/or accumulated for the printing of totals at the end of certain card *groups*.

punched card verifier   A machine used to ensure that data punched into *punched cards* was the same as the data on the original documents from which it was punched. The process of manual punching from original documents was repeated and the machine recognized any difference in key depression. ⟡ general article on *Data Preparation*.

punched paper tape ⟡ *punched tape* and general article on *Paper Tape*.

punched tape A tape of fixed width into which information can be recorded by means of a pattern of punched holes. Tape is normally of paper, approximately 0.004 in. thick. The width of tape is referred to by the number of *tracks* or *channels* it holds, i.e., the number of holes which can be punched across it. The usual widths are 5-track ($^{11}/_{16}$ in.) 6- or 7-track (⅞ in.) and 8-track (1 in.). Also known as *Paper Tape*, under which heading there is a general article.

punch, eleven ⟡ *X-punch* and *Y-punch*.

punch, hand (card) ⟡ *hand punch*[1].

punch, hand-feed Synonymous with *hand punch*.

punch, hand (paper tape) ⟡ *hand punch*[2].

punching, normal stage ⟡ *normal stage punching*.

punching positions The places on a *punched card* into which holes could be punched. A punching position was at the intersection of a *row* and a *card column*.

punching rate The rate at which information could be punched in the form of holes in *punched cards* or *paper tape*. In the case of cards the rate was normally measured by the number of cards which could be punched per unit of time and in the case of paper tape by the number of *characters* per unit of time.

punchings, designation Synonymous with *control holes*.

punching station The position within a *card punch* at which a *punched card* was punched.

punching track The part of a *card punch* which moved the *punched card* through the machine.

punch, keyboard Synonymous with *key punch*.

punch knife The part of the mechanism of a *card punch* which made the hole in a *punched card*.

punch position ⟡ *punching positions*.

punch tape ⟡ *paper tape*.

punch tape code ⟡ *paper tape codes*.

punch, twelve ⟡ *twelve punch* and *Y-punch*.

punch, zone ⟡ *zone digit*.

punctuation bits *Bits* used in *variable field record* systems to indicate the beginning and end of items of information.

push down list A method of storing a list of items of information; as each new item is entered into the list it occupies the first location in the list, all the other items moving down one place in the list. Contrasted with *push up list*.

push down store A *store* which works on the principle of a *push down list*, so that as new items of data are added to the store, previous items are moved back, the latest item occupying the first *location* in the store. This arrangement of data can be performed either by *hardware* or by *program*.

Also known as cellar.

push–pull amplifier An amplifier in which the input signal is accepted simultaneously by two amplifying units which operate in opposite phase to produce two output voltages with opposite signs but of the same magnitude.

Also known as double-ended amplifier.

push up list A method of storing a list of items of information; each new item is entered into the list after the last item, so that the other items do not change their relative positions in the list. Contrasted with *push down list*.

Q

corrent process. Technically a quit function will include arithmetic processes for further processing functions available to the user, or dequent that or the result produced by dividing one number by another, in respect of these two resulting process is presented by the way in which these resulting process is performed. The quit station depends on the way in which these resulting process the termination of termination.

quality assurance   Most large computer departments and professional computing organizations incorporate a quality assurance (QA) function, with the overall responsibility of ensuring that *hardware* and *software* systems are fully tested before being handed over to the user. The QA unit will normally be separate and independent from the development unit and will set standards for acceptance criteria, documentation and general data processing standards.

quanta   Plural of *quantum*.

quantity, double-precision   ◊ *double-precision arithmetic*.

quantization   Dividing the range of values of a variable into a finite number of distinct subdivisions or *quanta*.

quantizer   A device for converting an *analog* quantity into its *digital* equivalent.

quantum   One of the subdivisions made as a result of *quantization*.

quartz delay line   A form of *acoustic delay line* in which quartz is used to recirculate sonic signals.

quasi instruction   An item of data present in a *program* in *instruction format* but never in fact executed as an instruction.

query   A term used in information retrieval to refer to a particular request for information. ◊ *query language*.

query language   A formalized method of formulating queries in an *information retrieval* system.

queuing theory   The application of probability theory to the study of delays or queues produced at servicing points.

QUICKTRAN   QUICKTRAN is a subset of the programming language *FORTRAN*, designed primarily for use with *multi-access* systems. The basic program statements are compatible with FORTRAN, but the language is extended to include extensive facilities for controlling the *testing*, *debugging* and *operating* of programs. The use of special statements enable the user to *compile*, test and *run* a program from a *remote terminal*.

quinary   Synonymous with *biquinary*.

quit   A function in a *program* which allows the user to terminate the current process. Normally a quit function will include a menu of options for further processing functions available to the user.

quotient Part of the result produced by dividing one number by another: a *remainder* may also be produced. In a digital computer the precision given in respect of these two resulting *operands* is governed by the way in which the arithmetic process is performed. The precision depends on the way in which the programmer specifies the termination of the operation.

qwerty The standard English typewriter keyboard layout, named after the initial letters on the first alphabetic row of the keyboard.

R

rack-up A method of presenting data on a *video* whereby each time the last line of the *screen* is filled, the first line is deleted and all lines move up one line, thus enabling a new line to be entered. Compare with *wrap round*.

radix The basis of a notation or number system, defining a number representational system by *positional representation*. In a decimal system the radix is 10, in an *octal* system the radix is 8, and in a *binary* system the radix is 2.

Also known as base.

radix complement The radix complement of a number is obtained by subtracting each digit of the number from one less than its *radix* and then adding 1 to the result obtained. (For example, the radix complement of the decimal number 171 is $999 - 171 + 1 = 829$.)

Also known as noughts complement and true complement.

radix complement, diminished ◊ *diminished radix complement*.

radix-minus-one complement Synonymous with *diminished radix complement*; usually a more explicit term is used, e.g., *nines complement* or *ones complement*.

radix notation A generic term embracing both *fixed radix notation* and *mixed base radix notation*.

Also known as *base notation*.

radix point The location of the separation of the integral parts and the fractional part of a number expressed in a *radix notation*. This location is marked in the decimal system by the decimal point (a dot in English usage, a comma elsewhere).

RAM Acronym for *Random Access Memory*.

RAMPS Acronym for *Resource Allocation in Multi-Project Scheduling*.

random access memory (RAM) *Memory* into which data can be written and from which data can be read. RAM may be static R A M or dynamic RAM. Static RAM retains any information it contains when power is switched off; dynamic RAM requires a continuous power supply to retain information. Contrasted with *read-only memory* (*ROM*).

random access storage A *storage* designed to give a constant (or almost constant) *access time* for any *location* addressed and regardless of the location previously addressed. ◊ general article on *Storage Devices*.

random number generator 1. A *hardware* unit designed to produce *random numbers* in specified quantities. 2. A *program* designed to produce random numbers in specified quantities.

random numbers 1. A set of numbers produced entirely by chance. 2. A set of numbers which for a specific purpose may be assumed to be free from statistical bias, i.e., the numbers have no predetermined sequence. The set may be produced by chance, but may also be derived by means of an *algorithm* designed to produce numbers sufficiently random for any desired degree of statistical accuracy.

random number sequence ◊ *random numbers*.

range 1. The difference between the upper and lower limits of a function or quantity. 2. A family of *processors* with similar characteristics, differing in power and size but usually using a common *machine language*.

range independence A characteristic of *software* which can be processed on any machine in a given *range*[2].

rank To arrange in a given order of importance.

rapid-access loop A part of *store* with a faster *access time* than the rest of the storage medium.

raster scan The production of an image on a *screen* by an electron beam tracing successive parallel lines.

rate, pulse repetition ◊ *pulse repetition rate*.

rate, residual error ◊ *residual error rate*.

raw data Data which has neither been subject to *data reduction* nor processed. It may be readable or converted to machine-sensible form (e.g., *punched cards*).

read To obtain data from one form of *store* (e.g., *magnetic disk*) and transfer it to another (e.g., the *main memory* of a computer). Contrasted with *write*.

read-around ratio The number of times information held in *electrostatic storage* at a specific spot can be referred to before the spillover of electrons causes data loss in the nearby spots. Data in the surrounding spots must be restored before this deterioration.

reader A device designed to *read*.

reader, magnetic tape ◊ *magnetic tape reader*.

read head An electromagnet used to read from a magnetic medium such as *magnetic tape, magnetic disk* or *magnetic drum*.

Also known as reading head or playback head.

reading head Synonymous with *read head*.

reading station That part of a *card track* at which holes punched in a *punched card* are sensed; e.g., by means of a photo-electric head.

read-only memory (ROM) *Memory* containing information which is present and permanent and which cannot be written to, but can only be read by *program functions*. ⬦ *PROM*. Contrasted with *RAM*.

read-only storage A device which holds permanent data that cannot be altered by *program instructions*.

read-out To *read* from the *internal store* of a computer and transfer it to an *external store*.

read-punch unit An *input/output device* capable of both reading punched data and then punching computed results. If the unit was reading and punching *punched cards* (as opposed to *paper tape*) it might also segregate the newly punched cards from the ones previously input.

read rate Number of units of data (e.g., *characters, words, blocks, fields, cards*) capable of being *read* by an input reading device in a given unit of time.

read time The time interval between the instant the transfer from a *store* begins and the instant it is completed. The read time is therefore the *access time* less the *waiting time*.

Also known as transfer time; related to *write time*.

read while writing The reading (⬦ *read*) into *store* of a *record* or group of records simultaneously with the writing (⬦ *write*) from store of another record or group of records.

read/write channel A channel connecting a *peripheral unit* with a *central processor*.

read/write head An electromagnet used to read or write on a magnetic medium such as *magnetic tape, magnetic disk* or *magnetic drum*.

ready-for-sending A signal sent by a receiving node in a network in response to a ready-to-send signal, indicating that the receiving unit has established connexion over the line and is ready to accept data transmission.

real address An *address* in *main store*; contrasted with *virtual address* from which the real address is obtained by reference to a table or by addition of a datum. Synonyms for real address include *direct address, absolute address* and *specific address*.

real file A collection of *records*, created from one or more *primitive files* by means of a *record access mechanism* in an *operating system*.

real store   A term used in contrast to *virtual storage* to refer to a specific *hardware* storage device in use for a particular activity within an *operating system*.

real time   Real time is an expression used to refer to any system in which the processing of data input to the system to obtain a result occurs virtually simultaneously with the event generating the data. Thus most process control systems operate in real time, since input data must be processed quickly enough to enable the results to be used as feedback information. In commercial data processing an example of a real time system is an airline booking system, in which each booking must be processed by the system immediately it is made so that a completely up-to-date picture of the actual state of affairs is maintained by the computer at all times. Real time systems normally require the use of *data communication* equipment to feed data into the system from remote terminal, *direct access storage devices* to store incoming data in large volumes and the use of *central processors* capable of *time sharing* the *programs* needed to validate data and control the input data, at the same time as using this data for the particular application required. Since the point of having a real time system is that the computer provides a picture of events as they occur such a system will also be associated with some form of *information retrieval* system, making use of equipment such as *visual display units, interrogating typewriters* or other forms of inquiry station.

real time clock   A device which generates readable signals at regular intervals of time. Such a device is used in *real time* systems to calculate the actual or *elapsed time* which passes between the occurrence of two events, in contrast to the time, usually much shorter, taken by the computer to compute the time interval. Such a device is also used to control the operation of certain equipment in accordance with a defined time scale. In this sense also known as *clock, digital clock*.

real variable   A variable expressed in *floating point* format.

recompile   To repeat the process of *compilation* of a *program*, usually as a result of *debugging*, or in order to create a version of the program which will run on a different *range* of equipment.

reconfiguration   Changing the availability or method of use of the component parts of a computer system, including the *operating system software* necessary to control the new *configuration*.

reconfiguration console   ◊ *console*.

reconnexion   The replacement of one *resource* by another, or the re-establishment of a resource which for any reason has been made inoperative.

reconstitution The restoration of a *file* to an earlier stage, e.g., as a result of a *dump and restart* procedure.

record access management ◊ *record access mechanism.*

record access mechanism Software within an *operating system* used to *access data* forming a particular *real file* by means of operations on the constituent *primitive files*.

record A unit of data representing a particular *transaction* or a basic element of a *file* consisting in turn of a number of interrelated *data elements*.

record blocking The practice of grouping *records* into data *blocks* which can be read and/or written to *magnetic tape* in one operation. This arrangement enables the tape to be read more efficiently and reduces the time required overall to read or write the file.

record count A total of the number of *records* in a file. Usually maintained and checked each time the file is *updated* to provide control information about the performance of a *program* or a specific computer *run*.

record format A description of the contents and organization of a *record*, usually part of a *program specification*.

record head Synonymous with *write head*.

record header A *data element* or *field* within a *record* set aside for information required by system *software*, but not available to the *user* of the record.

recording density Relating to the distance between the magnetized spots on a magnetic *storage device*. For example, on a *magnetic tape* the density of the *binary digits* recorded on the tape is measured in *bits* per inch. In the case of *magnetic disks* the density is expressed in terms of the number of *bytes* which can be recorded on the disk surface. The following are typical packing densities encountered on a 5¼ inch diameter floppy disk:

single density: 125 *K bytes*
double density: 250 *K bytes*

The speed at which data may be transferred to or from a tape is dependent upon the recording density and the speed of the *tape drive*. ◊ *transfer rate*.

record list Information held on a *file* presented in readable format.

record reference ◊ *reference listing*.

record section Where a *record* is held in more than one *block*, that part of the record held in one block.

record separation A *code* or *character* used to indicate the end of one *record* and the start of another, within the same *file*.

recovery Actions taken to restore a system to working order after a *failure*; depending on the type of failure, these actions may be taken by the *user*, the *operating system* or both.

recovery file A file holding details of all changes made in another file so as to enable *reconstitution* to take place in the event of *failure*.

red-tape operations Operations performed as part of a *routine*, but concerned mainly with the organization of the routine itself rather than with the processing of *data*. For example, to monitor the progress of *input/output* operations to ensure that data in input/output areas is not *overwritten* until it has been processed. The more general red-tape operations are known as *housekeeping*.

redundancy 1. The use of extra *characters* or *bits* which are attached to an item of data to provide a means for checking the accuracy of the data as in *redundancy check*. For examples ◊ *check digit* and *parity check*. 2. The recording of information by means of a bit pattern which is theoretically capable of distinguishing between a wider range of values than the information requires. 3. The availability of alternative means for performing a specific function. 4. The retention of more than one copy of a set of data to avoid the consequences of *failure*.

redundancy check Any checking operation which depends on extra *characters* or *bits* that are attached to *data* to permit the automatic detection of errors. The extra characters do not themselves contribute to the information content of the data, e.g., ◊ *parity check*.

redundant character Synonymous with *check character*.

redundant check ◊ *redundancy check*.

redundant code A code in which more *bits* are used than are strictly necessary for the information to be conveyed; e.g., a 7-bit *paper tape* code in which each character requires 6 *information bits* plus one *parity bit*.

reel 1. A roll of *paper tape* perhaps mounted on a cardboard or plastic former. 2. A flanged spool for holding a *magnetic tape*. 3. A general term to describe a magnetic tape and the spool upon which it is mounted. In this context it is common to refer to tapes by their *reel numbers*, when strictly the term *tape serial number* is intended.

reel number Where a file of data extends over more than one *reel* of *magnetic tape* each reel of the file is identified by a different reel number. If the file is sequenced the reel numbers will indicate the order in which the reels must be taken. ⬦ *tape serial number*.

Also known as reel sequence number.

reel sequence number   Synonymous with *reel number*.

re-entrant code   Synonymous with *re-entrant procedure*.

re-entrant procedure   A *procedure*[2] that may be entered before a previous activation of the same procedure has been completed, since no interference is caused between more than one activation.

Also known as re-entrant code.

reference address   An *address* used as a reference point for a group of *instructions* written to contain *relative addresses*. Thus, for example, an *absolute address* is obtained by adding a reference address to a relative address.

reference listing   A list printed by a *compiler* to show *instructions* as they appear in the final *routine*, including details of *storage allocation*.

reference picture   A *picture* which provides operations staff with information about their activities.

reference supply   A voltage source used in an electrical *analog computer* as a unit by which other voltages can be measured.

reference time   The time at which an electrical pulse used to initiate some action first reaches 10 per cent of its specified amplitude.

regeneration period   The time that elapses while the screen of a *cathode ray tube* store is scanned by an electron beam to regenerate the charges on the surface of the screen.

regenerative reading   A *read* operation involving the automatic *writing* of data back into the locations from which it is extracted.

regenerative store   A type of storage unit in which signals representing data are constantly being regenerated so that information can be retained for as long as required. When some new item of data is loaded the regenerating circuit is automatically broken to permit the old data to be *overwritten*. ⟨⟩ *dynamic memory*.

regenerative tracks   On a *magnetic drum* these tracks are associated with the *read* and *write heads* and are arranged in such a manner that signals are regenerated during each drum revolution to retain data recorded on the drum. Thus each regenerative track and its *read/write heads* acts as a *regenerative store*.

regional address   That part of an *address* which indicates that the address itself is from a specified set of addresses for a predetermined region of *memory*.

register   A special *store location* generally having a capacity equivalent to the *word size* of the computer concerned and having specific properties for use during arithmetic and/or logical operations. For example, in some computers arithmetic operations can be performed only if at least one *operand* is stored in a special register. A computer may have several registers each of which is designed for a specific function.

register capacity The limiting values, upper and lower, of the quantities that may be processed by a *register*.

register, console display ◊ *console display register*.

register, control ◊ *control register*.

register, current instruction ◊ *current instruction register*.

register, delay line ◊ *delay line register*.

register dump ◊ *dump*.

register length The number of *characters* or *bits* that can be stored in a particular *register* within the *register capacity*.

register, memory buffer ◊ *memory buffer register*.

register, program ◊ *instruction register*.

register, sequence control ◊ *sequence control register*.

rejection Synonymous with *nor operation*.

relational data base A *data base management* system in which the *data manipulation language* contains facilities which allow the user to define relationships between *data elements* and to treat these relational definitions themselves as items of data.

relative address A number used in the *address* part of an *instruction* to specify a required *location* with respect to a *base address*. The *absolute address* is obtained by adding the *base address* to the relative address.

Also known as floating address.

relative addressing A system of *programming* in which *instructions* are written so that they do not refer directly to *absolute addresses* in *memory*; instead a *base address* is added to the address component of each instruction when the program is loaded in order to create numbers that refer to absolute *locations*. Thus a *subroutine* consisting of 20 instructions might be written to ocupy 20 *words* commencing at a base address R, through R + 1, R + 2 . . . to R + 19. If R were set equal to 1200 in *absolute coding* the *subroutine* would occupy words 1200 to 1219 in memory. This method enables a programmer to write a program in several independent sections or *segments* without having to consider the absolute addresses required.

relative code A *program* code in which *addresses* are specified in respect to some *base address* or one in which *symbolic addresses* are used.

relative coding Writing *program instructions* using the techniques of *relative addressing*.

relative error   The ratio of an error in some computed result in respect to the quantitive value of the result. Contrasted with *absolute error*.

relay amplifier   A device used in an *analog* system for comparing two signals which incorporates an amplifier that drives a switch.

relay centre   A *switching centre* in which message signals are received and automatically directed to one or more output circuits according to data contained in the message itself.

release   1. As a result of an action performed by an operator, by a *program instruction* or automatically by an *executive program*, to release a *peripheral unit* or a *memory* area from the control of a particular program. The *hardware* released becomes available for allocation to some other *program*. 2. The act of issuing a piece of *software* for use, usually after exhaustive testing; a particular version of a program or package may be known as a release. ◇ *version number*.

reliability   The performance of a particular machine measured against some predetermined standard for operating without failure of the equipment, for example the ratio of *serviceable time* to serviceable time plus *down time*.

relocatable code   ◇ *relocatable program*.

relocatable program   A *program* coded in *relative code* in such a way that it can be stored and executed in any part of the *memory*. Such a system requires some form of *executive program* to be stored in memory to allocate required storage areas and to ensure that all *instructions* are executed in respect to the current *base address* for the program. ◇ *dynamic allocation*.

relocate   The automatic *modification* of the *instructions* in a *program*, undertaken to permit the program to be *loaded* and executed in any specified *memory* area.

remainder   Part of the result obtained from the arithmetic operation known as *division*; the *dividend* is divided by the *divisor* to give the *quotient* and the remainder.

remark   Synonymous with *narrative*.

remedial maintenance   Maintenance work performed on equipment to repair some machine fault; classified as *fault time* or *down time* and not as part of *scheduled engineering time*.

remote   Any *peripheral unit* which operates at a distance from the host, involving some form of *data communication*, is said to be remote.

remote batch printer   A *printer* which is *remote* from the *central processor* which accepts data in *batch processing mode* for subsequent *off-line* printing.

remote calculator A *keyboard* device connected directly to a *central processor* via some *data link* to enable users at remote locations to present problems requiring calculation to the computer.

remote computing system A *hardware* configuration in which *remote consoles* are connected directly to a computer to enable users to have direct communication with the *central processor*. Users are able to *compile, test, debug* and execute their *programs* from these remote terminals. Proven programs are stored centrally on some *mass storage* device and can be called into *memory* as required. ⇔ *multi-access systems*.

remote computing system exchange A device that handles messages and data transmitted between a *central processor* and *remote consoles*. The exchange device enables a number of remote consoles to be operated simultaneously without mutual interference. It will receive characters transmitted from these terminals and form them into statements for transfer to *memory, results* and *messages* being returned to the appropriate terminal as required. ⇔ *multiplexor*.

remote computing system language A language used for communication with a central computing system from *remote consoles*. Such systems are usually installed to give scientists and engineers direct access to a computer for solving problems expressed in a *scientific computer language*: for example, *program statements* are often written in *FORTRAN*. However, it is also necessary for the language to incorporate operating statements; e.g., instructions to *test, debug*, change and execute programs. ⇔ *QUICKTRAN*.

remote computing system log A record of events occurring during the operation of *remote consoles*; it may be printed but is often recorded on some other output medium to enable analyses to be subsequently generated. The log may record the volume of traffic for individual terminals to facilitate financial charging or to demonstrate the efficiency of the remote system. It will record the types of error made, the numbers of *statements* used and volumes of data transferred.

remote console A terminal unit used in a *remote computing system*. A number of these distant consoles may be available, each equipped with facilities to send and receive data to and from the *central processor*. Connexion to the processor is usually made via a *remote computing system exchange*. The console itself is a work station with a greater or lesser degree of intelligence. It will be supported by such devices as *visual display units* and *line printers*. Usually a *keyboard* operated device such as an *on-line* electric typewriter or a *teleprinter* is available to permit direct communication with the central computing system.

remote data stations Remote *terminals* capable of sending data to, and receiving data from, a central computer. Communication may be by means of a telegraph circuit or a telephone voice quality line. Unlike a *remote console* in a *remote computing system*, a data station has no direct operating control over the central computer but acts as an automatic *data collection* point. Equipment at these stations may include *punched card* and *paper tape input/output devices* and perhaps a keyboard-operated unit. A data station also requires special data transmission units to connect the terminal to the communications channel and to perform *automatic error correction*.

remote data terminal Synonymous with *remote data station*.

remote debugging 1. In the strictest sense, the testing and correction of *programs* from a *remote console* as used in a *remote computing system*. 2. ◊ *remote testing*.

remote inquiry, real time Pertaining to a system in which distant terminals are connected to a *central processor* to enable users to interrogate the system and obtain information from data files. The terminals may be connected over outside *data transmission channels* or over a *local area*. Such a system requires that files are stored on a *mass storage* device with facilities for *direct access* to data.

remote job entry The input of data direct to a central computing system by means of a device remote from that system.

remote processing Related to a system in which data is transmitted as messages from distant stations to be processed by a central computer. For this type of system the central computer is usually equipped with an *executive program* or *operating system*, capable of receiving random messages from distant points and of processing and transmitting data at unpredictable intervals. During periods of peak activity the executive program will store messages and establish priorities for processing them. Some form of *remote computing system exchange* will be used to handle messages passing to and from the *central processor*. But ◊ *remote processor*.

remote processor A *processor* which is located away from a computer's *central processor* and whose activities are under the overall control of the central processor's *operating system*.

remote testing Remote testing was a method for organizing the flow of work being processed through a computer system. Using this method, programmers did not accompany their *programs* when they were being tested on the computer, but supplied the programs and associated *test data* with comprehensive instructions to be performed by the computer operators. The purpose of this technique was to speed the flow of work through a computer room and also to provide a useful discipline in the testing and *debugging* of programs. This discipline was necessarily a part of remote testing, since the programmer responsible for completing the instructions to the operator had to consider all possible conditions which might arise during the operation of the program in order to provide comprehensive instructions. These instructions included all requests for any diagnostic aids required, such as *memory prints*, or prints of data on *backing stores*, and also contained details of all expected actions of the program, including messages requiring operator action. Being compelled to write down all actions required from the operators, the programmer had a detailed record of the actions taken at each test run: such instructions given verbally during in-attendance testing could easily be forgotten or overlooked. An installation in which testing was always remote was known as a *closed shop*. ⟡ *Debugging*.

removable plugboard   Synonymous with *detachable plugboard*.

reorganize   To copy *data* into a new part of *filestore*, either because the user requires changes to the data format, or because the current *storage* structure has become inefficient (e.g., because the file contains dead *records*).

repair delay time   Time lost due to the inability to repair equipment because of lack of test equipment, spare parts or service staff.

repair time   Time spent on repairing equipment faults outside the time allocated to *routine maintenance* and *supplementary maintenance*.

repair time, mean   ⟡ *mean repair time* and *repair time*.

reperforator   Synonymous with *paper tape reproducer*.

repertoire   A range of *characters* or separate *codes* available in a particular system of coding. It is also common to refer to the *instruction repertoire* of a particular *program language* or *machine code*.

repetition frequency, pulse   ⟡ *pulse repetition frequency*.

repetition instruction   An *instruction* that can cause an instruction, or group of instructions, to be repeated a specified number of times. Generally used in a *loop* to cause the required number of cycles to be executed. Often such instructions are made conditional on some other set of circumstances occurring in the *program*.

repetition rate, pulse   ⟡ *pulse repetition frequency*.

repetitive addressing   A system adopted in some computers in which, under certain conditions, *instructions* can be written without the quoting of an *operand address*. The *program controller* automatically assumes that the address is that of the *location* addressed by the previous instruction.

repetitive operation   Pertaining to *analog computers*, a technique in which a solution is generated successively using the same equations and *parameters*, in order to display the solution as a steady graph on a *visual display unit*.

replication The use of more than one identical *hardware* unit in a system in such a way that the units are interchangeable in the event of *failure*. A form of *redundancy*[3].

reply A *message* generated in response to an earlier message.

report A general term for any printed analysis of data produced by a computer. ◊ *report program*.

report generation The printing of information extracted from one or more computer *files* using the techniques associated with a *report generator*.

report generator A *generator* specially designed to produce *programs* which will print out information from any computer *files*, in which it is necessary for the user to specify the format of the files concerned plus the format and content of the printed report, along with any rules for creating totals, etc.

report program A *program* designed to print out an analysis of a data *file*. Usually the data will be in some sequence of *keys*, and the report will consist of totals or analyses performed for various groups of *records*, each analysis or total being produced when a key change occurs. Where key changes have different levels of significance they are known as *control breaks*.

report program generator A *general purpose program* that can generate other *report programs* to meet users' specific requirements for printing results, summaries, etc., for computer files.

representation, binary-coded decimal ◊ *binary-coded decimal representation*.

representation, binary incremental ◊ *binary incremental representation*.

representation, positional ◊ *positional notation*.

representation, ternary incremental ◊ *ternary incremental representation*.

reproducer A *punched card* machine capable of reading a *pack* of cards and transferring information to be automatically punched into another set of cards. Usually, a *plugboard* was used to control the format of the cards thus produced, so that the *fields* could, if required, be arranged in a format differing from the original cards. A standard model reproducer had two *card tracks* known as the reading track and the punching track.

Also known as reproducing punch.

reproducer, paper tape ◊ *paper tape reproducer*.

reproducing punch   A synonym for *reproducer*.

request slip   A statement of the requirements of *store* and *peripheral units* of a *program*. Used in conjunction with *dynamic allocation*.

request-to-send   A signal which is sent by a *terminal* in a *network* to indicate that it wishes to send information over the line to the receiving *node*. The receiving node must respond with a *ready-for-sending* signal before the necessary condition for data transmission can be established.

rerouting   Establishing a new *route* between two *resources* or between a *process* and a *resource*, in particular the route betwen *main store* and a *peripheral* resource.

rerun   To repeat the execution of a *program*, usually as a result of an error condition.

rerun point   A point in a *program* from which it is possible to *restart* following an error or a machine failure.

rerun time   ◊ *systems recovery time*.

rescue dump   A technique in which the contents of *memory* are periodically output to a *backing store*, so that the *data, intermediate results* and the *program* of *instructions* can be preserved as at a particular step. Thus, in the event of a subsequent machine failure the program can be constituted in memory to restart from the last rescue dump. ◊ general article on *Dump and Restart*.

research, operations   ◊ *operational research*.

reservation   The allocation of *memory* areas or *peripheral units* to a particular *program* in a *multiprogramming* computer.

reserve   To assign a *memory area* and/or *peripheral units* to a particular *program* operating in a *multiprogramming system*.

reserved word   In a *programming language*, a *data name* not available to the user because it has some specific significance to the *compiler*; or any *data name* or *label* which can be used only in a specific context.

reset   1. In *programming*, to set a *counter* to zero, or to return an *indicator* to some stable condition. 2. On a *punched card machine*, to zeroize a *counter*. 3. A *hardware* or *software* function which causes a computer system to enter a predefined initial status in which all variable hardware and software states are restored to a set of initial values.

reset cycle   To return a *cycle index counter* to its original value.

reset mode   Pertaining to an *analog computer*, a state during which the initial conditions are applied to the system.

Also known as initial condition mode. Contrasted with *compute mode*.

reset pulse   One of the pulses that control the state of a *storage cell*, specifically one that tends to restore a cell to the *zero condition*.

reshaping, signal ⟡ *signal regeneration*.

resident routine A *routine* which exists permanently in *memory*; e.g., a *monitor routine* of an *executive program*. Contrasted with *non-resident routine* which refers to a routine called into *memory* from an external *store*.

residual error An error generated during an experiment; i.e., the difference between an exact result calculated theoretically and one obtained empirically.

residual error rate In *data transmission*, the ratio of undetected or uncorrected errors incurred in transmitting a given volume of data.

residue check A check performed to verify an *arithmetical operation* in which each *operand* is divided by a number *n* which generates a remainder that accompanies the operand as a *check digit* in subsequent operations.

resilience The ability of a system to continue operating in the event of *failure* of part of it; in this event the system may be said to be operating in *crippled mode*.

resolution The number of individually addressable and variable *picture elements* available in a *graphic display*.

resolution error An error derived from the limitations of an *analog* computing unit to respond to changes of less than a given increment.

resolver On an *analog computer*, a *function generator* the input variables of which are polar coordinates of a point, the output variables being Cartesian coordinates.

resolving potentiometer A potentiometer employed to operate as a *function generator*, in which the output variables are Cartesian coordinates of a point and the input variables are polar coordinates.

resource Any part of a computer system or *configuration* which can be considered as a separate unit for the purpose of allocation (⟡ *allocate*) for the use of a specific *process*.

resource allocation in multi-project scheduling A system of *allocation* using a network analysis to assist in making the best use of resources which have to be stretched over a number of projects. Usually known by the acronym R AMPS.

response In an *information retrieval* system, the information returned to the user as a result of initiating a query. More generally, the visible result of any user-initiated return in an *interactive* computer system.

response duration The interval between the *time origin* of a pulse and the time at which the pulse falls below a specified operating value.

response time The time required to answer an inquiry. For example, the time needed to transfer an inquiry from a terminal to a central

391

computer and to receive a reply at that terminal. Includes the time required for transmission in each direction plus time for retrieving and processing data to meet the inquiry.

restart To return to a previous point in a *program* in order to begin again following an error or machine malfunction. During the processing of large *batches* of data a programmer may cater for various restarts at regular intervals in his program so that a job can be resumed following a failure without going back to the beginning of the data. A cold restart is a restart at an earlier *restart point*. A warm restart indicates the ability of a program to restart without having to return to a restart point. ◊ general article on *Dump and Restart*.

restart point A point in a *program* that allows the program to be re-entered in order to effect a *restart* following an error or machine failure.

restore To set a *counter, register, switch* or *indicator* to some previous value or condition.

result A quantity or value derived from some *arithmetical* or *logical operation* performed upon one or more *operands*. ◊ *final result* and *intermediate result*.

retained peripheral A *peripheral unit* which was previously used on one type or *range* of processors but is subsequently used on a different range of equipment.

retention period The length of time (measured in days/weeks/months) for which data on a *reel* of *magnetic tape* is to be preserved, i.e., before the tape may be *overwritten*. This information may be held on the *header label* of the reel, and is used to ensure data security.

retrieval The extraction of *data* from a *file* or files by searching for specified *keys* or *labels* contained in *records* stored on the file. Records may be selected according to logical relationships between *fields* and may be processed or summarized to produce the required information. ◊ *information retrieval techniques*.

return A function of a *personal computer* which makes use of the 'carriage return' key on the *keyboard* to initiate a previously entered command.

return address Synonymous with *link*.

return instruction An *instruction* performed to return to a main *routine* after the execution of a *subroutine*. The instruction is usually modified by a *link* which has been previously stored to ensure that the main routine is re-entered at a desired point.

return-to-bias recording A method of *return-to-reference recording* in which each storage cell is permanently energized to a predetermined bias condition.

return-to-reference recording A system for recording information in *magnetic cells*, in which each cell can be magnetized to represent the *binary digit* 1 by applying energy to alter the condition of the cell with respect to some predetermined reference condition. The reference condition may be the magnetization of a cell to a specified level or the absence of magnetization.

reverse video A method of representing *characters* on a *visual display unit* in a manner contrasting with other characters; e.g., displaying characters in black on a white background so as to contrast with 'normal' characters displayed in white on a black background.

reversible counter A *counter* in which the value stored can be incremented or decremented according to a specified control signal.

reversible magnetic process A process whereby the flux within a magnetic material returns to its previous condition when the magnetic field is removed. Contrasted with *irreversible magnetic process*.

reversible process Synonymous with *reversible magnetic process*.

revolver track On a *magnetic drum*, a track which acts as a *regenerative store*. ◊ *regenerative track*.

rewind To reposition a *magnetic tape* to the *load point* (i.e., so that the tape is ready to *read* from the beginning).

rewrite To retain data in an area of *store* by recording it back in the *location* concerned after reading from that *location*.

RGB The initial letters of red, green, blue, referring to the three primary colours used in a *cathode ray* display to create colour images. ◊ *RGB monitor*.

RGB monitor A *visual display unit* consisting of a colour *cathode ray tube* in which red, green, and blue *electron beams* are individually controlled by digital signals, thus producing a sharp colour display.

ribbon cable A flat cable containing a number of wires running parallel to each other, separately insulated. Ribbon cables are used to connect *peripheral units* to *processors*, typically via a *parallel interface*.

right justified Describing an *item of data* which is stored in such a way that it occupies consecutive positions starting from the right-hand end of the *location* assigned. Thus, if an item should contain less *characters* than are allowed, the left-most position will be blank.

right shift A *shift* operation in which digits of a *word* are displaced to the right. In *arithmetical shift* this has the effect of division.

ring ◊ *write permit ring, write inhibit ring*.

ring counter A series of interconnective storage elements arranged in a loop. Only one element at any moment in time can exhibit a specified condition, and as input signals are counted this condition is displayed by successive elements around the loop.

ring network A *network* in which the topology is that of a continuous circle, with *nodes* represented as points on the circumference. Messages between nodes must pass through all intervening nodes on the ring.

ring shift A *shift* operation in which digits expelled at one end of a register return automatically at the other end.

ripple-through carry Synonymous with *high-speed carry*.

rise time The time required for an electrical pulse to rise from one-tenth to nine-tenths of its final value.

RJE Abbreviation of *remote job entry*.

RJE mode A method of operating a computer system whereby *jobs* are submitted from *terminals*.

robot A machine which carries out a sequence of operations under computer control, when the sequence may be revised by program, and where the actions are controlled by *analog* and *digital* signals emanating from sensors.

robotics A science or art involving both *artificial intelligence* (to reason) and mechanical engineering (to perform physical acts suggested by reason).

role indicator A code associated with a *keyword* to identify it as a noun, verb, or adjective, etc.

roll Synonymous with *spool*.

roll in 1. Activating a *process* in an *operating system* by bringing parts of the process successively into *main store*. 2. An action performed by an electro-mechanical *counter* on a *punched card tabulator*, in which the counter unit receives impulses representing numeric values read from a *card field* or emitted from another counter.

roll off The process by which a *primitive file* is copied from a specific *physical storage medium* or *volume* into *low level filestore, overwriting* any version of the file currently existing in filestore.

roll on The process of copying a *primitive file* from *low level filestore* into a specific type of *volume*.

roll out 1. Removing a *process* from *main store*. 2. An action performed by an electro-mechanical *counter* on a *punched card tabulator*, in which the counter emitted electrical impulses representing the numeric value currently stored in that counter. The original value remained in the counter after the roll out function is completed.

ROM Acronym for *Read-Only Memory*.

round To alter the value of digits at the least significant end of a number, in order to allow for digits to be removed in *truncating* the number. ◊ *rounding off*.

rounding error An error in a result that is attributable to *rounding off*.

rounding off The process of adjusting the *low order* digits of a number so as to reduce the effect of *truncation*. For example, a value equalling half the *radix* may be added to some specified *digit position* so that *carry* digits may be generated to increase the value in the next *highest significant position*. The number may then be truncated by ignoring the specified position and all succeeding positions.

route 1. Synonymous with *channel*[1] but used in connexion with *operating system* and *network*. 2. The path taken from an index page to an *end page* in a *tree structured data base*, typically a *videotex data base*.

routeing A method of linking *records* within a *tree structured data base*. Routeing can be hierarchical, whereby there is an automatic route from records at the top of the tree to records beneath; or direct, where the route gives the specified *location* of a linked record regardless of its position in the tree structure.

routeing page Synonymous with *index page*.

routine Used as a synonym for *program*, but often used to mean part of a program. For example, a program may be said to consist of an *input routine*, a *main routine, error routines* and an *output routine*. This term may in fact be used to denote any major *software* procedure which performs some well-defined function in the operation of a *program* or system.

routine, assembly ◊ *assembly program*.
routine, checking ◊ *checking program*.
routine, closed ◊ *closed subroutine*.
routine, compiling ◊ *compiler*.
routine, debugging ◊ *debugging aid*.
routine, executive ◊ *executive program*.
routine, floating point ◊ *floating point package*.
routine, heuristic ◊ *heuristic program*.
routine, housekeeping ◊ *housekeeping*.
routine, interpreter ◊ *interpretive routine*.

routine maintenance Maintenance work carried out according to a schedule, usually as recommended by the equipment manufacturer, to prevent equipment failure; the work usually includes testing, repairing, replacing, cleaning and adjusting components.

Also known as scheduled maintenance. Contrasted with *corrective maintenance* and *supplementary maintenance*.

routine maintenance time   Computer time assigned for performing *routine maintenance* work. Usually planned by the user well in advance, and often entailing a written agreement between the user and equipment manufacturer.

routine, master   ⬦ *master control routine*.

routine, object   ⬦ *object program*.

routine, open   ⬦ *open subroutine*.

routine, test   ⬦ *test program*.

routine, trace   ⬦ *trace program*.

routine, tracing   ⬦ *trace program*.

routine, translating   ⬦ *translator*.

routing   Meaning *message routing* in a system in which a central computer is attached to a communications network to receive and direct messages to their required destinations. ⬦ *routeing*.

routing indicator   In *message routing* systems, a group of *characters* or *digits* forming part of a message and specifying a required destination.

row   1. A horizontal row in a *matrix*. 2. A row of holes punched across the width of *paper tape*; in this sense also known as *frame*. 3 Synonymous with *card row*.

row binary   Relating to *punched cards*, a method of representing numbers by considering consecutive *punching positions* on each *row* of a card as consecutive digits in a *binary number*. Contrasted with *column binary*.

row binary code   ⬦ *row binary*.

row pitch   The distance between the holes running lengthwise along a punched *paper tape*, measured from centre to centre of consecutive positions.

RS series   RS is an abbreviation for Requirement Specification, as set by the Electrical Industries Association of the USA. A number of these specifications refer to the interconnexion standards for computing devices. The most common RS series standard includes RS232, RS422 and RS423.

run   The performance of one *program* or *routine*. Related particularly to *batch processing* applications, in which the beginning of a run is characterized by the operating functions necessary to *load* the program and its data, and the end of a run by operator activity to unload and then load a further program and files. Usually a number of runs are combined to form a *job*, or *suite* of runs.

run book   An operating guide for assembling the necessary materials and data for running a job, including a complete set of *operating instructions* for a *run* or *suite* of runs.

run chart A *flowchart* showing a *run* or series of runs combined to form a single *job*. It indicates the files and data to be input and output and shows by means of standard *flowchart symbols* the various *peripheral units* required for each run. It is used, for example, as part of the *operating instructions* for a job, but is not suitable for showing the detailed procedure for a run. Contrasted with *logic flowchart*.

run diagram ◊ *run chart*.

run duration The time required to execute a particular *run*.

run length encoding A method of encoding graphics data whereby the coding scheme describes the characteristics of each horizontal line of the graphics image, e.g., by using parameters to indicate the alternating length of black and white elements of a line in a monochrome image.

run locator routine A *routine* that locates a specified *program* on a *program tape*.

run, machine ◊ *run*.

running accumulator A storage unit consisting of a number of *registers* connected in such a way that data can be passed successively from one to another. Only one of the registers is able to accept data from, or transfer data, outside the system. Thus, as this register receives successive *words* of data they are pushed down into the other registers, and as it emits a *word* or data the other words move back up the system.

run phase Related to *program compilation*, and used to denote the period at which the compiled *object program* is first tested and run.

run time The time during or at which a *program* is *run*. Contrasted with *compilation time*.

S

S-100 bus A 100 line *highway* standard for use in small personal computers.

sampling The process of recording the value of a *variable* at intervals of time.

sampling rate The ratio of measurements of recorded values to all the values available, e.g., if a variable is measured every millisecond the sampling rate is 1000 measurements per second.

satellite processor A *processor* which is part of a larger *data processing* system and whose function is to process *runs* which are subsidiary to the main work of the system.

save To transfer *programs* or data on to any *off-line storage device* such as a *floppy disk* or *magnetic tape*. An alternative expression to store².

scale The process of altering a set of quantities by a fixed quantity so as to bring the values within the limits capable of being handled by the equipment or routines being used.

scale, extended time ⋄ *extended time scale*.

scale factor The quantity used in scaling by which the quantities being altered are multiplied or divided in order to bring them within the desired limits. ⋄ *scale*.

scale, fast time ⋄ *fast time scale*.

scale of two Synonymous with *binary notation*.

scale, slow time ⋄ *slow time scale*.

scaling factor Synonymous with *scale factor*.

scan 1. To examine every item in a list, or *record* in a *file*, usually as part of an *information retrieval* system in which each item is tested to see whether or not it satisfies certain conditions. 2. To test the condition of *communication links* or *input/output channels* in order to determine whether or not the channels are in use.

scanner A device which automatically carries out *sampling* and initiates required operations according to the values obtained.

scanning The action performed by a *scanner*.

scanning rate The rate at which a *scanner* samples.

scan period   Synonymous with *regeneration period*.

scan rate   In *process control*, the rate at which a quantity being controlled is checked.

scatter read   The process of distributing data into several areas of *store* from a single *input record* or *block*. ⇨ *gather write*.

scheduled engineering time   Time spent on installing and performing regular maintenance on a computer.

scheduled maintenance   Synonymous with *routine maintenance*.

scheduling   The operation of the sequence and priority in which *jobs* are to be run, and the allocation of *resources* to jobs. Scheduling may be done manually by operators or may be part of the function performed by an *operating system*.

schema   A complete description of a *data base*.

scientific computer   A computer used for *scientific data processing*.

scientific data processing   *Data processing* for scientific purposes, usually requiring machines with great computational power rather than ability to handle large files of data in a backing store. Contrasted with *commercial data processing* and *industrial data processing*.

scientific language   A *language* designed for the writing of mathematical or scientific *programs*. ⇨ *ALGOL, FORTRAN*.

scratch pad memory   An area of *memory* reserved for intermediate results. Synonymous with *work area*.

scratch tape   Any *reel* of *magnetic tape* whose *header label* contains information indicating that the tape may be used for any purpose, i.e., a tape containing information that may now be *over-written*. Contrasted with *master tape*. Compare also with *work tape*.

screen   1. The surface of a *cathode ray tube*. 2. In *information retrieval*, to make an initial selection from a set of data according to specified conditions.

screen mode   A technique of operating a *video* by which pages of information are formatted for the device.

scroll   The display of successive lines of text on a *visual display unit* whereby new lines are entered at the bottom of the screen causing all lines to move up the screen, with the top line disappearing. Reverse scrolling causes lines to enter at the top and disappear from the bottom of the screen.

search   To examine each item in a set in order to discover whether it satisfies specified conditions.

search time   The average time required to identify an item of data satisfying a specified condition.

SECAM   Acronym for Sequential Coleur À Memoire. A colour television broadcast standard developed in France and used in a number of countries, including the Soviet Union. Colour difference signals are transmitted sequentially. SECAM uses 625 picture lines and a 50 Hz field frequency. ⟡ *PAL.*

secondary storage Synonymous with *backing store.*

second generation computers Machines built with transistors, as opposed to *first generation* (thermionic valves) and *third generation* (*integrated circuits*). ⟡ *fourth* and *fifth generations.*

second level address An *address* in a *computer instruction* which references a *location* in which the actual address of the required *operand* is to be found. Synonymous with *indirect address.*

second remove subroutine A *subroutine* which is entered from another subroutine; contrasted with a *first remove subroutine* which is entered from the exits to the *main program.*

section 1. Synonymous with *segment.* 2. A part of a *magnetic tape*, sometimes also used as a synonym for *block.*

section, input ⟡ *input area.*

section, output ⟡ *output area.*

sector A part of a *track* or *band* of a *magnetic disk* or *magnetic drum*; also used as a synonym for a *block* of data stored on a sector.

security Security in the context of computing is a large subject, and a short article necessarily is limited to considering a few major aspects of the subject.

Security implies protection from a risk. Computer installations are subject to three main types of risk: (i) Risk to *hardware.* (ii) Risk to *software.* (iii) Risk to *information.*

Hardware is subject to the whole range of physical risks which may affect any item of sophisticated electronic equipment. A properly organized installation will be protected against fire, flood, sabotage. This means devices to detect and report the occurrence of any physical disturbance of the computer's environment: fire detectors, burglar alarms and so on. Some physical dangers, however, are particular to computer systems. Adequate air conditioning and environment control are necessary to protect an installation against temperature, humidity and dust which go beyond the limits of tolerance specified by the manufacturers. This often means not only proper environmental control equipment but also proper staff discipline (no smoking, cleanliness, doors closed).

Software in a computer installation is a highly valuable and highly vulnerable asset. The library of user-developed and manufacturers' programs frequently has cost as much as the hardware to produce.

Moreover, while a damaged item of equipment can be replaced relatively quickly, or borrowed at short notice from another user, destroyed or damaged software may require as many months of painstaking effort to recreate as were required for initial development. Security measures must therefore be taken to protect software from physical hazards, loss by fire, theft, etc. Most important, however, the user must take proper measures to enable software to be replaced if loss does in fact occur. An obvious precaution is to store alternative copies of all system software away from computer installations.

This procedure is not as simple as it sounds. Not only must copies be stored, the stored copies must be kept as up-to-date as the currently used versions. In addition all associated *documentation* must be stored with the machine readable versions of the software. This imposes a rigorous discipline on the installation's management in order to ensure proper updating and control procedures are maintained.

Information is the end-product of a computer system, and is perhaps the most valuable and most vulnerable part of any installation. The information held within the computer may well be crucial to the viability of the whole of an organization's operations. Loss of fundamental records, customer accounts, payroll, engineering records, laboratory results may totally destroy an organization. Fraudulent use of information may cost a company far more than a 'conventional' burglary or payroll raid. Industrial espionage may give commercial rivals an overwhelming competitive position.

The risks to which computer-held information is subject again can be divided between conventional risks and those specific to computer systems.

Fire, sabotage, theft can destroy records. To prevent this, proper access control and physical security must be maintained. Again, in order to minimize the results of loss of information, it is advisable to hold copies of vital files in a location remote from the computer itself. As for software, proper control is needed to make sure that security copies of data files are updated regularly.

A *generation number* system is one technique for preserving copies of files together with the data required to update files ($\diamond$ *grandfather tape*). In very large systems, particularly those controlled by *operating systems*, standard software is provided which regularly *dumps* copies of master files for security purposes.

Information in a computer system is vulnerable to more subtle risks than the conventional physical risks referred to. Unauthorized modification of software may result in generating false information resulting in fraudulent gain. For example, false invoices may be generated and submitted for payment; tampering with payroll output may result in excessive payments. The incidence of computer fraud shows the greatest growth rate of any type of civil crime in the developed world, and as new security measures are adopted, new and more ingenious ways of manipulating computers are devised. A short article cannot hope to cover the variety of possible frauds and counter measures. Security lies fundamentally in the proper control of software, and in proper controls built into computer systems. In addition the user must take the usual care in selection and supervision of the staff he entrusts with these controls.

One method of controlling software is to preserve an 'audit copy' of all vulnerable software. This is a version of the software known, as far as possible, to be error free and 'honest', i.e., not perpetrating fraud. At random intervals the version of the program actually being used for the particular application can be removed and physically compared with the audit copy to ensure no unauthorized modifications have been made. Audit *test data* can be kept for the same purpose, run against a program, and results checked against standard test results to ensure that there has been no unauthorized change.

Auditing techniques have been widely extended and adopted to provide both internal and external auditors with a wide range of aids in auditing computer systems.

Such aids include audit software which enable auditors to call for sample data from computer files and selectively process samples against inquiry and report programs generated by the auditor himself. (⋄ general article on *Audit of Computer Systems*.) The incidence of large communication systems with extensive *on-line* inquiry facilities poses further security problems for computer based information.

Terminals enable a user both to examine and to modify data. Both these facilities can be abused either deliberately or accidentally. Data protection is a major subject in its own right. Hardware devices enable terminals to be controlled physically through the use of physical controls: locks and keys to allow a user to use a terminal, or to restrict the use of a terminal to an input mode or output mode only. Software controls allow for highly complex access control by means of hierarchies of *passwords*. Software may be developed which examines passwords submitted through the terminal: files may be restricted to the owners of certain passwords only, and the level and type of information also may be controlled by passwords. The ability to update a *file, record* or even *field* may be restricted to certain passwords. In addition to unauthorized access and use by people, sophisticated *operating systems* and *data base* systems must be secure internally to prevent unauthorized interference of data by software operations. Operating systems and data base systems are concerned with the manipulation of data held within a computer system, and a hierarchy of software controls limits the operations which can be performed on different levels of file structure within such systems.

Security in a computer sense is thus concerned with the whole spectrum of risks and hazards to which all aspects of computers, hardware, software and information, are vulnerable. Techniques used to protect computers from such risks range from basic physical protection to complex computer based techniques for monitoring the computer's own functions.

see-saw circuit Synonymous with *sign-reversing amplifier*.

seek Synonymous with *search*.

seek area In a *direct access* store (e.g., a *magnetic disk file*), an area of storage assigned to hold specified *records* and chosen to permit rapid access to the records concerned in accordance with the physical characteristics of the device.

Also known as cylinder.

seek time The time taken by a *disk drive* to move its *heads* from one *track* to another.

segment 1. To divide a long *program* into a series of shorter units (segments, also known as *chapters*). A program may be divided into segments for convenience of programming, all segments being present in *store* together when the program is run; or because the program is too long to be contained in store all at once, in which case segments are read in sequence. In this latter case, segments or groups of segments read into store together may be called *overlays*. ◊ *Programming, common area*. 2. A fixed length part of a *track*.

segmented program A *program* written in separate *segments* or parts. Only one, or some, of the segments may fit into *memory* at any one time, and a main part of the program, remaining in memory, will call for other segments from a *backing store* as and when required, each new segment being used to *overlay* the preceding segments.

segment mark A *character* used to separate sections of a *tape file*.

segregating unit A *collator* used to select from a card file *punched cards* satisfying certain conditions.

select To make a choice between alternative courses of action as a result of a *test*.

selecting A method by which the transmission of information to

403

remote *terminals* is controlled by carrying the *address* of the receiving terminal in the *block* being transmitted.

selection sequential access ⬦ *selective sequential.*

selective digit emitter A device in *punched card* machines which can simulate signals usually generated by particular punchings.

selective dump A *dump* of a limited area of *store.*

selective sequential A method of processing a *direct access sequential file* in such a way that selected *records* in the file are located by means of an index table and are presented to the processing *program* in *key* number sequence.

selective trace A *trace program* in which only specified *instruction* types or *store* areas are analysed. ⬦ *Debugging.*

selector A device which tests for the presence of specified conditions and initiates appropriate operations according to the result of the test.

selector channel Where several *peripheral units* are connected to a *central processor* by a single *channel*, the selector channel controls the transfer of data between each peripheral unit and the central processor.

self-checking code Synonymous with *error detecting code.*

self-checking number A number which has attached to it a *check digit* whose value depends on the values of the other digits in the number, enabling the number to be checked after being transferred between *peripheral devices* or between *locations* of *store.*

self-resetting loop A *loop* which contains *instructions* restoring all *locations* affecting the operation of the loop to their original condition as at entry to the loop.

self-test A method of automatically testing the performance of line terminating equipment, such as *modems*, by transmitting a test pattern through the equipment and analysing the returning pattern.

self-triggering program A *program* which begins operating as soon as it has been placed in a *central processor.* ⬦ *trigger.*

semantic error An error in the selection of the correct *symbol* to represent a given idea or meaning, e.g., using the wrong *instruction format* for the *operation* required.

semantics The study of the relationship between symbols and their meaning.

semi-automatic switching centre ⬦ *switching centre.*

semiconductor A material such as *silicon* whose conductivity at room temperature lies between that of metals and insulators, but increases at high temperatures and decreases at low ones. ⬦ *silicon chip.*

send channel In communication circuits connecting two channels, the channel used for transmission into a terminal; the other channel is known as the return channel, with respect to that terminal.

sense 1. To test the state of some part of *hardware*, especially the state of a *switch*[1] set either manually or in the course of the operation of a device. 2. Synonymous with read.

sense switch A *switch*[1] on an *operator's console*, which can set a *switch*[3] in a *program*, thus allowing the operator to determine which *branch* is selected in a program with alternative paths.

sensing station The position within a *punched card* machine at which a card was read, e.g., by means of sensing brushes.

sentinel A *character* which is used to indicate the occurrence of a specified condition, e.g., the physical end of a *magnetic tape*, or the end of a *variable length record* in *store*.

separator A *character* used to separate logical units of data, e.g., *fields*, *records*.
   Also known as data delimiter.

sequence 1. To place a set of items into some defined order of the *keys* used to identify the items, e.g., to place a set of names into alphabetic sequence. Also known as order[2]. 2. Any set of items or instructions which have been placed in a defined order.

sequence check A check designed to ensure that an ordered set of items is in the expected *sequence* of *keys*.

sequence checking routine A routine which checks that a set of items expected to be in a defined *sequence* is in fact in the correct order.

sequence control register A *register* whose contents determine the next *instruction* to be performed.

sequence error An error detected by a *sequence checking routine*, i.e., an error arising because the arrangement of items in a set does not conform to some defined order.

sequence register Synonymous with *sequence control register*.

sequential access storage A *storage device* in which data can only be *accessed* in the sequence in which it is stored in the device, i.e., an item can only be processed after all the preceding items have been accessed. An example of sequential access storage is *magnetic tape*. ⟡ *sequential processing*.

sequential control A method of computer operation in which *instructions* are stored in the order in which they are executed.

sequential processing Processing *records* in a data *file* according to some predetermined sequence of *keys*. This is contrasted with *serial processing* in which each record is processed in the order in which it is stored in a given *storage device*. The two expressions become synonymous when used for *magnetic tape* processing, in which records are held both in sequence and in series on the tape, but on *direct access* devices *sequential* and *serial* processing are distinct techniques: records processed serially may not be in a given sequence and in sequential work only selected records need be examined. ◊ *selective sequential*.

sequential-stacked job control A control system which ensures that jobs are performed in the sequence in which they are presented to the system.

serial To deal with items of information or *instructions* in sequence; contrasted with *parallel*.

serial access *Access* to *records* in a data file in the order in which they occur in a given storage device. ◊ *serial processing*.

serial attribute A coding system common in *videotex* and *teletext* systems, where the attributes of a character (e.g., colour, size) are represented by a code within the coding scheme which is transmitted and stored, but not displayed or printed (unless a special command is effected). The attribute code precedes the character(s) having the required attribute, and appears on a display or printout as a space. ◊ *parallel attribute*.

serial feeding A method of feeding *punched cards* in which a card entered the *card track* with (for 80-column cards) column 1 or 80 leading. Contrasted with *sideways feed*.

serial interface An *interface* in which *serial* transfer of data occurs between *peripheral units* and a *processor*. Contrasted with *parallel interface*.

serial processing Processing *records* in a data file in the order in which they occur in a given *storage device*. This is contrasted with *sequential processing* in which records are processed according to some predetermined sequence of *keys*. The two expressions become synonymous when used for *magnetic tape* processing in which records are held both in sequence and in series on the tape. However on *direct access* devices *sequential* and *serial* processing refer to distinct techniques.

serial transfer Transfer of data in which each unit of data being transferred travels in sequence. Contrasted with *parallel transfer*. It should be noted that serial and parallel transfers can occur together, e.g., a series of *words* may be transferred serially, although each *bit* within the word is transferred in parallel.

serviceability The reliability of equipment, based on some objective criterion. Various criteria for assessing serviceability are adopted, ◊ *serviceability ratio, utilization ratio, operating ratio*.

serviceability ratio The *ratio of serviceable* time to the sum of *serviceable time* and *down time*.

serviceable time The total time during which a machine is in a state where it can operate normally, including time when the machine is idle, but not time when it is unattended.

service bits *Bits* which are used in *data transmission* to convey signals monitoring the transmission itself (e.g., requesting repetition) rather than conveying information. Associated with *check bit*.

service programs Synonymous with *service routines*.

service routines *Routines* whose purpose is to perform all functions associated with the maintenance and operation of a computer and the preparation and correction of *programs*. Service routines are normally *general purpose programs*, and include *executive* routines, *compilers, generators* and *assemblers, debugging routines, diagnostic routines* for *hardware* checking, and general *input/output* routines.

Also known as utility routines, service programs, utility programs. ◊ general article on *Utility Programs*.

servo Synonymous with *servo-mechanism*.

servo-mechanism A powered device used to control operations which is activated by a difference in the actual and desired values of the quantity under control and acts so as to minimize the difference.

session level In the *ISO seven layer reference model*, this refers to the fifth level of codes which establish, maintain and terminate logical connexions for the transfer of data between end users.

set 1. To place a desired value into a storage *location*. 2. To give a *bit* the value one. 3. A collection of items having some common property.

set pulse A pulse which has the property of *setting* a *bit*.

set up To prepare equipment for operation, e.g., to place paper in a *printer*, cards in a *card reader*, etc.

set up time Time taken during the running of a job in *set up* procedures.

seven layer reference model A model for communication *protocols*, designed to allow *open system* interconnection between computer equipment with different protocols. The seven layers are: (i) *physical level*; (ii) *data link level*; (iii) *network level*; (iv) *transport level*; (v) *session level*; (vi) *presentation level*; (vii) *application level*.

several-for-one The association of several *machine language instructions* with a single *source language statement*.

shared data base A *data base* which can be *updated* and *accessed* simultaneously by users in different physical locations, communicating with the data base over a *network*.

shared files system   A system in which more than one computer is able to *access* information stored on one *direct access storage device*.

shift   1. To move the elements of a unit of information (*bits, digits, characters*) to the left or right. ⊘ *arithmetical shift, logical shift*. 2. Synonymous with *shift character*.

shift, arithmetic   ⬦ *arithmetical shift*.

shift character   A *character* in a communications code which designates which group of codes in the set follows the shift character. ⊘ *shift-in* and *shift-out*.

Also known as shift.

shift-in   A *shift character* used to indicate that the designated character set following the shift is the standard character set. Contrasted with *shift-out*.

shifting register   Synonymous with *shift register*.

shift, non arithmetic   ⬦ *non arithmetic shift*.

shift-out   A *shift character* used to indicate that the designated character set following the shift is an alternative or non-standard character set. Contrasted with *shift-in*.

shift register   A *register* in which the data stored can be subjected to a right or left *shift*.

Also known as shifting register.

shift, ring   Synonymous with *circular shift*.

sideways feed   A method of feeding *punched cards* in which a card is placed in the *hopper* in such a way that it enters the *card track* with one of its long edges leading. Contrasted with *serial feeding*.

sight check   Checking that holes punched in two or more *punched cards* were identical by holding the cards together and looking through the pattern of holes.

sign   An arithmetical symbol which distinguishes positive from negative quantities.

signal   1. Any electrical pulse transmitted over a *network* which can be used to represent *bits* which make up a message or control information. 2. A specific code in a network system which controls the handling of messages and the set-up, maintenance and clearing of connexions.

signal conditioning   Modifying a signal so as to make it comprehensible to a particular device.

signal distance   The number of corresponding *bit positions* which differ in two *binary words* of the same length, e.g., the signal distance between the two following 6-bit words is 3.

100101 and 001100

◊ *Hamming distance* and *Hamming code*. The *exclusive-or operation* performed between two words will result in a word which corresponds to the signal distance. For this reason the operation is sometimes known as the *distance* operation.

signalling rate   The rate at which signals are transmitted in a communications system; measured, for example, in *bits* per second.

signal normalization   Synonymous with *signal standardization*.

signal, nought output   ◊ *nought output signal*.

signal, one output   ◊ *one output signal*.

signal regeneration   Restoring a signal to its original specification; a form of *signal standardization*.

Also known as signal reshaping.

signal reshaping   Synonymous with *signal regeneration*.

signal standardization   Using one signal to generate another which usually conforms to more stringent conditions.

Also known as signal normalization, standardization.

sign bit   A *sign digit* composed of a single *bit*.

sign check indicator   An *indicator* which can be set when the result of an arithmetic operation either changes sign, or is either positive or negative. Appropriate action can be taken according to the state of the indicator, thus providing a check on the sign when arithmetic calculations are performed.

sign-changing amplifier   ◊ *sign-reversing amplifier*.

sign digit   A *character*, normally at the end of a value *field* or *word*, used to indicate the algebraic sign of the value. For example, it is a convention to represent negative *binary* numbers as *true complements* of the corresponding positive numbers, thus, the left-hand character of the binary word indicates a positive value if set to 0 but a negative value if set to 1.

signed field   A *field* containing a number which incorporates a *sign digit* indicating the *sign* of the number.

significance   In *positional notation* the significance of a particular *digit position* in a number is the contribution to the total of a digit with the value 1 in that position; e.g., the significance of the italicized digit position in the following decimal number is 100: 1*4*59.

significant digits   Those *digits* or *digit positions* in a number whose values are known and are relevant to the precision of the number, e.g., the number 123.4 has four significant digits, whereas the number 123 has three significant digits and the number 123,000, when known to be correct to the nearest thousand, also has three significant digits.

Also known as significant figures.

significant figures Synonymous with *significant digits*.

sign on, sign off ⊙ *logon*.

sign position The position in a number in which the *sign digit* or symbol is placed.

sign-reversing amplifier Pertaining to a device in which the output voltage has the same magnitude as the input voltage but is of opposite sign.

Also known as sign-changing amplifier, inverting amplifier.

silicon chip A device composed of the non-metallic semiconducting element silicon, which contains a set of *integrated circuits*, reduced to a very small size, with resulting low cost and high speed performance.

simplex A communications system which allows transmission in one direction only. Compare with *duplex* and *half-duplex*.

simplex channel A communications *channel* which allows data to be transmitted in one direction only.

simulation The mathematical representation of problems allowing physical situations to be represented mathematically as a means of solving the problems created by the factors of the physical processes.

simulator A system, either *hardware* or *software*, designed to perform the *simulation* of some real process.

simulator routine An *interpretive routine* designed to enable *programs* written for one computer to run on a different computer.

simultaneity A feature by which certain *operations* in a *program* can be performed concurrently with others. This term is usually applied where separate *hardware* features are available to perform the separate tasks, but is sometimes, perhaps unwisely, used as a synonym for *timesharing* or *multiprogramming*.

simultaneous ⊙ *simultaneity*.

simultaneous access Placing data into *store*, or retrieving data from store, by means of *parallel transfer* of all elements of the unit of data.

Also known as parallel access.

simultaneous computer A computer which contains a unit giving it *simultaneity* of operation.

Also known as parallel computer.

single address code Synonymous with *single address instruction*.

single address instruction An *instruction format* which contains only one *operand* address.

Also known as single address code.

single bit error A data transmission error in which a single *bit* in a sequence is inverted (i.e., 0 becomes 1 or 1 becomes 0). ⊙ *transmission error*.

single column pence coding A *punched card* code which enables the values 0 to 11 to be represented by a punching in a single *card column*.

single density The recording density for *data storage* available with the first generation of 8in. diameter *floppy disks* (between 50k and 90k bytes). ⟡ *double density*.

single-ended amplifier An amplifier which develops only one out-put signal. Contrasted with a *double-ended amplifier*. ⟡ *push-pull amplifier*.

single length The representation of numbers in *binary* form in such a way that the values of the numbers can be obtained in a single *word*.

single shot circuit *Circuits* or *logic elements* arranged to perform *signal standardization* in order to convert an imprecise input *signal* into one which conforms to the requirements of a particular machine.

Also known as one shot circuit.

single shot operation Synonymous with *single step operation*.

single sided A *floppy disk* which has data recorded on only one side surface. Contrasted with *double sided*.

single step operation A method of operating a computer in which the *instructions* in a *program* are performed one at a time in response to an engineer's or operator's intervention. Single step operation is usually performed during *debugging*.

Also known as step-by-step operation, single shot operation, one shot operation.

sizing Sizing is concerned with the evaluation of the resources and facilities needed to perform a data processing task, to achieve a specified service at a cost commensurate with the user's requirements. The service itself will require a number of aspects to be considered. For example, the workload required by the user's system may entail a given *throughput* of *transactions* in a specific time; the system may have to handle peaks of transactions at critical times; individual users of the system may require specific *response times* to be met. There can also be a requirement for *resilience* in the system and an overall *serviceability* requirement to be met. The user's functional needs must also be understood so that the complexity of the processing can be assessed.

A study of these aspects enables a statement of the end-user's work load to be formulated, against which the sizing exercise will determine the resources needed both to develop and run the required system operationally. The end result of a sizing study would normally include: a statement of the work load and its future growth; a statement of the *hardware resources* needed both initially and to cope with future growth; an outline description of the *software* resources needed (both existing software and bespoke software which needs to be developed);

a statement of manpower resources needed to develop and maintain the system; a statement of expected throughput and resource levels; the spare capacity within the system; and the planned system *up time*.

A sizing study may be initiated in a number of situations; e.g., when a company issues a tender to purchase a new computer it is to be expected that the manufacturer's staff will size the project before submitting responses to the tender; a data processing department should size every major development which it undertakes; sizing techniques can also be used to review the operational efficiency of an installation or of a specific application.

The methodology used in a sizing study will depend on the degree of precision required, and on the availability of information and time to complete the study. In principle a sizing study requires information in two basic categories – product information and work load information.

With product information we are concerned with the performance ratings of hardware devices and the performance of existing or planned software used by the system. Software performance entails measuring or evaluating *instruction* path lengths and calculating the performance to be expected in executing specific functions on specified hardware.

Compiling work load information entails collecting up-to-date data about the end-user's requirement, and this may be based partially upon an assessment of his existing procedures and workload and upon future developments planned. Sometimes programs have to be written to collect and analyse data from existing systems. In designing future systems one should also consider developing special routines known as instrumentation to collect data in an organized way for future sizing activity.

The sizing technique used will be dependent on the quality of the information available and the resources and time available to carry out the exercise. A sizing exercise may embody the use of analytical methods applied in the construction of hand-worked models, or it may involve the use of parameter driven *simulation models*. It is important not to use techniques which cannot be supported by the quality of data, and it is also important to use methods which allow for iteration easily and inexpensively to permit variations in work load and resources to be evaluated. It is also important to be able to check results using a different method.

The most common area for sizing activity is in the evaluation of hardware and software configurations needed to perform a given task or set of tasks. This is often done at a time when the full extent of the ultimate system is not known. Thus it is important to continue to use sizing concepts throughout the development of projects from the time of their inception through to efficient and effective live running. A study conducted after completion of a *systems definition* will be based on better information than one based upon an outline design or a functional specification. The performance aspects of a system can obviously be better predicted and controlled when detailed *program specifications* have been produced.

The sizing of a project will go through a change of emphasis as the project develops. The initial sizing is done to match the work load and the resources/facilities which are to be budgeted for the project. At this stage, usually based upon a functional specification, a number of trade-offs can be made according to the findings of the sizing study; e.g., reducing systems functions in favour of performance or lower cost, increasing hardware in favour of improved system resilience or increased capacity for future growth. Obviously as one approaches the later stages of a project subsequent sizing activity provides a basis for tuning the design of the system to provide the performance and facilities originally planned.

There are a number of problems which can arise in sizing studies and, therefore, all projects must be managed with the principles, concept and limitations of sizing in mind. Some of the problems are summarized below.

The requirements of a system are often changed by users during the development of a project. These are likely to invalidate initial sizing and imply the need for continual sizing studies throughout the project. There is also a tendency in project development to aim at achieving the timescales and facilities needed at the expense of software efficiency, thus resulting in dilution of original performance objectives. This must be monitored and performance targets and budgets maintained by reappraisal of sizing assumptions at key stages. The organizational environment may change during project development, thus presenting a different balance in the workload to that initially evaluated. Assumptions about the performance of hardware or software products may not be realized in practice, and this can affect the performance of the system in a major way.

The output from a sizing exercise is able to provide information permitting changes in the design and giving management the opportunity to exercise trade-offs in the best interest of the project and the organization. It is important, therefore, to budget for on-going sizing activity in a project, and to create within the data processing organization a responsibility for promoting and developing sizing disciplines. The objective of sizing is to provide a basis of decision for making trade-offs which balance the level of service, the facilities and their cost within a particular computing project or installation.

skeletal code An incomplete set of *instructions* forming part of a *general routine* and completed by means of *parameters*.

skip 1. A computer *instruction* in which no operation is performed other than a jump to the next instruction in sequence. 2. A device, on a *card punch*, enabling *columns* on a *punched card* on which no punching was required to travel rapidly under the *punch knives*.

skip-sequential access A method of *file access* in which each successive access requires a *record* with a *key* higher than that of the previous access.

slave store A *store* which compensates for the different speeds of operation of storage units which must interact. For example, a fast *pipeline* can be slowed because it is dependent upon access to a relatively slower *main store*. In such a case *instructions* and *operands* required by the pipeline will be transferred via a slave store which is designed to drive the pipeline at high speed.

slot An *interface* within a *central processor* which allows the interconnexion of different *printed circuit boards*, thus adding to the basic functionality of a computer system. ⇨ *daughterboard, backplane*.

slow time scale A *time scale* which is greater than the unit of time in the physical system being studied.

Also known as extended time scale. ⇨ *analog computer*.

smart card A plastic card like a credit card containing an updatable microprocessor.

smudge In *optical character recognition*, ink which appears outside the limits of the shape of the printed character. ⇨ squeeze out.

SNA Abbreviation of systems network architecture.

snapshot dump A *dump* of selected parts of *store* which can occur at various points during the running of a *program*, usually for *debugging* purposes.

socket 1. A device which terminates the permanent part of a circuit, into which a *plug* can be inserted to complete the circuit. 2. Synonymous with *slot*.

Also known as hub[2] (*punched card* machines) and jack (telecommunications).

soft copy Output from a computer process which is displayed on a *visual display unit*. Contrasted with *hard copy*.

soft dump Synonymous with *register dump*. ⇨ *dump*.

soft key   A *key* on a *keyboard* or *keypad* whose function is determined by *software* and may vary depending on the *program* in use.

software   In its most general form, software is a term used in contrast to *hardware* to refer to all *programs* which can be used on a particular computer system. More specifically, the term is applied to all those programs which in some way can assist all users of a particular type of computer to make the best use of their machine, as distinct from the specific programs written to solve the problems of any particular user. In this case, software is usually produced by the computer manufacturer, and indeed the importance of software is such that investment in its production is a major item in the development and marketing of computers. By intelligent use of available software the user of a computer can considerably reduce the effort that is required in devising a system and writing the programs required to implement it.

Software comes in all shapes and sizes; this article gives a brief description of the various types of software, from the simplest to the most complex. More information can be obtained by consulting the various main entries.

Subroutines are the smallest items of software normally provided by a manufacturer. These are usually routines devised to perform large numbers of routine calculations, e.g., tax calculations, multiplication and division (if these functions cannot be performed by hardware), editing of data for input and output (e.g., inserting cheque protection symbols when printing sterling values). Subroutines to perform input and output operations also form part of this category of software: these are also called *packages* or *housekeeping routines*. Large numbers of these routines are supplied by manufacturers and they usually form part of a software *library* held on some form of *backing store*. Subroutines of this sort are not independent programs but will be incorporated by a user in his own programs when required.

Assemblers and *compilers* are programs used to convert programs written in a symbolic *language* into the *machine code* required by the computer.

Executive programs and *operating systems* are programs which are held permanently in store and are used to control the operations of other programs, particularly in *multiprogramming* systems.

Generators are programs which are similar in action to compilers and assemblers but only *object programs* of a particular type can be produced from them.

Utility programs are programs devised to perform some of the basic data handling operations, such as file conversion (e.g., transcribing a *magnetic tape* file to *magnetic disk*) *sorting*, controlling the location of data in a *direct access* file. Utility programs are generally devised for each type of *peripheral unit*.

Debugging routines include programs for producing *printouts* of *memory* at various stages of a program, and also various forms of analysis of the progress of a program. Such programs are known as *trace* or *monitor* routines.

File processing programs are programs devised for performing operations on data *files*, such as editing, validation, comparing and *updating*.

The types of software so far described involve routines designed either to form part of a user's program or to assist generally in the utilization of a computer and associated peripheral devices. A further extension of the concept of software is the *application package*. This involves a set of programs designed to perform the routines associated with a particular example of a broad general system. Examples are payroll packages, *PERT* packages, packages for the solution of transportation problems, *inventory management, spreadsheet*, etc. The user wishing to use a package of this type defines his own requirements by means of *parameters* which are employed by the programs in the system to produce the specific results required.

solid state computer   A computer constructed mainly from *solid state devices*.

solid state device   A device whose operation depends on the electronic properties of solid materials, e.g., *transistors, ferrite cores*.

sonic delay line   Synonymous with *acoustic delay line*.

sort   To arrange items of information into groups according to the identifying *keys* of each item. The items will be sequenced if the arrangement of the keys follows some predetermined order. ⟡ general article on *Sorting*.

sorter   A *punched card* machine which fed cards into several *pockets* according to the punchings present in specified *card columns*.

sort generator   A *generator* in which the *object program* is designed to *sort* a set of items into a given sequence defined by the *parameters* specified to the generator.

sorting   Usually data which is to be processed requires to be ordered and presented in a predetermined *sequence*. The need for sorting arises after the data has been transcribed on to a computer *input medium*, e.g., *magnetic disk, magnetic tape*. The sorting of data after transcription may take place externally from the computer (*off-line* sorting) or internally on the computer (*on-line* sorting). Off-line sorting can be used only on data which is on a medium enabling each item of data to be handled separately, e.g., documents printed with characters which can be read by some form of *character recognition* device.

All forms of sorting depend on the sequencing of items of data according to some ordering of a *key*. For example, in a telephone directory names are sorted in alphabetical order, the key being the subscriber's surname. An alternative sequence of the names in a directory is that of the street directory. In this case the key is the street and number of the house. If the streets are listed in alphabetical order and the occupiers in each street in the numerical order of their house number, we can say that two keys are being used: street name and house number. The items are listed in number within street sequence.

Off-line sorting is done by means of mechanical devices known as *sorters*. Basically these devices can sense the value of a particular *column* in a card or *mark* in a character recognition *field* and cause all items having the same value to be placed together in the same batch or *stacker*. In all off-line sorting the time taken to sequence a file of data depends largely on the size of the keys, since a separate pass through the machine is required for each digit in the key.

In on-line sorting, the principle of sequencing by means of an ordering of keys remains. Normally the record is handled together with its key although in some forms of sorting time is saved by removing the record from the key and sorting only the keys. The most common form of on-line sorting is *magnetic tape* sorting. Methods of tape sorting are variants of a method known as *merge* sorting. The merge sorting method is made up of two logical phases:

(i) A *string generation* phase in which data records are read from the unsorted input file, formed into groups which are in sequence, and written as ordered groups or *strings* on to other tapes.

(ii) A *string merging phase* in which one or more strings are merged or combined to form longer strings.

A phase of a sort is known as a *pass*. The maximum number of strings that may be merged together in one pass to form a single string is called the *way* of the sort. The various different methods of tape sorting, e.g., 'classical sorting', 'polyphase sorting', 'oscillating sorting', 'cascade sorting', differ in the techniques used in distributing the initial strings between the available magnetic *tape decks*. The particular sorting technique used for any application will depend on three main factors: the number and type of tape decks available, the amount of *storage*

417

available for holding the data to be sorted and the time available for the sorting operation. It should be mentioned here that in contrast to off-line sorting, the size of the key in magnetic tape sorting does not have a significant effect on the overall sort time.

Most manufacturers supply *software* for performing sorts. This software consists of *sort routines* which operate on *parameters* supplied to the program at *run time*, specifying the keys, size of records, tape decks available, etc., and also *sort generators*, which are used to create specific sort programs for subsequent use.

Internal storage sorting is another method of sorting which does not require magnetic tape. In this method all records being sorted are present together in internal storage. The two basic techniques are 'exchange sorting' and 'extraction sorting'. An exchanging sort entails the sorting of complete records within the original data storage area, based on the comparison of the record keys and the movement of the records according to the result of the comparison. Different methods of comparing records may be adopted. One of the methods commonly used in the *dichotomizing search* or *binary chop*, in which the first key is compared with one half way through the group of data, then the second two keys of each half are compared, and so on until all the data has been covered. Further passes through the data are made, each time the distance between keys being compared being halved until finally each key is compared with the next. One of the most time-consuming features of an exchange sort is the transfer of complete records after a comparison. An extraction sort overcomes this difficulty by associating each key with the *address* of the record in store, then transferring the keys and associated addresses to another part of store in which they are sorted. After the sort is completed the associated addresses can be used to sequence the original records.

Sorting on other *storage devices* may make use of the same techniques as tape sorting, or internal sorting, depending on whether the storage device is used as a *backing store* or as a store of the same level as internal storage.

sorting needle A needle used to probe a *pack* of *punched cards* in order to establish that a particular punching was common to all cards in the pack.

sorting routine A *routine* which will arrange items of data into sequence according to the values contained within specified *fields* (*key words*) of the individual *records*. Various types of sorting routine are described in the general article on *Sorting*.

sorting routine generator Synonymous with *sort generator*.

source code ◊ *source language.*

source computer A computer which performs the *compilation* of a *source program*, contrasted with an *object computer*, which is the computer on which the *object program* will be run.

source document An original document from which data is prepared in a form acceptable to a computer.

source language A programming *language* which cannot be directly processed by the *hardware* of a computer but requires *compilation* into an *object program* consisting of *instructions* in a *machine language* which can be directly understood by the computer. Examples of such languages are *COBOL, ALGOL, FORTRAN, PL/1.*

source machine Synonymous with *source computer.*

source module A unit of *source code* that can be *compiled* as a single unit.

source program A program written in a *source language.*

space character Synonymous with *blank*.

space division system A system in which *multiplexing* is effected by *frequency modulation.*

space suppression Inhibiting the normal movement of paper in a *printer* after a line of *characters* has been printed.

span The difference between the highest and lowest values in the *range* of values which a quantity can have.

spanned record A group of one or more *record sections* which together constitute a record but which span consecutive *blocks*.

special characters *Characters* in a *character set* which are neither letters nor numerals, e.g., !, ", /, @, £, etc.

Also known as additional characters, *symbols*.

special purpose computer A computer designed to solve problems of a restricted type. Contrasted with *general purpose computer.*

specific address Synonymous with *absolute address.*

specification A precise and detailed statement of requirements. The requirements may refer to the system being developed (◊ *system definition*), to a program (◊ *program specification*) or to the equipment required to operate a system. Functional specification.

specific code Synonymous with *absolute code.*

specific coding Synonymous with *absolute coding.*

specific program A *program* written in *absolute code.*

speech synthesis The generation under *microprocessor* control of sound patterning which simulates a human voice.

Also known as voice synthesis.

splicer A hand-operated device used to join together two pieces of *paper tape* in such a way that they can be satisfactorily *read* by a *paper tape reader*.

split screen A display on a *visual display unit*, where information under the control of separate and independent *programs* is visible simultaneously, and where the user can interact with one *application* without affecting another.

split-word operations *Operations* which can process part of a *word*, as distinct from the whole word, which is the normal unit of data on which operations are performed. ⟡ *single-length* working, *double-precision arithmetic*.

spool Properly, the mounting for a roll of *paper tape*, but also used to describe a coiled length of paper tape. But ⟡ *spooling*.

Also known as *reel*[1], *roll*.

spooling A method of achieving effective use of *hardware* during *input/output* operations by decoupling slow devices from the main process which requires the input/output.

spot carbon Carbon paper which is treated on selected parts of its surface only, so that only the required part of the printing is reproduced.

spot punch A punch, operated directly by hand, capable of making single holes in a *punched card* or *paper tape*.

Also known as unipunch.

spreadsheet A popular *application package* for *personal computers* which allows the user to analyse information presented in tabular form, manipulating rows and columns and allowing vertical and horizontal *scrolling* when the physical capacity of the *visual display unit* cannot accommodate all the available data.

sprocket holes 1. Holes punched in *paper tape* whose function was to drive the tape, or more usually to generate a signal used for indexing or timing the tape. Contrasted with *code holes*. Also known as *feed holes*. 2. Holes at the edges of *continuous stationery*, used by a *printer* to drive the stationery.

sprocket pulse In a *paper tape reader*, the pulse or signal generated by the reading of the *sprocket holes* on paper tape.

squeezeout In *optical character recognition*, printing in which the ink has gone to the edges of a character, making them appear darker than the centre of the character. ⟡ *smudge*.

stability In *optical character recognition*, the ability of inks to keep their colour when exposed to light or heat.

stable trigger circuit Synonymous with *toggle*.

stack An area of *store* reserved for the temporary storage of data, usually on *input* or before *output*. ⟡ *buffer*.

stacker A receptacle for holding *punched cards* after they have passed through a machine. Contrasted with *hopper*.

stacker, card ⟡ *stacker*.

standard code sets Sets of codes which have been defined by national and international standards bodies, such as *ANSI* and *CCITT*.

standard costing Efficiency and profitability can be increased by the use of a system in which standards are set for performance and cost per unit: the actual results are compared with standards and the extent and reasons for variances are reported.

The system embraces many other techniques such as work measurement, methods study and *budgetary control*, and expresses the results in terms of performance and cost.

The steps in setting up a standard costing system are: (i) The standard unit of output is established. For example, a refrigerator factory might use a unit of a refrigerator, a brick works one ton of bricks or a haulier one ton-mile. (ii) The standard volume of output is established. Normally this will be slightly below the theoretical maximum capacity so as to allow for shortfalls. (iii) Costs of each department have to be assessed so as to arrive at the standard cost per unit at the standard volume of output. The standard cost per unit is made up of: direct materials; direct labour; indirect costs (overheads). (iv) The costs of those departments (cost centres) which only contribute indirectly to the output are divided over the direct cost centres. For example, part of the costs of a factory maintenance department (indirect) would be allocated to the metal cutting department (direct). The allocation is treated as an overhead on the direct cost centres. (v) The direct cost per unit is assessed by work measurement and methods study. Standard amounts of labour time and material content for each unit are set and the indirect overheads added to obtain the standard cost per unit. (vi) Some of the indirect costs vary with the volume of output and some are fixed. Costs have to be analysed into fixed and variable to establish what variances are due to the volume of output deviating from standard. (vii) Actual costs are recorded in the same way as the standards, and variances are calculated and the reasons for them identified. Because of the analysis done in setting the standards and recording the actuals, comprehensive information can be produced about the causes of variances. For example, it may be due to the volume of output, labour efficiency, materials wastage, price of labour rate changes. (viii) Standards need to be kept under constant review but should only be amended if there is permanent change. It will be seen that the advantages of standard costing in management control are: (*a*) work methods can be improved;

(*b*) costs are reduced; (*c*) performance is judged; (*d*) variances are identified; (*e*) a basis for selling prices is provided.

standard form *Floating point representation* in which the *fixed point part* lies within a standard range of values chosen so that any given number can be represented by only one pair of numbers.

standard interface A *hardware* system providing standard logic circuits and *input/output channels* for the connexion of *peripheral units* to a *central processor*. Each peripheral is coupled to the processor via a standard multiway connector plug which carries all wiring for the necessary control signals and data flowing between the processor and the peripheral unit. In this way a standard processor can be fitted with any number and type of peripherals according to the number of channels provided on the processor itself, thus allowing for the later expansion of the system with minimal alteration of the *hardware*.

standardization 1. The process of replacing the *floating point representation* of a number by its *normalized* form. 2. A synonym for *signal standardization*.

standardize To replace the *floating point representation* of a number by its *normalized* form.

standards ⟡ general article on *Data Processing Standards*.

standard subroutine A *subroutine*, designed to perform a function having application in more than one *program*, which can be incorporated into different programs as required. Standard subroutines are usually supplied by computer manufacturers and may be present on a *library tape*.

standing charge Part of a tariff in a telecommunication service, which is made to a user as a fixed fee for allowing usage of the system, in addition to the *usage charge*.

standing-on-nines carry Synonymous with *high-speed carry*.

star network ⟡ *network architecture*.

start bit The first *bit* of the series of bits representing a *character*, which signifies the start of characters in order to maintain synchronization between transmitting and receiving terminals.

start–stop time Synonymous with *acceleration time* and *deceleration time*.

statement A *source language instruction*. Also used for any expression which can be input to a *compiler*, including *narrative* statements and *directives* controlling the operation of the compilation.

statement number A serial number given to each *statement* in a *program* written in a *source language*.

state, one Synonymous with *one condition*.

static dump A *dump* performed when a program reaches an *end of run* condition or some other recognizable stage within the *run*.

staticizer A *logic element* which converts information from a sequence of signals arriving one after the other in time to a corresponding representation of the information held permanently in *store*. Contrasted with *dynamicizer*.

static magnetic cell Synonymous with *magnetic cell*.

static memory A term used to describe *random access memory* (RAM) in which information is retained as long as power is maintained, without the need for constant reinsertion of data. Static *memory* is simpler to use but more expensive, less compact, and uses more power than dynamic memory. Contrasted with *volatile memory*. ⟨⟩ *non-volatile memory*.

static store 1. A *store* in which each *location* has a fixed space, and access to information does not depend on the location being available at a specific time. Contrasted with a *cyclic store*. 2. A *store* which has no moving parts.

static subroutine A *subroutine* which always performs the same operation, i.e., which does not require *parameters* in order to alter its functioning. Contrasted with *dynamic subroutine*.

stationery Stationery is used in computer systems to record results produced on a *printer* or *typewriter*. Most printers make use of continuous forms, driven through the printer by means of sprocket holes at each edge. Pages are separated from each other by perforations. Form designs may be preprinted on each page, the computer supplying the variable information, e.g., invoice details. Multi-part sets of stationery enable several copies to be printed of each page, either by means of interleaved carbon paper or specially treated chemical surfaces. Computer stationery can be obtained in a variety of different form widths and depths, the maximum size depending on the capacity of the printer being used. Multi-part sets can be divided by means of a *decollator*, and individual pages separated from each other with a *burster*.

Stationery used on typewriters is usually in the form of a continuous roll of paper without separate page perforations.

statistical multiplexor A version of a *time division multiplexor* which improves efficiency in the use of data circuits by giving increased priority to certain *channels*, in accordance with statistical predictions of likely *loading*.

status word A *word* which contains information about the condition of a *peripheral unit*. This information includes, for example, warning information when a peripheral needs attention (e.g., when the *paper low condition* is present on a *printer*) and is entered into the status word automatically by hardware.

step   Synonymous with *instruction*.

step-by-step operation   Synonymous with *single step operation*.

step change   A change from one value to another as a single increment taking negligible time.

step counter   A *counter* used to keep count of the steps in those *instructions* such as division and multiplication which involve a succession of separate operations.

stock control   Synonymous with *inventory control*.

stop code   Synonymous with *halt instruction*.

stop instruction   Synonymous with *halt instruction*.

stop instruction, conditional   ◊ *conditional stop instruction*.

stop instruction, optional   ◊ *optional stop instruction*.

stop time   Synonymous with *deceleration time*.

storage   Synonymous with *store*.

storage allocation   The process of allocating specific areas of *store* to specific types of *data*. Storage allocation is one of the functions which must be carried out during preparation of a *program*, and one of the operations performed by a *compiler* is to specify the areas allocated to the various types of data. But ◊ *dynamic allocation* (*of memory*).

storage allocation, dynamic   ◊ *dynamic allocation* (*of memory*).

storage block   Any area of *store*, usually set aside for some particular purpose, e.g., *input area, work area*.

storage, buffer   ◊ *buffer store*.

storage capacity   The amount of information which can be held in *store*, usually expressed as the number of units of data (*words, characters*) which can be retained.

storage cell   1. The smallest physical element of a *store*, e.g., in a *core storage* a single core. 2. That part of a store which can contain a single unit of data, e.g., a *bit* or *character*.

storage compacting   A practice adopted on *multiprogramming* computers, in which *memory locations* are assigned to *programs* so that the largest possible area of contiguous locations remains available for any other programs that are to be run. Thus, when one program is finished the memory areas may be automatically reallocated. ◊ *dynamic allocation* (*of memory*).

storage, content-addressed   ◊ *associative store*.

storage cycle   In a *cyclic store*, the interval between the times when any given *location* can be *accessed*.

storage density   The number of units of data which can be stored per unit length or area of the medium, e.g., the number of *bits* per inch which can be stored on *magnetic tape*.

Also known as recording density.

storage devices   A modern *digital computer* consists of a number of storage devices which are used to store both *data* and *program instructions*. This storage may be considered in two categories: *main memory* and *backing store*. There are within these categories a variety of memory systems some details of which are given below; first of all we shall discuss main memory systems.

A computer program consists of a large number of individual instructions which are executed one by one to operate on data. An individual instruction may require only a few microseconds to complete its function, and this operation time must include the time needed to transfer the instruction from memory to the *program controller* and to interpret and execute the instruction, including extracting the required *operands* from memory and storing away the result. Thus it can be seen that the memory must allow for the storage of a large number of instructions and operands, which must be available as required, at high speed. Reliable storage systems of this type are very expensive, and in the past it has been usual to build only the main memory to meet this requirement, utilizing various backing store devices to provide mass storage facilities. It is not unusual to have a computer with a main memory capacity of several million *bits*, but the earlier computers had a capacity of perhaps only 80,000 bits in their main memory. This increase in memory size has been made possible mainly by improved techniques and materials for constructing memory storage units.

The physical size of components is a very important factor in computer design, because in miniaturized circuits signals have to travel over very short distances and this enables high signal speeds to be obtained. For example, in some of the earlier core memories a core could be *switched* in about twenty microseconds whereas switching speeds of a few *nanoseconds* are possible with *integrated circuits*.

The earliest computers used thermionic valves and capacitors in the construction of the main memory and *logic circuits*. Such systems were expensive to manufacture and maintain, and the physical size of the components placed severe restrictions on the storage capacity and speed available. Also the power consumption of such memory units was high, and they required comprehensive cooling facilities.

The use of integrated circuits for memory devices and the spectacular advances in the manufacture of *silicon chips* brought about a rapid change in the development of computer memories. In the 1950s, computers were constructed of discrete semiconductor components known as transistors. Also, at this time, main memory units were constructed of magnetic cores. These components had to be physically wired on to circuit boards. Throughout the 1960s and 1970s great advances were made in development and manufacture of semiconductors, and now in the mid-1980s 1,000,000 semiconductor devices can be fitted on to a small piece of silicon measuring 5mm × 5mm, known as a *chip* or *integrated circuit* ⬦ *Very Large Scale Integration*. Main memory components are now constructed using such chips, and even desk top *personal computers* can contain 1,000,000 *bytes* of main memory.

The key attributes of main memory systems are: (i) *Access* to any word in the memory system is by a direct *addressing* technique in which each memory location has a numbered address. The addresses are represented and selected by means of electronic impulses and no physical movement of the storage medium is required. (ii) Access time is very short (say one nanosecond) and is constant for any item of data stored in the memory. (iii) Reliability is high. (iv) Power consumption is low. (v) The components are small and a comparatively small unit can provide a large storage capacity.

The systems described above are sometimes described as *immediate access stores*, but more properly may be described as *random access* memories, since it is possible for any unit of data to be available on demand at a guaranteed access time of very short duration. However the requirements of most modern digital computers are such that it is uneconomic to consider storing all data and program instructions in such a medium. Computers are instead designed to provide a certain volume of such storage, with backing storage facilities to hold millions more characters. At any moment in time the main memory is used to hold current data and instructions, and other data and program *segments* may be called in as *blocks* from backing store as required.

Backing storage usually consists of magnetic storage media such as *magnetic tape, magnetic drum, magnetic card* or *magnetic disk* storage. These are all in the general category known as *dynamic store*, because the storage medium has to be physically moved past a magnetic *read/write head* to obtain access to storage areas.

Magnetic tape is a *serial* store: data is recorded as individual characters along a length of tape and processing can be achieved only by sorting records into sequence so that each can be examined in turn (⬦ general article on Magnetic Tape).

A magnetic drum is a *cyclic* store; the drum is revolved continuously and data stored upon *tracks* around the periphery of the drum is available at fixed points in the basic cycle time. For example, if each track has a single read/write head the average access time for any unit of data is one half the time required to complete one drum revolution. A magnetic drum might have a capacity of millions of words and it is possible to connect several drums to a central processor. Operating at about 7000 revolutions per second a high speed drum might provide an average access time of a few milliseconds and have a transfer rate of millions of bits per second. Magnetic drums are usually associated with very large and powerful *main frame* computers. Perhaps the most common form of cyclic backing storage is the magnetic disk. These systems are found in use with *microcomputers, minicomputers* and mainframe computers. The disk subsystem is a most important element in a computer system and may represent up to 50 per cent of the cost of the computer system.

Small desk top microcomputers were first introduced using *floppy disks*. These are so called because they consist of flexible plastic material upon which data is recorded in tracks on a magnetizable surface. Prior to the emergence of floppy disk systems, so-called rigid or *hard disk* systems were in use. The floppy disk came into being with the development of microcomputers, where it provided a relevant economic solution and a convenient mode of operation for unskilled users. It is probable that floppy disks will be supplanted by small hard disk systems developed in recent years and which are referred to as mini-disks. Floppy disks are described here to illustrate the principles of disk operation. Hard disks will be considered later. The floppy disk (sometimes known as *diskette*) is in fact sealed into a square plastic case, although the diskette is indeed circular in shape. Sizes can vary, but 5¼ inch or 8 inch diameter disks are popular at the time of writing. A 5¼ inch disk can hold more than 1,000,000 bits of information recorded in a binary format as a series of magnetizable dots on the disk surface. Typically, the disk would include thirty-five recording tracks each divided into sixteen sectors, thus containing 2048 bits of information (i.e., 256 bytes per sector). The diskette is loaded into a floppy disk drive which may revolve at 360 rpm. To read or write to the disk a recording head has to move to the right track, select the sector required and read it into main memory. An average access time to retrieve a sector is in the order of 230 milliseconds.

Some floppy disks allow data to be recorded on both sides of the disk, and have a higher packing density than the one described above, e.g., giving up to 16,000,000 bits of information per disk. It is also possible to connect more than one drive to a single computer, thus increasing further the auxiliary storage capacity.

Hard disk systems have long been used with minicomputers and mainframe computers. It is only in recent years that these systems have been reduced in size and used with desk top computers. Today when we talk of hard disks, we may be referring to compact 8 inch disk systems storing, say, ten megabytes of information, to *Winchester disks*, or to very large fixed disk installations with hundreds of millions of bytes of storage.

Direct access devices, such as disk stores are a compromise to obtain, at an economic cost, certain of the qualities exhibited by main memories. In general the access time for any particular record is measured in milliseconds rather than microseconds and in many cases the access time is not entirely independent of the location last addressed. However, the maximum access time is sufficiently short to permit them to be considered as truly direct access devices. With these storage units programs can be organized to process data as it arises, and during such processing transactions can be applied to many *files* in the same *run* without the need to sort transactions into a specific sequence.

A typical magnetic disk store consists of a number of rotating disks each coated upon both surfaces with a magnetizable material. Information is written to, or read from, the disk by a series of arms, one for each disk surface. Each arm contains one, or several, read/write heads, and the arms can be positioned above certain areas of the corresponding disks according to instructions received from the central processor. Each disk surface usually contains a number of recording tracks and these may be further subdivided into sections or bands; the instructions from the central processor can cause the recording arms to be positioned to read or write from specified tracks. As with magnetic tape, information is generally recorded as a series of eight-bit characters each with an associated *parity bit*. A device of this type might hold several hundred million characters, and access time to any chosen bit might vary between 20 to 100 milliseconds.

Hard disk systems are generally more reliable than floppy systems. Some hard disks are sealed into the drive unit and can only be accessed physically by an engineer, for maintenance purposes. However, it is extremely inconvenient if one fails, because, unlike a floppy system, the disk cannot be stored off-line and thus any damage to its surface may cause permanent loss of data.

Operationally this can be offset by taking frequent copies of files to another disk or magnetic tape.

There is, however, another class of disk known as an *exchangeable disk*, in which information is recorded on *cartridges* which can be removed and stored *off-line* for security purposes.

Most computer systems are provided with a disk operating system (DOS), which takes care of the more complicated aspects of programming direct access systems and managing disk files.

The development of *optical storage* techniques has resulted in such direct access devices as *compact disk read-only memory* devices and *laser* cards and storage continues to grow less and less expensive.

In time we may expect a further breakthrough in the design and manufacture of integrated circuit techniques, or of bubble memories, but a continued dependence on auxiliary storage devices seems likely for many years to come.

storage, direct access   ◊ *direct access storage*.

storage, disk   ◊ *magnetic disk*.

storage, drum   ◊ *magnetic drum*.

storage dump   Synonymous with *memory dump*.

storage, dynamic   ◊ *dynamic store*.

storage, erasable   ◊ *erasable storage*.

storage, internal   ◊ *internal store*.

storage location   Synonymous with *location*.

storage, magnetic   ◊ *magnetic memory*.

storage, magnetic core   ◊ *magnetic core storage*.

storage, magnetic disk   ◊ *magnetic disk*.

storage, magnetic drum   ◊ *magnetic drum*.

storage, magnetic film   ◊ *thin-film memory*.

storage, magnetic tape   ◊ *magnetic tape*.

storage, main   ◊ *main memory*.

storage, mercury   ◊ *mercury memory*.

storage, non-erasable   ◊ *non-erasable store*.

storage, parallel search   ◊ *associative store*.

storage register   A *register* located in *store*. Contrasted with, for example, an *instruction register* which is located in the *program controller*.

storage, secondary   Synonymous with *backing store*.

storage, Williams tube   ◊ *Williams tube storage*.

store   1. Any device or medium which is capable of receiving information and retaining it over a period of time, and allows it to be retrieved and used when required. ◊ general article on *Storage Devices*. 2. To place information into a storage device.

store, cathode ray tube   ◊ *cathode ray tube*.

store, core ◊ *core storage*.

store cycle time The minimum time required to retrieve an item of data from *store*.

stored program A *program* which is wholly contained in *store*, and which is capable of being altered in store.

stored program computer Any computer which functions wholly or mainly with *instructions* which are held in *store*, and which can themselves be altered and manipulated in the same way as other data. The term computer now almost universally refers to stored program computer.

stored routine Synonymous with *stored program*.

store dump ◊ *dump*.

store, erasable ◊ *erasable storage*.

store, magnetic ◊ *magnetic memory*.

store, magnetic disk ◊ *magnetic disk*.

store, magnetic drum ◊ *magnetic drum*.

store, magnetic film ◊ *thin-film memory*.

store, magnetic tape ◊ *magnetic tape*.

store, magnetic wire ◊ *magnetic wire store*.

store, non-volatile ◊ *non-volatile memory*.

store, random access ◊ *random access storage* and *direct access*.

store, secondary Synonymous with *backing store*.

store, volatile Synonymous with *volatile memory*.

store, Williams tube ◊ *Williams tube storage*.

straight line coding Avoiding the use of loops during the *coding* of a program by repeating a set of *instructions* instead of *branching* repeatedly to the same set. The purpose of straight line coding is to improve the speed of execution of the program, since the use of a loop is usually slower because of *instruction modification*. ◊ general article on *Programming*.

stream A data *route* from a *resource* to a *controller*.

string 1. Any set of items which has been arranged into a *sequence* according to some specific order of *keys*. 2. Any set of consecutive *characters* or *digits* present in *store*.

string break In *sorting*, a string break occurs when there are no more *records* with *keys* higher than the highest key so far written to the current ouput *string*[1].

string length In *sorting*, the number of *records* in a *string*[1].

string manipulation The process of manipulating *strings*[2] of *characters* in *store*, treating them as single units of data.

structured programming A methodology for *programming* which involves a systematic procedure for describing the program's tasks in a series of stages or modules, each described in increasing detail until the final stage of coding is reached. A strict adherence to modules eliminates the need to use many *branch* or GOTO instructions, thus simplifying the task of program maintenance.

Also known as top down programming.

stunt box Part of a teleprinter which decodes signals used to control the operation of the machine, as contrasted with the information to be printed.

style In *optical character recognition*, the distinctive proportions of the characters which remain constant whatever the size of the character.

stylus input device Synonymous with *light pen*.

stylus, light pen ◊ *light pen*.

stylus printer A *printer* in which each character takes the form of a pattern of dots produced by a stylus or number of styluses moving over the surface of the paper.

Also known as wire printer.

subprogram ◊ general article on *multiprogramming*.

subroutine Part of a *program* which performs a logical section of the overall function of the program and which is available whenever the particular set of *instructions* is required. The instructions forming the subroutine do not need to be repeated every time they are required, but can be entered by means of a *branch* from the *main program*. Subroutines may be written for a specific program or they may be written in a general form to perform operations common to several programs. ◊ general articles on *Subroutines* and *Programming*.

subroutine library Any collection of *subroutines* which have been written for general application and can be incorporated in different *programs* when required.

subroutines Subroutines are self-contained sections of a *program* which can be incorporated into a complete program. A subroutine can be entered from any point in the main program and is usually so constructed that, when the subroutine has been obeyed, a return *branch* is automatically made to the instruction immediately following the branch into the subroutine. The actions performed by the subroutine may be modified by the use of *parameters*. Parameters may be specified in the main program by setting values into certain reserved *locations* or by setting up *dummy instructions* in the program area immediately following the branch to the subroutine. Also, the subroutine may be modified to return to an instruction other than the one immediately after the branch to the subroutine.

There are two main reasons for using subroutines:

(i) Certain routines are of a general nature and are common to many programs. For example, calculations of mathematical functions such as square roots, routines associated with the control of *input* and *output* *devices*. This type of subroutine is generally provided by the manufacturer as part of the *software* supplied with the computer.

(ii) Certain sections of a particular program may be required at several different points in the main program. Storage space can be saved by making these sections into subroutines, thus storing them only once instead of storing them separately each time they are required. Subroutines of this type are written by the programmer at the same time as the main program.

The object of a subroutine is thus:

(i) To make programming easier and quicker by incorporating pre-programmed and pre-tested subroutines, or

(ii) To save storage space by writing a section or program only once, and branching to it only when it is required in the main program.

Where a program is written using a programming *language*, a common feature of many *compilers* is the facility for incorporating subroutines of the first type into the *object program* by means of *source language statements*. The usual method is to incorporate all subroutines whether supplied by the manufacturer or developed by the user, on some form of backing store, e.g., a *magnetic disk*. The compiler then extracts the required subroutine from this medium when required by the source program. A collection of subroutines of this type is known as a *library* and a magnetic disk holding subroutines will be known as a *library disk*. However the terms library and library disk are also used for collections of *general purpose programs* and other items of software.

subscriber station In *data transmission*, the connexion provided for linking an outside location to a central office, including the connecting circuit and some circuit termination equipment, and sometimes also associated *input/output* equipment.

subscript A notation used to identify individual members of a set of items, usually by means of a number added to the name of the set, e.g., the members of the set of items named 'Invoices' could be given subscripts 1, 2, 3, etc., being identified as 'Invoice$_1$', 'Invoice$_2$', 'Invoice$_3$' etc. ⟨⟩ *array*.

subset 1. Any identifiable group of items which themselves belong to a larger grouping. 2. A contraction of the words *sub*scriber *set*; synonymous with *modem*.

subtracter A device performing the function of subtraction using digital signals. It receives three inputs representing *minuend, subtrahend* and a *carry* digit, and provides two outputs representing the *difference* and a *carry*.

subtracter-adder ◊ *adder-subtracter*.

subtraction An arithmetic operation in which one operand – the *subtrahend* – is subtracted from another – the *minuend* – to form the *difference*.

subtrahend In *subtraction*, the subtrahend is subtracted from the *minuend* to give the *difference*.

suite (of programs) A number of interrelated *programs* run one after the other as an operational job.

sum In *addition*, the *addend* and the *augend* are added to obtain the sum.

sumcheck To carry out a check using *checksums*.

sum-check digit A *check digit* produced by a *summation check*.

summary A *report* which omits details from each *record* processed but provides information derived from such details.

summary card A *punched card* containing totals and descriptive data resulting from an associated group of detail cards.

summary punch A *card punch*, directly under the control of a *tabulator*, used for punching *summary cards* from data processed by the tabulator.

summary punching Punching *summary* information from a *report* prepared by a *tabulator* or other machine on to *punched cards*, which could then be processed at a later time, either as additional data or as totals carried forward from one run to another.

summation check A *check* performed on a group of *digits* which consists of adding up all the digits in the set and comparing the result with a previously computed total. If *overflow* is ignored on performing the summation, so that the result is always a single digit, this digit can be used as a *check digit*, and is then known as a *sum-check digit*.

sum, modulo 2 ◊ *modulo 2 sum*.

supervising system ◊ *executive program*.

supervisor ◊ *supervisory program*.

supervisory control A *control system* in which information about the processes under control is provided at a central location but controlling action is taken by an operator.

supervisory program A master program permanently resident in the memory of a computer to control *time sharing, input/output* and

433

multiprogramming functions. Usually considered as an integral part of the computer and often classified as being part of the *hardware* of the system. ⟡ *executive program*.

supplementary maintenance Maintenance work which is not *routine maintenance* or *corrective maintenance*, usually undertaken in order to improve reliability of the equipment by minor modifications.

supplementary maintenance time Time spent on *supplementary maintenance*.

suppression Preventing the printing of certain selected *characters* when specified conditions occur. ⟡ *zero suppression*.

surveillance The process of monitoring any resource by means of *software*, as part of ensuring *security*.

swapping Synonymous with paging.

switch 1. Any device for opening, closing or directing an electric circuit. 2. To alter the state of a *bit* from 1 to 0 or 0 to 1. 3. In *programming*, a *branch instruction* which selects one of a number of alternative paths; the particular path chosen is determined by the setting of the switch, i.e., by the *modification* of the branch instruction or by giving a specified value, either manually or by *program*, to a *location* which is tested by the instruction.

switched circuit Circuits formed by activating switches[1] within an exchange to connect one set of lines with another, the connection being maintained until one part clears the circuit. Contrasted with *packet switching* and *message switching*.

switched-message network A *data transmission* system in which data can be communicated between any users of the network. The telex system is an example of a switched-message network.

switching centre In *data transmission*, the location where incoming messages are directed to their correct destinations. Switching may be automatic, in which case the *routing* is done without operator intervention, or semi-automatic or manual, involving some degree of operator intervention.

switching, message ⟡ *message switching system*.

symbol Any character, set of characters or figure conventionally or arbitrarily accepted as representing some quantity, process, instruction, data item or any other object, relationship or operation.

symbolic address The form an *address* takes in a *source language*, in which it can be represented by an arbitrary *label* chosen by the programmer. The address is translated into an *absolute address* when the program is *compiled*.

symbolic assembly-language listing A *printout*, which may be produced at the time a *source program* is *compiled*, which gives the *source language statements* together with the corresponding *machine coding* generated.

symbolic assembly system An automatic programming system embodying the use of an *assembly language* and an *assembly routine*.

symbolic code Synonymous with *symbolic instruction*.

symbolic coding Writing a program in a *source language*.

symbolic debugging A method of *debugging* in which certain *source language* statements can be *compiled* together with a *source program* containing known errors in order to correct the errors.

symbolic instruction An *instruction* in *source language* form.

symbolic language A programming *language* in which *instruction codes*, *data items* and *peripheral units* may be assigned *symbolic addresses*. Synonymous with *source language* and contrasted with *machine code*.

symbolic name A *label* used in *programs* written in a *source language* to reference *data elements, instructions, peripheral units*, etc. Symbolic names often make use of *mnemonic codes*.

symbolic programming Writing a program in a *source language*.

symbol table A *table* containing *symbols* and their interpretation.

symmetric difference Synonymous with *exclusive-or operation*.

sync bytes *Bytes* or units of information which precede transmission of data in *synchronous working* order to notify the receiving station that a signal is about to be transmitted so that receiver and transmitter can synchronize their respective clocks.

synchronizer A *storage device* which acts as a *buffer* to counteract the effects of transmitting data between devices which operate at different rates.

synchronous computer A computer in which the timing of all operations is controlled by equally spaced signals from a *clock*.

synchronous data transmission A system of high speed *data transmission*, in which *clocks* in receiving and transmitting *terminals* are synchronized by means of *sync bytes*. Contrasted with *asynchronous* data transmission.

synchronous working Performing a sequence of operations under the control of a cycle of equally spaced signals from a *clock*. Contrasted with *asynchronous working*.

sync pulse Synonymous with *clock pulse*.

syntax The rules which govern the structure of language statements; in particular, the rules for forming *statements* in a *source language* correctly.

synthesis The combination of separate things or concepts to form a complex whole. Contrasted with *analysis*.

synthetic address Synonymous with *generated address*.

synthetic language Synonymous with *source language*.

system Any group of objects related or interacting so as to form a unit. In *data processing* the objects which are interrelated will be individuals and machines, the purpose of their interacting being to achieve certain defined ends concerned with the manipulation of information, e.g., to produce a payroll. System can also be used to refer specifically to a particular interrelated collection of machines (in this sense, the term *configuration* is also used). ⚲ general article on *Systems Analysis*.

systematic error checking code A form of *error-detecting code* in which a valid *character* consists of a minimum number of *digits* required to identify the character, together with a *check digit* designed to maintain the minimum *signal distance* between characters as required by an error-detecting code. ⚲ *Hamming code*.

system chart Synonymous with *systems flowchart*.

system checks Checks which monitor the performance of a system, e.g., *control totals, record counts* and *hash* totals.

system control language ◊ *control language*.

system, ducol punched card ◊ *ducol punched card system*.

system failure ◊ *failure*.

system generation Use of a set of utility *programs*, including the *updating* and *maintenance* of system *libraries*.

system, hybrid computer ◊ *hybrid computer system*.

system, information ◊ *information system*.

system, information retrieval ◊ *information retrieval*.

system, management information ◊ *management information system*.

system, real time ◊ *real time*.

system reliability The ability of a *hardware* system to achieve its defined objectives. ◊ *reliability*.

systems analysis Systems analysis as an activity existed long before computers were invented: the art of analysing methods of doing things and designing and implementing new and better methods has been applied ever since mankind organized itself into social groups. Out of this organizing activity have developed the modern sciences of organization and methods (O & M), work study, systems engineering and other associated techniques.

The advent of computers produced a very powerful tool, capable of handling huge amounts of information at enormous speed. Systems analysis is the name given to the technique of determining how best to put this powerful tool to work.

This article gives a brief description of some of the aspects of systems analysis. The range of activities which come under this concept, however, is not clearly defined. Some of the activities described may be performed by an individual employed as a systems analyst: others may be considered to be more appropriate to a *programmer* or to an O & M expert. Nevertheless, the activities described are all concerned with using a computer efficiently and profitably: this is the ultimate aim of systems analysis.

The work of a systems analyst can be likened to that of an architect. In designing a building the architect must first of all determine in consultation with his client what the building is for: teaching, nursing, family living, etc. He must analyse the activities to be performed in the building: eating, sleeping, cooking, etc. He must then determine the physical limitations within which his design must come: costs, materials, dates. He then designs a solution to the problem: this solution must be communicated to the user, to the builder, to the contractor, to his clients. Once the design is approved, he must monitor progress on the building and alter designs if requirements change (although he will hope to have to do as little of this as possible). Finally, when the building is complete, he must satisfy himself that it conforms to his design and to the client's requirements. He can then have the satisfaction of seeing his design realized, and performing the function for which it was created.

This is only a rough analogy: but it illustrates the main functions of systems analysis: (i) definition of the problem; (ii) investigation of the working of existing systems; (iii) analysis of the results of the investigation so as to help determine the requirements of a new system; (iv) design of a new system that is practical and efficient and makes the best use of available *hardware* and *software*; (v) communication of the new system to all parties concerned; (vi) assistance in implementation of the new system and its maintenance thereafter.

Each of these functions will form part of the analysis of any particular system: however, the relative importance of each step and the responsibility for undertaking it may vary considerably from system to system. The following remarks outline briefly the methods adopted at each stage.

(i) Definition of the problem: Before embarking on a systems project a clear statement and understanding of the problem must be made: otherwise, the answer produced will not meet the needs that it is supposed to and the whole project may well prove to be abortive. Thus the first important task of a systems analyst is to obtain a definition of the problem. The subject of the project, and its boundaries, as well as the objectives and hoped-for benefits must be specified as precisely as possible in a written systems project assignment. This will be the result of cooperation between the 'clients' or users of the proposed new system and the staff to be involved in the design of the new system.

(ii) Investigation of the working of existing systems: This stage can be divided into an interim survey followed by a full scale systems investigation.

The purpose of an interim survey is to provide a guide from which to estimate the time needed for a full scale investigation and the resources required to carry the investigation out. The interim survey will normally cover the following points: volume of work; staff involved; time involved; costs of present system. The interim survey will not propose solutions but obtain facts highlighting areas for further investigation and defining the extent of the problem.

A full scale systems investigation can continue indefinitely: it is thus essential to plan such an investigation carefully, breaking it down into a series of separate projects. One approach to the problem is the systems project team. The investigation is planned as a series of tasks, each of which is given to a team to solve. The team is given precise terms of reference and a limit is set on the time for completion. Team members are taken from those closely involved in the subject under investigation, as well as systems specialists. In assigning tasks and breaking down a detailed investigation into separate projects it is essential to determine what facts are to be looked for, so that unnecessary detail is not included. *Documentation* of the results of the investigation is essential, and several techniques are available, such as systems *flowcharting, horizontal flowcharts* and *decision tables*. In carrying out a systems investigation it is not sufficient merely to record what is formally laid down in company rules or other documents as being the situation: neither is the correct picture necessarily obtained from what any individual says the situation is. The real situation must be discovered by patient observation and discussion. From the results of the investigation can be determined the best way of meeting the real needs of the system.

(iii) Analysis of results: Once the detailed systems investigation described above has been completed, the results obtained must be analysed so as to determine the weak points of the system investigated and the relation between the existing situation and the overall objectives of the new system. This stage attempts to produce answers to the following questions: Is the present system doing what it is supposed to do, in the time allowed, with the required accuracy and at reasonable cost? Is the organization of the system adequate to its task, and is the staff adequate? Are the documents used and produced necessary and are they efficiently designed? On the basis of answers to questions of this type the new system can be designed more effectively.

(iv) Design of new system: The designing of a new system is a creative function and, as such, difficult to define in detail. However, in designing a new system some of the following activities normally take place: (*a*) Re-appraise the original terms of reference of the investigation in the light of results so far obtained. (*b*) Reflect again on the results of the analysis of the existing system, particularly any weak points and any unexpected discoveries. (*c*) Determine precisely what output will be required from the new system and how it will be used. (*d*) Determine the *data items* required in order to produce the required output. (*e*) Decide on the medium and format of all *input* and *output files*, taking into account hardware and software availability and timing requirements. (*f*) Devise efficient methods for processing input to obtain output, making use of software available and defining any special programs required. (*g*) Devise an efficient method of *data collection*. This is particularly important, since the results produced by the system depend on how accurate, complete and up-to-date the raw data input to the system is. (*h*) Define in detail all the clerical procedures and documentation (e.g., *turn around documents, source documents*) required at the data capture stage. (*i*) Decide how the system is to cope with changes and modifications. No systems design is perfect, nor can an analyst predict completely the requirements of any system in the future. Thus as much flexibility as possible must be incorporated into all parts of the system. This can be done using general purpose software (e.g., applications software, file processing programs) or by specifying programs which can be modified by means of variables input from *parameters*.

(v) Documentation: The general articles on *Documentation* describe the documentation which must accompany any new system. Such documentation is essential: *a*. As a record of agreement on all decisions. *b*. As a method of communication between the analyst and the programmers responsible for preparing all programs required. *c*. As a method of communication between the analyst and those responsible for operating the system, both the user and the specialist data processing personnel. The documentation should be signed as agreed by the users, the programming staff and also representatives of company auditors and accountants.

(vi) Implementation: Before a new system is finally operational, several stages of testing must take place. The first step is the detailed testing of individual programs, for which the systems analyst will provide *test data* and schedules of expected results.

Once the individual programs of the system have been proved correct against test data, the system as a whole must be tested, to ensure that all procedures, manual, off-line and on-line are working as planned. This form of test requires some simulation of the 'real life' situation. This can be achieved on a limited basis by means of a pilot scheme, where one small but representative area of the system is used to test the new procedures before these are extended to other areas. This may be sufficient test of procedures: but in some cases, full *parallel running* will be required. This means that the new procedures are operated at the same time as the procedures they are designed to replace. The results obtained by the two systems are compared and the old system dispensed with when the new one is operating successfully.

The pilot scheme and parallel run steps are also used to try out the provisions made for auditing and controlling the operations of the new system, so that control is established over the full implementation of the system.

A major function of implementing a new system is ensuring that all documentation is accurate and up to date. And modifications made to a system in the light of testing or operational experience must pass through the same acceptance and audit procedures as the original system. The analyst must ensure that this documentation is maintained accurately and is always up to date.

(vii) Conclusions: This article has discussed in general terms some of the activities involved in systems analysis. Great emphasis is laid on the necessity for the analysis of a system to be complete and thorough. However, too great a rigidity in a system can prove fatal to its ultimate effectiveness. Any worthwhile system must be capable of being changed without involving a complete revision of all that has gone before. With the increasing availability of general purpose application-oriented software the task of the analyst is considerably eased. By definition, general purpose software is designed to be used in a large number of related applications which differ in detail. Thus a system making use of such software will be more flexible than one using specially devised routines. Software is designed to be modified, whereas single-purpose routines generally will do one job only, and cannot easily be modified.

Thus the task of a systems analyst is as much to forecast how the system and its requirements will change, as it is to define the specific requirements of the system at a fixed point in time. *Telecommunications* systems by which the user is able to interrogate a computer, and control the input and output from it directly, mean that the systems analyst is less an intermediary between a user and the mysterious world of the computer, and more a teacher, explaining how to use and control a powerful tool in the simplest and most efficient manner.

systems analyst ⟡ general article on *Computer Personnel.*

systems definition The document produced by a *systems analyst* which defines in detail the system he has designed. This document explains all clerical procedures and includes *program* specifications.

Also known as systems specification. ⟡ general articles on *Documentation – Systems* and *Systems Analysis.*

systems design The investigation and recording of existing *systems* and the design of new systems. ⟡ general article on *Systems Analysis.*

systems flowchart A *flowchart* in which the *flowchart symbols* represent specific clerical, *data preparation* and computer procedures which are combined in *systems design.*

Also known as flow-process diagram, process chart. Contrasted with *program flowchart.* ⟡ general article on *Flowcharting.*

systems network architecture A *data network protocol* developed by IBM as a standard means of interconnecting *terminals* with *host processors* and allowing the sharing of separate *applications* in the host processor.

systems recovery time The period spent on recovery. Also known as *rerun time.*

systems, inquiry and communications ⟡ *inquiry and communications systems.*

systems specification Synonymous with *systems definition.*

system structure ⟡ general article on *Systems Analysis.*

system, time-sharing monitor ⟡ *time-sharing monitor system.*

table An *array* of data in *memory*, or on some other storage medium, which is so organized that individual items may be retrieved by the specifying of *keys*[1] stored as part of each item. Sometimes items may be located by specifying their position in the table.

table look-at The process whereby items in a *table* are obtained by calculation. That is, an *algorithm* is used to locate the position of the item in the table, rather than employ a search as in *table look-up*.

table look-up 1. A method of obtaining a function value from a *function table* corresponding to a specified *argument*. 2. Any method of searching a *table* to locate items relevant to a specified *key*.

table look-up instruction A *basic instruction* which may be modified to refer to data arranged in a *table*. An instruction used to search for an item containing a nominated *key*.

tablet Synonymous with *pad*.

tabular language A system for specifying programming requirements in terms of *decision tables*, in which the tables fulfil the role of a *problem-oriented programming language*.

tabulate 1. The accumulation of totals for groups of items, each group consisting of items bearing a common *key*. 2. On a *punched card tabulator*, the printing of totals for groups of cards, each line of totals being initiated by a change of *control data* between the end of one group and the beginning of the next.

tabulation 1. A printed report produced on a *punched card tabulator* consisting of *totals only*. 2. The automatic movement of the carriage of a typewriter or teleprinter through a series of specified positions in a succession of print lines.

tabulation character A *character* forming part of some data to be printed but which is not itself printed and instead is used to control the format of the printed output, e.g., to cause a throw to the next line; or, on a teleprinter, to initiate the *carriage return* function. A member of the set of characters known as *format effectors*.

tabulator A machine which was the heart of *punched card* systems. It automatically fed punched cards, reading data from them to be directly *listed* and/or accumulated for the printing of totals at the end of certain card *groups*.

tag 1. A collection of *characters* or *digits* attached to a *record* as a means of identification. 2. A short *record* inserted in a location of a *direct access file* to retrieve an *overflow record*. The tag usually consists of the *key* for the *overflow record* plus the current *address* of that *record*. 3. A perforated price tag which is attached to goods and which can be removed at point of sale and used in an *automatic processing system*.

tag converting unit A machine for reading *tags*[3] and for transfering the data thus sensed into some other medium such as *magnetic disk*. Some tag readers provide for direct input to computer *memory*.

tag format The layout and design of a *record* used as a *tag*[2] to locate an *overflow bucket*.

takedown The process of removing *magnetic tapes, punched cards, paper tape* and *printouts* from *peripherals* at the end of a computer *run* or suite of runs. To clear the equipment ready for *loading* the next job.

takedown time The time required to complete a *takedown* operation.

tally A printed list of figures produced on an adding machine.

tally reader A machine that can read data as printed characters from a *tally* list; e.g., by means of *optical character recognition*.

tandem system A system in which two *hardware* units are used to fulfil some processing operation. For example, some processing applications require the use of two *processors*, one acting as a slave performing routine processing operations under the control of the master processor.

tank Sometimes used as a colloquialism for *mercury delay line*.

tape A continuous strip of material for recording data, e.g., *paper tape* or *magnetic tape*.

tape alteration A process, achieved under *program* control or by operator intervention, whereby a program can be made to switch from one *tape deck* to another to minimize the time delay in changing from one *reel* to another when processing a *multi-reel file*.

tape bootstrap routine A *bootstrap* routine present in the first *block* of a *program tape*. When the routine is read into *store* it reads specified programs from the tape: it may also contain other *utility programs*.

tape, chadded paper ⋄ *chadded tape*.

tape, chadless paper ⋄ *chadless tape*.

tape cluster Synonymous with *magnetic tape group*.

tape code, paper ⋄ *paper tape code*.

tape comparator A machine that automatically compares two *paper tapes* which have been prepared from identical *source documents*. The tapes are compared *character* by character and the machine stops if a discrepancy is detected; if no errors are detected the initial preparation is assumed to have been correctly completed. In most systems of this sort a third tape is automatically produced as the comparison takes place. In the event of a discrepancy the operator can enter correct characters from a *keyboard*.

tape controlled carriage An *automatic carriage* which is activated under the control of a loop of paper or mylar plastic into which holes have been punched to provide a *program* for automatically feeding the stationery.

tape core A *magnetic core* constructed using a length of ferromagnetic tape wound as a spiral.

tape deck A device consisting of a *tape transport mechanism* for handling *magnetic tape*, along with an associated *read head* and *write head*. Sometimes a single tape deck is mounted in a free-standing unit, a number of which may be connected to a *central processor*. More often a number of decks, say four or six, are mounted in a single unit known as a *tape group*.

tape drive Used loosely as a synonym for a *magnetic tape deck*, but more accurately refers to the *tape transport mechanism* only. Also used to describe the mechanism that feeds *paper tape* in an automatic *paper tape punch* or *paper tape reader*.

tape feed A mechanism forming part of a *paper tape reader* or *paper tape punch*. That part of the machine which can feed *paper tape* to be read or punched.

tape file Synonymous with *magnetic tape file*; a series of *records* arranged sequentially on *magnetic tape*.

tape group A single unit containing two or more *tape decks*.
Also known as cluster. ◊ *magnetic tape group*.

tape labels Special *records* appearing at the beginning and end of a *reel* of *magnetic tape* to provide details about the *file* of *records* stored on the tape. ◊ *header label* and *trailer label*.

tape library ◊ *magnetic tape library*.

tape mark 1. A special *character* recorded on a *file* of *magnetic tape* in order to subdivide the file into sections. A tape mark is usually followed by a *record* providing descriptive data concerning the particular section of the file. Also known as control mark. 2. A special character that indicates the physical end of a *reel* of tape. In this sense, also known as *end of tape marker*.

tape, master instruction ◊ *master instruction tape*.

tape, perforated ⬦ *punched tape*.

tape plotting system A system for driving a *digital incremental plotter* from data recorded on *magnetic tape* or *paper tape*.

tape processing simultaneity Pertaining to a *time sharing system* in which several *magnetic tape decks* may be activated to *read* or *write* data at the same time while continuing to process data in the *central processor*. ⬦ *time sharing*.

tape punch A device for punching holes in *paper tape*; the term was generally used to denote a *keyboard* operated unit. Contrasted with *automatic tape punch* which refers to a unit that could be connected to a *central processor* or any communications circuit to punch data received from a channel.

Also known as paper tape punch.

tape punch, automatic ⬦ *automatic tape punch*.

tape, punched ⬦ *paper tape*.

tape reader A device which reads *data* recorded as holes punched in *paper tape*.

tape reader, magnetic ⬦ *magnetic tape reader*.

tape reproducer A device used to copy data from one length of *paper tape* to another. It could also incorporate facilities to enable the operator to interrupt this process in order to insert new data from a *keyboard* on to the tape thus produced.

tape serial number An identification number, usually recorded on a tape *header label*, which is allotted to a new *magnetic tape* and remains unchanged through the life of the tape even though all other identifying information (e.g., *file name, reel number*) may change.

tape sort A computer operation in which a *file* of data held on *magnetic tape* is sorted into sequence according to a *key* contained in each *record* of the file. ⬦ general article on *Sorting*.

tape splicer ⬦ *splicer*.

tape station Synonymous with *magnetic tape deck*.

tape thickness The least of the cross-sectional dimensions of a piece of *paper tape* or *magnetic tape*. Contrasted with *tape width*.

tape transport 1. The mechanism that drives a *reel* of *magnetic tape* past the *read* and *write* heads on a *tape deck*. Also known as magnetic tape drive. 2. A mechanism for driving *paper tape* through a *punching station* or *sensing station*.

tape transport mechanism Part of a *magnetic tape deck*; the mechanism that drives and controls the movement of *magnetic tape* past a *read* or *write* head.

445

tape unit Usually means a single *magnetic tape deck* and its associated control circuitry, but sometimes used as a synonym for *magnetic tape group* to mean two or more tape decks housed in a single cabinet.

tape verifier A device for checking the accuracy of data punched into *paper tape*. In one *data preparation* system the operator enters data from *source documents* to a *keyboard*, and the device automatically compares the *data* with holes previously punched into a paper tape by another operator. ⬦ *data preparation*.

tape width A piece of *paper tape* or *magnetic tape* has two cross-sectional dimensions: the greater of these is the tape width (the other being the *tape thickness*).

tape wound core A *magnetic core* made from a coil of ferromagnetic tape.

tapped potentiometer function generator A device, used on *analog computers* for generating functions of one variable, in which the input variable sets the angular position of a potentiometer shaft. A number of taps along the potentiometer are positioned to represent the table of values for the function.

target computer The specification of the particular system required for running a particular *object program*.
Also known as target machine.

target configuration Same as *target computer*, but referring to the particular combination of *peripheral units* and the number of *memory locations* needed to run a particular *object program*.

target language Synonymous with *object language*.

target machine Synonymous with *target computer*.

target phase During *compilation*, the phase at which the *object program* is first run.

target program Synonymous with *object program*.

tariff The charging scheme applied by *network* operators (usually national *PTTs*), covering both data and voice transmission, and *packet switch* charges.

teaching machines Traditional teaching methods rely on teachers and textbooks and both have their drawbacks: in a typical classroom or lecture, a teacher stands in front of a number of pupils and talks; this can be a one-way process with information being transmitted but with little indication of how well it is being received (particularly if the number of pupils is large). Often the teaching rate will be too fast for some students, who will become confused, and too slow for others, who will become bored.

The use of textbooks also has deficiencies. Like the lecturer, the textbook can make little provision for response on the part of the student. However, response is considered to play a vital role in learning, with the corollary that poor response should be immediately picked up so that remedial action can be taken.

Teaching machines have the following features:

(a) There is continuous and active response to each unit of information presented, e.g., questions are asked before the student moves on to new material.

(b) There is immediate feedback to the student's responses, e.g., he is told whether his answers were right or wrong.

(c) The student can work at his own pace and teaching material presented can be varied to suit individual capabilities.

A teaching machine consists of two elements, the *program* and the *hardware*. The program is of particular importance, since this is what does the teaching. Hardware used may range from interactive *on-line* computers to sheets of paper printed and bound in a special way (i.e., a special sort of book).

Computer teaching programs may be one of three varieties: linear programs, branching programs or a mixture of both.

All programs consist of a number of *frames* which present a unit of information and request a response from the student.

Linear programs are based on the operant theory of learning which has had considerable influence in the field. The typical unit of information consists of one or two sentences followed by a sentence containing blanks. The student's response consists of filling in the blanks with words, phrases or numbers. This is known as a constructed response. Once the student has made his response the right answer is revealed to him. Progress through the program is linear in the sense that one frame follows another in sequence, although there may be some provision for skipping some frames for able students, or going back to earlier frames for revision.

Branching programs have rather larger units of information, perhaps two or three paragraphs. Having read the frame the student responds by answering a multiple choice question. According to the answer he gives the student branches to another part of the program. The main path of a branching program is the path that a student follows if he always answers questions correctly. Branches off the main path are provided to give remedial teaching to those who answer questions incorrectly. Thus different students may see different sequences of information.

It is impossible to describe the whole range of teaching machines here, but the basic elements of most teaching machines can be outlined as a storage unit to hold the program, a display mechanism and a method of inputting response.

Computers are used at the heart of such units as language laboratories, where the main objective is to provide individual attention at the student's own pace. The student sits at a console (which may be a two-way typewriter or a *visual display unit*), receives instructions from the computer and types back a response. Interaction between student and machine is controlled by a program with the textual material for display called in from *backing store* rather than residing permanently in *memory*. In this way a large number of pupils can receive what amounts to individual attention from a teaching machine which has a particular eye for their problems and which is never impatient or forced to leave one pupil behind for the benefit of the others.

telecommunication The transmission and reception of data over radio circuits or transmission lines by means of electromagnetic signals. Telecommunications facilities have been used to extend the use of computers far beyond the boundaries of the computer room and *distributed* computing was made possible by the convergence of computing and communications.

teleconference The interconnexion of a number of end users through a telephone and/or *data network*, so that information can be shared in *real time*. Voice teleconference can be enhanced by the addition of *terminals* allowing the exchange of text and graphics and *telewriting*, and by the addition of pictures (video teleconferencing).

telegraphic communication Communication by means of signals in an on/off mode. For example, the earliest telegraph systems were operated by a manual key which interrupted current in a circuit to produce audible clicks for a distant operator. This technique was developed and the teleprinter (and associated equipment) emerged as the principal device for this form of communication. In this system the teleprinter is able to generate and respond to coded signals in which combinations of on/off pulses are used to represent numeric or alphabetic characters. Modern *multiplexing* techniques have largely invalidated the earlier distinction between telegraphic and *telephonic communication*. ⋄ *data transmission*.

telemeter Equipment for recording and transmitting measurements as data to a distant location by electromagnetic waves.

telemetering The recording and transmitting of measurements and data by electromagnetic means and the reception of such data at a distant point.

telephone data set A unit used to connect a *data terminal* to a telephone circuit, e.g., to transmit data from the terminal to a processing centre. A telephone data set converts signals from the terminal into a form suitable for transmission over a telephone circuit, and vice versa.

telephonic communication A method of communication in which signals are transmitted by electrical tones of different frequency over a *communications link*. In relation to *electronic data processing* this form of communication permits data to be transmitted at very high speed and by the use of *multiplexing* techniques several signals can be transmitted over a single channel. ◊ *data transmission, modem.*

teleprinter A device resembling a typewriter which can be connected to a *communications link* to receive or transmit data from and to a distant point. Incoming signals may be received on a print unit forming part of the teleprinter, and on some machines the incoming signals may also be automatically recorded on *paper tape*. Outgoing messages may be entered on a *keyboard* and, on some teleprinters, may be transmitted automatically by the passing of a message tape through a paper tape reading unit. Teleprinters are sometimes used for direct *input/output* to a *central processor*.

teleprocessing A term registered by IBM used to describe systems in which remote locations are connected to a central computer by *data transmission* circuits. For example, to facilitate the direct *on-line* control of industrial processes or of commercial systems.

teleprocessing monitor A *software package* which provides a set of facilities designed to assist the development and operation of complex *on-line* and *real-time applications*. The teleprocessing monitor (TPM) acts as an *interface* between user application and the *operating system* of the computer.

telesoftware The transmission of *software* from a central *store* or data base to a local *processor* over a *telecommunication network*, e.g., the telephone system. Once the software has been downloaded, the processor can operate the *programs* locally.

teletex An advanced form of *telex* service which interconnects *terminals* providing *word-processing* facilities, such as use of upper and lower case characters, and *text editing* commands. Not to be confused with *teletext*.

teletext A method of communicating information by using television signals. A normal TV picture is composed of a number of lines; some of these lines are not used to convey picture data, and the signal capacity of these lines is used to carry codes which can be decoded by a simple adaptor to the TV set and displayed on the screen instead of, or superimposed over, the TV image. In the UK, teletext services are provided by *Ceefax* (BBC) and *Oracle* (ITV). Not to be confused with *teletex*. ⇨ *videotex*.

teletext decoder A device which detects *teletext* signals on a TV broadcast and converts them into a text and graphics image displayed on the television screen.

teletext editing terminal A device for creating the text and graphics codes for a teletext transmission.

teletext standards The published *character codes* and *transmission* standards for a *teletext* system. The British *Ceefax* and *Oracle* teletext services use an *alphamosaic* standard.

Teletype The trademark of the Teletype Corporation of the USA, often used generally when referring to equipment or systems of *telegraphic communication*.

teletype grade A grade of circuit suitable for the transmission of signals for *telegraphic communication*.

teletype input/output unit A telegraphic terminal device specifically used for connexion to a central computer; e.g., a *teleprinter* used as an *input/output* unit.

teletypewriter A telegraphic terminal device, resembling a typewriter, used to transmit and receive messages in a telegraphic communications system. ⋄ *teleprinter*.

telewriting The use of computer *graphics* techniques to transmit handwriting and drawings in *real time* between communicating *terminals*, when the writing is created by use of a *light pen* or *graphics pad*.

telex An automatic exchange service provided for communication between subscribers using telegraphic equipment such as *teleprinters*.

template A specification of a structure which allows programmes to declare their own data types.

temporary storage *Storage locations* which have been reserved, during the operation of a particular *program*, for storing *intermediate results*.

ten position ⋄ *X-position*.

tens complement A number produced by subtracting from nine each digit of a number whose *radix* is ten and then adding one to the *least significant position*. For example, the tens complement of 291 is 709. ⇨ *radix complement*.

tera Prefix denoting one million million or 10^{12}.

terminal A device at which *data* may be input to or output from a *data communications* system. *Visual display units* are often known as terminals.

 Also known as *data terminal*.

terminal, data communication ⋄ *data communication terminal.*

terminal, job-oriented ⋄ *job-oriented data terminal.*

terminal, multiplex-data ⋄ *multiplex-data terminal.*

terminal symbol A symbol on punched *paper tape* to indicate the end of a *record* or some other unit of information.

terminal user A person using a *terminal*. Also known as transactor.

termination Conclusion of a series of actions. ⋄ *abnormal termination.*

ternary Pertaining to three. The ternary system of *number representation* uses the three *digits* 0, 1 and 2 to represent numbers expressed using a base or *radix* of 3. For example the number 5 is represented as 12.

ternary incremental representation Pertaining to *digital integrators*; a method of *incremental representation* in which increment values are rounded off as either $+1$, -1 or zero.

test To examine an element of data or an *indicator* to ascertain whether some predetermined condition is satisfied.

testbed A *software* system designed to simplify the testing of *programs* by providing *test data* and diagnostic information. ⋄ general article on *Modular Programming.*

test, crippled leapfrog ⋄ *crippled leapfrog test.*

test data Sample data, covering as many likely and unlikely combinations as reasonable, prepared as input to test a *program*. Expected results are also prepared and compared with the results produced by the computer.

testing envelope *Software* which provides an environment for the testing of a *program* or a *program module*. ⋄ general article on *Modular Programming.*

test pack A *pack* of *punched cards* containing both *program* and *test data* for a *test run*.

test program A *program* designed to check the correct functioning of the *hardware* units of a computer. It may also identify particular kinds of fault, but ⋄ *diagnostic program.*

test routine ⋄ *test program.*

test run A test, performed to check that a particular *program* is operating correctly, in which *test data* is used to generate results for comparison with expected answers.

text The information element of any message, excluding those *characters* or *bits* required to facilitate the transmission of the message.

text editing Facilities provided in a *word processing* system which allow the user to insert and delete words and lines, and manipulate complete sections of text by changing their location within a document.

thin-film memory An *internal storage* medium consisting of a thin layer (a few millionths of an inch thick) of magnetic substance deposited on a plate of non-magnetizable material such as glass. The film can be polarized for the representation of *digital* information, enabling data to be written or retrieved at speeds measured in *nanoseconds*. This type of *memory* has the characteristics necessary for miniaturized components which can operate at very fast processing speeds.

text editor *Software* which provides a range of facilities for text editing. ⟨⟩ *editor*.

third generation computers Machines built with *integrated circuits*. Related to *first generation, second generation* and *fourth generation*. ⟨⟩ *fifth generation*.

third party maintenance The maintenance of computer equipment by specialist organizations as an alternative to having a maintenance contract with the equipment manufacturer.

thrashing An error condition occurring with *virtual storage* systems, where the *processor* time becomes completely occupied with *paging tasks* to the exclusion of any processing.

thread A group of *beads*.

three address instruction An *instruction* in which three *addresses* are specified as part of the *instruction format*. When arithmetic operations are performed, one *location* will be used to contain the *result*, the other two containing *operands* to be used in the process.

three-input adder A *logic element* employed for performing *addition* using *digital* input signals. It will accept three input signals (representing digits of *addend, augend* and *carry*) and will produce two output signals, representing a *carry digit* and a digit for the *sum*.

three-input subtracter A *logic element* used for performing subtraction with *digital signals*. It will accept three input signals (*minuend, subtrahend* and *borrow*) and will produce two output signals representing a digit to be borrowed in the next *digit position* and a digit for the *difference*.

three-level subroutine A *subroutine* in which entry is made to a second, lower level, subroutine, from which a further entry is made to a third level.

threshold A specified value established to control the output from a *threshold element*.

threshold element A *logic element* having one output signal but several input signals, each given a specified weight. The output signal is dependent on the input signals being greater or less than some given value, known as the *threshold*. For example, in a *majority element*, if all *n* inputs are weighted as 1, the output is dependent on threshold equal to $(n+1) \div 2$.

throughput The productivity of a machine, system or procedure, measured in some terms meaningful to the process under consideration. For example, a payroll system may deal with 100 employee records per minute; an *information retrieval* system might handle 10,000 inquiries per hour.

tie-line A leased communications channel operating between two private branch exchanges.

tightly coupled twin One of two *processors* using separate *operating systems* but able to share *data* and *code* via an inter-processor *buffer* and to control access to *backing store* without mutual interference. Contrasted with *loosely coupled twin*.

time-derived channel A channel obtained by *multiplexing* several signals over a single channel, in such a way that each signal is separated from any other by time.

time-division multiplexing A system whereby a channel is made available to a number of terminal devices each occupying the channel for the transmission of *data* for short periods at regular intervals. The effect is such that all terminals appear to transmit simultaneously over one channel. ⟨⟩ *time sharing*.

time division multiplier An *analog* unit used for multiplication, in which there are two input variables and a single output. One input variable is used to control the amplitude of a square wave, while the other variable controls the *mark-to-space ratio* of the wave form. The output voltage is smoothed to derive the average value of the output as a product. Same as *mark-space multiplier*.

time, fault ⟨⟩ *down time*.

time, latency ⟨⟩ *waiting time*.

time, machine-spoilt ⟨⟩ *machine-spoilt work time*.

time, mean repair ⟨⟩ *mean repair time*.

time-of-day clock An electronic device which registers the time in hours, minutes and seconds over a 24-hour cycle, and which will transmit a signal to the *central processor* on request so that events can be logged. ⟨⟩ *timer clock*.

time origin A reference point during the generation of a pulse, i.e., the point at which the pulse reaches a certain percentage, usually ten per cent, of its full amplitude. All subsequent events related to that pulse are measured over time with respect to the time origin. ⟨⟩ *reference time*.

time, program development ⟨⟩ *program development time*.

time, program testing ⊳ *program testing time*.

timer An automatic timing device that provides clock signals within a *central processor*, for example, to register *elapsed time* for an event in millisecond increments. ⊳ *timer clock*.

timer clock An electronic device used for timing events that occur during the operation of a computer system. Situated in the *central processor*, it can provide data for charging out computer time, monitor operations to detect looping and similar error conditions and provide time in hours and minutes for maintaining an operating log.

time, routine maintenance ⊳ *routine maintenance time*.

time scale (factor) The ratio between the time for an event as simulated with an *analog device* and the actual duration of time for the event in the physical system under study. ⊳ *slow time scale* and *fast time scale*.

time, scheduled engineering ⊳ *scheduled engineering time*.

time series Data transmitted as a series of discrete elements distributed over time. Quantitative values are assigned to specific instants in the time series.

time shared input/output system A computer system in which independent *peripheral units* may be activated simultaneously under control of the *central processor* which shares its time in accepting or transmitting data to the peripheral units. At the same time the central processor may continue to process data internally by *time sharing* one or more *programs*.

time shared system Any system in which *hardware* is used more efficiently by using *time sharing* techniques to facilitate concurrent operations. For example, in a *multiprogramming computer*, several *programs* may be processed concurrently by switching from one to another in a fixed sequence to permit a certain number of *instructions* to be performed on each occasion. In some systems programs are given priorities before being loaded into the *central processor*, so that a program of highest priority is activated continuously until it is held up, say, for data from a *peripheral unit*, whereupon the program with next highest priority is activated.

time sharing A system in which a particular device is used for two or more concurrent operations. Thus the device operates momentarily to fulfil one purpose then another, returns to the first, and so on in succession until the operations are completed. This activity is performed at high speed according to a strict sequence, each independent operation being executed as a series of finite steps.

time sharing dynamic allocator An *executive program* which controls the activation of independent programs in a *multiprogramming* or *time sharing* system. This type of program also allocates storage *areas* and *peripheral units* to any program entering the system, and when a program is deleted it re-allocates storage for the remaining programs to ensure that the largest possible area of contiguous locations remains available for another program.

time sharing monitor system An *executive program* consisting of a number of routines which coordinate the operation of a *time sharing* computer, including the automatic switching from one program to another in a *multiprogramming* system and the control of all input/output operations so that several *peripheral units* may be operated concurrently while data is processed in the *central processor*.

time slicing Synonymous with *time sharing*.

time, start ⟡ *acceleration time*.

time study When the optimum method of performing an operation has been determined through method study the work content of that operation may be established by work measurement, which essentially determines the time required to carry out the operation to a specified standard of performance by a qualified worker. This enables standards of machine utilization and labour performance to be set. These standards have a number of applications: determining the manning necessary; providing the proper basis for incentive schemes; planning and controlling production; and establishing selling prices and delivery promises.

The main techniques of work measurement are time study, synthesis (from standard data, such as predetermined motion time standards) and analytical estimating. Time study is generally appropriate only for repetitive work and differs from the other two in that the time for an operation is determined by means of direct observations. An accurate specification of the operation must be recorded, including the method to be used and all relevant conditions. The operation is broken down into its constituent elements and times for each are obtained with a stopwatch.

These recorded times by themselves are not sufficient as a measure of the work content of the operation. It is necessary to take account of the effectiveness of the speed and effort employed, and to give this a numerical value by mentally comparing it with a standard of effectiveness. This process is known as rating, and the standard rate of working (usually taken as 100 rating) is defined as that corresponding to the average rate at which qualified workers will naturally work on the operation, providing they know and adhere to the specified method and provided they are motivated to apply themselves to their work. A basic (or normalized) time can thus be obtained for each element:

$$\text{basic time} = \text{observed time} \times \frac{\text{observed rating}}{\text{standard rating}}$$

Thus basic time is independent of the operator observed and is a genuine measure of the work content.

The basic time accounts only for the productive part of the work cycle, and allowances must be added for non-productive time. A process allowance is necessary if the operator is forced to be idle during part of the cycle owing to unbalanced work of men and machines; a rest allowance is given for recovery from the physical and mental stresses that may be involved; a synchronization allowance, to compensate for natural interference of men and/or machines; and a contingency allowance, to cover any irregular small delays whose precise measurement is uneconomic.

Careful assessment of the value for each allowance is made in the light of the work and conditions involved. The addition of these values to the basic time gives the standard (or allowed) time for the operation.

time, supplementary maintenance   ⋄ *supplementary maintenance time.*

timing considerations   The economics of designing a *file* or a system expressed in terms of the machine time or the overall *throughput* speed for a *run* or series of runs.

timing error   An error made in designing a *program*; e.g., one in which, when designing the program, the programmer has underestimated the time allotted for an *input/output* operation, as a consequence of which unnecessary delays are incurred during processing.

TLU   Abbreviation of *table look-up.*

toggle   A circuit or device which must always assume one of two stable states. ⋄ *flip-flop.*

toggle switch   A manually operated switch which can be set to either of two positions.

torn-tape   *Paper tape* which had been torn from a *paper tape punch* on receipt at a *switching centre* so that it could be taken to a transmitting *paper tape reader.*

torn-tape switching centre   ⋄ *switching centre.*

torsional mode delay line   A *delay line* in which mechanical vibrations are propagated by subjecting a material to torsion, with the object of introducing a specific delay in the transmission of a signal.

totals only   Describes the printing of a report using a *punched card* *tabulator*, or a computer *printer*, in such a manner that for specified groups of cards or input *records* totals only were printed; i.e., data from the individual records was not listed directly but was accumulated and printed when a *control change* took place.

total system A complete system of clerical and computer procedures embracing all the main activities of a particular company or organization. An integrated network of subsystems comprising all the data processing activities of an organization.

total time The total time available for utilization of a particular computer installation, including all *attended time* and *unattended time*.

total transfer A method for accumulating minor, intermediate and major *control totals* (⟡ *control data*) when preparing printed results on a *punched card* tabulator. The minor total was accumulated directly from a card *field* and higher levels of totals were created by accumulating from minor to intermediate, and from intermediate to major totals.

touch screen ⟡ *touch sensitive screen*.

touch sensitive screen A visual display unit which has superimposed over the screen surface a device (usually consisting of a pattern of infra-red light sensors) which can detect the location on the screen of a touch, and can cause software to be activated according to the location 'touched', e.g., for *menu selection*.

TP Abbreviation of *transaction processing*.

TPM Abbreviation of *teleprocessing monitor*.

trace program A *diagnostic program* used to check and locate errors in other programs. The output from the trace program may consist of selected *instructions* from the program being checked, as well as results obtained during the operation of the instructions.

trace routine Synonymous with *trace program*.

trace statement A statement available as part of the *source coding* for certain *programming languages*, enabling specified *segments* of a *source program* to be checked at the *source language* level.

track 1. A channel on a *magnetic memory* device for recording data, e.g., the tracks on a *magnetic disk*. 2. One of the longitudinal channels for recording data as holes punched in *paper tape*, e.g., 6-track tape.

trackball A palm-sized ball mounted so that it can spin freely, used to control the movement of a *cursor* on a *visual display unit*.

track labels Special *records* used to identify *tracks* on a *magnetic storage* medium; e.g., on a *magnetic card file* a card/track number might be used as a label at the beginning of each track of each card.

track pitch The physical measurement separating two adjacent *tracks*; e.g., on *paper tape* or *magnetic tape*.

track, reading ⟡ *card track*.

traffic The term used to measure the capacity and utilization of a *telecommunications* system, described in terms of the number of calls in the system.

trailer label A special *record* appearing at the end of a *file* stored on *magnetic tape* or other magnetic recording medium. It serves to identify the end of the file and usually provides certain *control data* related to that file, e.g., number of records.

trailer record A *record* which immediately follows an associated group of records, and which contains totals and other *control data* relevant to the group.

trailing edge Pertaining to a *punched card* – the edge that last enters the *card track* of a punched card machine. Contrasted with *leading edge*.

trailing end Relating to *paper tape*, the logical end of a length of tape, i.e., the end at which the last *record* occurs for that particular batch. Contrasted with *leading end*.

transacter A device which can be linked to a computer system to permit a number of data sources to be coupled with the system. For example, a number of input stations could be connected to a *central processor* via a transacter to provide a *real time data collection* capability within a factory.

transaction 1. Any event which requires a *record* to be generated for processing in a data processing system. Also refers to the record itself. 2. A set of exchanges between a *terminal user* and a computer system, including the processing of these exchanges which may also involve the *updating* of *files*.

transaction data A collection of *characters* or *digits*, representing one or more events, which requires to be accepted into a data processing system to *update* a *master file* or to generate results. In a *real time* system such data may arise at random and must be dealt with as it occurs; in a *batch processing* system transactions are batched to form groups which are sorted and applied to the *master files* at predetermined periods.

transaction file Synonymous with *change file*.

transaction log A physical record maintained on *backing store* of every *transaction*[2] taking place in a *real time* based system.

transaction processing The activation of a *central processor* by messages from remote locations, and its response to those locations. ⟡ *transaction*[2].

transaction record Synonymous with *change record*.

458

transaction tape A *magnetic tape* or length of *paper tape* containing a *transaction file*.

Also known as amendment tape, *change tape*.

transactor Synonymous with *terminal user*.

transborder dataflow When data is accessed from one country, held in another, and transmitted after processing to a third, the ownership and copyright implications are considerable. The problems are given the label of transborder dataflow problems.

transceiver A *terminal* unit which can both transmit and receive information from a *data transmission* circuit.

transcribe To copy from one medium to another, e.g., from *punched cards* to *paper tape*, or from *paper tape* to *magnetic tape*. This type of operation can be achieved by special *off-line* equipment or by a computer *program*.

transcriber A device used to transfer information from one medium to another, e.g., from *paper tape* to *punched cards*.

transducer A device that converts energy from one form to another. For example, in an *acoustic delay line* electrical energy is converted to sound energy.

transfer 1. As in a *transfer operation*, i.e., an operation to copy data from one part of *memory* to another. Effected by a *program instruction* which specifies the memory *locations* required. 2. To *transfer control* from one part of a *routine* to another, or to transfer control from one routine to another, by means of a *branch instruction*. 3. To transfer data to memory from a *peripheral unit* and vice versa – a *peripheral transfer*.

transfer card When a *program* has been loaded into a computer by means of *punched cards*, a transfer card executes the entrance into the program after loading.

transfer check A *parity check* performed to verify the accuracy of a *transfer operation*.

transfer control A *branch instruction* is said to transfer control from one part of a *program* to another part, i.e., the *program controller* jumps from one set of instructions to another. In a *multi-programming* computer an *executive program* transfers control from one program to another according to specified priorities for the completion of programs.

transfer function A mathematical expression which specifies the relationship between two phenomena existing at different points in time or space in a particular system.

transfer instruction 1. An *instruction* which copies data from one part of *memory* to another. 2. A *branch instruction* to *transfer control* from one part of a *program* to another.

transfer instruction, condition control Synonymous with *conditional branch*.

transfer instruction, control Synonymous with *branch instruction*.

transfer instruction, unconditional control Synonymous with *unconditional branch instruction*.

transfer interpreter A *punched card interpreter* which read information from a *punched card* and printed the information on to the same card or on to a following card.

Also known as posting interpreter.

transfer of control ⟡ *transfer control*.

transfer of control, conditional ⟡ *conditional transfer of control*.

transfer operation An operation in which data is moved from one area of *memory* to another, or from one medium of *store* to another.

transfer rate The rate at which data may be transferred between a *peripheral unit* and the *main memory* of a computer. Dependent upon the speed and operational mode of the *peripheral* and upon the speed of the memory. On *magnetic tape* the maximum transfer rate is governed by the speed of the *tape drive* and the *packing density* of the information recorded on the tape. For example, with a packing density of 256 characters per inch and a tape speed of 7 feet per second, the maximum transfer rate is 21,504 characters per second. Hence the expression *21kch/s tape decks*.

transfer time Synonymous with *read time*.

transfer, unconditional ⟡ *unconditional branch instruction*.

transfluxor A type of magnetic storage element, in which a small piece of perforated ferromagnetic material is used, which provides a *non-volatile memory*.

transform To convert data to another form without changing the information content, e.g., to *normalize* a *floating point number*.

transient As in 'transient fault', a rapid disturbance of a signal or circuit which then swiftly reverts to a stable or normal condition.

transistor A small solid-state semiconductor which can operate as an *amplifier* or as a switching device. Transistors are usually constructed of silicon or germanium; they are small and light and have very fast switching speeds.

transistor–transistor logic A common form of *integrated circuit* design which is low cost and flexible but has some disadvantages, including high power dissipation and inadequate speed for some applications.

transition 1. A change in a circuit from one operating condition to another. 2. Also known as *bridging*. ⟡ general article on *Transition*.

transition As computer systems become larger and more complex so the *software* associated with such systems increases in complexity. A typical software system on a larger machine will consist of an interlocking set of user-programs and manufacturers' software under the overall control of a larger *operating system*, possibly also making use of a sophisticated *data base management system*.

Transition is the term given to the problem of transferring such a system from one *range*[2] of equipment to another. This problem has a different order of magnitude to the associated but much simpler problem of transferring an individual program from one machine to another.

In the latter case, procedures are relatively straightforward. If the program is written in a *high-level language* such as *COBOL* or *FORTRAN*, the *source program* can be *recompiled* on the new machine. Usually this is sufficient to produce a version of the program which will run adequately, possibly with some minor amendments to cater for any differences of *configuration* or idosyncrasies of *compiler*. Even in the simple case, some problems arise in transferring *data files* to the new system. Hardware conventions may mean differences in internal format of data fields, differences in the *labelling* of files and so on. Some method of transferring simple data files from one convention to another is required. This usually takes the form of a special program which will read a file in one format and convert the data formats, labels, etc., into the new format. This process is known as *conversion*[2].

As systems become more complex so the transfer from one range to another becomes more complex. The task cannot be accomplished effectively by simply *recompiling* all programs and converting all files as in the simple situation outlined above. Where many hundreds of programs are involved, and the programs themselves are interrelated with each other and with the overall operating system and data base system, individual recompilation will certainly result in an incompatible set of new software.

One solution to this problem is known as *emulation*. This solution cuts the Gordian knot by making the new machine act as though it were the old machine.

This feat is performed either by special hardware, or special software, or a combination of both. The entire system: programs, operating system, data files, is taken on to the new machine in machine readable form, and the emulation process converts each instruction or data item into the new machine's version, executes it, and re-interprets the result in the old format.

In practice of course life is not quite so straightforward. No emulator is capable of behaving precisely as the old machine: some adjustment to software and data formats is necessary to ensure that the old system behaves exactly as before on the new machine. The more sophisticated the transition software, the less has to be done to change the old system to enable it to run on the new machine. Clearly, using this process does provide a considerable saving in the time and effort needed to convert each individual program and data file.

Using this type of software does however have a penalty. Interposing emulating software between the old system and the new machine means a loss of efficiency. To a certain extent the power and speed of the new hardware will compensate for this, and the system will be expected to run more efficiently than before. However, to exploit a new and more powerful machine fully, means that in the end an entirely new version of the system must be developed to make maximum use of more advanced facilities. Transition provides a bridge to the new machine, and allows the user time to develop more advanced systems while continuing to run his existing systems with minimum interruption.

transition card A *punched* card used to indicate the end of a *pack* of *program* cards. Thus, when the program pack was read into the computer, the transition card terminated the *loading* phase and initiated the execution of the program.

translate To change data expressed in one form into another form without loss of meaning. For example, to convert automatically from a *source language program* to an *object program*.

translater ⋄ *translator*.

translation An operation which converts data from one format to another without changing the meaning of the information.

translator A *program* which converts statements written in one *programming language* to the format of another programming language, e.g., from a *source language* to *machine code*.

transmission The transfer of *data* from one location to another by means of electromagnetic waves; e.g., by radio waves or over telephone or telegraph circuits. ⋄ *data transmission*.

transmission control character A character forming part of a message, specifically included to control the *routing* of that signal to its required destination.

transmission interface converter A device which converts data to or from a format suitable for transfer over a *data transmission channel*.

transmission loss Synonymous with *attenuation*.

transmission, parallel ⋄ *parallel transfer*.

transmission, serial ⋄ *serial transfer*.

transmission speed The speed at which data may be transmitted from a particular device or over a particular type of circuit. Measured as the number of data units transmitted over a unit of time; e.g., 10 *characters* per second, 2000 *bits* per second. ⬦ *baud*.

transmit 1. To send data from one geographical location to another via a *data transmission* circuit. 2. To *transfer* information from one *memory location* to another, *overwriting* any *data* previously *stored* in the new location.

transparency A characteristic of *data management software* which allows *application programs* to use *files* while remaining unaware of, and independent of, the structure of the *physical files*. The programs regard the data and file organization as those which have been stated in the program's requirements. ⬦ general article on *Data Base Management Systems*.

transport delay unit Pertaining to *analog* computing equipment, a device which outputs a signal as a delayed form of an input signal.
Also known as transport unit and delay unit.

transport level In the ISO seven layer reference model for communications protocol, this is the fourth level, and defines the physical method of communicating between *user nodes*.

trap A *branch* operation initiated automatically by *hardware* on the detection of some unusual condition during the running of a *program*. Usually traps are associated with some *operating system* or *monitor program* which automatically assumes control and corrects the condition or notes the cause of failure. Trapping is a feature of certain *diagnostic routines*, but can also be used in processing routines, e.g., to recover from *arithmetic overflow* or unusual *input/output* conditions.

trapezoidal integration A process of integration in which it is assumed that y, an input variable, is subject to a constant rate of change during a step. ⬦ *digital integrator*.

trapping A feature of *monitor programs* in which automatic checks are made upon the performance of other programs. A *trap* is designed to detect unusual incidents during the running of a program and will initiate an *unconditional branch* to some *diagnostic program* or recovery routine.

trap setting A *trap* is usually activated as the result of a condition detected in the running of a *program*. The program is automatically interrupted and a *hardware* or *software* device *transfers control* to a *routine* forming part of the overall *operating system* for the computer. Usually the *operator* has the power to determine the traps to be set for any particular *run*; this is achieved by the setting of manual controls on the *console*. Thus several traps may be associated with particular conditions but the operator can determine which of these are to be allowed to *interrupt* a program.

tree   A type of *decoder* in which the graphical representation of the input and output lines resembles a tree.

tree network   ⟡ *network architecture.*

tree structure   A form of *data base* design in which *records* contain *routeing* links to other records in the data base. Record identifiers in a tree structure are related, so that, for example, record number 123 can have as direct descendants 12300 to 12309. Records up the tree are known as parents, and down the tree as descendants. A descendant without a parent is known as an orphan. ⟡⟩ *videotex.*

triad   A group of three *characters* or three *bits*; a unit of data forming part of a *message* or *record*.

tributary circuit   A branch circuit that connects to a main communications switching *network*.

trigger   1. An electronic device which can be activated to adopt a particular stable condition. A switching device used in the logic circuits of a *central processor* or its *peripheral units*. 2. To trigger, to activate a machine or a *program* automatically; e.g., to *branch* automatically to the *entry point* of a program in *memory* after *loading* the program.

Also known as initiate.

trigger circuit, bistable   ⟡ *bistable circuit.*

trigger circuit, monostable   ⟡ *monostable device.*

trigger circuit, stable   Synonymous with *bistable circuit.*

trigger pair   Synonymous with *bistable circuit.*

triple-length working   Performing arithmetic operations on numbers which require three *words* in order to develop the necessary precision for the *result*.

trouble shooting   Searching for errors in a *program* or for the cause of some machine failure. Identifying and eliminating errors in a *routine*.

Also known as *debugging*, on which there is a general article.

true complement   ⟡ *radix complement.*

true-time operation   1. An *analog* system that operates coincidentally with the physical system being simulated. 2. Sometimes used as a synonym for *real time* working.

truncate   To suppress those digits of a number which are not significant according to some predetermined requirement for accuracy in a result.

truncation error   An error arising from inaccuracy in truncating a result.

trunk   1. Sometimes used to describe an *interface* channel between a *peripheral unit* and a *central processor*. 2. Synonymous with *highway*.

trunk circuit A channel connecting two telephone or telegraph switching centres.

trunk link An interface which allows *peripheral units* to *access* the *main store*.

truth table A *Boolean operation table* in which the values 0 and 1 given to the variables are interpreted as measuring 'true' and 'false'. ◊ *Boolean algebra*.

TTL Abbreviation of *transistor–transistor logic*.

TTY Abbreviation of *teletype*.

tube An abbreviation for *cathode ray tube visual display unit*.

turn around document A document produced as output from a computer system, circulated to initiate some clerical transaction external to the computer procedures and then re-input to the system to *update* computer *files*. Such documents are often found in systems that employ *optical character recognition* for data input. Documents printed by the computer are circulated, other data is then added and an OCR reader accepts data from the document into the computer once more.

turn around time The time required to complete a task; e.g., to collect data, transcribe it for processing, carry out computation and provide results to the user. ◊ *response time*.

turnkey operation The supply by a contractor of a complete computing operation, including *hardware, software* and computer staff for a user organization.

twelve punch A term once used to denote a hole in the topmost *punching position* of a *card column*, also commonly known as the 10 or Y-position. But ◊ *Y-position*.

twenty-nine feature A device used on *punched card* machines to enable values up to a maximum of 29 to be recorded in a single *card column*, the *punching positions* 11 and 10 being used to represent 10 and 20.

twin check Any checking method in which an operation is performed twice; e.g., to *read* data twice and perform an automatic comparison.

twisted pair The standard telephone line transmission medium, consisting of a single wire with an earth return, used for linking a telephone receiver with a local exchange, and also used for a wide range of computer *terminals*.

two address instruction An *instruction* in which the *addresses* of two *operands* are specified as part of the *instruction format*. When arithmetic operations are to be performed one of the *locations* addressed will be used to hold the *result* after the instruction has been executed.

two-core-per-bit store Descriptive of a *memory* in which each *binary digit* is represented by two *magnetic cores*.

465

two-dimensional storage Related to *direct access* devices; in which an area allocated to a particular *file* need not be a series of physically contiguous *locations* but instead will be specified as a number of *buckets* drawn from one or more *seek areas*.

two gap head ◊ *magnetic tape head*.

two input adder A *logic element* which performs *addition* by accepting two digital input signals (a digit of a number and an *addend* or a *carry*) and which provides two output signals (a carry digit and a digit for the sum).

two input subtracter A *logic element* used to effect the operation of *subtraction*. It accepts two input signals (a digit of a number, and a *borrow* digit or one representing the *subtrahend*) and produces two digital outputs, a borrow digit and one for the *difference*.

two-level subroutine A *subroutine* containing another subroutine within its own structure.

two-out-of-five code A code system in which *characters* or *digits* are represented by groups of five *binary digits*, any two of which may be set to 'one' while the other three are 'zero'.

two-plus-one address Pertaining to an *instruction format* in which two *addresses* are employed to specify separate *operands*, while a third address is employed to indicate the *location* for the *result*.

twos complement A *radix complement* for the *binary notation* system.

two state variable A variable that can be a value from a set containing two elements only.

two-valued variable Synonymous with *binary variable*.

two-wire channel A circuit which can either transmit or receive along two paths.

TWX A communications system providing two-way transmission for telegraphic communication over the switched telephone network.

type bar A *print member* embossed with a range of *characters* or *symbols*, e.g., forming part of the *print unit* for a *punched card tabulator*.

type bar, interchangeable ◊ *interchangeable type bar*.

type drum A barrel-shaped drum used on a *line printer* and containing a number of *print positions* each consisting of a band of about fifty characters embossed around the drum's circumference. A typical drum might contain 160 print positions. ◊ *Output Devices*.

type face The design of the characters printed by a particular *printer*.

type fount, optical ◊ *optical type fount*.

typewriter ◊ *console typewriter, interrogating typewriter, on-line typewriter*.

U

UCSD Abbreviation of University of California, San Diego; applied to *Pascal*, since the university supports a standard version of the language.

UHF Abbreviation of *ultra high frequency*.

UL Abbreviation of Underwriters' Laboratory, which sets the safety standards which electronic and electrical equipment are required to meet in order to be acceptable for insurance purposes in the USA.

ULA Abbreviation of uncommitted logic array.

ultra high frequency Radio waves in the range from 300 MHz to 3 GHz; used primarily for television broadcasts.

ultrasonics Supersonics: the study of pressure waves with frequencies which are above the audible limit (20 kilocycles per second), but which are of the same nature as sound waves.

unary operation Synonymous with *monadic operation*.

unattended time Time when a computer is switched off but not subject to maintenance work.

unbundle When a computer's software represented a comparatively small percentage of the cost, its price was included in that of the *hardware*. As software grew in percentage terms, it was separated out (unbundled) and sold on its own.

uncommitted logic array A form of *integrated circuit* which contains a number of logic components whose interconnexions, and hence function, are not defined at the time of manufacture, but may be specified at a second processing stage. An economic method of producing dedicated integrated circuits; however, there is some loss of power and efficiency compared with fully dedicated circuits.

unconditional branch instruction A *branch instruction* which results in control being transferred to another part of a *program*. This transfer is independent of any previous conditions or states of the program.

Also known as unconditional jump instruction and unconditional transfer instruction. Contrasted with *conditional branch*.

unconditional jump instruction Synonymous with *unconditional branch instruction*.

unconditional transfer instruction Synonymous with *unconditional branch instruction.*

underflow The generation of a result whose value is too small for the range of the number representation being used. Contrasted with *overflow.*

underpunch A hole punched in any of the *rows* in a *punched card* except those that were used for *zone* punching. That is, a hole punched in the lower nine rows of an 80-column card of twelve rows where the top three rows had zone significance.

undisturbed one output signal The output from a *store* previously set to one when it is subjected to a full *read* pulse.

undisturbed output signal The output from a *store* – previously set to one or zero – when it is subjected to a full read pulse with no intervening partial pulses. Related to *undisturbed one output signal* and *undisturbed zero output signal.*

Also known as undisturbed response voltage.

undisturbed response voltage Synonymous with *undisturbed output signal.*

undisturbed zero output signal The output from a *store* previously set to *zero* when it is subjected to a full read pulse.

unexpected halt A *halt* in a *program* not due to an *interrupt* or *halt instruction*; usually the result of a program error or *hardware* failure.

Also known as hang-up. Contrasted with *programmed halt.*

uniformly accessible store Synonymous with *random access store.*

union Synonymous with *inclusive-or operation.*

union catalogue A compilation of the listings of two or more catalogues (of libraries, for example).

unipolar An input signal is defined as unipolar if the same electrical voltage polarity is used to represent different logical states. Contrasted with *bipolar.*

unipunch Synonymous with *spot punch.*

unit, anti-coincidence ⟡ *anti-coincidence element.*

unit, card punch ⟡ *card punch.*

unit, card reader ⟡ *card reader.*

unit, central processing ⟡ *central processor.*

uniterm system An *information retrieval* system which makes use of cards distinguished from each other by a word, symbol or number which is unique and in some way describes the content of the card. The descriptors used are often designed on a coordinate indexing basis.

unit, magnetic tape ⟡ *magnetic tape unit.*

unit, manual input ⟡ *manual input unit.*

unit, manual word ◊ *manual word generator*.

unit, output ◊ *output devices*.

unit record A storage medium, e.g., a *punched card*, containing one complete *record* formed of several *data elements*. For example all data relevant to one staff number contained in one punched card.

unit string A *string* with only one member.

Unix An *operating system* designed by Bell Laboratories in the USA for use with *minicomputers* and small business computers, and widely adopted by many manufacturers.

unmodified instruction Synonymous with *basic instruction*.

unpack To recover original data from a storage location in which it has been packed along with other data. Contrasted with *pack*².

unpaged segment A *segment* which is not divided into *pages* and is thus transferred as a complete unit between *main store* and *virtual store*.

unplot A *command* which causes the pen on a *graph plotter* to be raised from the paper, and thus stop drawing.

unset Synonymous with *reset*.

unused time Time during which equipment is switched off and is unattended.

unwind To show in full, without *modifiers* or *red-tape operations*, all the *instructions* used during a *loop* of instructions. Unwinding may be performed by a computer.

update To apply *transactions* to a data *file* in order to amend, add or delete records and thus ensure that the file reflects the latest situation. ◊ general article on *Updating and File Maintenance*.

updating and file maintenance In ordinary office procedure a file is a receptacle for holding documents, usually partitioned into sections which are indexed in some way to help both the filing and retrieval of documents. Computer files are like this in that they are used to store information and they are indexed, but their outward form is different and information is coded, not stored as pieces of paper. Even so, they need to be updated and maintained, updating being the reflection of actual events changing the information and maintenance being the adding, deleting or correcting of material to ensure that the information properly reflects the real situation. For example, consider a computer file containing customer accounts, showing, for each customer, the account number, name and address, outstanding balance and credit limit. The customer may order items from the firm holding the file, in which case his account must be debited with the price, and he will make payments in which case his account will be credited: the original statement is updated to take account of these transactions. The maintenance of the file described might involve correcting an account that was showing a false balance, adding new customers or removing records of customers who are no longer doing business with the firm.

The file described above consisted of a number of accounts. Files might also contain quantities and descriptions of a number of stock items, or a list of the firm's employees with personnel details. The items different files might contain are commonly known as *records* and files are said to be composed of a number of records each of which breaks down into a number of *fields*. One of the fields within a record is known as the *key*: this is different for each record and will be used to identify it during computer processing. Examples of record keys are account numbers, works numbers and part numbers. Each file in a computer installation is given a name which enables the computer to identify it, such as 'Customer File', 'Personnel File' and so on.

To understand how computer files are updated and maintained it is necessary to appreciate the characteristics of the storage media used for files. Files are typically held on *magnetic tape, magnetic disks, magnetic drums* or *magnetic cards*; this type of medium is collectively known as *backing store*, as distinct from *main store*, which is the working *memory* of the computer and not used for storing permanent data. All data on backing store is recorded as a series of flux changes in a magnetic recording surface. Each flux change is regarded as a change of state from 0 to 1 or vice versa, i.e., a *binary* code is used to represent numbers or letters of the alphabet. Data is written to backing store by an output from main store, and subsequently read by an input to main store.

Magnetic tape is a *serial* recording medium, differing from magnetic disks, drums and cards which are *direct access* media. Serial files can only be updated serially, by copying from one file to another. Direct access files can be updated serially, but also randomly and *selective-sequentially*.

The characteristics of serial updating are as follows. Records are stored in sequential order according to the record keys. Sorted transactions and file records are each read in turn and the keys examined for a match. If a transaction does not apply the record is written unchanged to a new file. If a transaction does apply the record is updated and similarly written to the new file. Eventually a completely new updated file will have been created. The old file is usually retained for a while in case mistakes have been made during the updating, and usually several *generations* of a file are preserved, all at successive stages of updating. All these generations of a file will have the same file name, and to distinguish between them, each is given a unique number (known as a *generation number*).

The main features of serial updating are that the input transactions with which the file is to be updated are collected into a sizeable batch and sorted into record key order, and every record on the file has to be read and written to a new file whether or not it has been updated. The closer the batch size approaches the file size the fewer will be the number of unwanted records read and rewritten. Magnetic tape files, therefore, are most suitable when large volumes of data are being presented during the updating run. Magnetic tape is the most common method of storing files because of its relatively low cost; the extra flexibility of direct access processing, however, frequently justifies the higher price of the equipment.

The characteristic of direct access files is that *addresses* within the file can be specified, not necessarily in sequence. This permits selective-sequential or random updating. For selective-sequential processing the records within the file are held in key order and input transactions are sorted to this order, as with serial processing. Only those records for which there are transactions, however, are read from the file and, when updated, the records are written back to where they came from. Thus, unwanted records are not *accessed*, with a consequent saving in time, and the file is updated in situ, without copying. This increased efficiency brings with it two problems. First, updated records may not fit back into the file if they have been expanded and there may be no room for new records. Secondly, since past generations of the file are not preserved an alternative system of file security must be devised. The first problem is known as *overflow* and is catered for by having files bigger than they presently need to be. File security is dealt with by keeping copies of files, or copies of the parts that have changed.

Random updating of direct access files eliminates the need for batching and sorting the input transactions, which can be dealt with as they occur. There is no difference in principle from selective-sequential updating, but this implies an orderly progression through the file, while random access involves the need to access any part of the file at any particular instant and is most suitable for low volumes of data. Where response time is critical in file updating, however, for example in airline flight booking, random access is essential.

upper curtate Those *punching positions* of a *punched card* which had *zone* significance and which were usually grouped at the top of a card. Contrasted with *lower curtate*.

up time Synonymous with *serviceable time*.

usage charge   Part of a *tariff* in a communication service, which is based on actual usage by the subscriber, including number of calls made, duration, volume, distance, and time passed in which the call was made. Contrasted with *standing charge*.

user   1. A general term for any individual or group ultimately making use of the *output* from a computer system. 2. In an *operating system* an individual exercising control over, or using, a particular *resource*.

user data packet   A unit of information forming part of a message transmitted from one user to another in a *packet switch service*.

user defined character   A *character* in a *code set*, where the relationship between the code representation of this character and the symbol actually displayed or printed is determined by the user through interaction with *software*.

user defined function key   A *function key* whose function is selected by a choice made by a user. Related to *soft key*.

user friendly   An expression used to describe computer systems which are designed to be simple to use by untrained users, by means of self-explanatory or self-evident interaction between user and computer. A good example of a user friendly system is *videotex*. User friendly systems are sometimes said to be *philoxenic*.

user group   A group of users of a particular manufacturer's equipment. The group meets to discuss problems, exchange *programs* and generally exchange knowledge gained in installing and developing systems.

user hook   A facility provided by suppliers of *software* enabling users to alter, replace or bypass parts of the software.

user interface   A term used to describe any way in which a user accesses a computer system, for example, through a *visual display unit*, a *personal computer* or a *videotex terminal*.

user node   A *node* in a *network* at which a user *terminal* is stationed. Contrasted with a node at which control functions take place.

user port   A *port*[2] to which a user is connected to a computer in a *communications network*.

utility programs   Utility programs are part of the *software* of a system, devised to perform operations on *files* of data. Utility programs are not concerned with the specific contents of any file, but operate on whole files treated as units, transferring them from one medium of store to another, making copies of files and re-organizing their sequence.

Utility programs used for transferring data from one storage medium to another include *punched cards* to *magnetic tape* and *paper tape* to magnetic tape programs, magnetic tape to *direct access* storage, and *routines* for printing contents of *storage devices* on a *printer*. The purpose of transferring data from one type of medium to another is usually to place data required for subsequent processing on to a faster storage medium. Thus, for example, a punched card file may be transferred initially to magnetic tape. Once on tape, the file can conveniently be sorted into any required sequence and the data processed by several routines by being read from the magnetic tape. Such *file conversion* routines may also perform *editing* and validation on the basic data, ensuring that the formats on the new storage medium conform to the requirements for subsequent processing. The listing of contents of storage devices on a printer is usually performed for *debugging* purposes, or in the course of program testing, in order to provide a programmer with full details of the file contents. Such routines are seldom used as part of a normal production run, since although the output gives full details of the file content, the format will usually be inconvenient from a user's point of view.

Conversion routines are also usually provided for transferring data from a fast to a slow peripheral, e.g., magnetic disk to tape. Such a transfer would be performed if, for example, it were necessary to convert a data file from one type of magnetic disk to another, incompatible with the former. In this case, the data from the first disk would be read again and converted on to the second disk. In the case of direct access storage devices, it is usual to place the contents of storage on to magnetic tape or some other storage device from time to time, so that if the contents of the direct access file were destroyed in any way, the file may be re-created. This problem arises because with direct access storage updating a file may cause previous information to be *overwritten*, whereas with magnetic tape the original file is not altered in any way.

Utility programs are also produced for making copies of files on the same type of storage device: keeping copies of data files is an essential part of the security of a data processing system, particularly if the organization of the system does not permit re-creation of files through a *generation* system of updating or through *restart* procedures. Copies of files may also be made for use on other machines or by other users.

Programs for re-organizing the sequence of data files form an important section of utility programs. *Sorting* of files, either on magnetic tape or on direct access storage devices, enables the data items in the file to be placed in any required sequence, for subsequent processing. File re-organization also forms an important part of the techniques of storing data in direct access devices, where data is not held in a serial sequence as, for example, on magnetic tape. Using the technique of

473

storing data in *buckets*, whose address is derived from the *key* of the data item being stored, means that the buckets become full up and additional data items have to be stored in other buckets, access being achieved by means of storing the new bucket address in the original bucket. As more and more bucket overflow occurs, the storage device holds more and more addresses as well as data. Thus, in order to release the space taken up by addresses, re-organization of data must take place from time to time.

Other utility programs prepare storage devices to accept data files and check their performance and accuracy. Such programs give *labels* to files, remove labels from files which are no longer required, and can be used, for example, to check magnetic tapes for *parity* errors or direct access devices for flaws in bucket areas.

Utility programs are also used for handling files which hold details of programs and for transferring programs from one type of storage device to another. Such programs operate in the same way as data file utility programs, but also include programs to create and update program *libraries*. Programs for debugging purposes, such as *trace* programs, are also sometimes referred to as utility programs, but since such programs are more specialized than normal utility software the term should not strictly be applied to them. ⇨ articles on *Software, Debugging, Sorting*.

utility routines Synonymous with *Utility Programs*.

utilization ratio The ratio of *effective time* of an *automatic data processing* system to the *serviceable time*, i.e., the ratio of the time spent on productive work, *program* development and incidentals, to the total time during which the system is in a state where it can operate normally.

UVEPROM Acronym for Ultra-Violet Erasable Programmable Read-Only Memory. ⇨ *PROM*.

V

V.22, V.23, V.24 Examples of *V-Series* standards: (i) V.22 is a standard for *modems*, operating at 1200 *bits* per second (bps) in full *duplex* over the standard telephone network. (ii) V.23 is as for V.22 but for a modem operating at a split speed of 600 bps receive and 1200 bps transmit speed. (iii) V.24 is a comprehensive standard for the connexion of data terminal equipment and modems, covering the definition of some 40 control circuits.

validity check A check to ensure that data falls within certain prescribed limits, e.g., that numerals do not appear in a *field* which should have alphabetic characters only, that a field for days of the month does not contain a number over 31, etc.

value added network A service (e.g., *videotex*), provided through *telecommunicatons*, for which a charge is made, thus providing additional value to the basic network technology.

VAN Acronym for *Value Added Network.*

variable address Synonymous with *indexed address.*

variable block A *block* whose size is not fixed but varies (within certain limits) according to the data requirements. ⊘ *block mark.* Contrasted with *fixed block length.*

variable connector A *connector* which may be connected to more than one point in a *flowchart* depending on the path taken from a *decision box.*

variable field A field whose length may vary within certain prescribed limits according to the requirements of data. The end of the field is indicated by a *terminal symbol.*

variable length ⊘ *variable field.*

variable, two-valued ⊘ *binary variable.*

VDU Abbreviation of *visual display unit.*

vector In *graphics software, parameters* which indicate the direction and distance of one point from another.

vector mode display A method for presenting data on a *cathode ray tube visual display unit* in which vectors are displayed as straight lines between points on the screen.

verge-perforated card   Synonymous with *margin-punched card*.

verification   The process of checking the original punching of data into *punched cards* or *paper tape*. ⬦ general article on *Data Preparation*.

verifier   A *keyboard* operated device used to check the original punching of data in *punched cards* or *paper tape*. ⬦ *punched card verifier, paper tape verifier*. ⬦ *general article on Data Preparation*.

version number   *Programs* and *packages* are frequently revised, and in order to keep control over different versions of the same piece of software, version numbers are given to each successive *release* of a piece of software. Usually a decimal system is used; a change in the integer denotes a major revision, and in the decimal a minor revision.

vertical feed   The feed mechanism in which a *punched card* was placed in a *hopper* in a vertical position. Contrasted with *horizontal feed*.

vertical resolution   A measure of *resolution* determined by the number of *pixels* which can be displayed vertically on a graphic display.

vertical scroll   *Scrolling* of text up and down a screen, whereby as new lines of text are added at the bottom, existing lines disappear from the top, and vice versa.

very large scale integration   *Integrated circuits* which contain several hundred thousand transistors. ⬦ *large scale integration*.

video   A term generally used for a *visual display unit*.

videodisk   A storage device which makes use of the high data capacity of equipment designed to store television picture data on *disks*. Videodisks can be used to store images which can be accessed and retrieved. ⬦ *optical* storage.

videotex   A system of storing a large *tree structured* data base, consisting of pages of text and graphics data, with *user friendly commands*, and accessing *pages*[2] from low cost terminals, often videotex adaptors, using a standard domestic television set for the display screen. Data is communicated over standard telephone lines. A number of countries have established public videotex services, such as *Prestel* in the UK, and private videotex systems have become of major importance to a wide range of commercial and industrial organizations. Videotex is the internationally accepted term for the system originally called viewdata, in the UK. ⬦ *videotex adaptor, videotex decoder, videotex editing terminal, videotex standards*, and *teletext*.

videotex adaptor   A low cost device incorporating a *modem* and *videotex decoder* which when attached to a standard domestic television set and to the public telephone network allows a user to access a videotex system.

videotex decoder   A piece of *software* usually, but not always, held in

PROM on an *integrated circuit* which interprets *videotex* standard codes and generates a videotex *page* on a screen.

videotex editing terminal   A terminal which allows the user to create videotex pages and update a videotex system data base.

videotex standards . The standards adopted within a country or by a system supplier for the transmission of data within a *videotex* system. There are three main types of videotex standard: *alphamosaic, alphageometric* and *alphaphotographic*.

videotext   Sometimes used to embrace both *teletext* and *videotex*.

viewdata   Synonymous with *videotex*. Still used widely in the UK, but the difficulty of pronouncing it in many foreign languages has encouraged the use of the word videotex internationally.

virgin medium   A medium completely devoid of any information, e.g., a floppy disk which has not been *formatted*. Contrasted with *empty medium*.

virtual   Synonymous with *logical*.

virtual address   An address referring to a *store location* but which must be converted by *address mapping* to obtain a *real address* referring to a specific *main store* location. Has a meaning similar to *relative address* but is applied to computers providing *virtual storage* facilities.

virtual circuit   The path through a *packet switching network* for any particular message when the actual physical path taken by each message may vary according to the characteristics of the network.

virtual machine   The environment in which all *code* and *data* required to carry out a particular function is executed. ◊ general article on *Virtual Machine Environment*.

virtual machine environment   An environment in which several different users are able to operate their *applications* within a computer system in such a way that there is considerable sharing of *hardware* and *software* facilities. However, each user application is unaware of the existence of other applications, and is developed as though it alone occupied the computer.

In a virtual machine environment each user regards his program as consisting of a series of *instructions* to solve his particular application program. When the program is *compiled*, additional instructions are added to provide an interface with standard *system software* or *middleware*, e.g., input/output routines, or file handling routines. During the compiling process, a program is also allocated hardware *resources* including *peripheral devices*.

To the user, the various items of system software which operate in conjunction with his program are not thought of as forming his program

– indeed, they will reside in a separate part of the main store and be shared by several other application programs.

The importance of a virtual machine environment is that hardware and software resources are efficiently shared by all users without them being conscious of the fact and with full *security* and privacy for individual programs. Each user's virtual machine thus has protection from interference although it may co-exist with several other virtual machines each operating independently.

Each virtual machine contains a hardware and software mechanism to handle all requests for system software facilities and to pass control to relevant routines. The interaction of all co-existing virtual machines is governed by the *kernel* which is usually that central part of an operating system which interfaces directly with the hardware, and provides mutual synchronization and protection to processes active within the computer. The kernel is instrumental in mapping individual virtual machines on to the hardware, and controls the transfer of *segments* between main store and backing store. The kernel monitors virtual machines and their dependence upon events – e.g., the termination of a peripheral transfer – and controls the activation of virtual machines accordingly. It schedules processing time between active virtual machines, and manages peripheral transfers and interrupts within the system.

For the virtual machine concept to be effective it must be supported by hardware *architecture* which offers a comprehensive system of protection to all processes active within the system. Such a system provides protection for code and data within a virtual machine from errors internal to that machine, and from the effects of errors occurring in other virtual machines.

A virtual machine environment is one which enables each user application within a computer system to operate independently without interference with other user applications with which it must co-exist, the computer system being designed so that all user applications can efficiently share the resources of processing time, main storage, and system software.

virtual storage   A *store* management system in which a user is able to use the storage resources of a computer without regard to constraints imposed by a limited *main store*, and the requirements of other *applications* which may be using the system.

In a computer capable of *multiprogramming*, several application programs may operate at the same time, and must share the resources of the computer. The resources will include main store and *backing store*. This usually means that the programmer responsible for writing the application has to observe constraints on the amount of main store that he uses, and where a program exceeds a specified allocation of main store the programmer must arrange for *overlays* to be organized.

In more advanced computers, hardware and software mechanisms are used to relieve the programmer of the need to observe the constraints to a limited main store. The users of the system are able to assume that the main store is of infinite size. (In practice a program and its data are automatically considered to consist of *segments*, a limited number of the segments will reside in *main store* and the remainder will exist on a fast backing store device.) The maximum amount of storage allowed to any program is of such size as to present no practical constraint to the user. This facility can be provided only by computers with a large enough capacity of main store and backing store, and with an advanced *operating system* to handle the management of storage facilities and the *interrupts* which must occur to ensure that programs are provided with the application code and data from backing store when required.

One method of handling the management of storage in a virtual storage system is *paging*. The object of paging is to ensure that the physical storage capacity is efficiently allocated, particularly the main store. The paging system handles the moving in and out of segments to and from main store. The system operates in such a way that segments currently required for application programs are kept in main store, new segments are brought in as required and inactive segments are transferred to backing store to make room as necessary.

A segment is a large unit of data: segments may be of variable length but each occupying several thousand characters or *bytes* of storage. They are necessarily so, in order to ensure efficient transfers between main store and backing store; it would be very inefficient to call continually for smaller amounts of information from backing store. However, because the segment is a relatively large unit of store, it cannot readily be accommodated in odd areas of main store which may remain unused at any moment in time. To overcome this problem, segments are considered to consist of smaller units known as pages which can be handled by allocation to small unused areas of storage. A page may be about one thousand words or bytes in size.

Wastage of storage allocated in this way is sometimes referred to as *fragmentation*; a certain degree of main store fragmentation occurs in a paging system but it is much less significant than in a system in which segmentation alone is used.

It follows that if the pages of a particular segment are distributed over a number of areas of the main store, the system used to manage the store must be capable of handling pages so that to all intents and purposes they appear to the user as existing in contiguous areas of storage. A virtual storage system has to ensure that there is complete *security* and a lack of interference between segments and pages used by the different application programs. The principles of *virtual storage* systems can be extended further to the concept of a *virtual machine environment*.

Visicalc An early *spreadsheet* program which was very widely used when *personal computers* first entered the marketplace.

visual display unit A display unit that consists of a *cathode ray tube* which is used to display *characters* or graphics representing data read from the *main memory* of a computer. A visual display unit also incorporates a *keyboard* or *key pad* so that computer *files* can be interrogated from remote locations. Often also known as *terminal*.

VLSI Abbreviation of very large scale integration.

voice grade channel A *channel* capable of transmitting speech quality signals.

voice recognition The ability of computers to analyse sounds and, by comparing the *digital* representation of the speech patterns with a stored pattern, to recognize the meaning of the speech and respond according to a preset *program*.

voice synthesis ◊ *speech synthesis*.

volatile memory Memory which does not retain stored data when power is cut off. ◊ *dynamic memory*. Contrasted with *non-volatile memory*, *static memory*.

volume A unit of magnetic *storage* which can be connected to a computer system; e.g., a reel of *magnetic tape* or a *disk pack*.

von Neumann architecture Computer *architecture* with a stored *program*, and *input/output* units, and a function dictated by the reading of program instructions sequentially from memory. Contrasted with *non-von Neumann architecture*.

V-Series A series of standards recommended by the *CCITT*, governing data transmission over telephone circuits, using *analog* techniques, identified by the letter V and numbers 1–57. Common examples are *V.22, V.23, V.24*. ◊ *X-Series*.

W

waiting time The waiting time of a computer *store* is the interval between the moment a *control unit* calls for a *transfer* of data to or from the store and the moment the transfer begins.

Also known as latency.

walk down Successive *partial drive pulses* or *digit pulses* in an incorrectly operating *store* will cause a progressive *irreversible magnetic process* in a magnetic cell. Such a process is known as walk down or *loss of information*. In a correctly operating store, a *steady state condition* (where only *reversible processes* occur) is reached after the application of relatively few partial drive or digit pulses.

walkthrough ⇨ *dry running*.

WAN Acronym for *Wide Area Network*.

warm restart ⇨ *restart*.

waste instruction Synonymous with *do nothing instruction*.

wheel printer A *printer* which prints characters from the rim of a *print wheel*. The available characters are placed round the rim of each wheel and there is a wheel for each printing position.

wide area network A *network* connecting computers over long distances, usually using the telephone network or a *packet switch service*. Contrasted with local area network.

wildcard A *character* or group of characters which represent an undefined character *string*, used in *information retrieval* systems when the user is interested in retrieving items which must contain some specified characters, but where characters represented by wildcards are indeterminate.

Williams tube An electrostatic storage *cathode ray tube* which uses a cathode ray tube with only one gun assembly. The device was developed by F. C. Williams of the University of Manchester and was a significant advance in the development of digital representation.

Williams tube storage A method of storage using a *Williams tube*.

Winchester disk A *magnetic disk drive* which is similar in size to a *floppy disk* but overcomes speed and storage limitations by closer head alignment and denser recording, the mechanism being protected from dust by being in a sealed unit. A Winchester is a *fixed disk* system and is named after the 30-30 Winchester rifle, the original Winchester disk being 30 *megabytes* of data on 30 *tracks*.

window   A form of split screen where different *applications* can display their information independently on different areas of a *visual display unit*.

wire printer   Synonymous with *stylus printer*.

wire-wrap   A method of effecting electrical connexions without soldering, by wrapping a fine wire round small posts connected to components on a circuit board; a low cost method of creating prototypes for *printed circuit boards*.

wiring diagram   A diagrammatic representation of the electronic circuitry for components and *printed circuit boards* for a computer system. ⟡ *circuit diagram*.

word   A basic unit of data in a computer *memory*; the unit will consist of a predetermined number of *characters* or *bits* to be processed as an entity; i.e., a *program instruction* or an element of data. In many digital computers a *fixed word length* is used, but in other machines characters may be grouped to form words of variable length according to the requirements of the particular instructions to be performed.

word length   The size of a *word*, measured by the number of *digits* it contains, e.g., a 24-*bit* word will be able to hold numbers in the range -2^{23} to $+2^{23} - 1$.

word oriented   A computer is said to be word oriented if the basic element of data which can be individually *addressed* in *store* is a *word*. The individual *bits* or *characters* within the word may be *accessed* by the use of certain *instructions* if required. Contrasted with *character oriented*.

word processor   A *text editing* device usually consisting of a *microcomputer*, a *visual display unit*, a *printer* and a *software package*. Documents are initiated on a typewriter-like *keyboard*, and the software allows text manipulation and editing (such as error correction, insertion and tabulation), and storage for later retrieval and printing.

word time   The time required to process one *word* of information in *memory*.

work area   An area within *memory* in which items of data are stored temporarily during processing.
Also known as working storage, *intermediate storage*, scratch pad.

work assembly   The clerical function concerned with the assembly of the data *files* and materials necessary to run a *program* or *suite* of programs. The general coordination of data passing to and from a computer system, including perhaps the maintenance of *manual control routines* to validate the quality of the data received and/or generated by the system.

working, double-length ⟡ *double-precision arithmetic.*

working, real time ⟡ *real time.*

working storage Synonymous with *work area.*

work measurement The use of certain techniques to establish the time a worker should take to carry out a job. ⟡ *Time Study.*

work station Usually an *intelligent terminal* at which data can be *input* and *processed*, perhaps using data from a *host computer*, before results are sent to a host.

work tape A *magnetic tape* retained in the computer room for general use during processing; e.g., available for intermediate *passes* of a *sort program* or for use in program testing. An expired master file might be used as a work tape, or a set of tapes may be assigned a permanent role as work tapes. Compare with *scratch tape.*

work time, machine-spoilt ⟡ *machine-spoilt work time.*

wrap round Because the screen of a *visual display unit* cannot always present all the information called for, the wrap round technique allows further data to be displayed at the start of the top line of the screen, overwriting existing data. The rest of the existing data is then successively overwritten until the bottom line is again completed and the process is repeated. Compare with *rack-up.*

wreck Synonymous with *jam.*

write To transcribe data on to a form of *store* from another form of store, e.g., transcribing data on to a *magnetic tape* from the *main memory* of a computer. Data is 'written to' tape rather than 'written on' tape. Contrasted with *read.*

write head An electromagnet used to write on a magnetic medium such as *magnetic tape, magnetic disk*, or *magnetic drum.*

Also known as recording head or writing head.

write inhibit ring A *file protection ring* which is attached to the *hub* of a *magnetic tape reel* in such a way that it physically prevents any *writing* from occurring on the reel. Contrasted with *write permit ring.*

write permit ring A *file protection ring* which is attached to the *hub* of a *magnetic tape reel* in order physically to allow data to be *written* to the reel.

Also known as write ring. Contrasted with *write inhibit ring.*

write pulse A *drive pulse* which either sets the *one condition* of a magnetic cell or writes into the cell.

write ring Synonymous with *write permit ring.*

write time   The time interval between the instant transcription to a *storage device* begins and the instant it is completed. The write time is therefore the *access time* less the *waiting time*. Related to *read time*.

writing head   ◊ *write head*.

X

X.24, X.25 Examples of X-Series standards: (i) X.24 relates to interchange circuits between *data terminal* equipment and *modems* on public digital networks. (ii) X.25 relates to interchange circuits as for X.24, but for connexion of *packet switch services*.

xerographic printer A *page printer* (i.e., a printer in which the character pattern is set for a whole page before printing) using the principle of *xerography*.

xerography A dry copying process: the image to be copied is projected on to a plate causing an electrostatic charge to be discharged where the light falls and retained where the image is black. Resinous powder is then tumbled over the plate, adhering only to the uncharged areas. The resin is transferred to paper or other medium for use as a printing master.

X-position Usually the *punching positions* in the second *row* of a *punched card* starting from the top, also known as the 11-position; the top row was Y or 10, the second X or 11, the third 0 and the rest 1-9. Sometimes however, the notations X and Y were reversed, and it was as well to take great care when making reference to these positions.

X-punch A hole punched in the X-position of a *punched card* (usually the second *row* starting from the top, but ⬦ *X-position*).

X-Series A series of standards, recommended by the *CCITT*, governing the interconnexion of users' *data terminal* equipment and *modems*. The X-Series standards are an extension of the *V-Series*, recognizing the development of digital devices and their interconnexion with *analog* facilities. Examples are *X.24, X.25*.

X–Y cursor addressing The location of the position of a *cursor* on a screen, by reference to the X (horizontal) and Y (vertical) coordinate position of the cursor.

X–Y plotter ⬦ *data plotter*.

Y

Y-edge leading As the top *row* of a *punched card* was known as the Y-row, a card fed long edge first (*parallel feed*), with the top row nearest the read mechanism, was said to be fed 'Y-edge leading'. This contrasted with '*nine-edge leading*'; '*serial feed*, column 1 leading'; and, in an 80-column card, 'serial feed, column 80 leading'.

Y-position Usually the *punching positions* in the top *row* of a *punched card*, also known as the 10 position; the second row was then X or 11, the third 0 and the rest 1–9. Sometimes, however, the notations X and Y (10 and 11) were reversed, and it was as well to take great care when making reference to these positions.

Y-punch A hole punched in the Y-position of a card (usually the top *row*, but ◊ *Y-position*).

Z

zero 1. Nothing. 2. A numeral denoting zero magnitude. 3. The condition of codes recognized by a computer as zero, such *bit* structures often being different for positive and negative zero.

zero access storage This phrase was once in frequent use for describing storage with a very short *waiting time* or *latency*. A waiting time of zero, however, is not strictly possible, and the phrase has now fallen into disrepute.

zero address instruction format An *instruction format* with no *address* part. Such a format is used when no address is required, e.g., when an instruction refers automatically to another *location*, as in *repetitive addressing*.

Also known as addressless instruction format.

zero balance The result of a technique of balancing if details and totals are both correct: when both details and totals are processed together, with details as negative and the totals as positive, a balance of zero will be obtained if both accumulations are correct.

zero condition The state of a *magnetic cell* when it represents *zero*.

Also known as zero state and nought state.

zero elimination Synonymous with *zero suppression*.

zero fill To replace all data in a *store* or group of *locations* with the repeated representation of *zero*.

zeroize 1. To reset a mechanical register to its *zero* position. 2. To replace the contents of a *storage area* by pulses representing zero.

zero-level address Synonymous with *immediate address*.

zero loss A condition which arises when the gain in power in a circuit line to amplification is just sufficient to overcome the inevitable loss in power attributed to the line end associated operating equipment.

zero output ⟡ *zero output signal*.

zero output signal The output given by a *magnetic cell* in the *zero condition* when a *read* pulse is applied.

zero output signal, undisturbed ⟡ *undisturbed zero output signal*.

zero state Synonymous with *zero condition*.

zero suppression The elimination before printing of non-significant zeros, e.g., those to the left of significant digits. The suppression is a function of editing.

Also known as zero elimination.

zone 1. That area of, for example, a *punched card* in which *zone digits* were punched. 2. Part of a *magnetic disk* with a *transfer rate* which differs from the transfer rate of other areas on the same disk; this allows optimum utilization of the surface area. 3. A part of *main memory* allocated for a predetermined function.

zone bit For example, where six *bits* denote each *character*, the two most significant bits may be used in conjunction with the numeric bits to represent alphabetic and special characters. ($\diamond$ *zone, zone digit*.)

zone digit The numerical key to a section of a *code*; e.g., where a hole was punched in the *X-position* of a *column* of a *punched card* it gave a value to a hole punched in the 2-position of the same column of that card. If a hole were punched in the *Y-position* instead of the X-position, a different value would attach to the hole in the 2-position, and the X-, Y- and (if appropriate) 0 *punching positions* were thus zone digits. Zone digits could be used independently of other punchings for control significance, etc.

zone punch Synonymous with *zone digit*.

zoom A facility in *graphics software*, which allows the size of an image to be reduced or increased without the need to re-define the image *parameters*.